Desmond Ford: Reformist Theologian, Gospel Revivalist

by *Milton Hook*

Desmond Ford: Reformist Theologian, Gospel Revivalist
Milton Hook

Library of Congress Cataloging-in-Publication Data
Desmond Ford: Reformist Theologian, Gospel Revivalist
Milton Hook

pp. 341 (including photos and index).

1. Ford, Desmond, 1929–2019.
2. Seventh-day Adventists—Doctrines.
3. Seventh-day Adventists—Clergy.
ISBN: (paperback) 9798401395603
Imprint: Independently published

First edition:
Cover illustration: MacMouser Graphics, Portland, Oregon
© 2008 Adventist Today Foundation
Riverside, California

Second Edition:
Cover Illustration: Darren Baker, Bare Graphics
©2022 Desmond Ford Publications
Caloundra, Qld, Australia

Table of Contents

Abbreviations

AC	Avondale College (formerly Australasian Missionary College)
ACHR	Avondale College Heritage Room
AMC	Australasian Missionary College
AR	Australasian Record and Advent World Survey (now titled Record)
AST	Australasian Signs of the Times (now titled Signs of the Times)
ATS	Adventist Theological Society
BRI	Biblical Research Institute
GC	General Conference [of Seventh-day Adventists]
GCA	General Conference [of Seventh-day Adventist] Archives
GNU	Good News Unlimited [organization]
GNUB	Good News Unlimited Bulletin
Ibid.	From the Latin *"ibidem,"* meaning "in the same place"
KJV	King James Version
NIV	New International Version
NSW	New South Wales
PREXAD	[General Conference] Presidents Executive Advisory [Committee]
PUC	Pacific Union College
RH	Review and Herald (or Review, now titled Adventist Review)
SDA	Seventh-day Adventist

Foreword for the Second Edition

Desmond Ford died on 11 March 2019 at age 90 and one month. Despite deteriorating health after age 86, he remained active for most of his remaining days. He was still able to record videos and gave his last sermon in the home of Dr Ross and Natalie Sinclair. This was about three months before he died, and it was given to a small but rapt audience of about forty people.[1] After that, Des hoped to record his own funeral sermon on the Shepherd's Psalm (Psalm 23), but he was unable to finish it.

Des died, as he lived, by faith in the Son of God who loved him and gave himself for him. His raison d'être was to serve and preach Christ and his cross and resurrection. To make Christ central meant making a shambles of parts of traditional Adventism. Des was not a Fundamentalist himself, but believed the Fundamentalist errors of his denomination must be confronted head on, while some scholars preferred to just ignore them. Thus, Des leapt through the brick wall in 1979 and 1980 to the detriment of his own earthly career. He lost his reputation, his job, his ministerial and teaching credentials, and later, his ordination.

Though he was always focused on Christ, the denomination called him apostate, and leaders tried repeatedly to have his membership removed. When Des handed in his membership at Pacific Union College on his return to Australia in 2000, some said, "See, he left the denomination," while covering up their own continual demand for such for the previous twenty years. Being married to him, I was given the same discipline.

Stating all this may merely reflect my pain at watching the treatment he received. On the other hand, Des and I went on to have another wonderful ministry with Good News Unlimited. God provided for us at every step. Des preached, wrote, and fellowshipped with many saints, our gospel friends. In fact, most people did not treat us any differently when we met them individually. Therefore, we had nothing to complain about and cannot say we suffered. Leaving Adventism was a stepping-stone to another ministry where Des was free to preach the gospel.

Des had not one skerrick of bitterness for the way his brethren treated him. He believed and taught that salvation was all about God's forgiveness, and that we who receive this love, must manifest the same forgiveness 70 times seven.

> [21]Then Peter came to Jesus and asked, 'Lord, how many times shall I forgive my brother who sins against me? Up to seven times?'
> [22] Jesus <u>answered, 'I tell you, not just seven times,</u> but <u>seventy-seven times!</u>' (Matt 18:22–23)

Some see this text as referring directly back to Daniel 9:24, which mentions "seventy-sevens" and links it with the "end of sin and the bringing in of everlasting righteousness," predicted here long before the cross.[2]

> [24] 'Seventy "sevens" are decreed for your people and your holy city to finish transgression, to put an end to sin, to atone for wickedness, to bring in everlasting righteousness, to seal up vision and prophecy and to anoint the Most Holy Place.'

The parallel text to Matthew 18 in Luke 17 is slightly different. It uses seven times seven instead of seventy-sevens, and adds the statement 'if he repents':

> [3]'Watch yourselves. If your brother sins, rebuke him; and **if he repents,** forgive him. [4]Even if he sins against you seven times in a day, and seven times returns to say, "I repent," you must forgive him'

Des stuck to Matthew 18. He not only forgave those who said, "I repent"; he went one step further. He forgave them anyway, repentant or not.

It was, therefore, not his courage, nor his brilliant mind, nor his amazing ability to speak and answer questions, nor his natural charisma and energy for which he should be remembered, but rather for this sentence, "He forgave his enemies for Christ's sake." I watched him closely until the end and wondered at the beauty and transparency of his spiritual life. It was my privilege to witness this wonderful man close-up. Like all saints, he did not think much of himself.

Gillian Ford
Little Mountain, QLD, Australia
8 December 2021

P.S. The work of Des's later ministry, after his severance from the ministry of the Seventh-day Adventist Church, was called Good News Unlimited. This continues to run in the United States, but is most active under the direction of Dr Eliezer Gonzales in Australia. Des's works—documents, videos, podcasts, and books are all to be available as time permits on his website at www.desmondford.org.

Endnotes
1. This sermon can be found on Phil Butler's You Tube page, https://www.youtube.com/watch?v=Cb4-3F4FWYo&t=105s (2018.11.17. Christian Assurance).
2. Many commentators have seen this connection but not all agree.

As a comment on this new edition of his book, Milton Hook wrote:

Increased Seventh-day Adventist church membership statistics do not indicate the blessing of God. They simply mean more people are cast into a dilemma about their salvation, to a large extent reliant on their performance of good works and the ever-elusive attainment of moral perfection.

Some dickering around the edges of the investigative judgment theory has taken place, leaving members in a cultic time warp that has no foundation in Scripture. The mistaken assertion is still held that sacrificial blood in the Hebraic services always defiled the sanctuary except in the Day of Atonement service.

The year-day theory is still maintained despite the historical failure of the formula every time it is applied. The invention of a two-phased ministry of Christ, a pre-1844 ministry in a heavenly first apartment, followed by a post-1844 ministry in a heavenly second apartment, is still proposed—despite the testimony of the Book of Hebrews declaring that Christ entered into the very presence of God at His ascension.

Daniel 9 is still interpreted as the divine answer to the time period of Daniel 8, despite the obvious contextual sense that the time period of Daniel 9 is unrelated to Daniel 8, its simply being in response to Daniel's prayer in the early verses of chapter 9.

(See Appendix A for more).

From Milton Hook to The Reader

Most of the personalities discussed in this book intersected not only Desmond Ford's journey, but mine as well. As a lad I listened to Lawrence Naden preach at camp meetings. At Carmel College I sat in Alfred Jorgensen's Bible and English classes. Later, at Avondale College, I was instructed by Gordon McDowell, Desmond Ford, and Alwyn Salom. There, too, I listened to Erwin Gane's chapel talks. As a young minister I worked alongside Llewelyn Jones. Robert Pierson visited my remote mission station in the highlands of Papua New Guinea. I was impressed by his rapport with third-world people. At that same time, I assisted George Burnside in an evangelistic crusade at Madang. Later, during studies at Andrews University, I occasionally filled in for William Murdoch when he was unable to teach his classes. My understanding of the gospel was expanded by Hans LaRondelle's seminary lectures. My love of church history was quickened by Mervyn Maxwell. My family and I stayed for a week in the home of Colin Standish at Columbia Union College, while I did research for my dissertation. Keith Parmenter visited my parish when I returned to Australia. Robert Parr was my conference president during the 1980s, while I cared for various churches in Sydney. The list could be lengthened considerably. This book is a stage on which personalities well known to me play important parts.

As I have written about my contemporaries, I have experienced both joy and sadness. Readers will readily recognize those I learned to love as saints. Those I found to be scoundrels are just as easily identified. I do not belong to the school of thought that believes written history should be entirely dispassionate and clinically objective. Arguably, there is no such thing as absolute objectivity. Even the history found in Scripture is written from a national or tribal perspective, but historians follow certain guidelines designed to give reasonable objectivity. I have made every effort to stay within those boundaries.

Soldiers who have recently survived a war cannot avoid emotion as they retell their experiences. So, it is with me. I was filled with despair when confronted with biblically illiterate church members posturing as judges of other men's theology. I was dismayed by the invective directed at Desmond Ford and the efforts to demonize him within his own church. I became alarmed when I realized my church was rejecting the gospel of Jesus Christ and resisting the Spirit, when confronted by Scripture. I believed my church was falling short of Protestant tradition by enlisting Ellen White as an equal to Scripture. I felt helpless as scores of my fellow ministers were dismissed or were betrayed because of their stand for the gospel. I laughed at the humor in Robert Parr's letters. I wept when I wrote about the tragedy of Gwen Ford's premature death. I have tried to be as objective as possible, but this account is unashamedly passionate and frank. It is intended to rouse readers' emotions and remind them of the apostolic gospel that will never be quashed.

When the chill of the Glacier View meeting struck me in 1980, I realized that something monumentally historic had occurred and would, in time, have to be critically assessed. I began to gather documents for that purpose. Two other men, Trevor Lloyd and Graeme Bradford, own a collection of tape recordings, documents, and interviews relevant to the topic. I am indebted to these men for happily sharing their collections with me when they learned of my project, and I have used material from the archives at Avondale College, Cooranbong, New South Wales, as well.

The prime source of documentation comes from Desmond Ford, himself. He readily admits that he has the world's worst filing system, but when his vast letter and manuscript collection was collated chronologically, it provided the basis for this saga. Hundreds of letters are preserved in his holdings—some written in his courting days, others penned to his first wife, Gwen, during her illness, and some to his mother while he was overseas. Later ones concern theological controversy. More were posted to his second wife, Gillian, during his world itineraries for Good News Unlimited. Desmond and his family graciously shared all of these with me, as well as a wide selection of photographs. The letter collection speaks of an extraordinary man—one devoted to his family, genuinely committed to Christ, frugal, highly disciplined in his habits, thoughtful of others, and given to a wry sense of humor. The interpretations of these various collections are entirely my own.

There will, no doubt, be other histories written about this era and these personalities, together with the theological issues surveyed. I encourage historians to do so. More of the saga lies hidden in some church archives awaiting release. My manuscript is simply one contribution, one view, one evaluation. A few will perhaps disagree with some of my interpretations of the history. More will deny my interpretation of Scripture, especially perfectionists, traditionalists, or fundamentalists. I believe the writing of neither history nor theology has finality or perfection. Perfect objectivity and perfect truth belong to a heavenly land.

Some of the documentation for this book, such as the *Review and Herald, Ministry,* and *Spectrum,* can be found readily in Adventist archival holdings around the world. Other documents used for this volume are lodged in Australia, with Avondale College archives, and in America at Loma Linda University archives, arranged in sequence according to the End Notes.

Finally, I wish to thank Arnold Reye and Lynden Rogers and his wife, Julie, for methodically working through the draft of my manuscript, looking for embarrassing gaffes and poor expressions. It is tedious work, unrelieved by the historian's thrill of discovery that comes when sleuthing among old documents.

Milton Hook

Chapter One:
A Passion for Books

In the bright Saturday afternoon sun of August 23, 1980, a large crowd converged on the Andrews University Seminary chapel at Berrien Springs, Michigan. A delegation had just returned from the Glacier View meetings in Colorado, where more than one hundred Seventh-day Adventist (SDA) Church leaders met to discuss Desmond Ford's thesis on the Investigative Judgment theory. The air was alive with anticipation. Their concern was just as focused on the man as it was on his theology, because he had attracted a significant following of devotees enthusiastic about his gospel preaching. They wondered, "What was to be the fate of Professor Ford and the church's belief in an Investigative Judgment?"[1]

The crowd became so large that the Seminary chapel could not contain the crush, so the meeting was moved to a larger chapel on campus. Not within living memory had so much interest been generated by religious debate. The man, Desmond Ford, who had brought the high-level discussion to a head, was he who had, "more than any other one person, made Adventists care passionately about theology."[2]

Many among the Andrews University crowd were stunned to hear the claim that Ford's thesis was largely rejected at Glacier View and the man himself was being threatened with disciplinary action. A short time later they were grieved to learn that he had been defrocked. This man was no ordinary individual, and in the meetings at Glacier View there were shades of Martin Luther at his trial.

Why would a Christian church, in the enlightened and progressive Twentieth Century, deliberately deprive itself of one of its best theologians, who at the same time was loyal, industrious, and arguably their most dynamic preacher of Christ's gospel? This inexplicable action far exceeded the mythical stupidity of shooting oneself in the foot. The carefully premeditated shot was deliberately aimed at the heart. How can such corporate foolishness be explained? As in the practice of primitive medicine, this bleeding of the body corporate was supposed to bring healing. Instead, it brought bruising and fractures, deep wounds and depression. Many believed the very Spirit had departed from their church.

For a serious attempt at rationality, we must seek out beginnings—the roots of an unusually gifted boy born some fifty-four years earlier in Queensland, Australia. We must carefully watch the impact of his contemporaries, his training, and the divine influence in his life. The saga traverses a number of key biblical topics of debate and raises the question, "How could one man exert so much theological momentum in the culture of Seventh-day Adventism, a group so protective of its traditions and so resistant to change?" What led Ford to trial, and was it really an ignominious end to a brilliant gospel voice?

Ford's odyssey begins in the Land Down Under, where his influence grew, and then extends to America and throughout the world.

Childhood in Queensland, Australia

"You can have a shilling for every book you read," Wilfred Ford promised his young son, Desmond. It was a family tradition. Years earlier, Wilfred's father had used the same incentive on him, a ploy that molded him into a well-read man.

And so, Desmond earned many a shilling. He vividly remembers reading a book for his father on the sinking of the German cruiser, Emden, in World War I. Over time he absorbed volumes of classics and penny-dreadfuls with little discrimination. He developed a prodigious passion for fiction, to be replaced later by an all-engrossing love of sacred themes.[3]

Desmond's father also encouraged him to recite poetry. Standing on a bench seat in their home when seven years old, he recalls reciting "The Slave's Dream."

Some piety ran in Desmond's veins. His paternal grandmother, who lived a healthy one hundred years, was of Scottish Covenanter stock. Her father knew the original biblical languages and would read the English version morning and evening to his children. He had memorized most of the Psalms. All their kinsfolk were uncompromising in religious debate, their grim dourness giving way to geniality and good humor only at family gatherings.

Both lines of Desmond's family were pioneers in Queensland, Australia. The Ford lineage boasted hardy farmers and cattlemen of English and Australian colonial stock. His maternal ancestors, the Simpsons, were English, Irish, and Chinese immigrants to Australia. George Simpson, Sr., Desmond's great-grandfather, was a saddler, hotelier, one-time mayor of Townsville, and editor of the Townsville Bulletin.[4]

Desmond was born in Townsville, Queensland, on February 2, 1929. His only sibling, brother Val, was four years older. They were sprinkled as Anglicans (Episcopalians) because their parents were nominal members of that faith. In practical terms his father was virtually an atheist. His mother, Lillian, Desmond recalled, always maintained "a religious facade."

While rearing his family, Desmond's father worked as a post-office telegrapher. He never cared much for religion, but he did motivate Desmond to read from an early age and arranged for him to join the local library. Desmond also devoured books from the good library of English classics owned by Grandfather Simpson, who lived just across the road.

As his father weeded the carrots or dug the potatoes, Desmond would read to him. He would read alone while his schoolmates played marbles. He would take his bicycle, a sack, and a book and read while standing in queues at the Townsville ice works. Rarely was a book out of his hands. By the age of nine, reading was a virtuous obsession for him.

Elementary years at West End Townsville School were typical of a government-sponsored education—rustic conditions, but sound in the Three Rs. In the tropical north it was customary to wear straw hats with ventilation holes in the top. Shoes were never worn until the teenage years. Decorum in the classroom sometimes gave way to more than games in the playground. Teams of boys would face each other across a short no-mans-land and stage stone-throwing fights. To this day Desmond carries small scars to the mouth and eyebrows but is thankful that boyish bravado did no long-term harm to his eyesight or speaking capabilities.

Wilfred's cousin, Lionel Smith, Sr., was a Seventh-day Adventist, and later, he and his family became Desmond's firm friends. The Smiths were acquainted with Raglan Marks, an earnest Adventist living in Townsville. But it was before Desmond was born, in his mother's early stages of pregnancy with him, that a Seventh-day Adventist colporteur named Lindsay Roland happened to call at their home, beginning a long chain of events that would shape Desmond's life.

Lillian showed some interest in what the colporteur had to say, especially about nutrition, and he returned to give a few Bible studies to her and Wilfred. As a child Wilfred was fed mainly soup—almost all that his mother had time to prepare while caring for a news agency. Wilfred, consequently, suffered with digestive problems in his adult life and gave ear to any promise of remedial nutrition. Nevertheless, when the colporteur began shifting from nutrition to biblical topics and the Saturday Sabbath,

Wilfred, especially, grew uneasy and the studies were terminated.

Lillian was attractive, intelligent, and articulate, but not a good cook. The traditional colonial menu, consisting of staples like beef and potatoes, had been called into question. Lillian's kitchen was now opened to better ideas. She now wished to help establish sound dietary habits for her husband's benefit and for the rest of the family's. So, she remained interested in the Adventist Church, experimenting with whatever proved to be simple and healthy. Desmond remembers that if the food was palatable in its raw state, Lillian preferred serving it that way. The benefits for Desmond were incalculable. His mind began to take in the principles of health that proved vital to his career. Later, Lillian bought the home health guide, *Ladies Handbook,* from another Seventh-day Adventist colporteur. She, with Desmond, also attended some Adventist evangelistic programs and a camp meeting at Bowen in 1939.

Desmond found the Bowen camp meeting to be dull, but he enjoyed the breakfast dish, Granola (from the camp kitchen) and visiting the beach and a small nearby bookshop. Charles Bird, the North Queensland Mission superintendent, noticed his fondness for reading and presented him with a Bible. He and his wife, Ruth, no doubt prayed for seeds of thought to be sown if Desmond should ever read it. He did, indeed. Over a period of three years, he absorbed it from Genesis to Revelation, completing it at about the same time he finished elementary school. He was embarking on a spiritual odyssey.

Desmond had scarcely begun this spiritual journey when his parents separated and later divorced for reasons of incompatibility.[5] The experience was no doubt both bewildering and sobering for a nine-year-old, but one that Desmond came to accept. Val and Desmond remained with their mother, temporarily moving into a flat adjoining the Simpson grandparent's home, across the road. Desmond's father went to Canberra, eventually moving into the Prime Minister's Department to supervise staff that handled secretly coded telegrams during World War II. He rarely provided financial support for them. They were thrust into poverty with the wolf at their door.

Bird and his wife began calling on Lillian to give Bible studies. Ruth would always leave the children's church paper, *Our Little Friend,* for Desmond to read. At this time a flirtation began between Lillian and Charles Bird, escalating into Bird's ceasing his church employment and divorcing his wife (though in later life he would return to Ruth. Bird moved to Sydney and started a dry-cleaning business in the inner-city suburb of Kensington. Lillian followed and worked for him, stringing him along, but refusing to marry him, despite his entreaties.

Southward Bound

When Lillian, Val, and Desmond made their way to Sydney by train, Desmond would hop out at some station stops to search the platforms for any rack of free Adventist *Signs of the Times* or *Our Little Friend.* He enjoyed reading the children's stories. On arrival they first found rooms at the Salvation Army "Peoples Palace" (so called), on Liverpool Street. Bird was living there, too, in a separate room.

Now, in 1941, it was wartime. Desmond remembers the naval ships in the harbor, the high-pitched scream of air-raid alarms and Australian and American servicemen on the streets. He recalls, too, the time when midget Japanese submarines penetrated the defenses of Sydney Harbor, everyone scrambling into underground shelters as the shrill sound of warning sirens pierced the air. The real threat of Japanese forces overwhelming the allied armies in the Pacific region filled the newspapers of the day. With anxious minds even schoolboys like Desmond followed progress of the battles.

Val initially found work in Sydney at Tooth's Brewery but joined the air force radar section in mid-1942. He served mainly in the Papua New Guinea region, without injury.

Lillian soon located a more permanent home at 23 Lily Street, Enfield, west of the city. It was austere, consisting of one room that had only a bed, an empty bookcase, a typewriter, and a picture on the wall of camels and the pyramids of Egypt—a spot Desmond would later visit.

In Sydney, Desmond and his mother continued their association with the Anglican Church by going to a service most Sundays. During the week Desmond attended Crown Street High, a government-operated slum school in Surry Hills, passing his Intermediate Examination (1943) in Bookkeeping, Elementary Science, two English units, and two Mathematics units. English was his favorite subject, although Science became a fascination. His expanding horizons also included stamp collecting in albums provided by the Eta Peanut Butter Company.

Arthur Hall, headmaster at Crown Street High, exhibited Christian values and earned Desmond's respect. During one vacation, Hall arranged for Desmond to get some drill and athletic training so that he could return and take charge of marching his peers to and from their

5

sports afternoons at nearby Moore Park. Some of Desmond's natural abilities also received further training. He won a prize for a story published in the school paper, and he was given regular duties in his school library in addition to the kindergarten library next door.

In school classes the teachers challenged his mind with theories of evolution. An Adventist friend loaned him some books by George McCready Price to provide balance from a creationist's viewpoint. Unfortunately, family poverty did not allow Desmond further years at high school. He felt he was deprived in this respect until he was able to attend college later.

It was Desmond's headmaster who advised his mother not to dally in finding him employment after leaving high school. Soldiers would soon be returning in large numbers from the war, he predicted, and would absorb the best jobs. Having some heritage in the publishing world and considering Desmond's love of all things literary, his mother took him for an aptitude test at Associated Newspapers on Elizabeth Street, Sydney. He was soon employed as a copy boy in the compositor room and also began attending journalism classes in the same building.

Desmond observed the proofreaders in their den above the Linotype machines, noticing that the room had no natural light and that the men were overweight because of lack of exercise. He was unsettled by the prospect that one day he might end up in the same room. Later, when promoted to the editorial room because of his own published material, his ears were offended by the constant profanity, so he determined not to spend his life in that environment. During lunch hours he would take the three-minute walk to the city library and search for books on creation and evolution. There he also uncovered a dusty set of Thomas Scott's *Commentary on the Scriptures,* the most extensive publication of this nature that he had seen.

Working at the same publishing office was a young man about Desmond's age, Fred Nossal. The two became good friends. They seemed to share similar interests, often discussing the meaning of life. Desmond gave him a book about the Bible to nurture his spiritual journey and in years to come occasionally corresponded with him.[6] Here, perhaps, lie the first indications that Desmond would spend his adult life in gospel evangelism.

Almost all of Desmond's wages went to his mother for their living expenses, but he gradually saved enough to buy a second-hand set of *Encyclopaedia Britannica.* In its pages he found for the first time the disturbing higher-critical views on the book of Daniel. His grandmother Simpson sent him a little pocket money that he spent on used six-penny records for his gramophone (phonograph) and cheap seats in the Sydney cinemas.

Working under Jack Lillis, a kindly Roman Catholic and editor of Pocket Book and World News, Desmond soon began to write for the *Sun Junior,* another publication under the umbrella of *Associated Newspapers.* He had been an avid reader of fiction for years and now produced a few penny-dreadfuls and shilling-shockers of his own. A sample title was 'One Night in Berlin,' penned in the context of World War II. Nowadays, Desmond wouldn't mind if silverfish ate the few surviving copies resting in a remote corner of his vast library.

Near the tram stop that Desmond used each day he conversed at times with a Plymouth Brethren shoe-repairer who shared the gospel with him. This cobbler's Christian witness was an excellent role model for Desmond. Traveling to work each morning with lofty thoughts in mind, Desmond would often muse on the jostling crowd spilling from Wynyard underground railway station. It would be a noble work, he thought, to learn the Scriptures and teach them to the masses.

As a teenage journalist Desmond's meager income hardly raised a rattle in a tin can, and pecuniary interests were never paramount in his life. But like his mother's, his path kept intersecting with Seventh-day Adventists, and a different interest intensified.

Closer Ties with Adventists
In about 1944 Desmond first heard the silver tongue of Lawrence Naden on Advent Radio Church, later known as The Voice of Prophecy. He wrote away and completed a Bible study course, the Schuler Series, offered on the program. Its proof-text method seemed very superficial, and Desmond found it disappointing.

On one occasion Desmond fell into conversation with another Adventist minister, Mervyn Ball, at the Sydney Central railway station, arguing against him about the sanctity of Saturday. Not only did the incident demonstrate Desmond's sociability, but it also indicated he had formed strong opinions early in his experience and was confident enough to advocate them.

Later, Harold Harker, Sr., working in conjunction with Advent Radio Church, walked miles to regularly study the Scriptures with him, carrying armfuls of books to prove his points. Desmond remembers that his studies were generally pallid but his prayers memorable. At one study Harker produced a dirty piece of rag from his pocket and covered it with a clean red piece to illustrate the efficacy of Christ's blood. Desmond never forgot that lesson. It was Harker, too, who sold Desmond meaty books like *Thoughts on Daniel and Revelation,* by Uriah Smith. He skipped the commentary on the last portion of Daniel 11, deeming it irrelevant. He read most of it while watering the garden.

More Adventist books kept falling into Desmond's hands. Archibald Hefren, a teacher at Burwood SDA High School, loaned him Ellen White's *Messages to Young People.* After reading much of it he was struck by the long list of ethical taboos it set for him—no more fiction reading, no more cinema-going, no more this, no more that, *ad infinitum.* These "messages" were in a similar vein to Ellen White's *Testimonies for the Church,* of which one child wrote with more candor than grammar, "The Testimonies is the things wot you musn't do."[7] Each dictum was like a bombshell dropped on Desmond's equilibrium. He read the last few pages of *Messages to Young People* under the streetlamp outside Hefren's home, before returning it to him. Its idealistic tone challenged him. He ended up dropping both fiction and the cinema.

Charles Bird, who remained a conservative Bible student and often discussed religion with Desmond, continued to feed his insatiable appetite for reading. In Bird's library Desmond read sections of non-SDA commentaries regarding the judgment scene in Daniel 7, noticing how they differed from Uriah Smith's interpretations. Bird loaned Desmond *The Outlined Bible* by Robert Lee, a Plymouth Brethren writer on gospel themes. He also loaned him a copy of *The Great Controversy,* another of Ellen White's books. Desmond read it on the Sydney trams and trains. This book made the most telling impact on his thinking and led to his conviction to join the SDA Church.

Eric Hon, in charge of social services among the SDA churches, also took a special interest in Desmond's welfare. In the winter of 1946, he and Thomas Sherwin, M.D., of the Sydney Sanitarium organized a rally for church members, especially the youth. During the meeting Sherwin called for the youth to dedicate themselves to God's service. Scores responded, including Desmond, who wrote a stirring report of the event for the SDA Church magazine, *Australasian Record.*[8]

Men like Hon, Harker, and Naden, among others, became role models for Desmond during his adolescence. He admired them for their genuine Christian graces. A psychologist might add that they acted as father figures. Certainly, together they nurtured him in the simple dynamics of Christianity.

Desmond was especially impressed with the writings of Ellen White. As he listened to Naden on the radio he was struck by incisive quotations used from White. It was, he said, their succinctness, their concise wisdom, that impressed him. He visited Naden, asking him, "Why isn't the name of God in the book of Esther?" He also quizzed him about the date of the writing of Daniel, because he had just picked up a second-hand book about it. Naden was unprepared but with his usual aplomb gave Desmond a study about the SDA view of the Mark of the Beast. A spiritual father-son relationship was kindled.

The decision to link up with the Adventists posed dilemmas for Desmond. How could he be a Saturday-keeper and remain working at Associated Newspapers? How could he avoid Friday evening classes as he attended night school, studying for his Leaving Certificate (final year of academy)? What, too, was he to do about his mother's displeasure? She and other family members strongly opposed the very thought of Desmond joining the church. She had shown some earlier interest herself but now was disenchanted and alarmed, fearing that Desmond would jeopardize his career and her means of support.

Some of these barriers were easily resolved. The boss at Associated Newspapers agreed that he could have Saturdays off. But the problem of Friday evening classes lingered. Naden arranged for Gordon McDowell, another young Adventist teacher at Burwood SDA High, to meet Desmond on a Sydney city street corner one day. McDowell offered to tutor him in the course content missed at night school. Desmond was impressed with McDowell's down-to-earth nature and was grateful for the offer, but chose instead to drop the studies altogether. The Adventist ministers who had befriended him could see possibilities of a different career path, with the church, and assured him his Intermediate Certificate (mid-academy level) would qualify him.

During the summer holiday of 1945 and 1946, Desmond rode the train to Melbourne with cousin Keith Dean, intent on searching the second-hand bookshops of Melbourne. As he was about to board the train, Bird pressed some pound notes into his hand, saying, "Buy a few good books." Desmond felt as if Father Christmas had emptied his entire sleigh-load into his lap.

Desmond first found the Melbourne library and after hours of reading happened on a book by Reuben Torrey that contained a useful appendix listing standard theological classics. He hastily copied the page. Armed with this wish list, he found a second-hand bookshop in Bourke Street and asked where the theology books were grouped. He then climbed a narrow, winding staircase to an upper room packed with a chaotic array of volumes. They were priced cheaply. Miraculously he found several titles he had listed earlier. Like a four-year-old in a candy store, he spent all his money.

Arriving back in Sydney with a box of weighty Christian classics, Desmond set about reading his treasure trove. Among them were W. H. Turton's *Truth of Christianity,* Charles Spurgeon's *Christ's Glorious Achievements,* William Paley's *Christian Evidences,* and Thomas Horne's 1839 *Introduction to the Critical Study and Knowledge of the Holy Scriptures* in five volumes, no doubt all coming from the estates of deceased clerics. They were now being relished by a young, fertile mind just beginning his journey. Tomes like these had an enduring influence on Desmond's understanding of Scripture and served as a bulwark against pervasive fundamentalist elements in his church. Horne's volumes, especially, established some basic principles of biblical exegesis that Desmond came to cherish. The conditional element of prophecy was a crucial principle based on man's free will and God's readiness to pardon offenders when they genuinely repent. Another was the principle of double applications that can be made of many Bible prophecies. Horne admitted that most German theologians rejected this principle, but cited at least seven learned church dignitaries who argued convincingly for its veracity.

Desmond's mother remained ill at ease with his attraction to Seventh-day Adventism, and she ordered a book from America that attacked SDA doctrines. It was called, *Forty-four Bible-supported Reasons Why You Should Not Become a Seventh-day Adventist,* by E. B. Jones. When it arrived, he chose to research the chapter on "The Soul," convincing himself that the Adventist position was biblical, and that therefore most of the other objections in the book were probably ill founded too. Despite his mother's continued reluctance, Desmond decided to be baptized and join the SDA Church. After all, there are some things a sixteen-year-old young man must decide for himself in order to shape his own eternal destiny.

Church Membership
So, Desmond was baptized at Waitara SDA Church by William Morris

on September 21, 1946. On the following Sabbath he was welcomed as a member of the Ryde SDA Church, located near the tram terminus and closer to his home.[9] At that time the Ryde church group met in a hired hall, and each Sabbath morning the members would clear the empty beer glasses off the piano, left behind after Friday evening community dances. At the Sabbath services Desmond's soul was stirred by good gospel sermons from ministers such as Robert ("Daddy") Hare and Robert Salton. Several of the members stand out in Desmond's memory as attractive, transparent Christians, including Cyril Evans, who told Desmond about the intriguing writings of C. S. Lewis. The Evans family, like many other Australians, had great affection for the defrocked SDA Bible lecturer, William W. Fletcher. One dark night, en route to meet Desmond's mother, Evans introduced Desmond to Fletcher, who happened to emerge from the shadows outside Burwood railway station while visiting the area. It was Desmond's only encounter with the so-called heretic who had retired to northern Queensland.

Ruth Bird, who had transferred from Townsville to Sydney, attended the same Ryde church and often invited Desmond home for Sabbath lunches. She was a real saint, a spiritual mother to him. She harbored no grudges against Desmond or his mother.

Desmond felt in his heart that he had made the right decision. He wanted to live as a Christian. From his reading of Scripture he believed the essentials of salvation in Jesus Christ. He understood the teachings of the Seventh-day Adventist Church. Much later, upon reflection, he admitted that at the time he was puzzled by only one Adventist enigma—the unusual interpretation of Hebrews 9 and further explanations of Christs heavenly ministry made by Ellen White in *The Great Controversy.*

Rationalizing the Great Disappointment of the Millerites, White had written that Christ entered the Most Holy Place in the heavenly sanctuary in 1844 to begin an Investigative Judgment of humanity.[10] But Hebrews 9 clearly places Christ in the very presence of God immediately after His ascension, not in 1844. Desmond had read that chapter more than once. Despite this solitary misgiving, Desmond later explained that he became an Adventist on the weight of evidence, seeing so many good things in Adventism and being generally impressed by White's books.

Having crossed his Red Sea, Desmond threw himself wholeheartedly into more Bible study, reading more of Whites books and Christian classics. He had no money for expensive volumes, so he ferreted among the second-hand bookshops in Sydney, such as Tyrell's, where he found a few more copies of White's writings—books such as Life Sketches, Ministry of Healing, and Education. Bird's library was also continually open to him, where he especially remembers soaking up the contents of Source Book for Bible Students and copying many of its pages with an antiquated typewriter.

Desmond's developing library was not everybody's bedtime reading, but there was now a long-range motive in his quest. He was thinking that he would like to study for the ministry at the Australasian Missionary College, Cooranbong, New South Wales (the denominations senior training institution affectionately known as Avondale). He had read a little about the beginnings and purpose of the college in *Life Sketches*. So, he, his mother, and Bird made an exploratory trip to the college, but the prospect of Desmond attending devastated his mother. She would not hear of it. Her hopes of Desmond becoming a good journalist with a reliable income looked bright, and she did not want him to risk losing that dream. And his brother, antagonistic toward religion and recently returned from the war, threatened, "If you go to that college, I'll drive my motorbike over a cliff." But Bird pleaded, "Let him go, and I will pay his fees." Mother relented, but big brother remained anti-church and angry about it for years.

Accordingly, Desmond quickly handed in his resignation at the press office and late in 1946 they all returned to familiar Townsville during the summer. Desmond worked briefly for a windmill company, then in the North Queensland SDA Mission office, and sold the denomination's health magazine from door to door.

By early February 1947, Desmond was on the train bound for Avondale. Gerald Peacock, the genial president of the North Queensland Mission for whom Desmond had done some weeks of secretarial work, smuggled him aboard the train to avoid his brother, Val.

Desmond sent a letter ahead to the college principal that concluded with the words, "...the prospects of attending college fill me with joy and gratitude to God."[11] A few months later his mother briefly revisited the college. She became reconciled to Desmond's attendance and wrote back to the principal, saying, "It is very comforting for me to know that he [Desmond] is perfectly happy at Avondale, and judging from my stay there, I can quite understand it."[12]

End Notes

1 Joel Valleray, "The Fate of Dr. Ford," *Concern,* Oct 14, 1980, p. 1.

2 Roy Branson et al., "Desmond Ford: Herald of Gospel Theology," *Spectrum,* Dec 1994, p. 4.

3 Biographical details in this chapter are from Desmond Ford, interviewed by Milton Hook at Caloundra, Australia, May 24, 25, 2001; Desmond Ford, interviewed by Trevor Lloyd at Sydney, March 12, 1995, and at Caloundra, Jan 7, 2001; Eleanor Hawke, "Sydney Newspaper Reporter is now a Senior Bible Teacher," *Avondale News,* May 1961, p. 4; Desmond Ford, *Physicians of the Soul,* (Nashville, Tennessee: Southern Publishing Association, 1980), pp. 95–137.

4 Elènne Ford, [Ford Ancestry], unpublished paper, June 30, 2001.

5 Note: In the 1970s Desmond renewed contact with his father and kept in touch with him from America during the 1980s. Val, in Australia, also renewed his association with his father. On one occasion, late in life, Wilfred and Lillian were persuaded to attend a family get-together but there was no real reconciliation. Both passed away in 1987, at eighty-seven years of age.

6 Desmond Ford to Gwen Booth, May 26, 1952.

7 T A B[rown], "The Home Letter," *Far and Near,* May 1922, p. 21.

8 Desmond Ford, "The Challenge of Service," *AR,* September 2, 1946.

9 Certificate of Baptism, Desmond Ford.

10 Ellen White, *The Great Controversy,* (Mountain View, California: Pacific Press Publishing Association, 1950), pp. 423–429.

11 Desmond Ford to the principal of AMC, Jan 9, 1947.

12 Lillian Ford to William Murdoch, May 14, 1947.

Excerpts from Desmond's 1942 diary

Saturday, January 3
I went to [municipal] library. Got "Chums" for one book. Read for 2 hours. 3 o'clock went swimming with Val. Manila taken by Japs. Went to church. Made ice cream. Val made lemon butter.

Tuesday, January 6
Met Jack Russell at 10:30. Went to Manly with him. Went swimming there twice. Grouse [Australian slang for "excellent"] baths.

Wednesday, January 21
It is a year yesterday since we all left Townsville. Sydney is a grouse place but I would like to see all my friends. Went to pictures and Hunters Hill by ferry.

Sunday, January 25
Read all the morning. Went to the very top of the Morris Hotel. 13 stories high. Went and had two 2d orange drinks at Happyland.

Monday, January 26
Australia Day [public holiday]. Went by 7:12 a.m. train to Katoomba. Raining and very misty. Cold as the dickens [Slang for "diabolically so"]. Grouse 3 hr train ride.

Wednesday, January 28
Japs suffer heavy losses. Met Jack [school friend] and went swimming. In the afternoon went to town with Jack. Went on all the escalators and lifts. Went in all the city buildings.

Monday, February 2
My birthday. Mum gave me 4/9, Val 3/7-half, grandma and grandpa 4/-. Wrote to John [Townsville friend]. Got two letters. Paid my debt.

Tuesday, February 3
Read all morning. Cracked 6 lbs nuts. Went to library. Went round town trying to buy a gramophone. Went swimming. Port Moresby raided by Japs. War very serious.

Friday, February 6
Started school. Lousy [Slang for "joyless"]. 2 compositions and page of definitions for homework. Sumatra bombed. All oil wells gone.

Tuesday, February 17
School. Physical training. Got 4 cuts [Slang for "a caning for misbehavior"] from Mr Pugh.

Friday, February 27
Japs bomb islands north of Queensland. Saw beach girl contest. Varnished my gramophone.

Sunday, March 15
Gave a talk at school on "Books I've Read and Enjoyed." I took about 2 hrs to prepare. Class and teacher liked it.

Tuesday, March 24
Mr Pugh chose Leon Gill and me to [rubber] stamp some things and we got out of 5 periods. Japs bomb Port Moresby again.

Wednesday, March 25
Finished stamping the things. Raining like the dickens.

Friday, March 27
Gave speech to 3rd year class ([Japanese] raid on Darwin). Gave talk on Sir A Conan Doyle to my class. Sport.

Tuesday, March 31
Finished reading "The Pirate." Started reading "The Paris Sketchbook" by Thackeray. Played three quarters of my records.

Sunday, April 5
Jap cruiser sunk. Went to the pictures and saw "Honky Tonk."

Saturday, April 11
Went to the Minerva and saw "Point Valaine."

Sunday, April 12

Church. Went to Luna Park. Went on the cars and the "Tilt a World."

Friday, April 24

Found out that I got top marks in English and History.

Saturday, May 2

Bought 9 new records. Did some of my homework. Read for about 1 and half hrs. Played cards.

Monday, May 4

Received my prefect's [monitor's] badge from Mr Hall at Assembly.

Friday, May 22

Leon Gill and I are now librarians of school library.

Monday, June 1

Japs two-man submarines raid Sydney harbour. No damage done except sinking of old ferry. 3 [Jap] subs sunk.

Chapter Two:
New Friends and Revised Understandings

Desmond's college experience over the next four years was naturally one of exciting mental and spiritual enrichment. His passion for books in the years prior to arrival at college served as a solid foundation for his studies. In the college library he discovered Charles Spurgeon's sermons, Arthur Pink's *Commentary on the Gospel of John* and *Commentary on the Book of Hebrews,* and classic histories of the Reformation written by J.A. Wylie and Merle D'Aubigné. Biographies of William Carey, John Wesley, Catherine and William Booth and many more were also found on the library shelves. Since then, over the years, he has purchased for himself about five hundred Christian biographies. These provided sermon illustrations and helped to sustain his courage in dark times.

Veteran schoolmaster, Charles Schowe, taught Desmond biblical Greek. His Bible teachers were Alfred Kranz, Nelson Burns, Anders Magnusson, and William Murdoch. Burns, he said, was "not a great scholar but a lovable Christian." Classes with Magnusson were "not the most inspiring," he remembered, but the man himself was the epitome of "probity." During class discussions, especially on Bible topics, Desmond was always an enthusiastic participant. Students quipped, "New Testament Epistles was taught by Pastor Kranz and commented on by Desmond Ford." Just a couple of years earlier, at his newspaper office desk, he had often pulled out Kranz's class notes and pored over them, not realizing that one day he would sit in the author's class.[1]

Murdoch made the most lasting impression on Desmond. He was an outstanding scholar and the first Doctor of Philosophy Desmond had ever met. He held him in awe. Like Lawrence Naden, Murdoch became a spiritual father and mentor. During some of his time at college Desmond worked as his reader and also did biblical research for him. One of those assignments was to do an Old Testament word study of *eduth* (witness or testimony). He also stepped in to take occasional Bible classes for Murdoch and Burns, whenever these men were called away to more urgent duties. The experience gave Desmond a lingering taste for teaching.

Murdoch was a man who thought outside the square. In his mind denominational doctrines were always open to refinement, even change. "It doesn't pay to put your stakes down too far," he repeatedly advised his classes, "because one day you may have to pull them up again." Murdoch was talking from experience. Earlier, he held to Uriah Smith's view that Turkey was the King of the North (Daniel 11), and Armageddon was a literal battle (Revelation 16). However, he later rejected these views in favor of a worldwide interpretation, running counter to church administrators back in England. For this reason, he had been exiled, as it were, to Australia in 1947.

After four years of association, Murdoch wrote of Desmond, "He is a brilliant student and a very good speaker."[2] He was not exaggerating. In Bible subjects and biblical languages Desmond's examination results were in the 90-percentile ranking.[3] "One day you must go to the [SDA] Seminary [in America]," Murdoch advised him under the jacaranda trees outside the chapel. Desmond went to his room and prayerfully opened his King James Version of Scripture. His eyes lit on the phrase "This is the thing that ye shall do...." (2 Kings 11:15). He admits now that it was a simplistic method of discovering God's will, but Murdoch's seed thought was not lost on him. The two men were, indeed, to repeat their teacher/student association at the Seminary a few years later.

A bicycle accident during Desmond's first year at Avondale almost cost him any future hope of being a public speaker. He was thrown to the road, smashing his teeth and badly lacerating his mouth, necessitating ongoing dental treatment to normalize structural problems. Fortunately, there was no legacy of a speech impediment.

In the men's dormitories Desmond shared a top-floor room with Les Parkinson, overlooking the Sanitarium Health Food factory, and another room later with Laurie Haycock. During term-end breaks Desmond sometimes went camping in the nearby Wattagan hills with these young men.

Like many other students Desmond made scores of friends for life at college. Later, in retrospect, he treasured memories of John and Mary (Buckingham) Trim, Geoff Helsby, Clem Christian, Lewis Lansdown, and Alec Moir (who later became best man at his wedding).

From the outset at college Desmond resisted the option of working nightshifts in the nearby Sanitarium factory. He would not jeopardize his health making health foods. Unnatural sleep habits enforced by the night work were anathema to him. Instead, he chose to work out in the sunshine and fresh air on the farm and orchard. Later he did some additional work in the library and dining room, to boost income for his fees. His godly grandmother would send him twenty-five cents a week for little necessities like soap and postage stamps. It was all she could spare. Charles Bird had obliged with the first-year fees, but the liaison with Desmond's mother deteriorated and his business suffered reverses, to the point where he could not fulfill his promise to finance Desmond's study. From then onward Desmond scrambled to find his own finances.

"At the end of each year," Desmond revealed later, "there was some threat about my return [to college], but the Lord always opened the way, strengthening my confidence in Him." For example, at the end of his first year, his brother demanded he bring all his goods home because he would not allow Desmond to return to college. However, Desmond found shelter in an Adventist home, away from his brother's anger, and sold books door to door in order to finance himself.

Desmond canvassed *Desire of Ages,* placing approximately one in every seventh home he visited. He admits that the work was an uphill grind, and that one morning his feelings were at ebb tide, but three sales in successive homes was all that was needed to buoy his spirits once more. He finally concluded it was simply God's goodness toward him that carried him through these efforts to earn college fees. Further reflection prompted him to believe the experience instilled some "social aggressiveness into one who was more inclined to retire with books."

No matter how hard Desmond tried to avoid the spectre of debt, it continually stalked him. In his graduation year he was deep in the red. Only with Murdoch's intervention was Desmond permitted to graduate, the debt being written off with the proviso that he be indentured to the church for a few years.

Throughout his time at college Desmond continued to use his literary skills. About a dozen articles for the church's missionary magazine, *Australasian Signs of the Times,* were published, beginning with one in 1948, titled "Pictures of Jesus in the Old Testament."[4] A series on books of the Bible followed in 1950.[5] Later, in 1952, he developed a regular Bible "Question-Corner"[6] in this paper that was to continue for nearly three decades. Not everyone, of course, agreed with his answers. Occasional articles also appeared in the denomination's *Australasian Record* and the college newssheet, *Avondale Forum.* Of special interest in the latter was an article titled, "A Study on Study," a virtual summary of the techniques he had garnered for the art of memorization. He declared, "The mind is like a camera. It cannot photograph in a fog." He wasn't talking about aesthetics for, admittedly, beautiful photographs can be taken in foggy conditions with subtle lighting effects. His thrust, instead, was against intemperate health habits and digressions of thought that clouded the learning process.[7]

Gaining knowledge, however, was only one aspect of college. There were also matters of the soul. Judging by an article Desmond co-authored about a week of prayer at Avondale, he was deeply touched by the preaching in the chapel.[8] Often his heart was persuaded, and his conscience needled. On one occasion the president of the North New South Wales Conference, David Sibley, was residing in the men's dormitories while visiting the college. At an opportune moment Desmond confessed to him that he had brought to college a pair of his brother's army shoes for his own use. It troubled him that perhaps he had wrongfully acquired government property. Sibley assured him nothing illegal had taken place and added kindly, "Blessed is the man with a tender conscience."

During these college years it was customary for students, especially prospective ministers and teachers, to give homilies at worship services. It was excellent training for Desmond, among others. He also took the opportunity to preach in small Adventist Churches nearby.

In conjunction with other ministerial students, Desmond also helped to enlist the student group into prayer bands, meeting early one morning each week. At 5:30 a.m. he often gathered the leaders of these small groups, giving a Bible study that they, in turn, would repeat in their prayer sessions. The themes of these studies were usually cutting-edge and ones being debated in the churches at the time—end-time topics from the Book of Revelation, such as Armageddon and the 144,000 saints.

What of the Heart?

Did Desmond find romance at Avondale? Cramming one's brain with theories on the age of the earth, the entire history of the world, and the philosophies and theologies of myriads of thinkers leaves barely a vacant corner to indulge in matters of the heart. But on one occasion he expressed concern for the health of a shy lass named Gwen Booth, who was studying long hours to struggle through her course. She was apparently moved by his interest in her welfare. Soon after, when he had finished addressing a group of student prayer-band leaders, she plucked up the courage to thrust a small filing folder into his hands. She whispered, "For your notes," and then fled the scene.[9]

Gwen had obviously developed some admiration from a distance. She noticed on several occasions that Desmond seemed disorganized with his preaching notes and thought her little gift would be a splendid way to help remedy the situation and also to say she cared about him. These sparks ignited a warm and tender friendship.

Desmond and Gwen assisted children in the local chapter of the church-sponsored Junior Missionary Volunteer Society and became better acquainted. Their paths often intersected at the library where Desmond plucked up the courage to ask Gwen her age. They wrote to each other during vacations. And as Desmond's graduation approached, they confessed their affection for each other on the steps of the college chapel.[10] It was the era when the faculty kept a strict eye on any budding romance. Taboos abounded. Nevertheless, within those restrictions Desmond and Gwen managed to mingle often enough to secure a fond regard for each other. In a brief note he passed to her on campus one day, he vowed, "Apart from my spiritual inheritance in Christ, you are my greatest blessing in the world."[11]

Gwen was reared under humble circumstances in Yass, New South Wales, by a mother with an anxious disposition and a quiet father who toiled on the local roads. Her elementary school was only a shack with six pupils and a teacher who had not completed high school. Seeking better learning conditions for her daughter, Mrs. Booth eventually found board for Gwen with Elder and Mrs. Albert Watts in Sydney. In the home she was a sometime Cinderella[12] but apparently was content in order to improve her lot in life. Gwen attended the SDA high school at Burwood, with Gordon McDowell and Archibald Hefren among her teachers. She was converted to Adventism at that time and later enrolled at Avondale College.

At college Gwen found work as a trainee elementary school teacher while at the same time studying for her teaching certificate. Among her fine qualities was first and foremost her devotion to Jesus Christ. Desmond spoke of her as his "twin soul." Thoughtful and unassuming, she was a quiet achiever and sensitive to the needs of others.[13] Occasionally she wrote articles on Christian principles of child training for the church missionary paper.[14] She and Desmond continued to keep in close contact after he left college.

Some Theology Refinements

In retrospect Desmond regards his Avondale days as often preoccupied with legalistic jousts and endless discussions over proper Adventist behavior rather than a sustained focus on the life of Jesus. He also admits his esteem for Ellen White's books caused him to give any topic a litmus test with her pages rather than on Scripture. Later, he learned she herself advocated that all sermons should quote the Bible alone.

At college it had been a rude shock for Desmond to learn that some of what he had read in Smith's *Daniel and Revelation* and other Adventist books was rapidly becoming passe in the denomination. His teachers and a few fellow students were suggesting some alternative views to Smith's textbook. Significant points concerned such matters as the interpretation of the King of the North (Daniel 11) and the Battle of Armageddon (Revelation 16).

Smith's charting of the fulfillment of Daniel 11 drew a number of demarcation lines between his successive world powers. Some of Des's peers believed Smith's transition points between the powers seemed arbitrary and strained. After describing some Seleucid history in verses 1 to 13 Smith proposed that the phrase "robbers of the people" (v. 14) introduced "a new power," i.e., pagan Rome. He did it without providing proof when sorely needed, for a transition is not obvious in the text.

Furthermore, Smith introduced a new power at verse 31. The "abomination of desolation," he believed, was papal Rome that abolished "the daily" (for Adventists of that era, pagan Rome). His brief discussion at this point was unconvincing.

A further transition took place, he alleged, at verse 36. The sentence, "a certain King shall do according to his will," he maintained, "clearly" introduced a new power and that power, he said, was Voltaire and the French Revolution. But it is not clear at all.

Smith then hurried on to verse 40, where he introduced Turkey as the King of the North. Apparently, he was aware some commentators pictured the papacy in these verses, but he brushed aside their view, saying it "is so evidently wide of the mark that its consideration need not detain us."[15]

Smith was like a sailor who had set out from New York for China, only to be found halfway up Chattanooga Creek without a sextant. Perhaps he was sailing under a false assumption. Today, it is imperative to ask, did Smith merely assume that chapters 10 to 12 of Daniel should navigate exactly the same sea lanes as chapters 2, 7, and 8? Is it a valid assumption that all of Daniels prophecies move through similar sequential empires to culminate in the Papacy and beyond? Or was Smiths interpretation colored with antagonism and fear engendered by the flood of Roman Catholic immigrants disembarking onto the Eastern Seaboard of America in his time?

It was clear to Desmond's teachers that Daniel 10–12 highlights the future history of Daniel's people, the Hebrews (10:14), but any link to the Papacy or the French Revolution or Turkey was debated. Furthermore, joining this vision with Armageddon in Revelation 16, they believed, introduced another dubious assumption, in addition to the extreme literalism employed by Smith.

Earlier thought leaders in the church had wrestled with the same problems of interpretation. In the 1860s and 1870s James White and Uriah Smith offered different interpretations to each other, White preferring the view that Armageddon was a war between earthly and heavenly powers rather than a battle between certain nations on earth.[16]

Later, Herbert Lacey, a prominent SDA Bible teacher early in the twentieth century, was convinced Daniel 11:1-30 found its fulfillment in Antiochus Epiphanes, and only the last portion of the chapter applied to the papacy. He also entertained the possibility that Antiochus Epiphanes could be regarded as "a type" or primary fulfillment in the entire chapter, and the papacy may then fit a secondary application.[17] Lacey was suggesting a long-accepted method of double applications in prophetic interpretation, as Desmond had read in Thomas Horne's volumes.

However, for decades the usual Adventist interpretation of Daniel 11 and Revelation 16 had changed little from Smith's viewpoint. Orthodox instructors taught that Turkey, as the King of the North (Daniel), would be squeezed out of Europe into Palestine, where it would be made vulnerable by the drying up of the River Euphrates. Japan and China, the alleged Kings of the East (Revelation 16), would then sweep into southern Asia and across the dry Euphrates. There the literal Battle of Armageddon would be fought, with the powers of Gog joining in (Ezekiel 38,39). Some thought Gog might be Russia or other European powers.[18] (No one thought to be consistently literal and believe the armies would use bows and arrows as portrayed in Ezekiel 39:3).

In sharp contrast to this view, one of Desmond's teachers, Alfred Kranz, had admitted in 1942:

[I] find myself leaning more and more to the view that

23

Armageddon is the conflict of the church with Babylon.... I must confess that as a result of my findings I have lost my belief altogether in the view that Scripture foretells a mighty international struggle centering in the Plain of Esdraelon in Palestine with the Asiatic nations playing their part in the conflict....[19]

This view gathered momentum in Australia. Walter M. R. Scragg, Sr., a church administrator and evangelist, reinforced Kranz's view when he cautioned at the same time:

I would warn against a centralization of prophetic interpretation to local Palestine. Armageddon and the Valley of Jehoshaphat must be viewed in the light of types of a world covered with the battle of God Almighty.[20]

By 1945 the traditional Adventist mishmash of Bible texts relating to Armageddon was being abandoned by many Adventist thought leaders. Their crystal ball was shattered by a different chain of events unfolding during wartime. Louis Were, an Australian Adventist evangelist who had studied Christopher Wordsworth's Bible commentaries, warned them in the 1930s and early 1940s of faulty exegesis in regard to the Apocalypse. He was dismissed on a pretext by a small group of vocal fundamentalists.[21] To attend any of Were's meetings after his dismissal was to court rejection by church leaders. Desmond was alerted to this danger by the college preceptor.[22]

By the time Desmond had reached college, most Adventist Bible teachers in Australia and America had abandoned Smith on Armageddon and were accepting a different scenario. At least two of his Bible teachers, Kranz and Murdoch, had wholly given up Smith's view and adopted the revised view of a worldwide spiritual battle between the forces of good and evil, as Were taught. Desmond came to agree with them. Keith Moxon, a fellow student, advised him, "You ought to read Louis Were's writings." Desmond took his advice and at the same time began correspondence with Were, whose books circulated widely. Despite the risk of guilt by association, Desmond later visited him in Melbourne about 1951.[23]

In college prayer bands Desmond and others aired the new views. This became common knowledge. Some parents of the students became alarmed, writing letters of complaint to college president Murdoch.

When Desmond was challenged by Murdoch, he produced the primary sources—Wordsworth's commentary and Joseph Angus's *Bible Handbook*—rather than Were's books. Murdoch immediately responded, saying, "Oh, Wordsworth and Angus are perfectly orthodox."[24]

Desmond emerged from Avondale with a broader view on many points of theology, graduating from the Ministerial Course after four years of study, 1947–1950. He completed the years with scholastic distinction[25] and undiminished zeal to share his religious experience. The blossoming friendship with Gwen was a wonderful bonus. She and Desmond would soon unite their lives in service for the church.

End Notes

1   Biographical details in this chapter are according to Desmond Ford, interviewed by Milton Hook at Caloundra, May 24, 25, 2001; Desmond Ford, interviewed by Trevor Lloyd at Sydney, March 12, 1995, and at Caloundra, Jan 7, 2001.

2   William Murdoch to Charles Bird, May 8, 1950.

3   AMC academic record transcript, Desmond Ford, 1947–1950.

4   Desmond Ford, "Pictures of Jesus in the Old Testament," *AST,* Feb 2, 1948, pp. 4, 5.

5   E.g., Desmond Ford, "The Book of Genesis," *AST,* Aug 7, 1950, pp. 6, 7.

6   Desmond Ford, "Question Corner," *AST,* Oct 6, 1952, p. 14.

7   Desmond Ford, "A Study on Study," Avondale Forum, [ca. 1949], pp. 6–8.

8   Ruby Peglar and Desmond Ford, "Week of Prayer at Avondale," *AR,* Aug 2, 1948, p. 5.

9   Desmond Ford, *Physicians of the Soul,* (Nashville, Tennessee: Southern Publishing Association, 1980), pp. 130, 131; Desmond Ford, unpublished memoirs, 1974, p. 2.

10 Desmond Ford to Gwen Booth, Jan 23, 1950, May 25, Aug 7, 1951, April 18, 1952.

11 Desmond Ford to Gwen Booth, ca. 1950.

12 Desmond Ford to Gwen Booth, June 19, 1952.

13 A[rchibald] Hefren, "Life Sketch of Gwen Ford," *AR,* May 25, 1970, p. 14

14 Gwen Booth, "Shaping Their Future," *AST,* Nov 13, 1950, pp. 12, 13.

15 Uriah Smith, *Daniel and the Revelation,* (Melbourne, Victoria:

Signs Publishing Company, n.d.), pp. 231, 255, 265, 273, 277.

16   Raymond Cottrell, "The Pioneers on Daniel Eleven and Armageddon," unpublished paper presented to the Bible Research Fellowship, 1949.

17   Herbert Lacey, Arthur Daniels et al., "Paraphrase of Daniel Eleven," unpublished transcript of discussion, [ca. 1919], GCA.

18   E.g., Horace Franks, *The Riddle of the Orient,* (Warburton, Victoria: Signs Publishing Company, n.d.); Carlyle Haynes, *On the Eve of Armageddon,* (Washington, D.C.: Review and Herald Publishing Association, 1924); A. W. Anderson, Through Turmoil to Peace, (Warburton, Victoria: Signs Publishing Company, 1932).

19   Alfred Kranz, "Armageddon and the Kings of the East," unpublished paper submitted to the Australasian Union Conference Committee on Special Study, Auburn Church, Melbourne, June 11, 12, 1942, p. 1.

20   Walter Scragg to Dear Brethren, [ca. June 1942], pp. 1, 5. Note: The "brethren" were members of the Committee on Special Study convening at Auburn Church, Melbourne, to discuss the teachings of Louis Were. Later, Scragg reverted to the traditional view.

21   Milton Hook, "Louis Were," unpublished paper [1986], Ellen G. White Research Centre, Avondale College, Cooranbong, Australia.

22   Ford, interviewed by Lloyd, March 12, 1995.

23   Desmond Ford to Gwen Booth, [ca. 1951].

24   Ford, interviewed by Lloyd, March 12, 1995.

25   AMC academic record, Desmond Ford, 1947–1950.

Chapter Three:
Seeds of Joy and Conflict

David Sibley thought highly of a man contrite enough to confess taking his brothers army shoes. When Desmond graduated from the Ministerial Course at the close of 1950, Sibley invited him to start his internship in the North New South Wales Conference of which he was president at the time.[1] Sibley was amiable and down-to-earth. His theological stance was broader than that of many administrators, and he was more tolerant and receptive of alternative views on contentious passages in Daniel, Revelation, and Hebrews. He would not badger Desmond with traditional views.

Initially, Desmond was assigned to begin work in New Zealand. Gwen was downcast at the thought of him going so far away. She shared her blues with Sibley on the college campus one day and he said, "If Desmond is interested in coming to North New South Wales Conference, then get him to give me a call." Desmond needed no second invitation. Alternative plans were quickly put in place for him to remain in Australia, and he relayed his jubilation to Gwen, confessing, "I must admit that the prospect of being nearer to you is a very pleasing one, and as I believe that our friendship is part of the Lord's plan this was a factor to be considered."[2]

Desmond's mother, still exercising her maternal role, insisted she must live with him wherever he worked in the conference so that he would be properly fed and well groomed.[3] A bed-sitter was therefore too small for them both. And finances would not stretch enough for a rented home. A caravan (trailer) was the only alternative. Maternal grandparents first came to the rescue with $500 to buy a jalopy, an Austin, but it had limited towing power. His plight was therefore to find a caravan big enough and bright enough for a woman of social tastes, as well as light and cheap. A colleague, not knowing of his perplexity, wrote to him quoting an Ellen White promise about God's relief in every difficulty. Less than an hour later, while walking the streets of Cardiff, a suburb of Newcastle, Desmond spotted a man building a caravan down an alleyway. He chatted to him and finally made a deal, buying it unlined, therefore lighter, and cheaper.

Desmond began his work under Sibley's direction by laboring on the construction site of the new Coffs Harbour church and assisting with Ingathering in the same area, i.e., soliciting for church mission donations.[4]

Gwen was appointed to teach in the elementary school at Auburn in Sydney. At Easter or other holiday weekends she visited Desmond and his mother. The young lovers usually spent the time together on long walks, becoming better acquainted and discussing plans for the future. Gwen brought Desmond little gifts of oranges or fruitcake. She took the time to knit him a cardigan for the winter. After one visit Desmond wrote playfully to her, "I have a complaint to make. A serious one—I have had over six of your cookies today and can now see the bottom of the tin!" Desmond reciprocated her thoughtfulness by typing up her articles that she began to submit for publication in church papers.[5]

In his first full year of church service, 1951, Desmond came face to face with Adventist fundamentalism when asked to assist evangelist George Burnside's crusade team in Newcastle. Young workers like Desmond were called on to advertise the program, manage the stage and visual aids, organize the ushering, and do some visitation of interested attendees.

Burnside had attended Avondale College in the Depression years without graduating from any tertiary course. Making the most of his oratory skills, he had conducted evangelistic crusades in Queensland, Tasmania, and his home country, New Zealand.[6] He was a John Wayne character. When he came on stage he was always pumped for a fight between the goodies and baddies, his powder tinder dry. First, he would ride out into the audience and shoot down the Roman Catholics. While his carbine was still smoking, he would then pull a Smith and Wesson from his side holster, as it were, and shoot from the hip at the so-called "apostate" Protestants. Before long much of the sizable audience was gone forever and gun-shy of SDAs. The remnant left behind was confined to the party faithful and a few who loved a religious dogfight.

This manner of evangelism was not unique to Burnside. It was, in fact, the general rule among Adventist preachers, a modified heritage from American Methodism in the Nineteenth Century. Lectures of the 1950s were dogmatic and contemptuous of other religions. The interpretation of Scripture sometimes started with dubious assumptions and proceeded along illogical lines with historical distortions and preposterous claims tossed in. One of Burnsides advertisements for the Newcastle meetings carried the lines:

> Will Christians own property on other planets? Hear George Burnside—harmonizer of science and religion. In this lecture Burnside will tell the exact location of heaven, what its inhabitants look like, and their occupation.[7]

Amazingly, some of the public loved this brand of speculation and were baptized. After the church granted them membership, they often generated dust storms of intolerance and became clones of militant dogmatism among their peers.

During evangelistic addresses it was the custom for the speaker to spend a little time answering a Bible query or two from a question box in the foyer. The evangelist himself usually salted the box with his own questions. Not only did he get to word the question, but he had also memorized an answer. Was it disingenuous or sanctified wisdom? Whatever the case, the ploy raised the credibility of the evangelist, many regarding him as a biblical sage or savant.

It was also the evangelist's custom to hold training sessions for his team—times for prayer, post-mortems on lectures, future planning, and questions from team workers. Answers by the evangelist had to be spontaneous. Unlike the question box, there was no opportunity for homework. On one occasion, after the topic of Armageddon had been presented, Burnside was speaking to his team when Desmond put up his hand and asked some searching questions. "If places," he asked, "like Sodom and Laodicea and Babylon, as mentioned in the Book of Revelation, are interpreted as figures of speech, then why is the site Armageddon in Revelation interpreted in a literal sense?" and, "Why is east, as used in the Book of Revelation, interpreted as east of Jerusalem when, since the end of the Temple and the sacrificial system, Jerusalem could no longer be regarded as the spiritual center of the world?"

Burnside was bewildered and his hackles were raised. By his questions Desmond laid bare some of the inconsistencies of the traditional literal view of Armageddon. The savant now looked silly.

With the meeting closed, Burnside immediately took Desmond aside, saying in a reproachful tone, "You've got a big head." With a show of piety, Burnside followed up by offering prayer, asking for God to bring Desmond into line.

Should Desmond have asked these questions? Yes. The church

encouraged the view that their evangelists were authoritative and proficient exponents of the Word. Evidence for this is found in the church custom of rewarding successful evangelists with administrative positions, in which they would sit in judgment at times on theological matters. Furthermore, the church argued for a spirit of inquiry, and the questions Desmond was asking were timely, not flippant ones designed to bring confusion. He simply wanted to open the subject up for some balanced discussion. The topics were already being discussed in whispered tones by the mission team. During these chats a hush came over the group whenever Burnside approached.[8]

Desmond knew that his Bible teachers accepted a revised view, different from the traditional view preached by Burnside. And Murdoch had shared with him the recent report of the College Bible Teachers Council in America, held soon after the 1950 General Conference Session.[9] Desmond did not project the names of teachers who held a different view than Burnsides to embarrass him. Instead, he simply asked the leading questions.

Desmond was always a sharpshooter. In this street duel he took three paces, turned, and shot the gun clean out of John Wayne's hand, while the bystanders looked on. It was certainly not the most politic thing to do, but Desmond exhibited a tenacious interest in arriving at biblical truth. Never again would Burnside publicly dispute with Desmond. Instead, he would first muster a small army of fundamentalist horsemen and whip them into battle.

Fundamentalism

Religious fundamentalism, or extremism, is one of the most dangerous elements in the world. It has many faces—Muslim, Roman Catholic, Protestant, Jewish, and more. It was instrumental in the death of Jesus, urged on by the Pharisees. It has caused inestimable hatred and bloodshed since the cross and, it seems, will feature prominently in the very last days of earth's history.

Is there a genetic predisposition to fundamentalism? It is commonly believed there may be some link. What is demonstrable is that fundamentalism rises from a cultural and sociological milieu and can only be understood in its context, often a society that is disadvantaged, unsophisticated, or frontier-like.[10] For example, among Christians it boomed during the Great Depression of the 1930s and the two World Wars. Poor sociological conditions breed anger and militancy.

The Islamic scholar, Imam Yusuf, made the blunt observation about fundamentalism among Muslims with these words: "There are Muslim fascists who are intellectually bankrupt. The only way they can argue is to eliminate the voices they don't agree with."[11]

The same applies to extremists in other religions. You can always tell a fundamentalist, but you can't tell them much! Adventists like to be regarded as evangelicals, but the reality is that there are many fundamentalists (in the general sense of the term) among them. These have a high regard for Scripture but misuse it, applying prooftext methods that often ignore the context and literary genre. It is unfortunate, too, that the word "infallible" is used of the Scriptures in the SDA Statement of Fundamental Beliefs.[12] Despite the official spin put on the word, it usually reflects, among Adventists, a belief in what amounts to be the verbal inspiration of the Scriptures. Some fundamentalist ministers have candidly made that claim, regardless of the fact most church officials would want to distance themselves from the idea.[13]

Parallel to Adventism's commonly held view of inspiration is the bias to literalize unnecessarily. Fundamentalists see almost everything in black and white. They usually miss the glorious colors in biblical language, the imagery or figures of speech, the context of the times in which it was written, and the nuances found in the original languages. They are often simplistic, biblically illiterate, and usually scorn intellectualism. They have zeal without knowledge. They proof-text to maintain prejudices and are consistently inconsistent. For this reason, they become easy targets for theologically trained sharpshooters.

Adventist fundamentalists also cloister themselves. Their rejection of the world drastically reduces their usefulness in the world. Their fortress mentality incorporates a belief in their impregnable nature and their possession of righteous answers and righteousness itself, together with an unfaltering conviction they will be exonerated in the end. Indeed, they teach that the last generation of Adventists, prior to the Second Coming, will be God's superlative trophies exhibited in front of an admiring universe. They breathe religious intolerance, not winsomeness and humility. They are usually humorless, critical to the point of demonizing any perceived enemy, and make miserable company.

They are also country cousins of traditionalists. Their spiritual forefathers, they believe, could not possibly have taken a wrong turn in the labyrinth of theology. Furthermore, some maintain that because their ancestors always used the King James Version of the Bible, it is therefore the only valid Scripture for them, reading sinister motives behind any variation in a modern translation. In the Adventist fundamentalist mind there are prayer wheels or rosary beads, as it were, on which they keep repeating the mantra, "We have the message. We have the truth. We have not followed cunningly devised fables. Stand by the ancient landmarks." They make stalwart missionaries and defenders of their faith—to the death, sometimes—but they are prone to defend quicksands on their turf simply because some lie within their inherited fence lines. They cannot bring themselves to build a new fence line that excludes perilous property.[14]

Loaded with these grenades—biblical illiteracy, religious intolerance, and a resistance to change—we must be careful when disarming them. It can only be done along gospel lines, with the Holy Spirit leading the way. They must first sense the depth of sin in human nature and experience the good news of divine forgiveness, then accept by faith God's perfect and accomplished atonement and live in a spirit of meekness and growth in all Christian graces. Along the way the Spirit re-educates in the better methods of Scripture interpretation. That is, the heart must first be broken before the mind is reshaped. Polemics and dialectics will not convert anyone. The milk of the gospel must permeate before the meat of Scripture is digested.

It is at this point where the John Wayne types failed miserably. They spent their time preaching sectarian doctrine, often of a dubious nature, rather than basic Christianity. In Desmond's first year of ministerial work, he undoubtedly did not fully appreciate the nature of fundamentalism but slowly and instinctively he resisted it, at the same time sensing a better method of evangelism. Early in his career he began to emphasize spiritual priorities that did not mesh with fundamentalism. For example, when relating an experience with some people who showed interest in the church, he told Gwen, "I suggested to them that on the Day of Judgment no one would be lost merely because they were sinners, but only because of the refusal to accept Christ's salvation from sin."[15] He made no mention of sectarian doctrine such as SDA remnancy. He was to spend much of his life trying to persuade fundamentalists to accept the good news of salvation.

Toward the end of Burnside's crusade in Newcastle the conference treasury funds were at a low ebb. Some of the mission team had no other choice than canvass church books to earn their living. Desmond was allotted territory in the suburbs of Newcastle, a city of shipyards and steel mills. Later he canvassed around the northern shores of Lake Macquarie at Toronto, Booragul, and Marmong Point. Then he went to the Upper Hunter region and sold more books in the country towns of Muswellbrook, Aberdeen, Scone, Murrurundi, and Ravensworth.[16]

Canvassing was not easy work. Inclement weather found Desmond dripping rainwater on people's doorsteps. He said his approach was much like Shakespeare's schoolboy—"creeping like snail, unwilling to school." The primitive campsites where he and his mother had to park their caravan often supplied unsafe drinking water, which resulted in a bout of sickness for Desmond. "Tomorrow, if there is no change," he declared to Gwen, "I will take castor oil with one hand and write a claim for a VC (Victoria Cross) with the other."[17]

By the end of the year, despite the privations, Desmond had sold 150 sets of books. "The Lord has more than rewarded my trembling faith," he rejoiced. When he completed his last delivery, he punched the air and shouted, "It is *finis.* Hallelujah!"[18]

Second Year

In 1952 Desmond was appointed to care for the pastoral needs of the Coffs Harbour district, under the watchful eye of a fundamentalist minister who met him with the discouraging words, "They'll never ordain you. You're too heretical." Desmond's earlier brush with Burnside was apparently not forgotten.

Desmond began by preaching the gospel and establishing friendships with the locals. Later in the year both men ran their public crusades—Desmond in Coffs Harbour Jetty and the other evangelist in the main township of Coffs Harbour. The fundamentalist baptized six converts and Desmond sixteen.[19] Subsequently, the fundamentalist was charitable toward Desmond, but because his crusade results were eclipsed this particular year, he was not happy. The conference president, Sibley, knew of it and promised Desmond a pastorate of his own for the following year.

Desmond's work in the Coffs Harbour district was intense. Finishing the building of the new church and the evangelistic campaigns were time-consuming. Desmond was in overdrive. His mother complained that he ate too fast, talked too fast, walked too fast, and drove too fast. It was partly due to his temperament, but when put into a situation requiring Herculean efforts he could rise to the occasion for short bursts.

Nevertheless, it taxed his emotional battery, so he promised himself that he would slacken the pace.[20]

Being located farther from Gwen during the year did not diminish their love for each other. Gwen managed to visit Coffs Harbour only during her brief holidays, between school terms. Their letters were prolific. At one point they confessed to each other that there was the typical Mars/Venus difference between them. Gwen admitted she was "very affectionate." Desmond described himself as "not outwardly demonstrative." But there was unmistakable warmth in their letters. Midyear was the first time a kiss appeared at the end of a letter from Desmond. With wedding plans for the end of the year, Gwen enthused in September, "Well, dearest Des, many hugs and kisses (be prepared for plenty after December to make up for your absence now)."[21] Desmond reciprocated, "The days are sweetened by the thought of the happiness our union will bring." He added, "To you, the dearest on earth, all my love and more than pen can say."[22]

Desmond sent Gwen a pair of stockings for her birthday. Commenting on the leggy illustration, he quipped, "The box maybe a bit vulgar, but I believe the contents are all right."[23]

Sibley could make the promise of a sole-charge pastorate for 1953 because he knew of Desmond's planned wedding at the end of 1952. It was the accepted norm that a pastor working with limited supervision should be married, in order to bring certain checks and balances to his ministry. This development was made easier when Desmond's mother tired of caravanning and its privations. Previously, Desmond had explained to Gwen that marriage would mean she would have to tolerate the presence and financial burden of his mother in their home. Gwen was graciously resigned to the fact of Lillian making up a threesome. But by now Lillian had had enough of New South Wales towns, especially the wintry conditions. Northern Queensland lured her back home. She would, in the future, only visit once a year "to maintain her [maternal] rights," as Desmond wryly stated later.

Throughout 1952 the letters between Gwen and Desmond reflected an increasing frenzy about wedding plans. Both were stretched in their duties with their minds on numerous urgencies. There was indecision about the caterer for the reception. The color of the suits Desmond and his best man should wear was debated. They were uncertain about finding time to buy Gwen's wedding ring. They mulled over the choice of a minister to perform the service and where the ceremony should take place—

Sydney or Cooranbong. And, initially, there was a misunderstanding over whether they should have one bridesmaid or two.[24]

Some things were certain. Based on Ellen White's writings they determined that there would be no ostentation at their wedding *(4 Testimonies,* p. 515) and a large sum of money was not going to be spent on photographs *(1 Testimonies,* p. 500).[25] The fact that White also forbad wedding rings *(Testimonies to Ministers,* pp. 180,181) was usually ignored by Australians, the cultural expectation of a bride receiving a ring being stronger than in America. Desmond and Gwen therefore followed Australian custom—the bridegroom placed a ring on the bride's hand during the wedding service.

Gwen planned meticulously for the grand day. Early in November Desmond himself was finally able to get to Cooranbong and Sydney to make final preparations. In the space of a day or two the date and venue were settled, invitation cards printed and posted, and the wedding ring purchased. Doug Martin, a personal friend, was chosen to sing during the service.[26]

Two Become One

Desmond and Gwen were wed on Wednesday, December 17, 1952, in the Avondale College chapel, a place of hallowed sentiment for many college students. The celebrant was Desmond's mentor, Dr. Murdoch, who was about to leave Australia and take up a new appointment as a lecturer at the SDA Seminary in Washington, D.C.[27]

Not many Queensland relatives were able to travel the long distance to attend the wedding, but Dess mother and Gwen's parents and sister, Linda, traveled south to be there. More relatives sent gifts and good wishes. Most of the guests were from Sydney and the Cooranbong district, including Alfred Kranz and his wife. Gwen's devoted schoolchildren sent a water set, a crystal set and a silver tray. Church members at Coffs Harbour had previously showered them with kitchen electrical goods and a set of cutlery.[28]

In wedded bliss Des and Gwen set out for Wollongong on their honeymoon in a flivver, a 1929 Chevrolet Tourer. Des had earlier crashed it on the way to a Bible study, rolling the vehicle over about four times on a rough and sloping mountain track near Megan, scattering his suitcase, tools, and prophetic charts all down the hillside. The windshield was smashed, the hood torn off, and two wheels were badly buckled. Fortunately, when it came to rest, he was still in the car, with only bruises and small cuts. He scrambled out and walked to the nearby farmhouse, gave his Bible study, and then his friends hauled the car into town.[29] Despite repairs it never ran as well again. Makeshift gadgets, such as a bath plug on a string to act as a choke, spoke of desperate measures to keep it going. It became so unreliable and embarrassing he often chose to hitchhike to appointments. However, it gave little trouble during their honeymoon.

In their first year together, 1953, Des and Gwen were assigned to the Quirindi pastorate in north New South Wales. Des conducted an evangelistic campaign in the local sports pavilion. His college friends, Alan Probert and his wife, Beryl, assisted with the music.[30] The Fords lived in a caravan and the Proberts in an old schoolhouse, all on church property. Des stored his growing library in a tumbledown shed onsite.

For the following eighteen months, 1954 to mid-1955, Des was appointed to minister further west at Gunnedah. On arrival he held evangelistic meetings in The Small Town Hall, arousing some mild opposition from the local Baptist minister who published a disclaimer, saying, "The Baptist Church is not in any way connected with the meetings at present being conducted by Mr. Desmond Ford." Des Mowday and his wife, Shirley, billed as "The Musical Mowdays," helped for most of the period in this country town.[31]

During those months appointments were extended even further west to the farming communities of Narrabri and Wee Waa where a few isolated Adventists lived. An elderly member at Narrabri, Mrs Wyatt, would give Des a room overnight and then she would drive him to Wee Waa in her little Austin 7. There, Dr. Ludowici, an Adventist physician, hosted Des while he conducted an evangelistic crusade in the townships School of Arts. Advertising for these crusade meetings showed a different approach than did Burnside's posters, especially with regard to the topics of Armageddon and Russia in prophecy.[32] After the meetings Des would quickly travel back home by train for further speaking engagements.

In mid-1955, Des and Gwen moved farther north in NSW to Inverell, remaining there until the end of 1957. Once again, Des launched into another public crusade with Butler Hall in the town center as the venue.[33] He was kept busy preaching and giving Bible studies, conducting an evangelistic radio program, and teaching Scripture classes in the local high school. (Government school regulations permitted clerics to voluntarily conduct a weekly class of their own denominational children and any others who chose to attend.) While Des was occupied with his duties, Gwen bravely tried some colporteur work, having some success despite her timidity.

Still ringing in Dess ears were the words, "You should go to the Seminary," spoken by Murdoch some years earlier. Both he and Gwen were convinced they should plan for further study overseas, but how would they ever raise the finance? They deliberately spent little on furniture during their first few years of marriage, but they found themselves repeatedly paying for repairs to their troublesome car. And some of their resources were devoted to the support of Des's mother.[34] No matter how frugally they lived, the meager ministerial salary was sorely tested. No clear avenue for study overseas was evident at the time.

In 1955 a move by some church administrators had almost changed Des's career path. Members of the Central Pacific Union Mission executive requested he be appointed to their field.[35] However, the top body, the Australasian Union Conference, advised the Missionary Appointees Committee that they preferred he remain in homeland evangelism, effectively sinking any plans the CPUM had for his services. In retrospect, it appears the continuance of Desmond's ministry in Australia hastened his prospects for study at the Seminary.

The Ford-Burgin Debate

Des's stay at Inverell established his future. First, it was at this time that he was ordained. Second, in 1955 he engaged in a public debate with a Church of Christ minister, Pastor Burgin, over the Sabbath issue. It brought some kudos for Des.

Burgin, a formidable opponent of Seventh-day Adventists, was accustomed to debating with Adventist ministers on the Sabbath issue. With the local Church of Christ Jubilee imminent it became known that Burgin would visit the celebrations. Some townsfolk saw an opportunity for a debate and let it be known to Des. For a month Des pondered the prospects. He obtained a copy of a Burgin diatribe against Burnside and studied the contents closely. An old SDA classic by J. N. Andrews, *The History of the Sabbath,* was also probed and searched at length, presenting him with several fresh lines of argument. He became so intense that it was hard to get to sleep at night. He worried that if such a debate were to be lost it would bring discouragement to his flock, and he himself would lose credibility as an Adventist pastor.

As soon as Burgin arrived in town he began preaching against SDAs, throwing down the gauntlet for anyone to prove that the Sabbath was instituted at Creation. Des resolved he would accept the challenge and try to arrange the debate in a private home. As expected, Des was invited to the Church of Christ celebrations, and it was there that he first met Burgin. Predictably, Burgin said to him, "I would like to have a public debate with you."

"Fine," said Des, "let's have it every day for a month."

"No," replied Burgin, "that would be unnecessary."

"What about every day for a week?" Des offered.

"No," Burgin insisted, "that's still too long."

"Would an all-day debate be adequate?" Des finally asked.

"No, just one evening would be quite sufficient," Burgin concluded.

It was first agreed to conduct the meeting in a private home, but the Church of Christ members insisted on a public meeting. They set the topic, "Is the Sabbath Binding on Christians?" Des agreed to the changed venue but wanted a more biblical title. Burgin suggested the qualified title, "Is the Old Testament Sabbath Binding on Christians?" On the spur of the moment Des agreed, but Gwen persuaded him the wording was biased against him, so he re-negotiated the title. After some haggling final consent was reached with the wording, "Is the Seventh Day or the First Day Binding on Christians?"

A couple of weeks before the appointed time, October 11, Des began advertising the debate widely. Harold Hollingsworth, his newly elected conference president, was informed and invited, along with other church officials. There were many prayer sessions. Des tried to relieve his stress by cycling and walking with Alex Moir, best man at his wedding and now his highly valued assistant in ministry. Alex advised Des at the time, "Remember, it's not what you say, but the spirit in which you say it."

On the day of the debate Des and Gwen had breakfast out in the sunshine, as was their custom. Then he secluded himself in the hills near his home. He walked, rehearsed arguments in his mind, prayed, and meditated.

A packed hall greeted both speakers in the evening, including representatives from other Christian churches. Burgin made the first presentation but had scarcely said three words before Des touched him on the shoulder and suggested the meeting should begin with prayer. The initiative immediately placed Des in a favorable position with the audience.

Burgin put forward his usual objections and Des met him at every turn with arguments that transcended the usual Adventist approach. Then Burgin resorted to sarcasm, losing further ground with the crowd. Increasingly his mouth and eyes twitched uncontrollably as he realized proceedings were slipping from his command. For the first time in his experience, he was really befuddled. At the close Des shook hands with him. Burgin did not wait around.[36] His loyal church members, however, believed he had gained the upper hand. SDA members left the hall declaring their man had won the battle.[37] A telegram was sent to head office, saying, "Ford slew the dragon." They replied, "Congratulations slaying dragon. When funeral?"[38]

Immediately after the meeting Des and Alex walked for hours, arriving home about 1 a.m., four hours past the usual bedtime! The following days Des spent cycling and gardening to revive his energy. Twice he tried listening to the tape recording of the debate, but he found it too exciting. It only stressed him further. The proceedings did no harm to the SDA cause, and later Des baptized some of Burgin's church members.[39]

Sibley was so impressed he had no qualms about recommending Des as a college Bible lecturer of the future—the long-term goal on which Des was focused. Even Burnside circulated eight pages of extracts from the debate.

The Ford Family Grows

Gwen was well advanced in pregnancy at the time of the debate. She had the option of remaining at Inverell and being admitted to the nearest hospital just prior to the birth, but instead she chose to fly to Sydney to be close to the Adventist Sanitarium and Hospital.[40] This proved to be providential.

In those days there were no special leave provisions for evangelists, so Des was expected to carry on as normal in Inverell. His public meetings were still in progress and church services, Bible studies, baptisms, and funerals filled his calendar.[41]

Gwen's labor pains had already begun when, not knowing her condition, Des scribbled a reassuring note, "I am praying for you constantly as you enter this short time of trouble."[42] Scratching a few lines to Des in between contractions, she began, "My dear husband Des and soon to be papa."[43]

Her "time" was far from short and crowded with trouble. The

birth was a prolonged, thirty-four-hour ordeal. Dr. John Letham had to anaesthetize her and use instruments because the babe was in the wrong position.[44] Finally, soon after midday on Saturday, October 29, little Ellen (now Elènne) Gwen entered her new world. Mother and daughter had to remain in hospital for about three weeks. Des signed off in one of his letters, "Your loving husband, now proud papa."[45]

With Gwen out of danger and recuperating in the hospital, Des and his assistant, Alex, snatched a three-day camping trip. The pressures of the year were causing Des to experience "floating specs" before his eyes. He desperately needed a break. They gathered some essential supplies and motored south to the Bundarra region, camping in a large outcrop of rocks with the wallabies and kangaroos nearby. They took long hikes during the day and rested by the river on their return. Des had baked four puddings to bring with him, made, he explained, from "rice, milk, eggs, sultanas, salt, honey, and coconut—and an ant or two from the honey."[46]

When Gwen returned with Elènne, Des was called away to conduct eight meetings at the annual church camp, but he could not free his mind from his precious ones back home. With fond lines he told Gwen, "I am glad you have her [Elènne] with you, for she represents us both and neither of us is far away when she is about."[47]

Greive's Contentions

While Des was at Inverell, some theological jousting was spearheaded by Robert Greive, then president of the North New Zealand Conference, who was making a vocal stand against perfectionism in the Adventist Church. He was also taking a step or two away from literalism, disavowing a two-apartment sanctuary in heaven and teaching that no record of sin is kept by God after a person has confessed and is justified by faith. [48]

Greive's chief antagonist was Francis Clifford, president of the Australasian Division, who maintained that a belief in the sinful nature of Christ was the orthodox denominational position. Greive, on the contrary, was preaching that Christ possessed a sinless nature during His incarnation.[49] At the time, Greive was corresponding with Roy Allan Anderson in the ministerial department of the General Conference and found that Anderson, on studying the issue for himself, had recently arrived at similar conclusions.[50]

Anderson was in the midst of co-authoring the book *Questions on Doctrine* with two colleagues at General Conference headquarters. Published the following year, it advocated, among other controversial topics, the sinless nature of Christ.[51] The authors were optimistic about weaning the SDA Church away from its fundamentalism,[52] but after the book's publication they were stunned by the vitriol from church fundamentalists such as Milian Andreasen.[53] However, the view regarding the sinless nature of Christ gathered support among some leading administrators in America. Clifford was silenced by this turn of events but, by then, it was too late for Greive and three other ministers, because they had all been defrocked for their stand on a raft of issues.[54]

Besides his view on the nature of Christ, Greive had also stood firmly by the Protestant dictum of *Sola Scriptura,* emphasizing that the Bible should be allowed to interpret itself. Clifford, on the other hand, advocated a belief similar to one found in Roman Catholicism and Mormonism, i.e., there are extra-canonical writings that are equally authoritative for doctrine and ethics, namely Ellen White's. Clifford is reported to have claimed, "If the servant of the Lord [White] declared there were picks and shovels in heaven, we must believe there are picks and shovels in heaven."[55]

Chief among the contentions raised by Greive was the issue regarding the Old Testament sanctuary services and what they taught about personal salvation. His positions were similar to those of William Fletcher, the Bible teacher at Avondale College in the 1930s. Des had met him briefly in 1946. Sibley, a Conference President and one who had seen Fletcher sacked for his views, astounded Des one day by blurting out in the course of conversation, "Fletcher was right!" Sibley explained that there never has been a church group without error, including SDAs, but that they can all be a blessing to others, nonetheless. Despite his inclinations, Sibley was obliged to make an effort to counter Greive, and he enlisted Des to conduct a series of meetings in Brisbane for that purpose. "Pray for me amid the controversy," Des wrote home to Gwen.[56]

Central to Greive's thesis was the rejection of a belief in a literal sanctuary in heaven. Greives inquisitors asked, "Was not a literal altar and literal incense and literal coals and literal smoke seen by John, as recorded in Revelation 8?" He replied, "Did John also see a literal pregnant woman in heaven, as recorded in Revelation 12?" The answer was quite obviously, "No." His point was that the symbols in Revelation carried little or no physical resemblance to the spiritual realities. Likewise, he stated, the symbolism of the Mosaic tabernacle bore no physical resemblance to what is commonly called the heavenly sanctuary. For example, the showbread, which represented Jesus as the bread of life, possessed no physical likeness to the person of Christ.[57]

Greive also found the SDA concept of a heavenly sanctuary with two apartments, separated by a veil and Christ moving beyond that veil into a Holy of Holies in 1844, un-Scriptural and positively un-Christian. It contradicts, he said, the Book of Hebrews. He accused Adventists of sewing up the torn veil of the Jerusalem Temple, as it were, relegating Christ's ministry in heaven to that of an ordinary priest from His resurrection until 1844, and only allowing His high priestly ministry to operate after 1844. Greive insisted that the Book of Hebrews clearly taught that Christ began His high priestly ministry from earliest Christian times, not 1844.[58]

Greive also maintained the supernatural tearing of the Temple veil in Jerusalem at the time of Calvary signified a completed atonement and ready access to the Heavenly Father through Jesus. In other words, all services that took place in the Mosaic tabernacle, including the entire Day of Atonement ceremony, prefigured the cross and found their complete fulfillment there.[59]

This teaching amounted to heresy in the eyes of most Australasian SDA Church administrators—Sibley, apparently, being one exception. SDA orthodoxy had taught that the first three festivals of the Jewish annual calendar—Passover, Unleavened Bread, and Pentecost—were fulfilled in the first Christian century. The fulfillment of the last three festivals—Trumpets, Day of Atonement, and Tabernacles, they claimed—were postponed until the Millerite preaching that trumpeted 1844, followed by the Investigative Judgment bringing final atonement, and then eternity in the new earth when Christ would tabernacle with the saints.[60]

SDAs never took this position to its logical conclusion. If their explanations were true, then any unfulfilled portions of the sanctuary services should have continued to be a part of religious services until the types met their antitypes sometime yet in the future. However, SDAs overlooked this fact and did not teach the annual necessity of sending a scapegoat into the wilderness or celebrating the Feast of Tabernacles (Numbers 29).

Greive pressed further. He maintained Christ's atonement at the cross was complete (Romans 6:10), just as the type indicated in the

Mosaic services.[61] After all, it is with somewhat monotonous regularity that Leviticus repeats the words "it shall make atonement" after the description of each offering. It does not read "it shall be a good start toward an atonement" or even "it shall go a long way toward an atonement." Instead, there exists a sense of finality and completeness about each service there and then, not a lingering of sin or an uncertainty about forgiveness or the need of a second, or continuing atonement at some later date. The opposite view was expressed from the earliest days of the Advent Movement, categorically arguing for an unfinished atonement at the cross.[62] SDAs argued that the daily Hebrew service prefigured the cross, bringing a "temporary or provisional atonement" and the annual Day of Atonement service prefigured a "cleansing" atonement or final blotting out of sins beginning in 1844.[63]

Greive was also adamant about the absolute forgiveness of sins immediately upon repentance. He insisted that when a person's sin was forgiven, not only was the guilt lifted, but the record of that sin was eradicated. It was a blotting out; a casting into the depths of the sea; a refusal by God to record them in some way; a reconciliation or reinstatement of the sinner, just as if the individual had never sinned (Isaiah 43:25; Acts 3:19; Romans 4:8; 8:33,34; Ephesians 2:18; 2 Corinthians 5:18,19; Hebrews 4:16; 10:19,20). This, he added, brought joyous assurance to the Christian believer. On the other hand, the Adventist scenario delayed a blotting out of sins until the record of the individual came up in an Investigative Judgment, sometime after 1844. Clifford reflected this position when he is reported to have said, "God neither forgives absolutely nor entirely [until the Investigative Judgment]." This situation, Greive said, understandably left SDA penitents uncertain of their salvation, apprehensive and unable to face either life or death with the Christian assurance of total forgiveness.[64]

In the substructure of the Adventist concept of an Investigative Judgment there lay a literalism surrounding the existence of heavenly books of record, innumerable lists of good and bad deeds housed on high. Fundamentalists pictured the angels hard at work scribbling in a heavenly scriptorium. They never imagined the Book of Life, for example, to be a figure of speech drawing on the Hebrew custom of keeping civic records so that legitimate citizens could enjoy legal, social, and religious privileges (Ezra 2:62; Isaiah 4:3; Ezekiel 13:9). Adventists, from time to time, even updated the meaning of these "books," seriously suggesting the records could be videos or perhaps even computer discs.[65]

Why are these heavenly registers kept at all? First, it is alleged, for God's reference so that He can decide in an Investigative Judgment whether or not an individual should be saved eternally. Secondly, for the saints' benefit, it is said, when they will later research these lists in heaven to convince themselves that God was absolutely fair in the judgments He had made. Further, it is alleged, the unfallen beings throughout the universe need some record of evidence that God has been just in His dealings with sin.[66]

The concept puts limitations on God's memory and places no significance on the fact that unfallen beings have been privy to God's righteous dealings with sin for eons. Surely the significance of Calvary brought the ultimate conviction that His ways are just and gracious.

Furthermore, the allegation that the Investigative Judgment is for the saints' benefit is based largely on 1 Corinthians 6:2 and 3 and joined arbitrarily with various references to figurative heavenly books. However, it is significant that Paul does not say when the judgments take place; under what circumstances they occur; why the saints take on the role of judges; what resources will be used; whether or not they are cursory or comprehensive in nature; or if they have any executive power. The verse is, as it were, a Pauline one-liner about which fundamentalists have written a conjectural essay.

This belief suggests the unthinkable—that humans who have some doubts about God's righteousness, who are not sure of His capacity to judge perfectly, will arrive in heaven to check up on God's judgment. They will, supposedly, sit in judgment on the Supreme Judge of the universe! What if they find Him in error? They will not, of course. So, what will be the point of their investigation? Will it be to quell any doubts they have of judgments they may read about lost individuals? This is highly unlikely and smacks of morbidity. On the contrary, the saints will conceivably have the utmost confidence in God's judgments before their ascension and glorification. Furthermore, the character of God is not on trial, begging an investigation. God's righteous and loving character was vindicated at Calvary. The trial is over. The finding of the universe forced the eviction of Satan and his angels from heaven (Revelation 12). Everyone now simply waits for the Advent and the executive judgment.

Some Key Voices Echo Greive

Greive's grievances concerning Adventism attracted the displeasure of church administrators, and he was dismissed in September 1956. A handful of sympathetic colleagues were also fired.[67] Des had made an effort to minister to two of them. One said that his former Bible teacher, Kranz, agreed with Greive in many points. In order to clarify the situation, Des wrote to Kranz, seeking answers about the sanctuary in heaven, Ellen White's writings, and the Investigative Judgment.

Kranz replied candidly. The following sample of extracts pictures him slaying a herd of sacred cows. He confessed concerning the heavenly sanctuary:

> We have erred in conveying too much of the idea of a material building with articles of furniture in heaven.... I have no doubt myself, although I have not taught it publicly, that the Book of Hebrews teaches that Christ entered the holy of holies at His ascension.... The whole purpose of the writer of Hebrews is to show that Christ has opened up a way into the unveiled presence of God.... Honestly, doesn't the view of an Investigative Judgment going on since 1844 seem more and more questionable as the years lengthen?[68]

Discussing Ellen White's writings, he declared:

> There can be no doubt whatever that Sr. White is unscriptural in many of her views. I could point to numerous errors in her writings and to interpretations of texts which are contradictory to sound exegesis. Even some of the things which she says she "saw" or "was shown" have been proved incorrect. And yet our leaders in general close their eyes to these things and refuse to discuss them, or, if they do admit them, fail to discern their import, and still lead our people to rely upon them as the word of God.... What worries me is that as a people we have virtually made Sr. White's writings the final word in theology and the touchstone of a person's loyalty. Consequently, we cannot make any progress in an understanding of the Scripture. How can we, so long as we believe in a divine commentary. Personally, I can see little difference between having a divine commentary and an infallible church or Book of Mormon, to tell us how we are to understand Scripture.[69]

Des also solicited answers from America, specifically from author Denton Rebok at General Conference headquarters. Rebok was on other business elsewhere and the letter was passed to the office of Roy Allen Anderson. Anderson pled that the pressure of work would not allow adequate answers and sent a new tract instead.[70] By that stage it seems he was reluctant to enter into the Australian debate. After all, Clifford had axed ministers for the very tenets Anderson was actively trying to promote.

Edward Heppenstall, a Bible lecturer in America, was less guarded than Anderson, answering Des in a forthright manner similar to Kranz's. The "hour of judgment" (Revelation 14), he said, excluded an Investigative Judgment because God was omniscient and could make innumerable assessments instantaneously. On the subject of Christ's atonement, he added:

> Christ's complete atonement is effected not at the point of entrance but at the point of sacrifice, not when He entered heaven. He entered into the presence of the Father *because* the atonement was complete. [Emphasis mine][71]

In order to assist his fellow ministers and understand the topical debate for himself, Des met Greive in person, even though Clifford forbad any contact with the so-called heretic.[72] He found Greive to be embittered by his experience. Des said little at the time. There appeared to be a growing concurrence between some of his own viewpoints and those expressed by Greive, Kranz, and Heppenstall. Nevertheless, judging by comments Des wrote in the margins of a document penned by Greive, he was not prepared to accede to every major point made by Greive. Des's theology was still in its adolescence.

The axing of ministers did not quell the questions. Des wrote further letters to America, seeking answers regarding the denomination's teachings about the Hebrew and heavenly sanctuaries. Professor Murdoch, now at the Washington Seminary, and Walter Read at General Conference headquarters, offered him some answers.[73] At the same time Clifford continued the battle with a challenge to Francis Nichol, the editor of the *Review and Herald.* Nichol was forthright in his reply to Clifford, urging that the SDA sanctuary doctrine could not be proved from the Book of Hebrews. He added a warning about treating the subject with too much literalism, as Clifford was prone to do.[74] Clearly, in 1957, there was a theological rift developing, and Des was trying to be conversant with the issues.

Throughout these years as an evangelist, Des continued to explore ways and means for further academic study. He was eager to fit himself for the task of college Bible teaching.[75] His library continued to grow with the addition of more second-hand books. He completed correspondence courses with the SDA Home Study Institute in America, at times disagreeing with his tutors there. All his inquiries made it evident he would need to gain a master's degree at the SDA Seminary, the prerequisite being a bachelor's degree then being offered at Avondale College. Finances were the stumbling block. He had scarcely three pennies in his piggybank.[76]

All obstacles to further study had disappeared, however, by October 1957. Some weeks earlier, plans were made by Avondale College and the Australasian Division, voting to sponsor Des to groom him as a prospective Bible lecturer at Avondale.[77] Des and Gwen were overjoyed. The barriers against advanced education had dramatically fallen over, enabling them to return to Avondale for further study in the 1958 college year.

A Further Addition

While these happy prospects for advanced education were in the air, Des and Gwen were anticipating the birth of their second child. Once again Gwen chose Sydney Sanitarium and Hospital and went south about the same time Des attended Avondale College for summer school. Little Elènne remained behind with church family in Inverell.

If the newborn should be another daughter, they would call her Grace. Paul was the name chosen for a boy.[78] With the arrival of the annual Christmas holidays, Des had virtually severed his ties with all responsibilities at Inverell and was able to be closer to Gwen for the occasion.

The birth progressed without complications, and a healthy boy was born on Friday, December 20, 1957. They named him Paul Wesley. Back in Inverell, Elènne proudly told her playmates, "I have a baby brother."[79] She accepted him without any feelings of rivalry and learned to love him dearly. During January 1958 the Ford family re-united and settled in at Cooranbong, preparing for the start of Des's regular college study program. The years of evangelism in rural towns of New South Wales had been rich with memorable experiences and had further developed his social and public speaking skills. These he took with him, refining and expanding them in the years ahead.

End Notes

1   Biographical details in this chapter are according to Desmond Ford, interviewed by Milton Hook at Caloundra, May 24, 25, 2001; Desmond Ford, interviewed by Trevor Lloyd at Sydney, March 12, 1995, and at Caloundra, Jan 7, 2001.

2   Desmond Ford to Gwen Booth, [ca. Dec 1950].

3   *Ibid.*

4   Desmond Ford to Gwen Booth, March 2, 6, 1951.

5   Desmond Ford to Gwen Booth, March 28, May 13, July 23, Nov 20, 1951.

6   Stanley Wood, "A M College Notes," *AR,* April 24, 1933, p. 3; A[lbert] Mitchell, "Wedding Bells," *AR,* March 2, 1936, p. 7; Bruce Manners, "Burnside: A Life of Evangelism," *AR,* April 30, 1994, p. 10.

7   Desmond Ford to Gwen Booth, April 4, 1952 (verso).

8   Desmond Ford to Gwen Booth, July 27, 1951.

9   Desmond Ford to William Murdoch, Nov 5, 1951.

10 E.g., Malcolm Bull and Keith Lockhart, *Seeking a Sanctuary: Seventh-day Adventism and the American Dream,* (New York, NY: Harper and Row, 1989); and "Through Islamic Eyes," Good Weekend insert, Sydney Morning Herald, Dec 1, 2001.

11 Quoted by Jack O'Sullivan, *Sydney Morning Herald,* Oct 11, 2001, p. 6.

12 Ministerial Association, General Conference of Seventh-day Adventists, *Seventh-day Adventists Believe...: A Biblical Exposition of 27 Fundamental Doctrines,* (Hagerstown, Maryland: Review and Herald Publishing Association, 1988), p. 4.

13 Austin Fletcher to Milton Hook, May 11, 2001.

14 On modern fundamentalism see, e.g., Norman J Cohen, ed. *The Fundamentalist Phenomenon,* (Grand Rapids, Michigan: William Eerdmans, 1990).

15 Desmond Ford to Gwen Booth, Nov 20, 1951.

16 Desmond Ford to Gwen Booth, July 3, 10, 17, 27, Aug 7, 24, 26, Sept 7, Oct 24, 1951.

17 Desmond Ford to Gwen Booth, July 17, Sept 3, Oct 30, 1951.

18 Desmond Ford to Gwen Booth, Nov 12, Dec 3, 9, 1951.

19 Desmond Ford to Gwen Booth, Nov 5, 1952.

20 Desmond Ford to Gwen Booth, June 2, 1952.

21 Desmond Ford to Gwen Booth, [ca. May], May 21, July 8, Aug 25, Sept 27, 1952.

22 Desmond Ford to Gwen Booth, April 9, Oct 27, 1952.

23 Desmond Ford to Gwen Booth, April 18, 1952.

24 Gwen Booth to Desmond Ford, Sept 27, Oct 10, 1952; Desmond Ford to Gwen Booth, June 19, Oct 17, 1952.

25 Ford to Booth, Oct 17, 1952.

26 Gwen Booth to Desmond Ford, Oct 10, 1952.

27 William Murdoch to Desmond and Gwen Ford, Jan 14, 1953; Desmond and Gwen Ford to William Murdoch, Jan 20, 1953; Bridal Bells, wedding book, Desmond and Gwen Ford.

28 Ford to Booth, Nov 5, 1952; Bridal Bells.

29 Desmond Ford to Gwen Booth, July 23, 1952.

30 Crusade advertising, [1953], Elènne (Ford) Lohrisch collection.

31 Crusade advertising, [1954], Elènne (Ford) Lohrisch collection.

32 *Ibid.*

33 Crusade advertising, [1955], Elènne (Ford) Lohrisch collection.

34 Desmond Ford to William Murdoch, Aug 13, 1957.

35 Australasian Union Conference Executive Committee minutes, Oct 25, 1955.

36 Desmond Ford Diary, 1955; Ford, interviewed by Lloyd, March 1995.

37 William Johnson, interviewed by Milton Hook, 19 Nov 2005.

38 Ford Diary, 1955.

39 *Ibid.*

40 Gwen Ford to Desmond Ford, [Oct 23, 1955].

41 Desmond Ford to Gwen Ford, Oct 24, [1955].

42 Desmond Ford to Gwen Ford, Oct 28, 1955.

43 Gwen Ford to Desmond Ford, [Oct 28, 1955].

44 Desmond Ford to Gwen Ford, Nov 2, [1955].

45 Desmond Ford to Gwen Ford, [Nov 4, 1955].

46 Desmond Ford to Gwen Ford, Nov 5, [7], [9], 1955.

47 Desmond Ford to Gwen Ford, [ca. Dec 1955].

48 R[obert] Greive, "Justified by His Blood," *AR,* Nov 22, 1954, p. 1; Lowell Tarling, *The Edges of Seventh-day Adventism,* (Bermagui South, NSW: Galilee Publications, 1981), pp. 180–182.

49 Robert Greive to Eryl Cummings, n.d.

50 Roy Allan Anderson to R[obert] Greive, Jan 19, 1956.

51 *Questions on Doctrine,* (Washington, D.C: Review and Herald Publishing Association, (1957), pp. 647–660.

52 Roy Allan Anderson to Robert Greive, April 23, 1956.

53 M[ilian] Andreasen, Letters to the Churches, (Baker, Oregon: Hudson Printing Company, [1959]).

54 R[obert] Greive, "The Administrative and Doctrinal Issues that Brought Four Seventh-day Adventists to Trial and Dismissal During the Year 1956," unpublished paper, [ca. 1956], p. 1.

55 Greive to Cummings, n.d.

56 Desmond Ford to Gwen Ford, [ca. 1957]

57 Greive, "Administrative and Doctrinal Issues," p. 15.

58 *Ibid.,* pp. 5, 6.

59 *Ibid.,* pp. 10, 12, 13.

60 Note: Very early reference to this point is found in O. R. L. Crosier, "The Law of Moses," *Day Star Extra,* Feb 7, 1846, p. 37, where he wrote, "All will admit that some of the types have been fulfilled and that others have not. As they are yet to be fulfilled, it becomes us to remember and study the law to learn their nature and import." This position became normative for SDAs. For elaboration see, e.g., M[ilian] Andreasen, *The Sanctuary Service,* (Takoma Park, Washington, D.C.: Review and Herald Publishing Association, 1937) pp. 216, 217; G[eorge] Burnside, *Announcing the Feasts of the Lord,* [Wahroonga, NSW: Burnside Press, ca. 1984], p. 12.

61 Greive, "Administrative and Doctrinal Issues," p. 15.

62 Crosier, "Law of Moses," *Day Star Extra,* Feb 7, 1846, p. 41.

63 F. C. Gilbert, *Messiah in His Sanctuary,* (Takoma Park, Washington, D.C.: Review and Herald Publishing Association, 1937), p. 71; Andreasen, *The Sanctuary Service,* pp. 177, 184–187.

64 Greive, "Administrative and Doctrinal Issues," pp. 15–17; R. A. Greive to W. E. Battye, June 1956; R. A. Greive to Bro Lawson, Dec 6, 1956.

65 E.g., Ralph Blodgett, *How Will it End?* (Boise, Idaho: Pacific Press Publishing Association, 1984), pp. 110–112.

66 *Ibid.*

67 Greive, "Administrative and Doctrinal Issues," p. 1.

68 Alfred Kranz to Desmond Ford, Jan 8, 1956.

69 *Ibid.*

70 Roy Allan Anderson to Desmond Ford, Dec 31, 1956.

71   Edward Heppenstall to Desmond Ford, Dec 29, 1956.
72   Greive to Cummings, n.d.
73   William Murdoch to Desmond Ford, Jan 2, 1957; Walter Read to Desmond Ford, May 20, 1957.
74   Francis Nichol to Francis Clifford, Aug 29, 1957.
75   Desmond Ford to Edward White, Dec 20, 1954, March 14, 1955, Aug 9, 1957
76   Ford to Murdoch, Aug 13, 1957; Eric Johanson to Edward White, Aug 19, 1957.
77   AC Board minutes, Sept 18,1957; Australasian Division Executive Committee minutes Oct 1, 1957.
78   Desmond Ford to Gwen Ford, [ca Dec 12, 1957].
79   Eileen Dwyer to Gwen Ford, [ca. Dec 22, 1957].

Chapter Four:
Reaching an Academic Milestone

Ford was in his late twenties with a young family when the opportunity presented itself for him to do further study. The next three years of tertiary education for him were significant in terms of shaping his future. He would forge lasting friendships with more academics and establish a solid foundation for an illustrious teaching and preaching career.

Late in 1957, preparations for Des to attend the 1958 college year at Avondale were marked by two bits of trivia. One was his estimated family budget for his second stint of study at Avondale. It showed a significant proportion was allocated for regular contributions to his mother's support and 12.5 percent tithe payments—donations he had habitually made since marriage.[1] It indicated he had a high sense of responsibility to his church and family, but the overall budget was a portent that Spartan living would persist. Payments to his mother became burdensome as she grew more demanding.

Second, church committee approval for some financial assistance to Des was made at about the same time as Erwin Gane requested money for his own theology training. Gane was a young teacher at Avondale, aspiring to earn a Bachelor of Divinity degree from London University.[2] On this occasion his petition was turned down by the denomination, partly because finances could not stretch to include more trainees. Furthermore, church executives did not imagine there would be a need for more theology teachers at Avondale in the foreseeable future. Gane's hopes of returning to Avondale one day as a leading Bible teacher were effectively cut off at the pass. For three years he persevered with his request, but was consistently refused.[3] A final attempt brought a qualified promise of assistance, the proviso being that he would be obliged to accept any type of church work after completing his studies. A Bible teaching position at Avondale could not be guaranteed.[4] His annoyance, coupled with a Wesleyan fundamentalist's perspective on salvation themes, later developed into hostility toward Des and his gospel emphasis.

A Lifelong Friendship Formed
During the summer of 1957/58, prior to the start of the college year,

a Seminary Extension School was held on the Avondale campus.[5] It was undertaken, in large part, to hose down the theology debate stirred by Robert Greive. Edward Heppenstall was the star lecturer, but it did not prove to be a watershed in ministerial understanding of the gospel or issues related to the sanctuary doctrine. Seeds were sown in this regard, but provocative lecturers like Heppenstall still had to be circumspect in the classroom, especially since he was operating in the shadow of Francis Clifford's fundamentalism.

Des attended, plying Heppenstall with more questions than anyone else in the class.[6] He had earlier corresponded with Heppenstall, but the classroom experiences initiated a close and durable friendship between the two men. For decades they would exchange theological insights, not always agreeing but mutually respecting each other's ideas.

The Summer School reminded Des of the elements of Greive's debate over the sanctuary doctrine. It prompted him to write again to Alfred Kranz, his former Bible teacher, and an acquaintance of Heppenstall. Six months later Kranz replied:

> I was interested in the few thoughts you gave me on his (Heppenstall's) views on Hebrews 9. I find myself in harmony with them. I am quite satisfied that no one would ever get our view of the cleansing of the sanctuary and the investigative judgment from the Book of Hebrews .... The question of where Christ is, is really irrelevant. The facts are that He is not limited to any place and has unrestricted access to the very presence of the Father. Christ's sacrifice qualified Him to enter the holy of holies at His ascension, there to intercede for us before the Father ....[7]

This letter from Kranz contained a few lingering denominational prejudices, but at the same time represented some cutting-edge thinking within the church. Understandably, he concluded with the words, "Regard my letter as confidential." At the time he was employed by the church in New Zealand but still under the control of Australian headquarters. He, too, had to be circumspect because the threat of censure from fundamentalist officials was real.

At this time Des and his family lived in Alton Road, Cooranbong, within walking distance of college classes. He found the location most distracting. His columns in the *Signs of the Times* had brought him some repute and a constant passing parade of well-meaning theology hobbyists, upward of a dozen each day, would visit to ask questions or air some supposed new light. He could choose to be rude and summarily dismiss them, but that was against his nature. Instead, frequently he retreated to the woods with books and paper in hand or took a handful of memory cards, rehearsing as he walked.[8]

While studying Des taught an undergraduate unit, titled "The Life and Teachings of Jesus," which helped to defray some of his expenses. Geoffrey Rosenhain, director of teacher training at Avondale, one day provided a critique of his teaching style. Des remembers him saying candidly, "You talk too fast, and you tend to answer your own questions before giving the students time to answer them."[9]

It was the time in his life, too, when he took up jogging for aerobic exercise. He had found walking and cycling to be beneficial before, but now, at times, he started something more vigorous. For a man naturally inclined to book reading and sedentary habits, this development was against the grain and a product of deliberate willpower. He habitually rose to study at about 3 a.m.[10] During the day he would get as much fresh air and sunshine as possible and then retire early, after a light meal. He wrote on one occasion of a simple supper of "prunes and oranges."[11] There was balance in his eating habits. He was never a vegan. Reading health research articles convinced him of the need for essential fatty acids. For this reason, he included eggs and some milk products in his diet.[12]

His intense application to pastoral work and study over the past seven years had, the year before, brought on a fainting spell during a minister's meeting. And while sitting in a history exam prior to starting his 1958 study program, a similar low-blood-pressure attack almost overcame him. He pulled through with great difficulty. An SDA physician, Dr. Boyd, had challenged him by asking, "Don't you believe the health message?"

"I watch my diet," Des lamely offered. Boyd warned, "You will not survive much beyond forty if you don't seriously initiate an exercise regimen to balance your study." This was vital advice, and Des wisely heeded it.[13]

A Significant Contemporary

His studies in 1958 brought Des into contact with Robert Brinsmead for the first time. They were classmates. Robert was invited home for meals with the Fords. They walked and talked on bush hikes together.

One of their classes was Art, under the tutelage of Morriss Kennedy. As he and Brinsmead applied their doubtful artistic skills, much time was absorbed in theological discussion. Later, Des admitted, Kennedy stretched the bounds of graciousness by giving him a pass in the subject The two students were unevenly matched in some respects. Des came with ministerial experience, wide reading in the evangelical classics and denominational literature, and a developing network of friends in SDA academia. Brinsmead, on the other hand, was a farm boy, steeped in ultra-conservative Adventism and out of contact with the foremost thinkers in the church. Nevertheless, their differences were balanced by significant similarities. Both were earnest Christians, intensely loyal to their church, devotees of Ellen White's writings, and keen debaters of topical issues with an infectious charisma that was persuasive when arguing their viewpoints.

In midyear Brinsmead and Archibald Hefren, now a college lecturer, had a friendly public debate about the biblical covenants. Hefren took the traditional SDA view that there were two separate covenants. Brinsmead, following what Heppenstall suggested at the Summer School, argued for one everlasting covenant.[14] The incident was an indication of Brinsmead's high profile on campus. He was also president of the student's Ministerial League[15] and conducted out-of-class discussion groups on biblical topics. It came as a rude shock, therefore, when he was refused entry for the following year, 1959, and could not complete his course.[16]

The matter had come to a head when a copy of Brinsmead's essay, "The Vision by the Hiddekel," fell into the hands of Clifford. It was the product of a class assignment and had been shared with Edward White, college principal, and Nelson Burns, college Bible lecturer. The contents created a stir wherever they were publicized.

In the manuscript Brinsmead rejected the idea of Turkey being a part of the fulfillment of Daniel 11. Furthermore, he was accused of equating Seventh-day Adventism with "the glorious holy mountain" (Daniel 11:45) that had become contaminated with Babylon because the church had rejected the message preached at the 1888 General Conference Session, in Minneapolis, Minnesotta.[17] The church had just published *Questions on Doctrine*, in which the sinless nature of Christ was espoused. The contamination that Brinsmead mentioned may have been an allusion to this view because, at the time, he believed in the sinful nature of Christ.

Brinsmead protested his innocence to church officials, claiming he was merely stressing what Ellen White had said about the dangers threatening the SDA Church prior to the Second Coming.[18] His protest fell on deaf ears. Clifford advised Avondale's principal not to re-admit Brinsmead, and he was dutifully shut out.

The pressure on Brinsmead caused him to pop up all over Australia, gathering sympathizers as he traveled and conducted seminars for SDAs. Claims and counterclaims were published throughout 1959 and 1960. Church authorities seemed unable to throw a telling theological punch, jabbing ineffectively with accusations about Brinsmead's improper protocol. He had not passed his manuscript before an investigative committee, they said; he was conducting meetings without the permission of the church; he was disruptive with debate while at college; his literature unsettled church members, and his paper had some misquotations from Ellen White's writings in it.[19]

At the time Des and his colleagues had no idea that matters would escalate into a deep schism. If Clifford had taken into account Brinsmead's immaturity and had allowed more time for discussion and counseling, the threads of conflict may not have strengthened. Instead, Brinsmead's chances for further study and maturation at Avondale were cut short within a month, and a denominational wrangle developed rapidly.

Des found himself out of harmony with most of Brinsmead's assumptions and conclusions. He believed in the sinless nature of Christ and opposed Robert's end-time perfectionism. Their discussions, both in and out of the classroom during 1958, were cordial and stimulating, but all that Des could do was to recommend some books that might broaden Brinsmead's understanding.

All Aboard for the USA
In or about July 1958 Gwen and the two children went north to Tannum Sands near Gladstone, Queensland, to be with her parents.[20] Des advised Gwen, "Get all the peace, exercise, rest and reading in [that] you can. Remember, this is a God-given opportunity for you to prepare for the next two or three years in a new atmosphere."[21] Preparations by that stage were well under way for Des and his family to sail to America for more study. Four months of R and R for Gwen proved to be a real tonic.

At the end of the college year Des graduated with his Bachelor of Arts degree, serving as chaplain of his graduating class.[22]

Des and family boarded the Arcadia at Sydney on November 28, 1958.[23] Their trip to New York took them via the Suez Canal, a longer route but one that enabled Des to familiarize himself with places of interest that might arise in Bible teaching.

During the first stage of the journey Paul was ill, and while crossing the infamous Great Australian Bight, both Des and Gwen became seasick. The family confined itself to the cabin for much of that time. Uncomfortable in the small space festooned with freshly washed diapers hung to dry, they longed for Fremantle harbor, Western Australia, and a stretch on *terra firma*.[24]

At Fremantle the ship made a one-day stopover. Des took the opportunity to visit the SDA college in the hills at Carmel. Later, in Singapore, the family inspected a mosque and the war cemetery and bought some clothing at the street bazaars.[25]

The ship called in at Colombo and Aden before going through the Suez Canal. On board they amused themselves in the swimming pool, and at the ping-pong table where Gwen especially excelled. Traveling companions included an Anglican minister. They also struck up a conversation with a lady on her way as a missionary to Sudan.[26]

In Cairo Des spent two hours in the Egyptian Museum. He also made a hurried trip to the Pyramids, dodging the street hawkers who were as "thick as flies and much more persistent."[27]

When the ship reached Malta, Des disembarked, leaving his family to travel on to England. He wished to visit Pompeii, Rome, and the Waldensian Valley.[28]

Des found the SDA Church in Rome. Its minister, a modern-day Jehu on a scooter, took him to many places of interest including the catacombs and the Vatican Museum.[29]

Traveling through the Alps to Switzerland, Des was impressed by the beauty of the mountains. In France he visited the SDA seminary at Collonges. Giving Paris a miss, he pressed on to London, anxious to re-join his family at Hull, where they were staying with Gwen's aunts.[30]

London proved to be packed with interest. For years Des had bought books from a second-hand dealer in the metropolis. He searched the bookseller's shop and found a few more additions to his library, including some works by F. W. Boreham, one of his favorite authors. He visited St Paul's Cathedral, Westminster Abbey and the British Museum, delighting in the sight of the Rosetta Stone, early biblical manuscripts, and Babylonian clay tablets that spoke of a great flood.[31]

The family reunited and met up with fellow Australian, Eric Magnusson, who had just completed his second Ph.D. in chemistry. Two years later Des and Eric found themselves lecturing together back at Avondale.

Before the boat left for America Des and his family spent three days at Newbold SDA College. Des took a chapel service and conducted a Bible class session in public evangelism.[32]

With their meager earthly possessions bundled up in cardboard boxes and a borrowed trunk, they sailed from Tilbury Docks aboard the Saxonia on January 17,1959.[33]

The Atlantic winter seas were so rough that Des and Gwen suffered seasickness again. They were confined to their cabin, unable to read or write, and so weakened they could barely talk. The crew was ill, too, but the children remained unaffected.

Des and Gwen were glad to disembark on January 25, after two months of traveling. They asked about their accommodations near the Washington Seminary, but were told that it was unavailable for another week, so a room was found for them at the New York SDA Evangelistic Center, off Times Square.

During their brief stay in New York, an SDA physician, Wayne McFarland, learned of little Paul's recurrent bronchitis. He kindly called at their room with a prescription and some American dollars to buy the medication. He advised, too, that they keep the air moist by boiling water on the stove all night. Paul soon made a complete recovery.[34]

Among Friends

William Murdoch, years earlier, had marked Ford as a man who should attend the Seminary, so he was especially pleased to welcome him. That both Murdoch and Heppenstall were lecturing there made Des feel at home.[35]

Des spent about twenty hours a week in classes, and an equal amount of time in the library. Gwen herself completed three units, scoring top grades in each. They found that living expenses were higher than expected, so Des took a part-time job, marking Home Bible Study answer sheets.[36]

Heppenstall, in his classes, based much of his material on Carl Henry's commentary, and Des enjoyed the insights. A couple of teachers were disappointing, one spending most of the time discussing archaeological findings and chronology, but dodging the exegetical mine fields in the

Book of Daniel. Another, who taught church history from moldy old notes, seemed to become lost in the minutia. With characteristic Aussie bluntness Des said to the seminary dean, "I wouldn't cross the road for some of your teachers here, let alone cross the world."

Another influential lecturer, Earle Hilgert, exercised student minds in non-traditional views that were akin to those of the ousted Australian Bible teacher, William Fletcher. Des wrote a paper on Daniel 9:24–27 for Hilgert, who promptly scribbled all over it, tearing his traditional arguments to shreds. Des had to face, head-on, these problems in the SDA viewpoint. Hilgert was clearly convinced that the expression "cut off" did not really mean cut off from a time period (such as 2300 days) but, instead, referred to a judicial decision by God. Des realized Hilgert was right. It led to his later decision to do a Master's thesis exploring the meaning of Daniel 8:14 and 9:24–27. In it he put forward the view that the New Testament used these verses in reference to the end-time, but not specifically to an Investigative Judgment beginning in 1844.

Further surprises met Des when he realized that lecturers such as Roland Loasby and Sakae Kubo had arrived at conclusions similar to his own in regard to Hebrews 9, i.e., that the passage allowed no grounds for an Investigative Judgment doctrine.

Des rubbed shoulders with other SDA thinkers and writers, such as Harry Lowe, Walter Read, Francis Nichol, and Don Neufeld, who expressed concerns that many traditional lines of SDA argument were ill-founded.[37]

Church academics were decades ahead of laity and administrators, and the prevalence of unorthodoxy alarmed Des, pressing him to question, "How can I return to Avondale and teach a raft of controversial issues?" The thought troubled him for months. One day while on his way home to Salisbury Hall, near the Seminary, he was overcome with a reassuring impression. It was as if a voice whispered, "It will be all right, Des." Later, on arriving back at Avondale, David Sibley's advice was more specific: "Tell students the problems and give them the best answers you can."

After two quarters of study, Heppenstall's assessment of Des suggested that he would be wasting his time to proceed there into the Bachelor of Divinity degree course. The Seminary, euphemistically called Potomac University, was not offering an accredited degree. It would be wiser, Heppenstall believed, for Des to attend a university that offered an accredited doctorate.

Heppenstall himself explored possible avenues for Des. A colleague of his, Winton Beaven, recommended that Des attend Michigan State University, where Kenneth Hance lectured. Hance was a Christian, closely associated with SDAs, and was considered tops in his field of expertise—the art of public speaking, or homiletics. He had written the article on rhetoric for *Encyclopaedia Britannica* and was president of the American Association for Speech.

Heppenstall dashed off a letter to Gordon McDowell, now education director at Australian headquarters, imploring him in urgent tones:

> We are all impressed here by Ford's ability in every way. He stands out here at the Seminary head and shoulders almost above all others.
>
> He has taken some of the most basic theological courses here at the Seminary, and in this area, he is ahead of some of the teachers to say the least.
>
> Frankly, I hate to see Ford leave the Seminary in one way; he has been the best student in my classes, and I hate to lose good students.
>
> ... We are fifty years behind the time as far as university degrees are concerned. But it is a shame for men like Ford to spend all this time and not get a fully accredited degree when he is capable and can get it done.
>
> If Des Ford is going to make the move, he must do it right away. In other words, he must move and get to Michigan for the Fall Quarter beginning early in September.[38]

McDowell agreed and was galvanized into action. He phoned his friend, Lawrence Naden, then secretary in the same offices, persuading him of the emergency. Clifford was flying back to Sydney that evening from a Papua New Guinea visit. On the trip from the airport, Naden convinced him that an immediate decision was imperative. So, the quorum of three—Clifford, Naden, and McDowell—met in Clifford's office about midnight, voted to authorize the transfer of Des to Michigan State University, then dispatched the message to America.[39]

The plans at the time were for Des to spend eighteen months in coursework and complete his major research thesis and for him to return to Avondale to lecture in February 1961. As it turned out that schedule was shortened.

At Michigan State University

Des and his family quickly relocated to East Lansing, near the university, and began regularly attending the Lansing SDA Church. The minister arranged for free furniture to be installed in their home, giving the Aussies a typically hospitable American welcome. Des and Gwen made good friends of many, especially three McKelmerys—a dentist, a medical doctor, and the wife of Art Kline. Des preached at Lansing and many more nearby churches so often that, prior to his departure, the Michigan Conference secretary sent him an unexpected check with hearty thanks.[40] [at the request of Neal Wilson's dad who was the President of the Michigan Conference] Des also kept in contact with Heppenstall, who, during the family's stay in Lansing, moved to Michigan. Heppenstall had come with the Seminary when it transferred to Berrien Springs, a relatively short drive from Lansing.

Gwen took typing lessons one evening each week, and Des put his studies aside on those occasions and devoted his complete attention to his youngsters. "What a great time we would have," Elènne fondly remembers. "He became our playground on those dark winter nights. We would climb all over him and ride on his back, and he would lift us up into the air on his feet. We would tumble and squeal with delight."[41]

As Des progressed through his coursework, he was able to incorporate some units related to religion, in preparation for his major thesis. He included studies in ancient and medieval history, Christian literature, the Protestant Reformation, and religion in American culture. By burning the midnight oil, he also made giant strides with his major dissertation, "A Study of Selected Pauline Epistles as Written Addresses." By the end of November 1960, he had completed that, too, ahead of schedule.[42] On hearing the news Heppenstall congratulated him:

> Praise the Lord for His goodness. Yours is a marvelous achievement by the grace of God. When you first went there, I was hoping that all the classwork could be completed, but never dreamed that your thesis too would be ready.[43]

There was one hiccough. Des found it irksome when he was asked by his professor to rewrite the first fifty pages before the final submission, honing it to perfection. It was the section treating the historical background for the thesis. On reflection this was providential, Des believes, because it was probably the only section of his thesis read thoroughly ten years later by F. F. Bruce, Manchester University lecturer, who was more of a historian than a theologian. Bruce favorably assessed his qualifications to enter a second doctoral program in England.

Heppenstall was eager to have Des join him at Andrews University and lecture in Systematic Theology after graduation, despite the reality of indenture to the Australasian field. Murdoch was less optimistic, knowing full well that McDowell was counting on Des to return to Avondale and would vigorously oppose the cancellation of plans.[44]

Two weeks later Heppenstall surrendered to the inevitable. Writing to Des. he admitted:

> It appears to me that once you get back to Australia, we will have considerable difficulty in getting you back again. That is the way it goes. Murdoch will not press the matter with your superiors in Australia.[45]

In the same letter was found a gift of cash for Des and Gwen. Heppenstall wryly teased:

> Now just don't say a thing about the enclosed; buy yourself and your good wife anything you have in mind. I know your inclination to argument, but this is no time and no subject for your discussion. Stay on theology, just keep your hat on.

On December 12,1960, Des was granted his Ph.D. *summa cum laude.* Of the 105 possible credit points, 97 of them were graded A— almost a perfect record. Heppenstall loaned him an academic gown for the ceremony to save the expense of renting one[46] and wrote further to him:

> That you have completed this work so early in life will mean a great deal to you in the future. Now you can spend your energies in your first love—the Bible and Biblical theology. There is no doubt in my mind that with this degree, other doors will be open to you in the world.... I have already spoken to Dr. Murdoch to urge that you be given a definite call to teach at the University [Andrews] as soon as this is possible. He agrees with me. Of course, you never know how long you [meaning Murdoch or himself] are to be around, and there "ariseth one who knows not Joseph." I have no doubt that

in the next few years you will establish yourself as one of our top men in Biblical Theology. And with this the financial obligation to your Division will not be considered any obstacle [to a transfer to America].[47]

For Des and his family these three years of study were filled with privations and stress, but at the same time it was an exhilarating experience. Des had easily earned academic qualifications to achieve what he wanted to do more than anything—to teach the Scriptures to active, inquiring minds. His return to Avondale in 1961 as a fulltime Bible lecturer heralded momentous times in his career.

End Notes

1   Desmond Ford to Edward White, Aug 9, 1957.
2   Erwin Gane to AMC Board, Aug 25, 1957.
3   Lawrence Naden to Erwin Gane, Jan 18, 1961.
4   Gordon McDowell to Erwin Gane, Dec 6, 1961.
5   John Trim, "Pillars of the Faith Strengthened," *AR,* March 3, 1958, pp. 1, 2.
6   Gordon McDowell, interviewed by Milton Hook at Sydney, May 7, 1997
7   Alfred Kranz to Desmond Ford, Aug 19, 1958.
8   Desmond Ford to Gwen Ford, [July 27, 1958].
9   Biographical details in this chapter according to Desmond Ford, interviewed by Milton Hook at Caloundra, May 21, 25, 2001; Desmond Ford interviewed by Trevor Lloyd at Sydney, Jan 7, 2001.
10   Desmond Ford to Gwen Ford, Aug 8, [1958].
11   Desmond Ford to Gwen Ford, July 22, [1958].
12   Desmond Ford to Gwen Ford, Sept 1, [1958].
13   Ford, interviewed by Lloyd, Jan 7, 2001.
14   "Lions to the Spoil," [Avondale] *College News,* July 3, 1958, p. 8.
15   "Topical Taps," [Avondale] *College News,* Feb 27, 1958, [p. 6].
16   Nelson Burns to Gordon McDowell, Jan 1, 1959; AC Faculty minutes, Feb 5, 1959.
17   Francis Clifford to Robert Brinsmead, March 11, 1959; "Notes by F. G. Clifford," [ca. 1959], unpublished paper, Box 362, ACFIR, Cooranbong, NSW.
18   "Copy of Letter Written by R. Brinsmead Concerning Charges Made Against Him," Oct 14, 1959.

19 Australasian Division Headquarters, Wahroonga, "A Reply to R Brinsmead's Circular Dated October 14, 1959," Oct 21, 1959; Keith Irvine to [West Australian] Conference Workers and Church Elders, Nov 20, 1959; Anon, "Illustrations of the Wrong Use of the Spirit of Prophecy in the Writings of R. Brinsmead and Others," n.d.; [Harold Hollingsworth], "Address by the President of the [North] New South Wales Conference," July 2, 1960, Box 353, ACHR, Cooranbong, NSW; R[obert] Brinsmead, "Crisis in Australia." [ca. July 1960], box 353, ACHR, Cooranbong, NSW; L[awrence] Naden. "What Do the Brinsmead Faction Really Believe?" Sept 14, 1960, Box 362, ACHR, Cooranbong, NSW.

20 Desmond Ford to Gwen Ford. [ca. July. 1958].

21 Desmond Ford to Gwen Ford. July 22. [1958].

22 Kevin Moore, ed,, Jacaranda, ([Cooranbong, NSW]: Avondale Press), 1958, [p. 35].

23 Desmond Ford to Gwen Ford. Sept 12, [1958].

24 Desmond Ford to Lillian Ford. [Nov 30, 1958].

25 Desmond Ford to Lillian Ford, Dec 10, [1958].

26 Desmond Ford to Lillian Ford. [Dec 4], Dec 10, [Dec 12, 1958].

27 Desmond Ford to Lillian Ford, Dec 21, [26], 1958.

28 Desmond Ford to Lillian Ford. [ca. Dec 28, 1958 - Jan 2, 1959] .

29 Desmond Ford to Lillian Ford, [ca. Jan 2, 1959].

30 Desmond Ford to Lillian Ford, [ca. Jan 6, 1959].

31 *Ibid.*

32 Desmond Ford to Lillian Ford, Jan 22, 1959.

33 Desmond Ford to Lillian Ford, [ca. Jan 6], 22, 1959.

34 *Ibid.*

35 Desmond Ford to Lillian Ford, Feb 14, [1959].

36 *Ibid.,* Desmond Ford to Gwen Ford, Aug 31, [1959], Potomac University academic transcript, Gwen Marie Ford, Aug 21, 1959.

37 Desmond Ford to Gwen Ford, Aug 28, [1959].

38 Edward Heppenstall to Gordon McDowell, Aug 10, 1959; Desmond Ford to Gordon McDowell, Aug 11, 1959.

39 Gordon McDowell to Edward Heppenstall, Sept 11, 1959; (Gordon McDowell to Desmond Ford, Sept 11, 1959.

40 Desmond Ford to Gordon McDowell, Sept 21, 1959.

41 Elènne Ford to Milton Hook, June 26, 2005.

42 "Transcript for Desmond Ford," Academic Records, Michigan State University, 1960.

43 Edward Heppenstall to Desmond Ford, Nov 27, 1960.
44 Edward Heppenstall to Desmond Ford, Sept 8, 20, Oct 17, 1960.
45 Edward Heppenstall to Desmond Ford, Nov 5, 1960.
46 "Transcript for Desmond Ford," Michigan State University, 1960, Edward Heppenstall to Desmond Ford, Dec 1, 1960.
47 Heppenstall to Ford, Nov 27, 1961).

Chapter Five:
Back to Beloved Avondale

Any qualms Ford had about leaving America were compensated by the joyous expectations of returning to Avondale College to teach theology. For years he had climbed the mountain toward this goal. Now there appeared a plateau. Anticipating a smoother run, he was unaware the decade would be a bittersweet ride.

Leaving Michigan, Des and his family went to San Francisco to board the ship for Australia. Before embarking they stayed briefly at the denominations Pacific Union College to the north of the city. Des took the opportunity to talk with Graham Maxwell, a resident theologian. During the discussion Maxwell freely admitted there were serious problems with traditional SDA interpretations of Daniel and Hebrews.[1] Their conversation reinforced what Des had heard at the Seminary.

It was Christmas time. Five-year-old Elènne and three-year-old Paul were delighted to discover some gifts left at their door by Ivan and Phyllis Higgins. The Higgins family had recently returned from a stint of service at Avondale College. These parting gifts were in keeping with the American thoughtfulness and generosity received during the two-year term of study.

On the high seas there was time for reflection on class preparation for the coming year and, more importantly, prolonged hours of family togetherness. For Elènne, especially, the trip was full of treasured memories with father in hand—sharing his cabin, exploring the ship, and indulging in cherry pie and cream for breakfast while mother and Paul were still asleep. "We took pineapples back to the cabin for them, but no cherry pies!" she confided later.[2]

Campus Living
The Fords took up residence on the college estate, as was expected of all lecturers. Their weatherboard cottage was located near the little cemetery dubbed "God's Acre." Habitually, Des woke about 3 a.m. to study and write. Then he cooked a hot breakfast or at least had the vegies in the oven for the family before they finished slumbering.

After each meal Des and Gwen went for a twenty-minute walk, hand in hand. Acting on Ellen White's advice, the children did not attend school until they were eight years old. Family worship with Scripture and prayers followed, and then Des went off to classes while Gwen remained to read stories to the children. With no television in the home, both parents found time to read stories to the kiddies for several hours each day. Jungle Doctor books and *Pilgrim's Progress* were favorites well beyond the age when Elènne and Paul could read for themselves. Des or Gwen often reached the end of a book only to hear "Read it again" and then go back to the beginning once more.

Parenting, of course, was not easy. Elènne readily admits she was often argumentative and forever testing the cautions of her parents. On one occasion she backchatted (became sassy with) her mother, who sent her to Des in his study. He tried to explain to her how it hurts parents deeply when children misbehave.

"I don't believe you," she said scornfully.

"Then, instead of a spanking," Des replied, "I want you to hit my hand as hard as you can so you will understand how it hurts me."

He held out his hand.

"I cannot hit you," she stammered through her blubbering. "But you must," Des pressed.

"No, I will never hit you," Elènne insisted.

Des tenderly reached forward, took her by both hands and she fell into his lap sobbing.

The spirit of love in the home was palpable because both Des and Gwen possessed even temperaments. "I really tried the patience of both of them to the limit," Elènne recalls. "I only remember my father losing his cool on one occasion—he was upset to find my brother and me listening to music he thought was inappropriate."

Sobering memories like these were overwhelmed by recollections of the frequent times of laughter. Des loved a joke, often spontaneously clapping his hands or slapping his thighs with boyish delight.

Des was frequently called on to preach at local church services and to conduct meetings at SDA camp sessions both in Australia and New Zealand.[3] These often took him away from his family or reduced his holiday time with them, but he always sent letters. On one occasion the family went north to holiday in Queensland with Gwen's parents. He had to remain behind to take meetings at the local Eraring campsite. He wrote to six-year-old Elènne:

I have thought about you much since I left and missed you and Paul and Mummy very much. Do you remember Mr [Walter] Kilroy? I am sure you do. He sent a present along for you. Today he told me that your talks with him made him feel very happy inside. Isn't it wonderful that we can, with Jesus' help, use our words to make people feel happy?[4]

At another time Des was conducting meetings in Adelaide, South Australia, on Gwen's birthday, but words of endearment were worth more to them than gifts. Before he departed for Adelaide, he had left an envelope addressed poetically to "Miss Thirty-two. To be read April 22." Inside, the note read, in part:

A better wife no man has ever had, and our union is the sweeter year by year although our program continues to be a busy one. I hope the kiddies will always remember, as I do, your untiring devotion to we three other family members. God bless you dear and give you a happy birthday and many happy years to come.[5]

Gwen was the untiring home anchor—a spiritual and practical right hand for Des. She loved to grow vegetables and flowers. Des himself tried his hand at it. But he says he gave up because callers continued to drop in and hinder this backyard exercise. The family's version has an added spin. The story is told that one day Des took the spade and with great gusto turned over sod after sod in Gwen's newly planted corn patch, burying most of the seeds so deep they rotted in the ground.[6] Time would tell, however, that his gardening skills would improve.

Currans Road
It was a fact, however, that the frequency of visitors who wanted to mull over minor theological questions became unmanageable again, just as it had when living in Cooranbong in 1958. For that reason, eighteen months after arriving back from America, Des found a home away from the campus on Currans Road, more off the beaten track but still within walking distance of the classrooms.[7]

Gordon McDowell, as college principal, liked to have all his lecturers living on the estate. The move to Currans Road was therefore met with some initial resistance from him, but he acquiesced graciously. It irked him, however, that Des got into the habit of avoiding attendance at evening meetings, gatherings at which teachers were expected to be present in those days.[8] Des, of course, being such an early riser sought bedtime about 8 p.m. Des was never a handyman, although he did excel himself with some maintenance work on the unpainted house at Currans Road, only falling off the ladder once and knocking his head on the concrete.

Soon after arriving on the college campus, Des bought a second-hand motorbike and sidecar. "There were many close shaves," his daughter remembers, "when he would be thinking of his next sermon instead of concentrating where he was driving." He would often drive the family the short distance to Beauty Point for a swim.

The family's recreation also included camping trips to the Wattagan hills, within sight of the college, just as he had done in his student days. They rode two bicycles loaded with a tent, supplies, and the two children. Later, when Elènne got her own bike, Des would tie a rope to hers and pull her up the hills. They would find a spot to pitch their tent and then enjoy long hikes.

Des also bought a heavy, old rowing boat from a local and would take the family down Dora Creek to Pulbah Island in Lake Macquarie. They hiked over the island, counting the venomous, red-bellied black snakes in their travels. When it came time to eat, Des waded out into the lake up to his waist and scooped up some clean water to make a stew. He had a tasty recipe that pleased the family. Before rowing upstream for home on one trip they all had to sit out some stormy weather, huddled in the tent listening on their little radio to the likes of "Puff the Magic Dragon."

Later, when the motorbike was pensioned off, Des bought an old Peugeot car. The family ventured south to Canberra in it during one holiday, traveling back via Wollongong and up the Bulli Pass. The engine groaned and wheezed all the way up the steep and winding track. Periodically, Des pulled to the gutter, allowing the long line of trapped drivers behind him to pass. During rainstorms Gwen had to manually operate the windshield wipers so that Des could see the road ahead.

Their hapless fortunes with old motor vehicles continued, generous students sometimes passing around the hat to keep wheels under foot.[9] Even at Currans Road some people persisted by dropping in for a theological pow-wow. Often at mealtimes, the entire Ford family decamped to the bush for privacy. And students, if they needed to ask questions about their classwork, were encouraged to visit before classes began at 7:30 a.m. Could the Fords be branded as anti-social? No. On the contrary their congeniality attracted villagers and students alike. On occasions entire theology classes were invited to a breakfast of gem cakes, muesli, and apples. Des's recreation included swimming with some teachers and students.

It was vital, however, that time be jealously guarded. Des had a full teaching load, was appointed to several committees (including the Division's Biblical Research Committee), and was a popular speaker at youth gatherings and camp-meetings. So incessant were calls for Des to address church members in Australia and New Zealand that Lawrence Naden, who had succeeded Francis Clifford as Division president, had to instruct his subordinates to restrict their demands. Alter all, he reminded them, "Dr. Ford has more than a full-time job at the college."[10]

Des also had publishing commitments to fulfill. He continued his "Bible Question Corner" in the church paper. One Sunday he typed out fifteen pages to mail away to Robert Parr, the editor.[11] The welcome checks that came in return from Parr were usually accompanied with the advice, "Don't spend it all on lollies [candies]."[12]

In the classroom Ford was scintillating. He fired like a Gatling gun. Delivery was never extemporaneous. On the contrary, he prepared each lesson, and by the time he stood in front of his class he was able to recite it from memory. Only occasionally would he dash a word or two on the blackboard, and students hardly had time to scribble notes. They got the gist and caught the enthusiasm. His teaching strategy was to set a tough exam for the end of first term in order, he claimed, to improve the students' productivity in the remaining two terms.[13]

Generous college administrators initially allowed anyone to sit in on Dess classes, including some adults from nearby Cooranbong village. Eventually, as the scramble for seats edged out paying students, a stop was put to this practice. His style was in sharp contrast to the dreadful droning of some other lecturers, who labored through their handwritten notes or complex blackboard schemes.

Significantly, Des inspired his students to read the books he recommended. They followed in his footsteps, accepting the same principles and precepts. His enthusiasm for biblical classics was infectious and one student became a part-time dealer by importing from a second-hand bookshop in Wales. If his students didn't get time to read all the books on his list, they would leave college with an excellent library for personal study and further intellectual growth.[14]

McDowell was impressed with the results. The Life and Teachings of Jesus class, he noted, converted many to a genuine Christian experience.[15] Whenever Des was off campus on speaking appointments, he attracted more young people than any other lecturer to the idea of attending college. Student numbers grew rapidly, and classes filled quickly.

Professor Ford's Theology

Des arrived at Avondale with a theology unlike traditional SDA preachers of that era. He taught Louis Were's ideas of latter-day events more confidently than Alfred Kranz or William Murdoch dared. And he openly urged the principle of recurring fulfillments in prophecy. He could teach these points, because denominational literature (specifically the *SDA Bible Commentary* and George McCready Price in *The Greatest of the Prophets)* now aired similar views. Veteran SDA preachers simply did not keep abreast of this phenomenon.

Essential foundations to Des's doctrine of salvation were tenets such as the sinless nature of Christ[16] expounded by Roy Anderson and Edward Heppenstall, and original sin preached by Charles Spurgeon, the famous Protestant evangelist. Des also underscored the verbs in the present tense in Romans 7:14–25, demonstrating a Christian's lifelong battle with sin, always striving but never arriving at perfect morality. He offered God's grace and imputed righteousness as the sinner's remedy, although at that time some of the finer points of salvation were not clearly defined. (At that stage he had not read *Examination of the Council of Trent]* by Martin Chemnitz, Luther's foremost apologist). Des preached memorable sermons about the certainty of God's forgiveness and the sublime assurance that follows with full acceptance of Christ. But he admits there still lingered in his thinking some traces of the Wesleyan justification plus sanctification model of salvation, so pervasive in the SDA Church. Much of his gospel preaching had its origins in Spurgeon's *Christ's Glorious Achievements,* Hannah Whitall Smith's *The Christian's Secret of a Happy Life,* and John Knox's little pamphlet on righteousness by faith.

Des was also loyal to the official statement of SDA beliefs that spoke of Christ's "two phases of ministry" in heaven, but he debunked the popular image of a literal fully furnished heavenly building. And his published articles on the Book of Daniel were sincere explorations for better answers to the problematic SDA interpretations.[17]

He possessed a high regard for Ellen Whites writings, more so than many others. Hope (Brinsmead) Taylor said somewhat derogatively, "Des was always using only Spirit of Prophecy."[18] His frequent use of White's writings may have given the mistaken impression to some that he held them as equal to the Scripture. But he never really thought of her writings as so elevated. He tried to walk the fine line of respect, found somewhere between total rejection and sycophancy.

This raft of teaching was bound to become more evident. As chairman of the theology department, Des's beliefs permeated the staff and students. The graduates entered church employment and happily shared the lessons with church members. Interest in Bible study revived.[19] His lectures on eschatology at the Seminary Extension School, held on campus during the summer of 1965/66, provided older ministers some exposure to the revised views about end-time events.[20]

In 1966 five scholars submitted a three-page minority report to the Daniel committee, a small study circle at headquarters in Washington, D.C. The committee was formed in the 1930s to discuss traditional interpretations that were problematic. They themselves experienced difficulties. Some members were scarcely aware of any exegetical problems in Daniel. They simply wanted to issue a statement to church members supportive of the *status quo*. Others, like Bible lecturer Raymond Cottrell, were better informed, knowing the biblical languages and the anomalies these posed for Adventist interpretations. Des was concerned that no alternative interpretations were being seriously explored, no satisfactory answers that might meet with some level of agreement and respectability among academics, so he had submitted some monographs to the committee that seemed to influence the committee's report.

This minority report proposed that the committee should look to the New Testament for inspired reinterpretations of Daniel. They also advised the establishment of "a Seventh-day Adventist Institute of Biblical Studies along the lines of the Geo-Science Institute" with a full-time staff to address problematic theological issues.[21] The suggestions fell on deaf ears at the time, causing some frustration. Nevertheless, Des himself continued to study the areas of concern and published his convictions in denominational magazines. His articles tried to develop better arguments for SDA distinctives, but years later he concluded that much of the evidence was thin.[22]

Answering Brinsmead

When Des arrived back at Avondale in 1961, Robert Brinsmead's perfectionist teachings were well established throughout Australasia. They were also finding fertile ground in America because Brinsmead himself was living there, speaking and pamphleteering across the country. A significant bone of contention concerned the timing of the sealing of the saints in the last days. In 1964, Des published a booklet, titled "The Sealing of the Saints—Before or After the Loud Cry?" [23] It was designed to confront and correct Brinsmead who, of course, could not resist a defense.[24] Both men quoted Ellen White at length because her writings contain the definitive SDA scenario of latter-day events.

The standard scenario employs esoteric motifs such as "The Sealing," "The Latter Rain," "The Loud Cry," "The Shaking," "The End of Probation," "The Death Decree," and "The Time of Jacob's Trouble."[25] The end-time plot is plausible but completely absent from the denominational creed, suggesting that it is unimportant or too speculative. Much of the construct is based on analogy. Des argued that the sealing occurs at or after the loud cry. Brinsmead's position was that the sealing occurs beforehand, to perfect the saints so that they can give the loud cry of warning to the world. Some of the elements may have some veracity, but to argue dogmatically over their exact timing or sequence seems fruitless. Years later, after his change of heart, Brinsmead derisively summed up the elements of the scenario by saying, "They are all fictitious.... The whole thing is a joke.... We [were] only arguing about imaginary events."[26] Des would not be so damning of the future scenario.

This was perhaps the most public arm-wrestle Des ever had with Brinsmead. He preferred to counter variant views by teaching and preaching a positive message of his own. At camp meetings, where there were Brinsmead sympathizers, he put the accent on God's grace and Christian assurance. In the classroom and chapel talks he gave a similar emphasis. His strategy was successful, for during the 1960s Brinsmead's theories exerted no influence on the Avondale campus.

The real thrust of Brinsmead's "Awakening Message" was perfectionism.[27] True, it was a brand to be experienced in the last days of earth's history, but since it was advocated simultaneously with a belief that the last days were already at hand, it made little difference whether perfection could be had then or in the future.

Waggoner and Jones

Dense vapors of perfectionism have always risen from Seventh-day Adventism. For decades prior to Brinsmead, perfectionists in the church promoted the ideas of Ellet Waggoner and Alonzo Jones, nineteenth-century SDA ministers—especially the messages they believed were given at the 1888 General Conference Session in Minneapolis. Brinsmead hauled his water from the same well.

The actual sermons Waggoner and Jones gave at Minneapolis are not extant. To deduce their theology, we must depend on their books and American *Signs of the Times* articles, beginning about 1884.

Christ, they taught, had a sinful nature but became perfectly obedient to the law of God.[28] Human beings today, they argued, find themselves with the same nature, and the only way to keep God's law is to totally surrender one's will to God,[29] (They evidently did not understand that doing so, if it really could be done, would render humans robotic.) This initial step, the reasoning continued, brings God's forgiveness for past sins and the application of God's imputed righteousness. By grace, God's power—they said—then enters the Christian's life, implanting a godly nature, infusing and imparting righteousness to the point that it enables the person to keep God's law perfectly.[30]

"What wonderful possibilities there are for the Christian! What heights of holiness he may attain!" Waggoner enthused in 1889.[31] Jones chimed in:

> What now is the great thought and purpose of His dwelling in the hearts of the people? The answer is, Perfection, the moral and spiritual perfection of the worshipper. Perfection of character is the Christian goal—perfection attained in human flesh in this world.... He [Jesus], having attained it, has become our Great High Priest ... to enable us to attain it.[32]

Waggoner amalgamated imputed and imparted righteousness by stating, "When the law cannot give us righteousness, we turn to Christ and get it.... This is righteousness put upon us and created in us." Biblical expressions like "Christ in us" (Galatians 2:20; 4:19) were interpreted stiffly, in a literal sense, rather than in the contextual and obvious figurative sense.

There seemed to be a notion that Christ's righteousness, like some divine chemotherapy, would literally permeate the human body and eradicate the cancerous sinful nature. These *elixir vitae*—especially references to imparted righteousness—rang the bells of the Wesleyan and Roman Catholic models of salvation.

It is not surprising that many SDAs did not warm to Waggoner and Jones at Minneapolis. Furthermore, it is understandable that during the 1890s Waggoner and Jones, among others, made the natural progression into pantheism. It is a logical step. If it is possible for Christ or the Holy Spirit to literally dwell within us, then it is also possible for God to dwell in other areas of His creation, such as animals and stars. (In the 1970s, when the denomination reprinted Waggoners 1900 book, *The Glad Tidings*, the editor and advocate for perfectionism, Robert Wieland, tampered with the original document and disingenuously deleted the embarrassing pantheistic bits).[34]

The Wesleyan strand had rope-like proportions in early Seventh-day Adventism and persisted at length. In 1952 William Branson, General Conference president, wrote:

> Perfection, then, is possible for us. The God who demonstrated His power by bringing Jesus from the dead can also make you perfect—perfect in every good work to do His will. How is this accomplished? It is by Christ working within us and through us the things that are well pleasing in God's sight.[35]

Brinsmead was nurtured from childhood in the Waggoner and Jones model. He refined it, giving it a sharp eschatological tang. A Christian, he declared, "grows in sanctification through imparted righteousness."[36] He talked much about the need for "the soul temple" (the Christian's body) to be filled with the Holy Spirit, so that sin would be eradicated in the life. The individual would then be able to stand as a righteous person, he claimed, without a mediator in the heavenly sanctuary after the close of probation.[37]

Brinsmead's thrust carried echoes of Samuel Wesley's hymn:

The temple has been yielded,
And purified of sin;
Let Thy Shekinah glory
Now shine forth from within.

There were sentiments from Ellen White, too—expressions to the effect that sanctification involves "the indwelling Spirit of God,"[38] and "the sanctification of the soul by the working of the Holy Spirit is the implanting of Christ's nature in humanity."[39] She added, "Those who are living upon the earth when the intercession of Christ shall cease in the sanctuary above are to stand in the sight of a holy God without a mediator."[40]

Brinsmead and his followers were prone to cull many perfectionistic statements from Ellen White. For example, they taught:

> As he [the Christian] advances toward perfection, he experiences a conversion to God every day; and this conversion is not completed until he attains to perfection of character, a full preparation for the finishing touch of immortality.[41]

It should be noted that Ellen White also made many statements clearly opposing perfectionism.[42] Brinsmead's antagonists made the most of these, but their efforts to nullify his influence were hamstrung because their theology ran almost parallel to his. Heppenstall himself, when reading an early Brinsmead booklet, admitted, "There are some points of variation, but so far, I do not see anything here to get excited about accept [sic] on the nature of Christ."[43]

Furthermore, any objections to Brinsmead's writings, highlighted in a published General Conference response, appeared to be nit-picking. Administrators' chief concerns surrounded the Brinsmead family connections to the German SDA Reform Movement; "the subversive nature of Robert's work"; his unwillingness "to work along the lines of organizational 'restraint and discipline;'" his "acceptance of tithe": and his insinuation that his teachings were the solution to any faults in the denomination.[44] They threw all the mud they could find against him but very little of it came from the theological bucket. The General Conference response was more of a personal attack. They played the man, not the ball.

Naden's little 1964 booklet, "The Perfecting of the Saints," written as a countermeasure against Brinsmead, perpetuated the notion that sanctification involved a lifetime of personal effort, slogging upwards to moral perfection with decreasing amounts of Christ's imputed righteousness and increasing amounts of alleged imparted righteousness.[45] And the 1966 book, *Preparation for the Final Crisis*, printed by the church as another thrust at Brinsmead, only reiterated much of what Brinsmead was saying about sanctification and latter-day events.[46]

In stark contrast, about the same time (1964) Ford published *Unlocking God's Treasury*. It was a comprehensive collection of Bible studies in which he made it clear that "God imputes perfection to us."[47] Rightly so, there was no mention of any such thing as imparted righteousness so prevalent in other SDA literature.

Why is there a need to understand the Brinsmead phenomenon of the 1960s? It is imperative in order to fully appreciate the turn of events of the 1970s and understand the position in which Des was cast. The 1960s saw concerted church strategies against Brinsmead, efforts that had minimal results because Brinsmead's theology was, to a large extent, in harmony with traditional Adventism. This became more obvious as perfectionism in the church blossomed in the 1970s under the *aegis* of the General Conference. By that time Brinsmead himself had discovered Reformation theology, renounced his perfectionism, and become a vocal proponent of Christ's imputed righteousness alone. He was then in close agreement with Des, who was never disposed to perfectionism, but fought it vigorously throughout the 1960s and onwards, earning the wrath of perfectionists.

Des published against Brinsmead in the early 1960s but did not get involved in a protracted dialogue. Whenever Brinsmead visited Cooranbong, he would call on Des, have a meal with him and then they would walk together in the bush. Des urged him to read the Reformers. Often Des discussed Brinsmead's activities with Naden, but all his association with Brinsmead was based on transparent friendship rather than secret collusion.[48] Teaching responsibilities and preaching assignments did not allow much time for lengthy dueling with anyone. He was focused on his family and campus tasks. In addition, his published articles indicate his mind was generally working through problematic passages in the Book of Daniel.

Opposition Simmers

There were two further concerns for Des in the 1960s. One was his wife's deteriorating health and the other was a developing covert operation mounted by traditionalists against his teachings.

Almost as soon as Des set foot back in Australia, George Burnside began a censorship campaign. Increasingly, Burnside found himself edged out of the camp meeting pulpits because Des preached a more appealing message.[49] Only on rare occasions was Burnside asked to speak at Avondale. College president, Gordon McDowell, was not a Burnside devotee. These matters seemed to irk Burnside, and when he realized Des was still advocating the new view, Were's view, about Armageddon and the King of the North, he publicly belittled Des during meetings with other SDA ministers.[50]

Similar criticism came from Walter Scragg, Sr., a crusty warrior who, unlike Burnside, did not stoop to a covert operation. Scragg never walked in any man's shadow. He did his own thinking and fought his own battles. He sent Des some of his manuscripts written against Were, promoting traditional views about Armageddon in addition to Christadelphian tenets expressed in Albert Anderson's 1930s book, *Through Turmoil to Peace*. In the 1940s, Scragg apparently agreed with much of Were's interpretations, but now was definitely opposed to them. Des gave Scragg's manuscripts a poor review, earning his dismay and opposition.[51]

The students who were trained at Avondale carried Des's views into their own pulpits. One intern was reprimanded because he used the word "eschatology" in a church service. Older ministers with little more than a high school (academy) education hadn't heard the word before and took offense, accusing the young man of bragging about his undergraduate training at Avondale.

Rumors were circulating, also, that college students no longer believed in a literal sanctuary in heaven with two separate rooms and golden furniture. Letters of concern were sent to Naden, who passed them on to McDowell. McDowell, in turn, sprang to the defense of Des and Avondale's theology department, citing denominational literature to prove Avondale's orthodoxy. At the same time, he clearly implied the rumormongers were marching out of step in the rearguard.[52]

Soon after, in January 1965, Burnside conducted a service at the Melbourne camp meeting in Victoria, where he seemed to deliberately address the rumors by speaking about the heavenly sanctuary in very literal terms. An intern had the temerity to confront Burnside and challenge the view put forward. All the alarm bells rang in official circles. The interns were assembled and read the riot act by conference administrators, insisting that only traditional views would be tolerated. Interns learned to be more circumspect, and the dust settled.[53]

Closer to home someone in Cooranbong village, thought to be Raglan Marks, circulated an anonymous letter calling for something to be done to "arrest the apostasy" at Avondale. "Icobod [sic]," he decried, "should be written over the old chapel, or, perhaps better still, placed up on the principal's TV antenna, which was the first in this Adventist community." He huffed and puffed against the Bible department's teaching that the earth could be more than six thousand years old and then put his sword into Des. "Dr. Ford," he concluded, "would now have us believe that the heavenly sanctuary is only an object lesson, with no real articles of furniture, in fact it does not even have walls, in other words there is no sanctuary in heaven."[54] Letters such as this one spoke for themselves, highlighting the sad kindergarten level of theology held by many church members.

Solomon had prayed to God at the dedication of his temple in Jerusalem, "The heavens, even the highest heaven, cannot contain You" (1 Kings 8:27), but SDA fundamentalists wanted to confine God to one most holy room in heaven!

Rumors continued swirling, encouraged by snide remarks from leading evangelists such as John Conley in Victoria, who was bitterly opposed to Were. He was known to point northwards to Avondale's theology department and say with a sneer, "The King of the North (a biblical vandal against the saints) is up there."[55]

Matters were brought to a head in 1969 when Burnside was preaching near Cooranbong at the Eraring camp meeting. He made a thinly disguised jibe at Avondale, saying, "Heresy is being taught at an institution not far from here." As ministerial secretary of the Division, he was virtually attacking the credibility of a major training institution in his own territory. Naden had had enough and summoned a meeting of twelve Bible teachers and administrators, including Burnside himself. Burnside was bluntly asked, "Were you referring to Avondale?" He said, "No," but not everyone believed him.[56]

In the meeting Burnside did, however, express the same sentiments as the circulating rumors. His major gripe concerned the doctrine of inspiration. Students graduating from Avondale, he claimed, did not have a high regard for Scripture and Ellen White's writings. Burnside thought they should hold to the view of inerrancy. Des cited White's writings and leading SDA Churchmen, demonstrating that the doctrine of inerrancy was not to be found in these orthodox publications. Rather, he recounted, the church favored plenary or thought inspiration (the reliability of Scripture), not verbal or dictation-style inspiration (the inerrancy of Scripture).[57]

It was perhaps one of the easiest and most fundamental issues that Burnside could have raised. He did not have any theological background for deeper waters. At the meeting Des answered his critics with ease. Naden dashed off a letter to Des that same day, kindly reassuring him:

> I want you to know that the brethren here at the Division have absolute confidence in your leadership of the Bible Department at Avondale. I think that the Lord blessed you in your presentation of your views, and it was very encouraging to note that all your associates in the department are one hundred per cent behind you.
>
> I pray that in spite of the many burdens that have been resting upon your shoulders of recent weeks, God will bless you with courage and with good health and that you might continue to serve Him in your present position for many years to come at Avondale College.[58]

Some months later Burnside was not re-elected to his post as ministerial secretary. Instead, he was relegated to a minor position in the local conference. The wounding drove him further underground in his uncharitable smear campaign against Des and Avondale College.

Gwen's Illness

"The many burdens" that Naden's letter mentioned no doubt concerned the deep anguish over Gwen's deteriorating health.[59]

In 1963 Gwen was diagnosed with malignant breast cancer and underwent surgery. There was every hope of a permanent recovery, but it proved to be false. The deadly specter of fatality returned about four years later, and her brave fight for survival assumed epic proportions. Her natural timidity left her, and an inner resolve took over. However, the cancer spread to her bones.

Simultaneously, the family was in the process of moving from Currans Road to the lakeside suburb of Silverwater. Des, Elènne, and Paul often peddled their bicycles the eight miles (12 kilometers) to and from the campus for classes. If Des needed to arrive early or the weather was inclement, he drove their old Kombi before dawn, taking a hot breakfast for the kiddies to eat along the way. He would leave the vehicle at the footbridge across Dora Creek—the back entrance to the campus.[60]

Traveling in the winter months was most uncomfortable. Des

found that his fingers and feet remained frozen, even after arriving in the classroom. He tried pepper in his socks as a desperate remedy.[61] Gwen was confined to bed much of the time. Charles and Ruth Bird had reunited and settled nearby. Ruth baked savory dishes for the Fords and sometimes did their laundry.[62] Des did the grocery shopping and frequented the second-hand shops in Newcastle, hunting for clothes.

As Gwen grew progressively worse, she could not keep her food down, vomiting and retching repeatedly. Elènne and Paul emptied the bowl, counting twenty to forty times each day. Dehydration became a problem. Des often stayed awake at night, listening to ensure she was still breathing. The ambulance came many times to take her to the hospital for intravenous feeding and a little recuperation.

The older children did what they could to help, especially caring for infant Luke, who had been born in the Sydney Adventist Hospital in 1966. If he cried a lot at night, Elènne and Paul often pushed him along the dirt road in his stroller, ducking for safety behind bushes when the headlights of a car appeared. Early one morning, when Luke was a toddler, they wheeled him in the stroller to a nearby jetty, still clad in their pyjamas and slippers. They took turns gathering handfuls of little stones for him to throw into the lake. When their backs were turned momentarily, he toppled into the lake. Elènne dived in, clothes and all, to fish him out.

By the time Elènne started high school, she had learned to assume a supportive role beyond her years. Besides care for Gwen and little Luke, she often took Paul by train into Newcastle for shopping trips. They sometimes stayed briefly with Gwen's half-sister, who babysat Luke at times.

Des and Gwen learned that a doctor practicing up north near the Brinsmead family was using some new treatment for cancer sufferers. In desperation they agreed to try it. Most of the medical profession could only offer Largactol to limit the vomiting and antibiotics to guard against infections that might further debilitate her body.[63] It was a two-edged sword, for the antibiotics weakened her immune system. Experimental and natural remedies seemed to be the only avenues left.

In January 1968 Gwen went north to stay in the Brisbane home of a friend, Mrs. Gealer. A month later she transferred to the home of Lawrence and Verna Brinsmead because she needed Verna's nursing skills on a daily basis.[64] The children stayed at John and Carlene Brinsmead's farm, but it was not long before Elènne chose to remain with Gwen, taking Luke with her. A couple of months later they both returned to their familiar home at Silverwater. For a few weeks Luke was taken daily to the campus primary school and spent the time playing on the floor of a classroom, while a teacher kept an eye on him. Then a housekeeper was briefly employed to care for him, living in a downstairs room at their home. Finally, a fine Christian woman named Ivy Harker began assisting and became very attached to Luke.

At one time, when Des was visiting Gwen, John Brinsmead said to him, "If you cast in your lot with the Brinsmead family, accepting our teachings, then God will heal Gwen." Des was appalled at the bribe. He regarded the Brinsmeads as friends, but was not prepared to compromise his conscience by joining the "Awakeners."[65]

What did Naden think of Des associating so closely with the Brinsmeads? Not for one moment did he think Des would accept their beliefs, but he was apprehensive, particularly about what it might do to the reputation of Avondale College and Des himself. Nevertheless, he realized the gravity of Gwen's condition.

But rumors quickly spread. In Western Australia it was said that Gwen had received healing from the Brinsmeads, and that Des had subsequently cast in his lot with them. Keith Parmenter, president of the Queensland Conference, began to believe reports that Des had taken meetings for Brinsmead followers and had accepted their teachings. The truth of the matter was that Des had conducted a couple of devotional studies in a home of one of the Brinsmead family while he was visiting Gwen. Des set about tracking down a recording of the meetings to pacify Parmenter.[66]

Part of Gwen's treatment involved the drinking of large quantities of carrot juice and herbal mixtures, as a cleansing regimen. Des sent her books to read, in addition to dried figs, nuts, sesame seeds, and olives to supplement her diet. His prolific letters exuded a positive balm: "It is so good to know of your upward soaring," he penned. He encouraged her to take a dip in the ocean whenever she found strength. "The massage of the water and the sunshine should hasten your progress," he added.[67] His optimistic stimulus was constant:

> Soon you will be able to see the clearing. I feel sure you are almost out of the woods now though the building up will take some time. Your faith and love are precious. God keep you in good spirits hour by hour. Look no further than the blessings and provisions of

the present moment.

Good reading will add to your vitality. The mind energizes every cell in the body or depresses it according to our thoughts. You are rebuilding your Rome so don't expect all in one day. I am proud of your courage, dear. But a brief part of your experience might have finished me. May He continue to sustain you. Just rest in Him when you can't pray or read. He understands and cares.[68]

Gwen was further buoyed by the arrival of her book, recently published in America, of a collection of stories for children. "This book will live on in many homes in many countries," Des affirmed, "and with His blessing will accomplish much good." She was also cheered by the baptism of her mother. Despite her illness Gwen had endured the round trip to briefly visit her parents for the joyous occasion.[69]

Paul returned to Des about the same time, April, and Des kept Gwen informed of their many hours together—gardening and playing cricket and ping-pong.[70] Paul loved fishing in the lake. He scribbled to Gwen in his best elementary hand:

Dear Mother,
I hope you are feeling well. On Sunday Stuet [Stewart] came out and we caught six exta big witing and about 20 others. How is Luke settling in. Dus Luke go fishing with poper [Poppa].
Love, Paul[71]

Elènne, too, shared her delights with Gwen. On a telegram form in the post office one day, she scratched a quick note:

Dear Mummy,
I'm in Newcastle now and Daddy has bought me a purse and shoes and socks to go with the dress you brought [sic] me, and a jumper with diamands [sic] shapes, all different colours and a skirt, ribbons and stockings.
Love, Ellen[72]

Expenditure for new clothing like this was rare. Des had written to Gwen saying he was about to take the trip to Newcastle and quipped, "I hope someone leaves us a bequest first."[73]

The "stockings" went against Dess inclinations. It was "silly," he felt, for a twelve-year-old "to wear such unnecessary frills," but Gwen's feminine instinct had given permission and Des was in no frame of mind to argue matters of dress.[74]

This was around the time when the college dean of women had asked Des to speak to the resident young ladies to try to persuade them against fashion fads. He was quite conservative in these matters but would rather have spoken on any other subject. He was feeling dyspeptic at the time but light-heartedly wrote to Gwen, "Poor sermons are the result of indigestion." He jested that if his nausea did not pass, he might preach so poorly that the ladies would be doomed to spinsterhood, "clad in carpet bags—bags for hags."[75]

Elènne was at the age when she was enthusiastically involved in school swimming carnivals and Pathfinder campouts. She made a long list of things to take on one outing, including "rice bubbles and sweets." Des reported to Gwen, "She is a well-organized little Miss even though possessing many residual Gentile tastes." After returning from one trip to Browns Falls, Elènne wrote to Gwen excitedly, describing the long trek, stories around the campfire, water fights and a midnight snack. Des was overwhelmed at times by her zest. "She can talk as Vesuvius can bubble," he commented.[76]

Trying to cope on his own with a blossoming teenager had its testing moments. "I have read her [Elènne] the riot act," Des despaired. "Next will come the riot." She tried every slick trick in the book. On one occasion when she was sick with a cold and wanted to watch a comedy on TV at a neighbor's home, she put it to Des that "laughter is the best medicine, and it might cure my cold."[77]

Des's domestic pressures were compounded by serious troubles in the theology department. One lecturer was recommending that students read Bertrand Russell's, "Why I Am Not a Christian," and now Des was counseling one lad who had become an agnostic because of reading it. Another lecturer was in hot water for advocating a raft of personal opinions that unsettled the students. He lasted six months until dismissal. Des found it hard to sleep at night because of the turmoil and suffered stomach pains. He was given free access to a guest room in the men's dormitories to rest between classes and wondered to himself if he should become a postman to avoid all the stress.[78]

Des's mind was continually on Gwen. Tragically, the natural

remedies only brought temporary relief for her. The cancer invaded her bones. So many hopes were dashed. In July she returned to Silverwater, emaciated and hardly able to walk.[79]

Gwen was in constant pain but never complained. She used to say it was Des's love that kept her alive. A cordotomy was tried as a means of reducing her pain. It was unsuccessful, leaving her paralyzed from the waist down and still in pain. She wasted away, weighing only a Belsen-like sixty pounds. Home care became impractical and inadequate. She was therefore admitted to nearby Eralyn Nursing Home, a private facility run by a church member. She said her goodbyes to Luke, and he was taken to New Zealand in the care of Ivy Harker. Elènne and Paul often called in after school to visit with their mother. Sometimes Des would drive Gwen and the children to the Wattagan hills, place her in a well-cushioned wheelchair, and push her for miles along the forest tracks. She enjoyed the fresh air and natural landscape. When those outings became too strenuous, she would be brought home in the car on Sabbath and Sunday afternoons. Des and Paul gently lifted her in and out of the vehicle to minimize her pain. Toward the end her spinal column could not bear any weight at all, and she had to remain lying in a stretcher position.[80]

Gwen bravely faced her inevitable demise. She wrote of her confidence in the Lord, and this touching testimony was published in the church journal.[81] Like any mother wanting the best for her brood, she talked with Des about prospects of a remarriage after she was gone. Both Des and Gwen were aware that some women had been making a play for Des's attentions as early as two years prior to her death. He deliberately shunned any hint of an advance.[82]

Gwen went ahead and thoughtfully made a list of those women close to them whom she believed were most suitable to assume her role after her death.

Witnessing Gwen wracked with pain and wasting away before his eyes, Des apparently had to wrestle with the choice of allowing palliative drugs that reduced pain but invariably hastened death. As Gwen lay dying, he aired the ethics of this form of euthanasia with his closest confidante, Norman Young, then a student at Manchester University. Young was too upset and recoiled from the sad news, only managing to answer, "I do not feel free to write on mercy termination of life while in your present trials."[83]

On April 22, 1970, Gwen turned forty. Gillian Wastell, an assistant at the nursing home who bonded with Gwen, had taken Elènne and Paul to stay with friends on an isolated farm near Wauchope, leaving Des by Gwen's bedside. She drifted into a coma-like state. Two days after her birthday, as the Sabbath began on Friday evening, she roused, gently pressed Des's hand, and said, "Thank you for a lovely life," and went to her rest peacefully.[84]

Word was sent to Gillian that she should call Des. She took Elènne and drove in the night to a telephone where they received the sad news. By the time they returned Paul was asleep. The next morning, Elènne recalls:

> I remember Paul's sad lonely figure sitting outside on a bench. He knew something bad had happened but was just sitting there waiting to be told. I was told to go and tell him. I sat down next to him, and he asked me if mother had died. I angrily replied, "Of course."[85]

Both Elènne and Paul developed tough exteriors to hide their pain. They, with Des, had known for a long time that the evil day would come. Luke, barely four years old, did not understand the enormity of the situation. The bitterness of any theological debate was mild compared to the sinking grief experienced by the family. Gwen's funeral service was conducted by Archibald Hefren, at the time a fellow lecturer with Des. She lies in "God's Acre," the college campus cemetery, until the resurrection.

Final Tribute to Gwen

When [the writer of] Hebrews 11 ran out of time to name more examples of faith he left the way open for later generations to include the likes of Gwen.

Norman Young[86]

End Notes

1   Desmond Ford, interviewed by Trevor Lloyd at Caloundra, Jan 7, 2001.

2   Elènne Ford to Milton Hook, June 26, 2005.

3   E.g., Desmond Ford to Elènne Ford, Dec 9, 1961; Desmond Ford to Gwen Ford, [Dec 1962].

4   Desmond Ford to Elènne Ford, Dec 9, 1961.

5   Desmond Ford to Gwen Ford, [April 1962].

6   Elènne Ford to Hook, June 26, 2005.

7   Desmond Ford to AC Board, June 6, 1962.

8   Gordon McDowell, interviewed by Trevor Lloyd at Sydney, March 25,1999.

9   Elènne Ford to Hook, June 26, 2005.

10   Lawrence Naden to John Keith and D[avid] Sibley, July 6, 1964.

11   Desmond Ford to Gwen Ford, [ca. Feb 25, 1968].

12   Desmond Ford to Gwen Ford, [ca. Feb 16, 1968].

13   Desmond Ford to Gwen Ford, [ca. May 1, 1968].

14   Personal recollections of the author, a student at Avondale 1960–1964.

15   McDowell, interviewed by Lloyd, March 25, 1999.

16   Desmond Ford, "Nature of Christ," address given at Western Australian camp meeting, 1964.

17   Desmond Ford, interviewed by Trevor Lloyd at Sydney, March 12, 1995, March 10, 1996; Desmond Ford, "The Reality of the Heavenly Sanctuary," unpublished paper, [ca. 1962], Box 436, ACHR, Cooranbong, NSW.

18   Hope (Brinsmead) Taylor, interviewed by Trevor Lloyd at Duranbah, April 8, 1996.

19   McDowell, interviewed by Lloyd, March 25, 1999.

20   Ken Low, "Seminary Extension School," *AR,* March 14, 1966, p. 1.

21   "Minority Report of the Committee on Daniel," unpublished paper, April 19, 1966; Ford, interviewed by Lloyd, March 10, 1996.

22   E.g., Desmond Ford articles, *Ministry*, Feb, June 1964; Oct, Dec 1965.

23   Desmond Ford, "The Sealing of the Saints—Before or After the Loud Cry?" n.p., [ca. 1964]

24   R[obert] Brinsmead, "The Timing of Revelation 18 and the Perfecting of the Saints: An Answer to Dr. Desmond Ford and Pastor L. C. Naden," n.p., [ca. 1964].

25 E.g., Fernando Chaij, *Preparation for the Final Crisis,* (Mountain View, California: Pacific Press Publishing Association, 1966).

26 Robert Brinsmead, interviewed by Trevor Lloyd at Duranbah, March 18, 1996.

27 E.g., Robert Brinsmead, "How is Perfection Possible?" in *Is Perfection Possible? Versus How is Perfection Possible?* Fred Metz, ed., n.p., January 1964.

28 E[llet] Waggoner, *The Gospel in the Book of Galatians,* (Oakland, California: Pacific Press Publishing Association, 1888), p. 45.

29 E[llet] Waggoner, *Christ and His Righteousness,* (Oakland, California: Pacific Press Publishing Association, 1890), p. 93.

30 E[llet] Waggoner, *Signs of the Times,* Feb 3, 1890, p. 70, June 30, 1890, p. 390.

31 E[llet] Waggoner, *Signs of the Times*, Jan 21, 1889, pp. 38, 39.

32 Alonzo Jones, *The Consecrated Way to Christian Perfection,* (Mountain View, California: Pacific Press Publishing Association, 1905), pp. 76, 84.

33 Waggoner, *Signs of the Times,* June 30, 1890, p. 390.

34 E[llet] Waggoner, *The Glad Tidings: Studies in Galatians,* (Mountain View, California: Pacific Press Publishing Association, [ca.1973]: originally published 1900.

35 D[enton] Rebok, ed., *Our Firm Foundation,* vol 2, (Washington, D.C.: Review and Herald Publishing Association, 1953), p. 595.

36 R[obert] Brinsmead, *Judgment Hour Sermons,* vol 4, (Conway, Missouri: Gems of Truth [1964]), p. 50.

37 R[obert] Brinsmead, *A Doctrinal Analysis of "The History and Teachings of Robert Brinsmead"* (Los Angeles, California: Sanctuary Awakening Fellowship, [ca. 1962]), p. 45.

38 Ellen White, *The Great Controversy,* (Mountain View, California: Pacific Press Publishing Association, 1888), p. 469.

39 Ellen White, *Christ's Object Lessons,* (Mountain View, California: Pacific Press Publishing Association, 1900), p. 384.

40 White, *Great Controversy,* pp. 425, 614.

41 Metz, ed., *Is Perfection Possible? Versus How is Perfection Possible?* p. 9.

42 E.g., Ellen White, *The Sanctified Life,* (Washington, D.C.: Review and Herald Publishing Association, 1937), pp. 7, 81.

43 Edward Heppenstall to Desmond Ford, Dec 1, 1960.

44 General Conference Research and Defence Literature Committee,

The History and Teaching of Robert Brinsmead, (Washington, D.C.: Review and Herald Publishing Association, 1962), pp. 2, 5, 10, 12, 16.

45   L. C. Naden, *The Perfecting of the Saints,* (Warburton, Victoria: Signs Publishing Company [1964]), [p. 30]

46   Chaij, pp. 16, 44–48.

47   Desmond Ford, *Unlocking God's Treasury,* (Warburton, Victoria: Signs Publishing Company, 1964), p. 18.

48   Ford, interviewed by Lloyd, March 12, 1995.

49   McDowell, interviewed by Lloyd, March 25, 1999.

50   Jim Johanson, interviewed by Milton Hook in Melbourne, Oct 10, 1996.

51   Walter Scragg, Sr., to Lawrence Naden, Jan 4, Dec 2, 1968; Walter Scragg, Sr., to Robert Frame, Jan 11, 1971.

52   Gordon McDowell to John Keith, Sept 21, 1964.

53   Personal recollections of the author, one of the slightly bemused interns.

54   [Raglan Marks?], circulated letter, Cooranbong, Sept 9, 1965.

55   Ford, interviewed by Lloyd, March 12, 1995.

56   McDowell, interviewed by Lloyd, March 25, 1999.

57   "Summary of a Discussion Concerning Bible Teaching at Avondale," unpublished paper, Wahroonga, Dec 22, 1969.

58   Lawrence Naden to Desmond Ford, Dec 22, 1969.

59   Details in this section are from Elènne Ford to Milton Hook, June 26, 2005.

60   Desmond Ford to Gwen Ford, [ca. June 1968, A].

61   Desmond Ford to Gwen Ford, [ca. June 1968, B].

62   Desmond Ford to Gwen Ford, [ca. May 24, 1968].

63   Desmond Ford, to Gwen Ford, [ca. Feb 25, 1968].

64   Desmond Ford to Gwen Ford, [Feb 13], 21, [1968] .

65   Ford, interviewed by Lloyd, March 10, 1996.

66   Desmond Ford to Gwen Ford, [Feb 9], March 19, 1968.

67   Desmond Ford to Gwen Ford, [Feb 12, March 21, ca. March, A, 1968]; Gwen Ford to Desmond Ford, fragment, [ca. June 1968].

68   Desmond Ford to Gwen Ford, [ca. Feb 5 ,9, ca. 27, ca. April, A, ca. June, C, 1968].

69   Desmond Ford to Gwen Ford, April 24, [ca. May 1968].

70   Desmond Ford to Gwen Ford, [ca. April 23, 30, 1968].

71   Paul Ford to Gwen Ford, [ca. May 4, 1968].

72 Elènne Ford to Gwen Ford, [ca. Feb 1968].

73 Desmond Ford to Gwen Ford, [ca. April 1968, C].

74 Desmond Ford to Gwen Ford, [ca. May 1, 1968].

75 *Ibid.*

76 Desmond Ford to Gwen Ford, [ca. Feb, March 21, ca. March, C, D, 1968].

77 Desmond Ford to Gwen Ford, [April 25, ca. April 30, 1968].

78 Desmond Ford to Gwen Ford, [ca. April, D, May 6, fragment, ca. June, E, ca. July 11, 1968].

79 Desmond Ford to Gwen Ford, [July 9, 1968].

80 Desmond Ford to Gwen Ford, [July 9, 1968]; Desmond Ford to Norman Young, April 2, 1970; Desmond Ford, unpublished life sketch of Gwen Ford, [1974], pp. 5, 6.

81 Gwen Ford, "Testament of Faith," *AR,* May 25, 1970, pp. 12, 14.

82 Desmond Ford to Gwen Ford, [ca. April 27, ca. June, F, 1968].

83 Norman Young to Desmond Ford, March 12, 1970.

84 Ford, life-sketch of Gwen Ford, [1974], p. 7.

85 Elènne Ford to Hook, June 26, 2005. .

86 Norman Young to Desmond Ford, April 14, [1970]

Chapter Six:
"I've Come for a Rest"

How does a family regain normalcy after witnessing the slow death of a loving wife and mother? There is rarely a full recovery. Many children, despite courageous veneers, retain fragile interiors that weep or simmer angrily. Des's children struggled for years to come to terms with their family tragedy. "Suffering," says Des, "makes you bitter or better."

He himself was buoyed by Gwen's faith and his belief in the resurrection. He maintains, too, that in all times of anguish he found strength by reading stories about Christian martyrs and missionaries who braved dreadful episodes.[1] In a positive philosophical frame of mind, just before Gwen's death he mused:

> There are arbors for pilgrims on the way to Zion and they are put there by the Prince of the City, not by the devil. It is remarkable that so few have ever thought about discussing the problem of good and yet so many discuss the problem of pain and evil. Life, for most of us, has a great deal of the former and the latter stands out because it is exceptional rather than the rule.[2]

Early in Gwen's illness Des had experienced one touching bit of cheer. His long-estranged brother, Val, came to their home seeking reconciliation after numerous letters Des had sent to him. When he found that Des had taken Gwen to a Sydney hospital for treatment, he was genuinely upset by the news of Gwen's illness. Uncertain of which hospital, Val set out desperately to ask at the most likely places. Emerging from the underground Town Hall railway station in the vast metropolis, he fortuitously spotted Des. He tapped him on the shoulder and said, "You're Des, aren't you?" Des was overwhelmed. Their astonishing rendezvous marked the renewal of an enduring brotherly bond. "I have written more letters to him than any other person on earth," Des claims.[3]

After Gwen's death Des felt he would like a break from the relentless duties both on and off campus. He revived prospects of doing a second doctorate, something that Gwen wanted him to do. Church leaders were also convinced there were distinct advantages for their college accreditation purposes if lecturers, especially heads of departments, owned a doctorate from a university conducted on the British system of education. Some Australian accreditation officials were prejudiced against the American education system.

In 1966 Des had corresponded with F. F. Bruce, a respected lecturer at Manchester University in England. He sent Bruce a copy of his major thesis completed at Michigan State University and received a very favorable reply.[4] Now seemed the opportune time to realize those earlier plans. He applied for study leave and in September 1970 the Avondale College Board voted to sponsor him to begin a Ph.D. at Manchester in 1971.[5]

These plans were endorsed at Australian church headquarters at the same time as Lawrence Naden, president, was being replaced by Robert Frame. Frame said to Des, "What are your plans for remarriage?" Des was in no rush to wed again. He thought he might wait until after study in England, but even then, there was no urgency. His reluctance arose from the fear of having another ill partner, a repetition of the trauma with Gwen. However, both Frame and David Sibley urged him to reconsider, warning that while he remained single, he would be pursued by "nuisance women." This was good advice because their concerns were well founded. On one occasion Des answered a knock at his front door and was met by a woman who said she had had a vision. "God has told me I should marry you," she gushed. Des maintained his poise and politely told her, "If that is the case, I would have been given a similar vision, but I haven't!"[6]

Elènne harbored a different fantasy. She wished for her favorite schoolteacher to become her new mother. At the same time, she sensed her father's only preference was Gillian Wastell, better known as Gill, a prospect Elènne resisted at first. In her diary she wrote about her misgivings and then hid them in a broken portion of her bedroom wall. Des happened on the diary one day and learned the truth about her thoughts about Gill. He and Elènne then went for a long walk, hand in hand, as he tried to mollify her tears and reservations. She finally accepted her father's choice.[7]

Gill had been born in England but migrated to New Zealand with her parents when she was sixteen. It was there she became a Seventh-day Adventist and then went to Australia at twenty-one to attend Avondale College as a relatively new adherent. During her five years on campus, she helped to pay her fees by working in the cafeteria and as a dean and assistant preceptress. For one year she did secretarial work for Des. During Gwen's illness Gill spent many hours painting a picture for her birthday.[8] She thought highly of Gwen, and the respect was reciprocal, but at the time Gwen made her list of possible wives, she hardly knew Gill.

Gill proved to be a bright student, beginning with the Bible Instructor's Course, but changed over to the bachelor's degree in Education. One of her early classes was the study of Daniel and Revelation, with Des as lecturer. She found it a daunting task to write a forty-page essay at the end, but she had brought to college a Reader's Digest book on the Bible that contained a history of Antiochus Epiphanes. She used it, together with other sources, to write her essay on Daniel 11 and Revelation 13, proposing a recurring fulfillment she had heard about in class. Des gave her a straight A for it. Soon after, Des confessed to her, "If I had written [and published] that essay I would have been put out of my job."[9]

Robert Parr, Des's editor and long-time friend, was told in confidence of wedding plans for the two. With his usual panache he wrote to Des:

> I have met your Gillian, of course. I well understand your feelings for the lass; she is a cut above the ordinary. A touch of class, she has, old boy. I first detected it in her when I received her first submission for the Signs of the Times. I took the unusual step of accepting the first article she submitted, and the second, also. I don't know that I have ever done that before to a hitherto unpublished writer. One thing I beg of you.
>
> Please do not court the lady by correspondence. NEVER write her a letter. In your own hand, that is. She will go absolutely bonkers trying to decipher it. And when next you see her, she will be a gibbering frustrate, a wild-eyed paranoiac who went off her rocker trying to make sense out of that spidery scrawl that you euphemistically refer to, in your lighter moments, as "writing." If there must be correspondence, please use a typewriter.[10]

Des and Gill were married in the home of Cooranbong friends at 7 a.m., college graduation day, November 22, 1970. David Sibley conducted the service. Later that day Gill received her degree, a B.Ed., with a French and German major.[11]

While the newlyweds were enjoying a brief honeymoon, Elènne recalls, "Paul and I, with the help of our much-loved teacher, packed up the house, putting some things into storage and some into suitcases and boxes, for Manchester."[12] Four-year-old Luke was returned from New Zealand after a year's absence, and that same night the Ford family of five boarded the boat for England.[13]

What a daunting task it was for a young woman to start married life with three children already in the household! Gill had given some prayerful thought to her marriage, especially the reality of suddenly having to care for three children, but she proved to be equal to the task. Baby Luke responded to "Mummy Gill," as he called her, and a good relationship was forged. Paul, being sensitive and quiet as a child, did not reveal his emotions so overtly but seemed to accept Gill into his boyish world. Elènne spent only brief periods in the home after the marriage. Des sacrificed a large chunk of his meager income to send her to boarding school in England. She only came home during holidays. Then she returned to Australia ahead of Des to attend Avondale College, sometimes staying with friends but later, for about eighteen months, with Des and Gill when they returned from England. Elènne finally boarded as a college student and then returned to England for law studies.[14]

Overseas Again

During their stay at Manchester, Des and Gill found an old stone house to rent. In the winter it was bitterly cold and so damp in some rooms that the wallpaper fell off. But the spring and summer months were delightful, with bold little birds flitting in and out of their open windows.

Earlier, F. F. Bruce had told Des that the university required a minimum of two years residence for him to earn the doctorate. When Des first met with Bruce at the university, he shared some of the pressures and trauma he had endured in recent years and confessed, "I've come for a rest!" Bruce responded compassionately and assured Des he would receive every assistance available to guarantee an untroubled stay on campus.

"What do I do first?" he asked Bruce.

"Learn German," was Bruce's blunt advice. "And then you will need to give me a statement of where you are going to aim at [in your research] and what you are going to do."[15]

The English system differed from the American method of earning a doctorate. American universities required classwork, culminating in comprehensive examinations, with a major research project and an oral defense of the project. But English universities accomplished all the classwork at the graduate level, leaving the doctoral level entirely for a major research project with an oral defense. So, Des sat in none of Bruce's classes and concentrated entirely on his own research.

Bruce had identified the lack of German language studies as the single weak spot in Dess preparation so far in his career. So, Des began a crash course of study, assisted by Gill, and her earlier study of German at Avondale proved to be gold bullion. German classes had been offered at Avondale for two years only, and she happened to be there during that very period. So as Des delved into German sources for his research, he understood enough to identify the pertinent passages, and Gill would translate those many pages by hand. Her work was of immeasurable value, though after this time, she never had reason to use the German language again.[16]

For two years, Des focused on biblical prophecy. First, he submitted his topic, "The Abomination of Desolation," in the prophetic passages of Daniel and the New Testament, and Bruce gave the go-ahead.

"I thought about it in the libraries," Des recalled, "I thought on the train, as I walked, as I ate at the meal table, during church services, in the bathroom and toilet, and at night when I should have been sleeping."[17]

Once he and Bruce sat in Bruce's study discussing some of the research, and Des said that he believed Daniel 8:14 is the pivotal verse in the Book of Daniel, because it summarizes the theme of the whole book, i.e., vindication. Every chapter, he maintained, pictures the saints in trouble until God intervenes and is vindicated—that is, God's saving power and His justice are vindicated as righteous.

"Have you noticed," Des continued, "that the *niphal* [passive] form of *tsadaq* [Hebrew for "vindicated" or "justified"] in Daniel 8:14 is the only time it is used in the Bible?"

"Are you sure?" Bruce queried.

"Well, to tell you the truth, I'm not one hundred per cent sure," Des admitted, "but somewhere along the way I've gained that impression."

"We'll find out right now," Bruce determined. Leaning back over his chair and reaching into his reference books, Bruce found the spot and blurted out, "You're right, it's the only time!"

Des was then confirmed in his belief that the word, properly translated as "vindicated," had special significance, indicating a climax involving

95

God's intervention, a culmination to dramatic events concerning His people and the vindication of His character.[18] Des later published these words in Ministry magazine:

> Our interpretation of Daniel 8:14, linking it with the judgment, is strongly supported by the key word of the text which expresses a concept now common to all students of eschatology.[19]

As his thesis developed in his thinking, Des also began to realize that the SDA dependence on Historicism[20] set a narrow view.

That is, Adventist prophetic interpretations proposed only pagan and papal Rome as fulfillments of "the abomination of desolation." Preterism, he concluded, likewise narrowly confined the application by restricting the fulfillment to Antiochus Epiphanes in the Second Century B.C. Similarly, Futurism limited the interpretation, but to a future antichrist at the end of time. Employing the principle of recurring fulfillments, the apotelesmatic principle, Des suggested that all these narrow interpretations had some value. By including the best elements of these three views and linking them together, he proposed, there would emerge the broad picture painted in Scripture. That is, Antiochus Epiphanes should be taken as the initial fulfillment of "the abomination of desolation," followed by pagan and papal Rome as possible fulfillments in the Christian era. Then, at the end of time, there would arise the mother of all antichrists who would persecute Christians but be annihilated in the last great judgment day.[21]

This approach promised understanding of other passages in apocalyptic prophecy if the principle was applied. Later, as his thesis became better known in academic circles, it was applauded and cited by a number of respected scholars.[22] One Oxford lecturer, for example, remarked, "I regard [it] as one of the most illuminating and worthwhile studies of New Testament eschatology that I have come across."[23]

Brinsmead's Backflip

While Des was caught up in the trauma of Gwen's illness and death, followed by his remarriage and preoccupation with studies at Manchester, significant developments in Australia were taking place that would influence the next decade.

Though most church members were unaware of it, Walter Scragg, Sr., a retired SDA Church administrator, was circulating his views among the Brinsmeads. Scragg's theology was a curious mixture of the traditional SDA beliefs and the revised views. He promoted the old view of Armageddon and the sinful nature of Christ based on what Ellen White had said; however he compiled a list of thirteen theological errors he said were made by White. Many of his views were unorthodox. These included the idea that the seal of God is more than just the keeping of the seventh-day Sabbath; that "the beast" of Revelation 13 is more than the Roman Catholic Church; that the word "cleansed" (KJV) in Daniel 8:14 is best translated "justified" or "vindicated;" that the daily atonements of Leviticus 4 and 5 brought about perfect forgiveness that needed no second forgiveness in the Day of Atonement service; that Antiochus Epiphanes fulfilled Daniel 8; and that the SDA view of an Investigative Judgment of the saints is not scriptural.[24]

Scragg produced a draft manuscript arguing these lines, titled "Hour of Faith," which he shared with Tom Brinsmead. After reading it three times Tom made this startling evaluation of Scragg's opinions:

It is a stimulating and radical approach to the Sanctuary and the Judgment. You cannot expect these views to be acceptable to the establishment. Yours is far more radical than Robert's sanctuary studies.

Just as Rome tenaciously fights against any attempt to deprive her of the doctrine of Apostolic Succession... so the SDA Church will never give up the General Conference interpretation of what happened in 1844, i.e., [the] sanctuary in heaven commenced to be cleansed (wrong translation).

Around this point the Establishment will fight you like fanatical Moslems, and they will grind their teeth at you in self-righteous anger.

Like the Jews of old they pride themselves on their traditions and they have presented tradition for truth. To win your points you have to de-rate the status of the S[pirit] of P[rophecy] and here again you will meet the immovable nonsense that these are inspired. If you had lived or rather brought these views to their notice 25 years ago you would have been declared an arch heretic.... For a long time, I have believed that the righteous are judged by the gospel daily and that there is no recounting [in an Investigative Judgment].[25]

These views were aired among the Brinsmead clan in 1971, and some were publicly voiced a little later, causing a theological tornado across the Western world among SDAs.

Scragg was in close touch with Robert Brinsmead too, seeking to influence him. In August 1970 Scragg told his son:

On our way back from Brisbane we [Scragg and wife] spent another two hours with him [Robert] when he tried to prove [that] his fantastic theory on a sinless life was right. I looked at him after a while and said, "Now, Robert, tell me, how far have you advanced in the last twenty years to this sinless state you talk about?" He [Robert] looked at his wife and she glanced at him and said nothing. Poor fellow.[26]

This prod in the right direction did not meet with much resistance from Brinsmead, because he was already in the throes of reconsidering his perfectionist views. Earlier in the year, prior to the papal visit to Australia in April 1970, Brinsmead had publicly questioned the right of the Australian government to spend so much taxpayers' money on a tour by a religious head. His protest made the local press and TV. Consequently, a local Roman Catholic dignitary challenged him to a debate. He took up the offer and threw himself into a study of Roman Catholic theology to prepare for the confrontation.

Brinsmead interviewed a Roman Catholic scholar at Banyo Seminary near Brisbane and studied their viewpoints about salvation. He discussed issues with local Lutheran ministers and read widely in the Reformation classics, just as Des had encouraged him to do years earlier. Much to his surprise he discovered that the red cardinals taught much the same as he himself did about the dynamics of salvation. The Roman Church, he found, believed justification was a forensic verdict, an imputation of Christ's righteousness, but they joined it with sanctification by saying salvation also depended on the imparted grace of God working in you and making you really righteous.[27] That was exactly what Waggoner and Jones had espoused. The view was prevalent in the SDA Church. In the 1960s Brinsmead had simply sharpened the theory with an eschatological whetstone.

With a change of heart Brinsmead was eventually led to declare:

They [Waggoner and Jones] were ignoramuses .... They didn't know bees from a bull's foot.... They were ignorant and foolish and didn't know what they were talking about on very simple and fundamental things of exegesis.[28]

Needless to say, Brinsmead's debate with the Roman Catholic cleric never materialized. He became so engrossed in his Reformation studies that he let the offer slide.

With this thorough reversal, the Brinsmead family first took truckloads of perfectionist literature to the dump. Then they launched into a prolonged and vigorous campaign to preach righteousness by faith alone. They also thought it proper, in about 1971, to apologize to the General Conference officials for all the divisiveness and distress they had caused the church.[29] For this reason Robert and John Brinsmead, with American sympathizer Dr Jack Zwemer, attended a meeting at Washington headquarters. It turned into a weeklong conference on a range of theological issues. Naden was there from Australia, and Ford was flown in from England as an academic representative.

One morning Des spoke on "the blotting out of sins" (Acts 3:19), inferring the apotelesmatic principle in his exposition. When he finished, the chairman asked for a response. Zwemer commented that Des had just demonstrated he was a bit "heterodox" for the SDA position. The chairman immediately called a recess. Another academic in the group sidled up to the Brinsmeads and Zwemer and with a wink and a nudge asked, "Do you know why they called a recess?"

"Why?" they chorused.

"Because they have gone off to find out what "heterodox" means!"[30]

Little good emerged from this and a subsequent meeting. General Conference administrators kept the Brinsmeads at arm's length, asking for their rebaptism and insisting they did not need their help in preaching about salvation. The Brinsmeads were not impressed by the administrators' apparent lack of interest in the gospel. They detected little knowledge of the Reformation doctrine of righteousness by faith alone.

Studies Finalized

At the time of the visit to Washington, Des, of course, really had his mind focused on his thesis. He capitalized on the trip by spending as much time as possible in the nearby Library of Congress, ferreting for material relevant to his research and then quickly headed back to England.[31]

Des completed his thesis in record time, six months before it was required. Bruce is said to have declared, after reading the manuscript, that it was the fastest thesis of quality he had ever witnessed.

During the eighteen months, Des had also accepted various speaking engagements, such as a graduation address at Newbold College and local church services. He always spoke on simple gospel themes, rather than laboring the heavier research that had occupied his mind.[32]

Troubles at Home

The speed with his research project was the more remarkable in view of the fact that serious domestic problems haunted Des.

At a premarital check-up, Gill was advised to use a birth control pill that contained synthetic progestin. It threw her hormonal system into confusion. She described her condition as a periodic "emotional fog," causing her to be "panic-stricken" and "terrified."

She wrote of the onset and worsening crisis:

> During our trip to England, Des and I had our first real argument, and I went into a gradually deepening depression and withdrew into sullen silences, punctuated by sudden uncontrollable outbursts of anger, retreating into my bedroom for hours and days at a time.
>
> I started to question my marriage. I had thought that God had led me into marriage, and that I had done the right thing taking on the family, and suddenly it seemed like a disaster. I felt terrible that I was making everyone miserable, when inside I wanted to be part of their healing.[33]

Thinking back over that time years later, Paul is said to have remarked, "There was a shadow over our home, and I did not know what it was."[34]

For a decade Gill tried all sorts of remedies—surgery for supposed polycystic ovaries, different types of birth control pills, psychiatric treatment and anti-depressants, and various hormonal supplements. Finally, regular implants of estrogen brought balance and relief to her body.[35] But in the meantime, there were desperate times when Des, too, questioned the marriage.

Having finished writing his thesis, Des decided (after discussing it with Gill) that they should make a tour of Europe with Paul and Luke. He spent forty pounds on a second-hand car and his fellow student, Norman Young, and wife, Liz, joined them. It proved to be the real rest that he had sought for so long. When he returned to face the oral defense of his thesis, he succeeded without a hitch and was granted his Ph.D. (Theology) at a graduation ceremony in December.[36] The dedication page of his thesis read:

> To the memory of Gwen Ford, who encouraged this project though aware she would not live to see it; and to Gill Ford, whose whole-hearted help made the hope a reality.[37]

Des and his family, except for Elènne, arrived back at Avondale in the summer of 1972/73. Des himself was fully rested and eager to resume lecturing again in the familiar halls of Avondale College.

Once again, however, he found himself back among his persistent critics, and they stepped up their opposition, making the next few years a time of confrontation between Adventist fundamentalism in Australia and Des's clarion calls for church members to accept the apostolic gospel.

End Notes

1   Desmond Ford, interviewed by Milton Hook at Caloundra, May 24, 2001.
2   Desmond Ford to Norman Young, April 2,1970.
3   Desmond Ford, interviewed by Trevor Lloyd at Sydney, March 10, 1996.
4   F. F. Bruce to Desmond Ford, Feb l4, Sept 20, 22, 1966.
5   A. C. Board minutes, Sept 10, 1970.
6   Elènne Ford to Milton Hook, June 27, 2005.
7   *Ibid.*
8   Desmond Ford to Gwen Ford, [ca. May 1,1968].
9   Gillian Ford, interviewed by Trevor Lloyd at Cooranbong, Jan 6, 1997.
10 Robert Parr to Desmond Ford, Nov 17, 1970.
11 Gillian Ford, interviewed by Lloyd, Jan 6, 1997.
12 Elènne Ford to Hook, June 27, 2005.
13 Gillian Ford, *Listening to Your Hormones,* (Rocklin, California: Prima Publishing, 1996), p. 5.
14 Elènne Ford to Hook, June 27, 2005.
15 Desmond Ford, interviewed by Milton Hook at Sydney, Feb 2, 2002; Desmond Ford, interviewed by Trevor Lloyd at Sydney,

March 12,1995.

16 Gillian Ford, interviewed by Lloyd, Jan 6, 1997.

17 Desmond Ford, interviewed by Lloyd, March 12,1995.

18 *Ibid.*

19 Desmond Ford, "Seventh-day Adventism and Eschatology," *Ministry,* March 1971, p. 42.

20 Historicism is a method of prophetic interpretation favored by Protestant reformers that regarded pagan and papal Rome as the definitive persecutors of Christs true followers. In contrast, Preterism is a method that regards end-time prophecies as having been fulfilled by about the end of the first Christian century. Futurism holds the opposite view, i.e., the end-time prophecies will find their fulfillment in a literal antichrist who will persecute Christ's followers on a global scale just prior to the Second Advent

21 Desmond Ford, interviewed by Lloyd, March 12, 1995.

22 E.g., George Beasley-Murray, *Jesus and the Last Days,* (Peabody, Massachusetts: Hendrickson Publishers, 1993).

23 David Wenham to University Press of America, Dec 5, 1985.

24 Walter Scragg, Sr., to Walter Scragg, Jr., Aug 30, 1970; Walter Scragg, Sr., to Robert Frame et al., Dec 15, 1970; Walter Scragg, Sr., to Lawrence Naden, Nov 21,1970, June 21, 1971; Walter Scragg, Sr., "Some of Sr. White's Mistakes," unpublished paper, box 437, ACHR, Cooranbong, NSW.

25 Tom Brinsmead to Pastor and Mrs. Scragg, Jan 19, 1971.

26 Scragg, Sr. to Scragg, Jr., Aug 30, 1970.

27 Robert Brinsmead, interviewed by Trevor Lloyd at Duranbah, April 18, 1996.

28 *Ibid.*

29 *Ibid.*

30 Jack Zwemer to Trevor Lloyd, Oct 22, 2004.

31 Desmond Ford, interviewed by Lloyd, March 12, 1995.

32 *Ibid.*

33 Gillian Ford, *Listening to Your Hormones,* pp. 6–8.

34 Desmond Ford to Milton Hook, July 16, 2005.

35 Gillian Ford, *Listening to Your Hormones*, pp. 9–23

36 Desmond Ford, interviewed by Milton Hook, Feb 2, 2002.

37 Desmond Ford, *The Abomination of Desolation in Biblical Eschatology,* (Washington, D.C.: University Press of America, 1979), p. iii.

Chapter Seven:
A Posse of Mossbacks

Avondale College held an attractive ambience for Des. Despite the loss of Gwen, it was the place of a thousand happy memories—early student days, friendships forged, vibrant classroom experiences, and its rustic setting. It was a joy to return to its halls in 1973.

Des and his family settled in at Currans Road. Elènne was boarding with friends and continuing her studies. Paul finished high school, and then flexed his independence and decided to go north to stay with maternal relatives in Queensland. There he first worked with his uncles in real estate. Later he partnered a plant nursery with an aunt. More recently, he has developed a very successful importing and wholesale business. Luke, of course, was only elementary school age and attended the campus school within walking distance of home.[1]

Once again, Des took up his lecturing duties and frequent speaking appointments. Whenever time permitted, he wrote articles for the denominational press. His critics carefully scrutinized them and made him a target of vilification. Des, however, was not the type to be intimidated by diatribes. If he believed he had a contribution to the ongoing quest for truth, he did not hesitate to share it publicly.

Before Des left Manchester, the editor of the Australasian *Signs of the Times*, Robert Parr, had arranged with Des to publish a series on the Book of Daniel, a reflection on its major themes after the doctoral studies, especially the "abomination of desolation" motif.

Parr had written with tongue in cheek:

> I am well aware of the fact that you are to the right (or the left) of Uriah Smith, W. M. R. Scragg, and sundry others. I know that the publication of your views of the King of the North, Armageddon and sundry other material, will bring W. M. R. Scragg out in the full flurry of his confused penmanship and, when I defend what I am doing, he will thenceforth not speak to me for the space of some weeks. For this reason, I am not terribly upset. Indeed, I would not consider it a hell on earth if good old Brother Scragg did not write to me very often.

I emphasize that it [your series] must be fairly simple.... I believe that you will not plunge into the inner recesses of prophecy to such an extent that only those who have four Ph.Ds. will be able to interpret it.... Be gentle on the Catholics, and don't get into any confusion about the King of the North. Obviously, that is Japan. Or Communist China if you are not too fussy about magnetic north.[2]

Des subsequently churned out twelve articles in as many weeks on arrival back in Australia. "Thank you for your marathon effort on Daniel," Parr responded, "Your STUFF came this a.m., and right glad I was to have it."[3]

These articles were reprinted in Ministry magazine, extending into 1974, and in 1975 the American *These Times* accepted submissions on the books of Genesis, Romans, and Colossians.[4] He was also asked by the General Conference Sabbath School Department to begin preparing a Sabbath School lesson quarterly with a book to complement the same topic.[5]

Contact with denominational editors was cordial, especially with homeland Parr, who was sometimes invited to share in Fordian hospitality when visiting Avondale. Making light of Des's abstemious living habits while responding to Gill's invitation to dinner on one occasion he kidded:

I know this invitation comes from your own generous heart and not from Old Spider-Scrawl [Des himself].... I cannot tell you how I'm looking forward to that baked orange peel. But please limit me to TWO glasses of the strained celery water. It's heady stuff and I have to play Hefren at golf on Sunday a.m., and I don't want a hangover.[6]

Parr saved some badinage for Des by asking, "Are you giving yourself a treat and coming on Sat. night [to the concert]? Aw, go on! Give yourself a break, whydoncha?"[7]

Aftermath of the Daniel Series

The articles on Daniel were an engaging series but remarkable for their traditional content. The treatise on Daniel 9, for instance, still did not address the immediate context, i.e., Daniel's prayer for enlightenment that grew out of his reading of Jeremiah's prophecy of seventy years' captivity in Babylon. Des seemed to maintain the assumption that Daniel 9 was occasioned by Daniel's residual consternation over the prophecy in Daniel 8, about ten years earlier. The "seventy weeks" time period of Daniel 9:24–27 was "cut off?" he said, "from the longer period of the 2300 years."[8]

Following Parr's admonition to be kind to Catholics (for many of them read *Signs of the Times*), Des simply alluded to them as "an illicit union of church and state" in the Middle Ages. Furthermore, when explaining the final chapters of Daniel, he made no mention of Turkey or Russia as the King of the North. And the word Armageddon was skirted completely.[9] For this reason, Walter Scragg, Sr., was unimpressed, writing letters of complaint to Robert Frame, the Australasian Division president, about what he regarded as serious omissions of orthodox views.[10] Frame, however, defended Des.[11]

Another critic came to the fore at this time. A retired Australian minister, Llewellyn Jones, had made a mild protest about three years earlier, raising an objection to the principle of dual fulfillments of prophecies that Des used in an October 1969 *Ministry* article. Now, having read the first few instalments of Des's articles on Daniel in the August 1973 *Ministry* magazines, he sent a letter post haste to the editor, hoping the final instalments would not speak of any dual fulfilments.[12]

Jones became alarmed when the instalments on the last chapters of Daniel were published, first by Parr in the Australasian *Signs of the Times* and then by Robert Spangler in *Ministry* magazine. Des clearly proposed not just dual fulfillments for the prophecies, but multiple ones. He cited the well-known New Testament scholar George Eldon Ladd as a recent commentator who agreed with the principle. Des disagreed with the traditional SDA commentator, Uriah Smith, and found that Antiochus Epiphanes did, indeed, fulfill Daniel 11:21–35. He added that "the abomination of desolation" also found a later fulfillment in pagan Rome, continuing fulfillments throughout the Christian centuries and, finally, "an ultimate accomplishment at the end of time."[13]

Jones was incensed, accusing Des of becoming a Futurist under the influence of Professor Bruce at Manchester.[14] Des had not sat in any of Bruce's classes, but the false allegation spread widely, and Jones even sent his poison letter to William Murdoch at Andrews University.

Murdoch informed Des:

I have told him [Jones] that I feel he has approached your

presentations with a definite bias that you belong to the Futurist School of interpretation. This bias runs throughout his criticism. I have told him that this is not so, that the Futurist builds his theory on the gap between the 69th and the 70th week [Daniel 9:24–27]. You have no such intimation in your documents....

Elder Jones begins with the supposition that when an Old Testament prophecy has one fulfillment that it is not possible to have a second. We do not agree with this proposition, as I have told him, and I cited Hosea 11:1 as the prime example.[15]

Edward Heppenstall, too, heard of Jones's grumbles and sympathized with Des:

I am quite appalled that you can be called in question at all on such points of interpretation taken by Uriah Smith. I thought we had settled that question long ago as to the nature of Smith's authority. I was always under the impression that Australia was the place for largeness of mind and heart in theological matters; that the brethren down under were more than eager for all the truth that could be brought to light and worthy of serious consideration.[16]

Nevertheless, some non-traditional elements that Des had written into the Daniel series did not meet with Heppenstall's view. For example, Heppenstall could not see that clauses, such as "bring in everlasting righteousness" (Daniel 9:24) might have an end-time application. However, he did agree with other major elements not found in traditional SDA literature. He explained:

What we have in this chapter is literal time and a literal fulfillment in the history of the Jews.... I do not see any future beyond AD 70 indicated in this chapter. Daniel's sole concern is with literal Jerusalem and the Jewish nation.... He knows nothing about 1844. Consequently, Gabriel seeks to enlighten him as to the fulfillment of Jeremiah's prophecy and the destiny of the Jewish nation. For me, your interpretation appears to be contrived.[17]

If Jones had known of Heppenstall's stand, his writing pad would have ignited, the ashes spelling out "SDA heretic," for Murdoch's letter had made no impression on him. Heppenstall was broadminded and unperturbed by what Des had written, stating good-naturedly, "I am not disturbed by your interpretation."[18]

Both Heppenstall and Murdoch were more concerned by the prospect of criticism doing irreparable damage to Des's reputation. "This can be very disastrous to a man's career," Murdoch advised Des, "and I must stand by you in this time of crisis."

Heppenstall chimed in, "If there is real danger of your standing and authority as a teacher being undermined, then please let me know. It is time to move, before men have so tarnished your stature."[19]

For twelve months Heppenstall explored the possibilities of Des teaching religion at Loma Linda University, but nothing came of it. Murdoch, on the other hand, wrote letters of support for Des to Robert Frame and Robert Pierson, then General Conference president.[20]

Frame was not a theologian but an accountancy specialist. Yet he had a good grasp of practical Christianity and a nose for detecting phony ethics among church critics. At times he was quite blunt in his letters to them. He wrote to Scragg, telling him that Albert Anderson's book, *Through Turmoil to Peace,* which Scragg was defending, did not represent SDA views but was, instead, "Christadelphian."[21] That assessment was correct. On another occasion he told Scragg it was wrong to single out Des as "the bête noire" [French for "black beast"] because he was not the only teacher at Avondale who molded budding evangelists.[22] Eventually he despaired of Scragg, confiding in Des:

> I think the less I write [to Scragg] the better, for it is practically impossible for him to see beyond his own theories and points of view. He discounts the *[SDA Bible] Commentary* to suit himself, and even though we do mention to him that what is taught at the College is recorded in the Commentary it may not weigh very heavily with him.[23]

Detractors Increase

Playing church sheriff, George Burnside had begun in the 1950s to gather around himself a posse of extreme conservatives, first attracting the likes of fellow evangelist John Conley. Despite his denial of a personal vendetta,[24] Burnside's opposition to Des intensified after a confrontation over the doctrine of inspiration in the summer of 1969/70, which directly resulted in his demotion.

Burnside set up a little printing press in his basement and began publishing mainly anonymous leaflets against Des, thinking all the time that only his closest colleagues knew their origin, but a distinctive typeface, layout, illustrations and other features later identified the issues as Burnside's work. One entitled, "Dr. Ford D.D.: Doctor of Doubt," was a trivialized and erroneous caricature of Des (who does not have a Doctor of Divinity degree). Burnside followed up with another scurrilous pamphlet (1975), "Dr. Des Ford's Dangerous Doctrines." Both issues were circulated freely at SDA camp meetings. Burnside's earlier denial that he had criticized Avondale at the Eraring camp now looked patently thin.

Burnside also published an interchange of letters between Scragg and Des, casting Des as one reluctant to face Scragg's supposedly watertight theology. Des was quoted as writing to Scragg, "It may help you to understand some things if I say that my programme here [at Avondale] just does not permit my doing one-fifth of things calling out to be done, and if I talked or wrote at length to everyone with whom I wished to converse I would have to give up eating and sleeping."[25]

Des was in a no-win dilemma. If he chose to avoid endless dialogue with critics, he was branded as aloof, uncooperative, and having no real answers. On the other hand, if he found the time to engage his critics, the discussion seemed interminable, with no promise of a satisfactory resolution. The best advice seemed to come from Jesus: "You cannot pour new wine into old wineskins" (Matthew 9:17).

Burnside's posse of elderly ministers continued to grow. Frank Breaden made submissions to Wahroonga church headquarters, alleging that Des and Gill were advocates of dissident views on the nature of Christ and righteousness by faith. Arthur Jacobson and Ron Heggie in the Cooranbong district acted as self-appointed theological watchmen over Des and Avondale College.[26] Nearby, Ormond Anderson, renowned as a wily mischief-maker, actively smeared Des and Avondale while moving among the churches on the north and central New South Wales coasts.[27] Frame appealed to Roy Anderson, Ormond's brother at General Conference offices in America, to dissuade Ormond from gossiping, but there was simply a closing of ranks with Burnside.[28]

Two ministerial retirees in Sydney who were friends of Burnside—James William Kent and John Keith—then joined the fray. When they read Des's articles on Daniel, they recognized some new lines of argument but were more responsible than Ormond Anderson, going directly to Frame with their concerns, reiterating the thrust of Llewelyn

Jones's manuscript.[29]

Crucial to the developing web of criticism was the entrance into the debate of the Standish twins, Colin and Russell. Russell was a medical doctor in Melbourne, in close contact with Jones. He gathered information in Australia to pass on to Colin in America. Colin held a Ph.D. and had lectured in Avondale's education department, before transferring to Jamaica and then Columbia Union College in the shadow of General Conference headquarters. The real danger of the Standish twins lay in the fact that they were men with tertiary degrees who postured as if their training were in theology. Many of the laity were later to put their trust in this facade. Colin acted as one line of communication to church leaders in America, feeding them with information on the twists and turns in the ongoing saga in Australia.[30]

Were these critics intelligent and lucid men? Certainly. Were they loyal to the church? Yes. Were they trained theologians? No. They had an aura of pretense, but Des could never bring himself to say an uncharitable word about any of them. He was honest: "There are many of them that are good men," he once said. "Their problem was their education."[31] On another occasion he expressed to Frame:

> Dr [Colin] Standish is one of the finest Christians I know. I wish he could be multiplied a million times. He is a very fine Adventist and one whom I feel I could trust in any situation—any situation, that is, bar the cause he has now espoused [biblical support for a six-thousand-year chronology].[32]

Other SDA theologians, most of them in harmony with Des, never attracted the same vitriol. For two decades the church had invested millions of dollars in higher education for their lecturers and youth, in addition to the infrastructure to operate it. By the 1970s the fruitage was evident. A wide gap had developed between the lecturers and graduates, on the one hand, and the older generation on the other. The greying church members generally knew of only two systems of biblical interpretation—the proof text method with generous lashings of literalism, and the accumulation of Ellen White quotations on any given topic. Des found himself in that milieu. Then why didn't other Bible lecturers, who shared similar beliefs with Des, attract the same criticisms? It was because of his high profile in church publications, an unwillingness to obfuscate, and his earnest quest to plug the many holes in SDA lines of argument. This set him up as a shooting target. Other theologians were less communicative or would only say their piece on debated issues behind closed doors. And, of course, there was the long-standing simmering rage of Burnside.

Perfectionism at the Highest Level
The 1970s brought a double-barreled barrage. Issues over prophetic interpretations were packed into one compartment, while in the other lurked explosive issues regarding the doctrine of righteousness by faith alone.

During the 1960s Robert Brinsmead's mailing list contained thousands of SDAs, many of them influential leaders. Closet sympathizers from all levels of administration, in addition to some American college lecturers, would meet secretly with him in ones and twos. When he jettisoned his perfectionism and took on board righteousness by faith, his erstwhile friends became bitter opponents.[33] At church headquarters Robert Pierson and vice-president Neal Wilson had made it clear they did not want any of Brinsmead's help in preaching the gospel. These officials told him bluntly, Brinsmead says, "Why not leave Adventists alone and share your faith with outsiders,"[34] So, he did just that.

In his magazines of the 1970s, Brinsmead appealed even to the Lutherans to revive their dynamism for righteousness by faith alone. He wrote about the drift toward Rome of many Protestant churches and the imbalance created in the charismatic movement when the focus was taken off Christ and placed on the Holy Spirit. He also highlighted end-time events as they related to salvation and the dangers of antinomianism (literally, anti-law as a means of salvation). Many SDAs were included on Brinsmead's 1970s mailing list, which was once again mushrooming.[35]

The irony of the 1970s lay in the fact that American church leaders, who professed to be preachers of the gospel, were anti-Brinsmead because of his emphasis on righteousness by faith alone and his exposure of their perfectionism. Brinsmead's new stance was in stark contrast to a revived and embellished brand of perfectionism being promoted by a number of key church leaders.

First and foremost in the vigorous drive was Robert H. Pierson, the General Conference president himself. At the Annual Councils of 1973 (Takoma Park) and 1974 (Loma Linda) the messages found their ground in the frustrated question, "Why has the Lord delayed His coming?" The answer given was that the messages of righteousness by faith had been spurned at the Minneapolis Conference of 1888 and the church needed to repent of that action. Church members were called to "perfectly reproduce" "the character of Christ" in their lives. Allegedly they would then be equipped to powerfully preach righteousness by faith to the world, and then Christ would return.

"Finishing the church's task" was the cliche used. "God was willing to bring His work to a swift triumph following 1844, in 1888, and again in 1901," it was said.[36]

This scenario inferred that church members had failed Jesus. They had delayed the Second Advent, it was claimed, because they were not perfect in character and therefore could not preach the gospel as they should. It raised the questions, "How will church members know they have reached the required level of perfection?" and "How perfect was the character of Christ that members were to replicate?"

Furthermore, "finishing the task" seemed to imply that members were working toward a qualitative or quantitative goal that when reached would allow them to declare, "We have finished, now Christ can come." SDAs, in other words, were supposed to possess the key for the timing of the Second Advent. Or was all this drum beating simply sanctified mumbo jumbo?

Brinsmead claimed that he had buried the bone of perfectionism and that the church had dug it up again.[37] The metaphor highlights the fact that the SDA Church leaders in the 1970s were really advocating what they condemned Brinsmead for teaching in the 1960s. The metaphors weakness was that the church had always retained a firm grasp of the perfectionism bone. In the 1970s it merely stuffed it into a vegie-link sausage as a marketing ploy.

Leaders like Kenneth Wood, the Review and Herald editor, and Herbert Douglass, his assistant, promoted perfectionism through the church media in the 1970s. The themes they emphasized were the sinful nature of Christ; Christ's victory over His sinful nature; personal adoption of Christ's example in sinless living; personal surrender of the willpower to facilitate victory over sin; and the development of a sinless life as a demonstration to the universe that it can be achieved, vindicating God's law as the moral standard and making Him proud of the saints' efforts.[38]

In 1975 Thomas Davis, a book editor at the Review, wrote *How to Be a Victorious Christian*. Pierson claimed in its foreword, "He [Christ] is waiting for His people to gain the victory over sin, so that He can trust them with heaven." The book contained numerous Ellen White quotations of a perfectionist nature. Ringing endorsements for the book came from a wide spectrum of church leaders.[39]

This volume came in the wake of a special issue of the *Review and Herald* devoted entirely to the topic of righteousness by faith, typically a mixed bag on the subject. One SDA theology lecturer, Jonathan Butler, wrote a fine column on Christian assurance.[40] But other articles muddied justification with sanctification. For example, Pierson wrote, "His [Christ's] imputed and imparted righteousness shall forever be my righteousness because of Calvary!"[41] Douglass, after citing much from Ellen White, concluded:

> Living, saving faith, kept Jesus from sinning. Such faith will keep any Christian from sinning. But this is what God wants proved. Such faith will characterize a significant group of people [loyal SDAs] before the end of time.... Such a group becomes a living exhibit of righteousness—of Christ-like behavior.[42]

Mervyn Maxwell, a leading SDA Church historian, contributed an article about Waggoner and Jones at the 1888 Minneapolis Conference, pointing out that Waggoner's remedy for sin was in the power of positive thinking. That is, because Christ promises to dwell in the Christian's heart and give victory over sin, Christians should believe it and praise God for it, and "while we are doing this our minds are wholly taken from doing evil, and the victory is ours."

"No wonder," Maxwell concluded, "1888 and the truth of righteousness by faith are inseparably linked in Adventist history!"[43] He accurately portrayed Waggoner, whose *Signs of the Times* articles of the 1880s are germane to perfectionism. For this reason, perfectionists in the church think of Waggoner as a spurned prophet.

This perfectionist slant on righteousness by faith was exacerbated in some 1974 week-of-prayer readings, specifically those written by Pierson and Morris Venden. The latter, at the time, was the pastor on the then-La Sierra campus of Loma Linda University.[44]

The church's predicament in the 1970s was compounded by Pierson's administrative style. Not a theologian himself, he misunderstood the rising Evangelicalism in the church and labeled it Liberalism.[45] He deliberately set out to emasculate the influence of church Evangelicals, restructuring the Biblical Research Institute and the Geoscience Research Institute so that it was under the control of non-academics like Willis Hackett and Gordon Hyde. If the triumvirate ever sought theological direction, they invariably turned to arch conservative Gerhard Hasel. Pierson was not open to a broad spectrum of specialists. He governed with a tight *curia* and a sense of winsome infallibility.[46]

Evangelicals Rally

In the closing months of 1974, some repudiations of the *Review* special issue were circulated. Robert McCurdy, Jr., of Washington State, presented a viewpoint from Scripture and the Reformation. "If the final generation is to demonstrate that the law can be kept," he declared, "they must keep it with the same absolute infinite perfection with which Christ kept it. The copy must equal the Pattern, or it will prove nothing."

He hoped that this doctrine would not be given opportunity to reach its logical conclusions with a replay of the Holy Flesh fanaticism in the denominations camp meetings.[47]

Brinsmead, too, penned a few pages, titled "A Statement to My SDA Friends." Having immersed himself in Reformation theology, he cited Martin Chemnitz, one of the best exponents of Lutheranism, and sought to define the biblical meaning of righteousness by faith: "In no instance does the apostle [Paul] ever equate righteousness by faith with inward renewal and sanctification," he summarized. "It is, without exception, 'the righteousness of One,' 'the obedience of One,' 'the righteousness of God in Him'" Romans 5:18, 19; 2 Corinthians 5:21."[48]

Charles Hodge's *Systematic Theology* was quoted by Brinsmead as support. The righteousness of faith, Hodge claimed, "is always declared to be not anything done by us or wrought in us, but what was done for us. It is ever represented as something external to ourselves."[49]

> They [Adventists] never separated sanctification from the article of righteousness by faith," Brinsmead continued. "They always included it and they always ended up in the mire of Roman Catholic spirituality with more emphasis on the 'in us' than the 'for us' and never any confidence [of their personal salvation].[50]

On December 10, 1974, Brinsmead met with a small group of denominational officers in Takoma Park. Both he and the officials reiterated their views, finding no harmony. Wood and Douglass prevailed with their belief that, in practical terms, righteousness by faith meant that Christians were to live a sinless life, just as Christ lived it.[51]

Not every SDA thought leader agreed with Wood and Douglass. Even one of their associates at the publishing office, Don Neufeld, wrote some excellent editorials to the contrary. Notable was his three-part series on the biblical phrase, "Be ye therefore perfect" (Matthew 5:48), explaining that the parallel phrase, "Be ye merciful" (Luke 6:36) is closer to the Aramaic and Hebrew meanings of "perfect." It was wrong, therefore, for Bible interpreters to impose Western nuances on the word.[52]

Theologians Edward Heppenstall and Hans LaRondelle publicly acknowledged their anti-perfectionism in the 1975 book, *Perfection: The Impossible Possibility*—a tome in which Douglass and Maxwell also outlined their views.[53] Later, one perceptive reviewer of the book noted that Douglass and Maxwell were largely dependent on Ellen White to support perfectionism, while Heppenstall and La Rondelle were heavily dependent on Scripture to establish their positions. Pressing his point, he concluded, "It is difficult to deny that Ellen White taught that God's people in the last days would reach such a state of holiness that they could stand faultless before God without a mediator; many of her statements are simply too plain to be explained away."[54]

Evidence of a widening chasm between the protagonists was also apparent in Australia, where some had given the cold shoulder to free copies of the *Review* special issue, handing it out among church members with great reluctance because they didn't believe its sentiments.[55]

A Fecund Period of Gospel Witnessing
Brinsmead's Reformation thrust was making an impression in non-Adventist and Adventist circles alike, especially in America and Australia. Some SDA youth in Australia arrived at Avondale College with his sentiments, sharing their newly discovered views with other students. When Ford arrived back from Manchester University, Avondale was ripe for revival.[56]

It is reported that one young person, Noel Mason, handed a copy of Brinsmead's pamphlet (probably *A Letter to My SDA Friends)* to Des soon after he arrived. He read it, and then checked the Reformation sources.[57] He shared it with Norman Young, also recently returned from Manchester. As a result, Des came to see righteousness by faith in sharper focus. Simply put, Brinsmead said that justification is Jesus plus nothing, and he stated what sanctification was not. He readily admits his debt to Brinsmead in this respect.

Any sermons preached by Des were characterized by an emphasis on justification by faith. It was his style not to attack perfectionism head on and divide his audience into those in agreement with perfectionism and those against it. Instead, he tried to keep them all onside so that they would hear a positive gospel. He preached the theology of righteousness by faith with language that the laity could understand, often using vivid imagery, analogies, parables, and Bible biography, all laced with pithy one-liners.[58]

His published articles were in the same tone. He could not be so bold as to say the perfectionism advocated by some of his church leaders was akin to Roman Catholicism's doctrine of sanctification, as Brinsmead was doing. However, his writing bore no references to "imparted righteousness," "victory piety," or the imperative to duplicate Christ's sinless life. His shafts against perfectionism were, nevertheless, pointed. In February 1975 he published in the *Record:*

> We stumble our way to the kingdom of God in [a] progressive growth in holiness ... that is manifested in an increasing awareness of sinfulness.... The chimera of sinlessness in this life is not a New Testament hope. Romans 7:14–25 and Galatians 5:17 show that the flesh strives against the spirit continually throughout the Christian's experience.... The legalism in the New Testament was not the belief that we are saved by works, but that we are saved by faith and works. Adventists are in danger of this error. We are not saved by faith and works but by faith that works.[59]

This reflected some of the best of Reformation thinking. It was, however, in sharp contrast to some of Ellen White's statements being used by the perfectionists, such as:

> Let us not be deceived by the oft-repeated assertion, 'All you have to do is to believe.' Faith and works are two oars which we must use *equally* .... if we [would] press our way up the stream against the current of unbelief.[60]

> It is the righteousness of Christ, His own unblemished character, that through faith is *imparted* to all who receive Him as their personal Saviour.... Christ in His humanity wrought out a perfect character,

115

and this character He offers to *impart* to us.[61]

The white raiment is purity of character, the righteousness of Christ *imparted* to the sinner.[62]

The *whole* character is to be transformed, the image of Christ is to be revealed in words and actions. A new nature is *imparted*. Man is renewed after the image of Christ in righteousness and true holiness... (Emphases supplied).[63]

More Critics

Des's February article in the *Record* was sent by a Queensland church member to Douglass at the Review office. In reply, Douglass revealed that the top level of the church was on the warpath against the gospel advocates. He confided:

I can imagine that the picture looks somewhat bleak 'down under' when the prevailing winds seem to blow from a new and strange Ford-Brinsmead mateship.

If Ford's 'The Two Faces of Redemption' is typical of his thinking today, I can understand your consternation.

There are many in Washington who are beginning to see the magnitude of this present diversion, that it is a distinct digression from solid, historic Adventist thought. The historic view regarding the human nature of Christ as best set forth in *The Desire of Ages* is now being given its proper emphasis here in Washington, and the aberrant position since the publication of *Questions on Doctrine* is now being seen in its proper light....

We are reaping the results of years of rudderless theology—but Elders Pierson, Hackett and Wilson are reversing all that, believe me.... Please keep me up to date regarding publications and whatever that reveals the outreach of the above-mentioned mateship.[64]

Contrary to the allegation, the "Ford-Brinsmead mateship" was neither "new" nor "strange." Ford had been a friend of Brinsmead since college days, whether they agreed on theology or not. There was nothing sinister or collusive or strange about it. But Douglass seemed threatened by the friendship, citing support for himself in high places. This support was real, with Pierson banning Parr from publishing any more articles on righteousness by faith until some agreement could be reached on the topic.[65]

Des's preaching and writing about righteousness by faith attracted more critics. One was John Clifford, a young man who had earlier absorbed perfectionism while staying in the home of Hope (Brinsmead) Taylor. He proved to be another would-be theologian. His training was in medicine, but he tossed theological terms around with abandon, labeling Des's views as "antinomianism," "universalism," and "liberalism."[66] The tags were slanderous, for Des represented none of these belief structures. When the gospel is preached, then legalists often resort to these allegations. The apostle Paul experienced the jibes of the Judaizers for the same reason.

Clifford mustered fellow members at Croydon, Victoria. Forty-one of them signed a letter to the executive committee at Australian headquarters, asking "for clarification of a reported decision by some [anonymous] leaders in this field, that the current teachings of R. D. Brinsmead are no longer unacceptable to the Australasian Division."[67]

The field secretary, Alfred Jorgensen, delegated to reply, asked the Croydon members to first place their request before their local conference, together with "any supporting documentation," which they did. But when the matter later came to his desk for a second time, he found no documentation. For that reason, he vowed, his committee would not consider the petition unless Croydon members divulged who made the allegations and who, specifically, was supposed to have made the decision regarding Brinsmead's teachings. "You will understand, Brother Reid," Jorgensen appealed, "that it is a fundamental principle of the operation of the Seventh-day Adventist Church throughout the world never to involve itself in anonymous reports."[68]

If Croydon members could get an official statement from headquarters that agreed with Brinsmead's gospel thrust, then they would have proof of a split between American and Australian leadership. They would also be able to demonstrate that Des was not in line with the Americans. But Jorgensen called their bluff and it all fell in a heap, because Clifford and his colleagues would not, or could not, provide confirmation that Brinsmead's teachings on righteousness by faith found agreement among Australian church officials. However, opposition from Croydon members intensified.

Gill Ford Enters the Fray
During these same months Gill was teaching a Sabbath School class for young marrieds at the Cooranbong Village Church. The themes for the quarter's lessons included the nature of Christ and righteousness by

faith. With two different views circulating among SDA believers, she found her class quite confused about the issues.

Gathering material from Des, in addition to class notes she was taking in Norman Young's lectures at the time, Gill began composing a manuscript that grew to fifty pages. It was submitted to the six theology lecturers at Avondale College under the title, "The Soteriological Implications of the Human Nature of Christ," and subsequently used in college classes. (A companion document, a compilation of Bible studies on similar tenets, appeared under the title, "For Saints and Sinners").[69]

The confusion among church members was partly due to the fact that both anti-perfectionists and perfectionists were quoting Ellen White, who seemed to exhibit no uniformity. For example, on one occasion she claimed, "The coming of Christ does not change our characters; it only *fixes them forever beyond all change*"[70] (Emphasis supplied). In another publication she declared, "A character formed according to the divine likeness is the only treasure that we take from this world to the next.... And in heaven we are *continually to improve*"[71] (Emphasis supplied).

What did she mean? With great difficulty some White apologists attempt reconciliations between statements like these, but this example, among many, illustrates the dilemma in which the laity often find themselves. They are left bewildered.

Gill had been an SDA for only a few years and innocently outlined what she had been taught by the minister who baptized her and what she had learned at Avondale. She did not deliberately set out to confront the perfectionists. In her manuscript she discussed the essential foundations of the doctrine of righteousness by faith—the nature of sin, the nature of man, and the nature of Christ. She cited pages of Ellen White's gospel quotes that were contrary to those quoted by the likes of Wood and Douglass. The real strength of her arguments lay in her heavy use of Scripture and her word study on "perfection," much of it a mirror of Neufeld's *Review* series. She also clarified many terms used in the debate. Her position was unequivocal, that "sanctification is imputed," not imparted.[72] Also, she wrote a page in the booklet called "The True and the False Gospel," which upset a lot of traditional people. This set the cat among the pigeons.

Des sent a copy of the manuscript to Raoul Dederen at Andrews University, who replied, "I agree with you as far as the substance is concerned." He confided that he was worried about Douglass's view that Christ had a sinful nature, declaring, "This is no minor, peripheral issue."[73]

Ray Stanley, ministerial secretary at Australasian headquarters, read Gill's paper, too, but could not agree with her definition of sin— "a state [of human nature] rather than merely a committing of wrong acts." He asked for some Ellen White quotations that would support Gill's view. That would apparently be conclusive for his mind.[74]

This distinction was vital. A perfectionist assumed that sin was merely wrong acts, and that if a person could whittle those down to virtually zero, then moral perfection lay close at hand. Gill's view put sin at a deeper level, an innate condition of humanity, a result of the first sin in Eden, and a condition that a person always suffers with until glorification. This condition can, nevertheless, be covered by faith with Christ's righteousness. Gill had described the innate condition with the use of Romans 7, but the thrust of Scripture[75] apparently made no impression on Stanley. He simply wanted Ellen White quotes.

Willis Hackett, a vice-president of the General Conference, visited Australia in the closing months of 1975. "I came away with a firm conviction that we are all saying the same thing, only arriving at our conclusions in a little different manner," he wrote to Des.[76] Clearly, he was not listening very carefully. Or was it because he did not fully understand the debate?

Cooranbong resident, Raglan Marks, launched a diatribe at Jorgensen about Gill's paper, complaining that it should have been scrutinized by the Biblical Research Committee. Jorgensen did not mince words in his reply. Only matters that "contribute some new dimension in our understanding of truth" come before that committee, he pointed out. "You are opposed to her [Gill's] position on the Person of Christ, as representing a partisan view," Jorgensen reasoned, "but, by the same token, you are circulating material (as witness your recent circularization of the worker force of the North New South Wales Conference with the Burnside reprints of Prescott and others on the post-fall Adamic nature of Christ) which others regard as equally partisan!" Then, like an Olympian fencer, he lunged with his foil, "Listen, Raglan, you and I are in the same peer group, and I can therefore talk to you man to man.... Now get this straight," the usually stoic Jorgensen persisted, "I'm not writing this letter to necessarily justify Gillian Ford in producing her document or in support of any theological position relating to the Person of Christ. I'm simply putting it to you: if you are going to charge the Fords and others with creating division by the material they publish, you won't stop the fire by throwing a tin of petrol [gasoline] from the other side!"[77]

Australian Talks Convened

Not even strong words could mollify Marks and the growing number of reactionaries, or mossbacks. Thirty-nine signed a letter to Australasian headquarters calling for a representative meeting of Avondale Bible lecturers and their antagonists. Signatories included Burnside, Russell Standish, J. W. Kent, Frank Breaden, J. B. Keith, Raglan Marks, O. K. Anderson, Heggie, Clifford, and some from the Croydon church.[78] It was evident that all the letters written to these men, and all the previous discussion that had taken place to resolve the issues, had made no impression. As far as they were concerned, SDA tradition with respect to doctrine was infallible. In many respects they paralleled Catholicism right down the line, except for the puff of chimney smoke.

The delegation wanted to discuss righteousness by faith, the age of the earth, the inspiration of Scripture and Ellen White's writings, Daniel 9, and the nature of a two-apartment sanctuary in heaven. The common denominator in all topics seemed to be, "What did Ellen White say about it?" Her authority versus the authority of Scripture was at stake because the critic saw everything through her crystal ball.

The meeting was duly convened at Avondale College on February 3, 1976. Discussions were continued the following day at Division headquarters in Wahroonga. Frame chaired the meetings. The full contingent of theology lecturers was present, together with church officers and a dozen or more critics. Des was given right of reply off the cuff to all papers presented by his critics. All attendees were welcome to take part in the discussion periods.[79]

The discussions at Avondale were civil, but the tone changed dramatically on the second day at Wahroonga. Des listened patiently to the presentations and scribbled a few notes as papers were read by his antagonists. He had brought with him a suitcase full of Ellen Whites books and other denominational literature. During the lunch break he tore off little bits of paper and placed them in the pages of the books, marking excerpts he planned to read in the afternoon.

After lunch he launched into his answers, reading quotation after quotation that destroyed the positions held by his critics. One by one he threw the books down on the table in front of them and challenged them to admit their error. Some of his closest colleagues felt he was too provocative. His assailants were livid. Burnside became blue in the face. Outside, office secretaries showed alarm, hearing shouting coming from behind the closed doors.[80]

It was a high point in the theological debate, a defining moment. After more than a decade of constant sniping, Des and his supporters were tiring of the barrage. They were emboldened to counterattack. Their victory, however, only caused the opposition to lick its wounds and hope to ambush on another day. Des, they determined, must be chased out of town.

A sample of personal anonymous assessments, made by those present at the meetings, indicate some important impressions:

I believe there were far too many topics introduced at this meeting for adequate discussion.

Even though not all the items were discussed, there was still insufficient time to draw meaningful conclusions. It was unfortunate that personal feelings were at times introduced with some degree of vehemence and this tended to destroy the dignity and decorum of the meeting.... It appeared that personality rather than principle was at stake.

While the meetings have not reached finality in any area, they did help to remove pressure on both sides.

I believe that much more could have been accomplished had the ministers [the critics] presented their papers to the theological faculty and requested that written answers be provided.

On the theological side of the discussion, I feel that there was nothing conclusive.

I believe it was helpful for Dr. Ford to demonstrate that his interpretations can be substantiated by current denominational literature. However, it was probably at this point that many of the older men [critics] faced a problem that caused them considerable trouble. They were faced with the dilemma of either admitting their failure to correctly understand the Biblical position or charging the denomination as a whole with heresy.

I do not think that there was a single doctrine that was canvassed at the meeting that was exclusively Fordian. Therefore, we must be extremely careful that we do not pillory one man when he is in fact teaching exactly what the leading theologians of the church have taught and are teaching.

It seems that Pastor [Elwyn] Martin [a retiree] feels that young men who leave the ministry do so because of Doctor Ford's theological positions. Let it be clearly understood that young men have left the ministry before Doctor Ford appeared on the scene and they will do so after he has left it. I suppose we could find young men whose faith has been shattered by G. Burnside, J. W. Kent, R. R. Frame, L. C. Naden and A. S. Jorgensen if we looked hard enough. Two examples out of the hundreds who have passed through Doctor Ford's hands hardly seem to be cause for concern. There are literally dozens of young men who are stalwarts in the ministry today because of Doctor Ford's strong leadership of the Theology Department.[81]

Predictably, at the end of the meeting twenty-two voted in support of Des and the sixteen critics remained opposed.[82] Jorgensen, as field secretary, was a key man in the discussions. Russell Standish had looked to him for support but did not get it. Bitterly disappointed, he returned to Victoria and chastened Jorgensen in a stinging letter, saying:

> Many of us in private conversations have been told of your clear theological differences with Doctor Ford on perhaps all the major points discussed yesterday. How we longed for you to express these convictions as forcefully as you did the weaknesses you perceived in our arguments....
>
> On every occasion the evident tenor of your remarks was to weaken the case of Truth [the critics viewpoint]...and strengthen the arguments of the man [Des] whose views you privately do not share. Many men who attended have concluded in my hearing that this is a policy you have long adopted in this matter. I was alarmed at the clear preference you showed.... Never once did you point out the many weaknesses in Doctor Ford's arguments.[83]

In an apparent attempt to make trouble for Jorgensen, Standish forwarded a copy of his letter to Pierson. Des received a copy, too, and replied with a defense of Jorgensen. He also elaborated on some points of difference with Standish. He wrote:

> The term 'righteousness by faith' is literally 'justification by faith'—and that does not mean that sanctification is ignored or downgraded but merely that it is the FRUIT and not the ROOT. You should see the article in our own Andrews [University] Journal (vol ix, 1971) by A. J. Mattill. All our Andrews New Testament men

know and are agreed on this and we at Avondale stand with our American brethren and indeed the whole field of New Testament scholarship.[84]

Standish was not persuaded, as was the case with most of the other critics. Nevertheless, letters of support for Des came in from all quarters, including Lawrence Naden, one of the scores of retirees who did not join the critics. Of Brinsmead's gospel emphasis Naden admitted to Des, "I find myself defending him at times." He concluded his letter by saying:

> God bless you, dear boy. May He guide you continually and may your sweet ministry to the church of God be enriched even by the 'fiery trials'. We love you and know that God has greater things for you to accomplish before the great and glorious day of His return.[85]

Shilly-shallying at Palmdale

Des was to face one more "fiery trial" that year, 1976. The ongoing theological wrangling was not just with a tiny group of vocal critics in Australia but also with a small and powerful group at American headquarters, specifically over the issue of righteousness by faith. Once again, the crux of the problem was the veracity and authority of White's writings. Would they put her writings aside and resolve the question by using Scripture alone? Or would the custom of quoting selected passages from White continue by both groups to suit their arguments?

Throughout 1975 Frame became increasingly alarmed by the promotion of perfectionism in American SDA literature. Naden echoed the concern when he wrote, "It has been distressing to me to note that at least two men in the States have been preaching and publishing the old Brinsmead view on the nature of Christ and sinless perfection; namely, [Herbert] Douglass and Mervyn Maxwell."[86]

There were more names, of course. Naden didn't mention Wood and Davis, and even Pierson himself.

Frame repeatedly discussed his concern with Pierson. American reluctance to address the problem was based partly on a belief that many church officials thought the differences over righteousness by faith were merely a matter of semantics.[87] That view was probably sincere but ignorant.

Des had been quietly dropped from the Biblical Research Committee.[88] It appeared Pierson was trying to diminish the Australasian voice while at the same time strengthening the hand of the American perfectionism group, perhaps hoping that the American view would prevail in time. But the Australian situation was at boiling point and could not continue without serious repercussions. There was no waiting time left. Frame finally persuaded Pierson that it was wiser to call a meeting where both parties could sit down and try to sort out their conflict face to face.[89]

On April 23-30, 1976, nineteen men were scheduled to meet at Palmdale, an isolated and desolate spot in California, specifically to discuss the topic of salvation. Des was chosen to attend as a representative from Australia. So also, were Alwyn Salom from Avondale College, editor Parr, and church administrators Frame, Jorgensen, Stanley, Claude Judd, Stuart Uttley, and Naden. The American field was represented by Raoul Dederen and La Rondelle from the Andrews University Seminary, Robert Olson from the White Estate, editors Wood and Neufeld, and administrators Pierson, Hyde, Hackett, Duncan Eva, and Neil Dower. Inexplicably, Douglass was conspicuous by his absence.[90]

As a talking point Hyde and Eva prepared a tentative statement about righteousness by faith and circulated it among the others for comment prior to meeting.[91] It exhibited the typical SDA amalgamation of salvation by faith plus works. "I could say Amen to almost every line of it," Des commented, "but at the bottom of the page the writer recants by affirming that righteousness by faith includes sanctification as well.[92] Des advised Frame of some key matters that must be resolved when they talked bluntly at Palmdale, emphasizing that they must come to some decision about the nature of Christ.

The perfectionist argues that Christ had a sinful nature like all mortals, and because He overcame it, human beings must do likewise. Yes, they say, we accept by faith the righteousness of Christ (that is justification) and then we do righteousness for the rest of our lives (that is sanctification). In other words, salvation is dependent on both the accepting of what Christ has done, together with the Christians doing.

On the other hand, the non-perfectionist believes that Christ, like Adam in Eden, possessed a sinless nature, and, unlike Adam, continued to resist temptation. His righteous life is accounted to the believers when they accept that gift by faith. This is known as the justification of the sinner. Out of gratitude for this gift the Christian performs Christ's ethics to the best of his or her ability, but the doing is never a part of the righteousness that saves. It is Christ's righteousness alone that saves.

"It is absolutely certain that the New Testament does limit the gift of righteousness which comes by faith to justification," Des clearly outlined to Frame. "Sanctification will be present in every soul but not as the righteousness which saves him." He predicted that if the Palmdale conference did not deal with these core subjects, then "they will come up again and again ... as though we had never met."[93]

Since Brinsmead's success at preaching the gospel haunted American headquarters, Des feared that Palmdale might degenerate into nothing more than a personal attack on Brinsmead. Therefore, he advised Frame further:

> We could siphon all the air out of the Brinsmead balloon if we followed the E. G. W[hite] counsels to agree with our opponents wherever we can conscientiously. They [Brinsmeads] have caught up on a few points since their recantation, and they have even passed some of our brethren who have gone backwards (witness the *R[eview] and H[erald]*). Wherever they [the Brinsmeads] are speaking according to Scripture and the Spirit of Prophecy, let us say so—and take all the wind out of their sails, to change the metaphor. This is certainly the best tactic.[94]

When the meetings got under way, Wood presented a two-hour paper quoting from SDA authors in an attempt to prove that the orthodox position maintained a sinful nature for Christ. When he was finished Des observed, "It's very interesting but quite irrelevant. All that matters is what the Bible says."

Then he proceeded to list texts such as Luke 1:35 and Hebrews 7:26 to prove the sinless nature of Christ. Pitting Scripture against SDA tradition was potentially volatile in such august ears, but Des believed the foundation for discussion had to be squarely based on Scripture alone.

Another of the American delegation gave a presentation and Des became so exasperated he blurted out, "Well, that was Roman Catholic theology, lock, stock and barrel." Some more timid souls were aghast. Frame and Salom pled with him later "to go a bit easy on the American brethren."[95] It was not wise to be so candid in public, but behind closed doors, with such a vital topic at stake, someone had to spell it out clearly. They had not come all that distance and spent all that money just to tiptoe around the daisies. Those advocating an indwelling Holy Spirit; the possibility of keeping God's commandments perfectly; salvation by faith and works; and sanctification being imparted righteousness, apparently did not understand that they were arm in arm with Roman Catholicism. They had to decide whether or not they would teach sanctification from a Catholic perspective or a truly Protestant perspective. Anyone who claimed that the whole debate was inconsequential or purely semantic just did not understand the issues at stake.

Des himself read three papers he had prepared on the key topics as he had earlier expressed them to Frame. He covered similar ground to Gill's "Soteriological Implications of the Human Nature of Christ," some of it verbatim, paragraph after paragraph. Salom gave a vital word study on "righteousness," as found in both the Old and New Testaments, concluding with the crucial statement, "Because our theology must be based on the Bible, and the Bible alone, it is evident that our use of the term 'righteousness by faith' should be restricted to its biblical use as an equivalent for 'justification by faith.'"[96]

At the close of the meetings the participants agreed they would remain tight-lipped until a statement of proceedings and findings was published in the church press. However, someone, thought to be Wood, leaked it to one of the Standish twins. Russell was handing it around in Australia before it was published in America, which irked Parr in particular.[97]

Generally speaking, the time together provided opportunity for all to air their views and get to know each other better. Des walked with some of them on his early morning jaunts.[98] By all accounts the tone of the meetings was amicable.

Did they put to rest the notion that their differences were merely semantic? Most certainly, for the discussions highlighted the real differences. Some participants may have seen that for the first time. However, a careful reading of the published Palmdale statement, "Christ Our Righteousness," demonstrated that the meetings were largely a waste of time because the document lacked definition. The contributors to the discussion were guaranteed failure before the gathering convened, because two fundamental tenets were never on the agenda—the nature of man and the nature of sin.

The introduction to the statement noted that it was "designed to stimulate further study and to help create a greater bond of unity among Adventists." But no unity emerged. The obdurate mossbacks kept up their carping. Later, Des reflected on the years following Palmdale and concluded the subject "was neglected and forgotten and buried."[99]

The substance of the Palmdale statement did admit "that when the words 'righteousness' and 'faith' are connected (by 'of,' or 'by,' et cetera) in Scripture, reference is to the experience of justification by faith."[100] This was one point that Des wanted them to arrive at, and which he seized upon when he returned to Australia, putting as much positive spin on the results as he possibly could.[101] But the statement would have been made stronger by saying "justification by faith alone" specifically separating it from sanctification. As it stood, the statement still left the ship SS Justification near the Sea of Sanctification, and that is exactly where the rest of the statement drifted. "Righteousness," it alleged, is concerned with "both imputed righteousness and repentance and imparted righteousness by faith and obedience."[102] The ship remained within sight of Trent.

In its three rambling pages the statement extolled the messages of Waggoner and Jones, inserting some of the perfectionist catch phrases such as "the indwelling Christ," "victory over sin," and adopting Christ as our example for overcoming sin. On the nature of Christ, the conclusions were ambivalent. Space was given to the question, "Was Jesus ever really tempted?" That, however, was never an essential issue. And great emphasis was placed on the assertion that the topic is an unfathomable mystery.[103] They would not admit that the mystery lies not in what Christ's nature consists of but rather in how a sinless Person could be conceived in a sinful person. The mystery is in the manner of His conception, not in the constituency of His nature. Christ's nature is clearly revealed in Scripture.

Furthermore, mention was made of Jesus being "in the likeness of sinful flesh" and "made like His brethren in every respect,"[104] leaving the laity with the inference that Christ had a sinful nature. It was imperative, however, to follow up with the simple admission that the Greek word for "like" means "similar to," rather than "identical." Accurate definition would have dispelled any inferences of a sinful nature.

A fork in the road confronted the church at Palmdale, offering a crucial opportunity to walk the path of righteousness by faith alone or continue to scramble through the thickets of perfectionism. Some small advances were made, but its confused and ambivalent wording left everyone unsatisfied and content to hold the same views they brought to the meetings. As Des predicted, the topics arose again, and further inching forward took place, but some important basics remain unresolved. For example, the 1980 Statement of Fundamental Beliefs still retains elements unlike the purest form of the apostolic gospel, with the inclusion of the words imparted righteousness.[105] After Palmdale, perfectionists still had plenty of scope in which to move, and Ford therefore remained vulnerable as he continued to teach and preach against perfectionism. An immediate fix seemed elusive. Would the church wholeheartedly embrace the doctrine of righteousness by faith alone?

End Notes

1 Elènne Ford to Milton Hook, June 27, 2005; Desmond Ford to Milton Hook, Aug 10, 2005.

2 Robert Parr to Desmond Ford, Nov 14, 1972.

3 Robert Parr to Desmond Ford, March 19, 1973.

4 Kenneth Holland to Desmond Ford, Jan 21, 1975.

5 Robert Parr to Desmond Ford, Nov 14, 1972.

6 Robert Parr to Desmond Ford, Aug 27, 1973.

7 Robert Parr to Desmond Ford, March 19, 1973.

8 Desmond Ford, "How Long, O God?" *Ministry,* Sept 1974, pp. 14–16; Desmond Ford, "Arithmetic Proves Christianity True," *Ministry,* Oct 1974, pp. 16–19.

9 Desmond Ford, "The Crisis at the Close," *Ministry,* Nov 1974, p. 22; Desmond Ford, "Midnight and Morning," *Ministry,* Dec 1974, pp. 34–36.

10 Walter Scragg, Sr., to Robert Frame, Feb 9, Sept 16, 1974.

11 Robert Frame to Walter Scragg, Sr., Feb 7, Aug 9, 1974.

12 Llewelyn Jones to Robert Spangler, Dec 5,1969, Aug 1, 1973.

13 Ford, Ministry, Oct 1974, p. 16; Ford, *Ministry,* Nov 1974, p. 22.

14 Llewelyn Jones, "A Review of the New Interpretation of the Seventy Weeks. Prophecy," Vermont, Victoria, unpublished paper, [ca. 1975].

15 William Murdoch to Desmond Ford, April 2, 1975.

16 Edward Heppenstall to Desmond Ford, March 17, 1975.

17 *Ibid.*

18 *Ibid.*

19 Murdoch to Ford, April 2, 1975; Heppenstall to Ford, March 17, 1975.

20 Edward Heppenstall to Desmond Ford, March 27, 1976; Murdoch to Ford, April 2, 1975.

21 Frame to Scragg, Feb 7, 1974. Note: Anderson's affinity with Christadelphian views is principally found in his promotion of

the idea that the Jews have a continuing role in the fulfillment of Bible prophecy with Jerusalem literally becoming the center of Gods kingdom on earth. This is in contrast to the SDA view that the Jewish nation is no longer God's elect.

22 Frame to Scragg, Aug 9, 1974.

23 Robert Frame to Desmond Ford, Sept 18, 1974.

24 George Burnside, "My Dear Fellow Adventist," [Wahroonga], [ca. 1974].

25 Desmond Ford to Walter Scragg, Sr., Aug 22, 1974, quoted in "Pastor Scragg's Letter to Dr. D. Ford," [Wahroonga], [ca. 1974].

26 Frank Breaden to Robert Frame, March 1, 1976; Arthur Jacobson, untitled paper, Cooranbong, Jan 25, 1976; Ron Heggie to George Burnside and Ray Stanley, Nov 1, 1975; Ron Heggie to Desmond Ford, Jan 26, 1976.

27 Tom Crabtree to Desmond Ford, Feb 20, 197[4]; Graeme Loftus to Eric Magnusson, Oct 23, 1975.

28 Robert Frame to Desmond Ford, Jan 22, 1975.

29 Robert Frame to James Kent and John Keith, April 21, 1975; James Kent to Robert Frame, May 7, 1975.

30 Colin Standish to Walter Scragg, Sr., May 8, 1975.

31 Desmond Ford, interviewed by Trevor Lloyd at Sydney, March 12, 1995.

32 Desmond Ford to Robert Frame, June 14, 1973.

33 Robert Brinsmead, interviewed by Trevor Lloyd at Duranbah, April 18, 1996.

34 Ray Martin, "Objective Digest Report: What is Happening in Australia," n.p., [ca.1976], p. 2.

35 *Ibid.*

36 Robert Pierson, "A Message from the 1973 Annual Council," n.p., Oct 1974, p. 8.

37 Robert Brinsmead, "Someone is Following Brinsmead," [ca. 1973].

38 Martin, "Objective Digest Report," pp. 2, 3.

39 Thomas Davis, *How to be a Victorious Christian,* (Washington, D.C.: Review and Herald Publishing Association, 1975).

40 Jonathan Butler, "Dare a Person Say 'I am Saved?'" Righteousness by Faith, *Review and Herald* special issue, [1974], pp. 19, 20.

41 Robert Pierson, "Good News for You!" Righteousness by Faith, *Review and Herald* special issue, [1974], p. 28.

42 Herbert Douglass, "Why God is Urgent—And Yet Waits,"

Righteousness by Faith, Review and Herald special issue, [1974], p. 23.

43 Mervyn Maxwell, "Christ and Minneapolis 1888," Righteousness by Faith, *Review and Herald* special issue, [1974], p.18.

44 See Readings for Seniors, *AR,* Sept 14–21, 1974, pp. 3–18.

45 Evangelicalism is the Protestant view that the doctrine of salvation by faith alone should be the essence of Christian witness. Liberalism, in the theological sense, is the view that much of the Christian tradition is dispensable and needs to be contemporised with modern thought

46 Raymond Cottrell, "Our Present Crisis: Reaction to a Decade of Obscurantism," [ca. Aug 1981].

47 Robert McCurdy, Jr., "An Examination of the Teaching of Righteousness by Faith as Presented in the Special Issue of the *Review and Herald,* Vol 151: No 20, 1974," [ca. 1974], p. 13.

48 Robert Brinsmead, "A Statement to My SDA Friends," Fallbrook, California, [ca.1974], pp. 3, 4.

49 *Ibid.,* p. 4.

50 Brinsmead, interviewed by Lloyd, April 18, 1996.

51 Martin, "Objective Digest Report," p. 3.

52 Don Neufeld, "Jesus and Perfection," *RH,* March 13, 1975, p. 9.

53 Herbert Douglass *et al., Perfection: The Impossible Possibility,* (Nashville, Tennessee: Southern Publishing Association, 1975).

54 Timothy Crosby, "Do the Authorities Conflict on Perfectionism?" *Spectrum,* Jan 1977, p. 64.

55 Martin, "Objective Digest Report," p. 3.

56 Lowell Tarling, *The Edges of Seventh-day Adventism,* (Bermagui South, NSW: Galilee Publications, 1981), p. 204.

57 Brinsmead, interviewed by Lloyd, April 18, 1996.

58 Ford, interviewed by Lloyd, March 12, 1995; Desmond Ford, *The Cross and Other Sermons,* (Steam Press, 1977).

59 Desmond Ford, "The Two Faces of Redemption," *AR,* Feb 10,1975, p. 13.

60 Ellen White, *Welfare Ministry* (Washington, D.C.: Review and Herald Publishing Association, 1952), p. 315. Note: One of the clearest treatments of Whites perfectionist stance and her difference with the best of Reformation theology is found in Leroy Moore, *The Theology Crisis* (Corpus Christi, Texas: Life Seminars, 1980).

61 Ellen White, *Christ's Object Lessons,* (Cooranbong, New South

Wales: Avondale Press [ca. 1900], pp. 310, 311.

62 Ellen White, Testimonies for the Church, vol. 4 (Mountain View, California: Pacific Press Publishing Association, 1948), p. 88.

63 Ellen White, Letter 2a, 1892.

64 Herbert Douglass to Paul von Wieldt, March 11, 1975.

65 Robert Parr to Graeme Loftus, April 9, 1975.

66 Hope (Brinsmead) Taylor, interviewed by Trevor Lloyd at Duranbah, April 8, 1996; John Clifford, "Question Asked of Doctor Ford," Oct, 1974.

67 H. Reid *et al.,* to K. S. Parmenter, March 1, 1975.

68 Alfred Jorgensen to H. Reid, March 6, 25, 1975; H. Reid to Clive Barritt, March 14, 1975.

69 Gillian Ford, interviewed by Trevor Lloyd at Cooranbong, Jan 6, 1997. [The pamphlet she was teaching from was called Faith in Action, Summer 1975 and was written by Herbert Douglass. Gill had not heard Douglass's view of the nature of Christ before and did not realise it reflected traditional Adventism.].

70 Ellen White, *Testimonies for the Church,* vol. 2 (Mountain View, California: Pacific Press Publishing Association, 1948), p. 466.

71 Ellen White, *Christ's Object Lessons,* (Washington, D.C.: Review and Herald Publishing Association, 1941), p. 332.

72 Gillian Ford, "The Soteriological Implications of the Human Nature of Christ," [Cooranbong], n.d.,p. 36. Note: Soteriological means that which pertains to the doctrine of salvation.

73 Raoul Dederen to Desmond Ford, Sept 15, 1975.

74 Ray Stanley to Desmond Ford, Dec 1, 1975.

75 Gillian Ford, "Soterological Implications," pp. 5, 49; Gillian Ford, "For Saints and Other Sinners," [Cooranbong], n.d., Lesson 5.

76 Willis Hackett to Desmond Ford, Sept 30, 1975.

77 Alfred Jorgensen to Raglan Marks, Nov 7, 1975.

78 Russell Standish et al. to the Committee of the Australasian Division of Seventh-day Adventists, Dec 18, 1975.

79 "Records of Proceedings: Biblical Research Institute, Australasian Division," Feb 3, 4, 1976, [pp. 1–7].

80 Eric Magnusson, interviewed by Milton Hook, Nov 19, 2005.

81 "Records of Proceedings: General Statement," 1976, [pp. 23–27].

82 Martin, "Objective Digest Report," p. 5.

83 Russell Standish to Alfred Jorgensen, Feb 4, 1976.

84 Desmond Ford to Russell Standish, Feb 17, 1976.

85 Lawrence Naden to Desmond Ford, [ca.1976]; Linda Driscoll to Robert Frame, Feb 16, 1976; Don Bain to Desmond Ford, March 12, 1976; Graeme Olsen to Desmond Ford, March 18, 1976.

86 Lawrence Naden to Robert Frame, Nov 13, 1975.

87 Robert Frame to Alfred Jorgensen et al., Nov 7, 1975; Gordon Hyde to Robert Frame, Jan 20, 1975; Hackett to Ford, Sept 30, 1975.

88 Gordon Hyde to Desmond Ford, Nov 13, 1975.

89 Robert Frame to Desmond Ford, Sept 29, 1975.

90 [Palmdale statement], "Christ Our Righteousness," RH, May 27, 1976, pp. 4–6. Note: Also appeared in *AR,* May 31, 1976, pp. 1–3.

91 Frame to Jorgensen *et al.,* Nov 7, 1975.

92 Desmond Ford to Robert Frame, Nov 10, 1975.

93 *Ibid.*

94 *Ibid.*

95 Ford, interviewed by Lloyd, March 12, 1995, March 10, 1996.

96 Jack Walker, ed "Documents from the Palmdale Conference on Righteousness by Faith," (Goodlettsville, Tennessee, Aug, 1976), p. 22.

97 Robert Parr to Desmond Ford, July 13, 1976.

98 Desmond Ford to Gordon Hyde, May 24, 1976.

99 Ford, interviewed by Lloyd, March 12, 1995.

100 [Palmdale statement], *AR,* May 31, 1976, p. 1.

101 Desmond Ford, "Chapel Talk," [Avondale College], May 18, 1976.

102 [Palmdale statement], *AR,* May 31, 1976, p. 1.

103 *Ibid.,* pp. 1, 2.

104 *Ibid.* Note: The sinless nature of Christ was eventually clearly declared in *Seventh-day Adventists Believe ...* (1988), p. 49.

105 *Seventh-day Adventists Believe...* (Hagerstown, Maryland: Review and Herald Publishing Association, 1988), p. 123.

Chapter Eight:
Reactions to the Palmdale Conference

The ambivalence of Palmdale was never conclusively resolved. It left a vacuum in the SDA Church where the different views persisted, and the apostolic gospel could not be preached with consistent clarity. Quarreling intensified, both in Australia and America.

Upon his return from Palmdale to Avondale College, Ford was asked to address the faculty and students about the developments at the meeting. He did so in two Tuesday-morning chapel talks, May 18 and 25.[1] He would rather have ad-libbed from a memorized outline, according to his custom, because reading notes, he said, was like "kissing someone through a paling fence."[2] But in order not to be misunderstood or misquoted he kept close to a prepared speech that was later freely distributed.

He recalled the story of the prodigal son in order to illustrate the relationship between justification and sanctification. Justification, he explained, occurred the instant the boy decided to return to his father. Sanctification, he added, took place on the road back home—every day making a fresh decision to keep walking, every day still smelling of pigs, every day bruising his bare feet or stubbing his toes. He really did not get increasingly righteous while walking along the road. The main goal was to stay on the right road until he reached his father.

Des noted that the Roman Catholics take the position that salvation means making righteous, i.e., as the prodigal son walked home, he became more righteous with each step. Catholicism, he added, also distorts the doctrine by imposing the idea of an infused or imparted righteousness in the term "sanctification," giving the sense that the righteousness is literally owned by the prodigal because he has put in the hard yards, walking and working. Des disagreed with this basic tenet. Changing the metaphor, he remarked, "Sanctification should not be understood as the battery principle, as though God is pouring it into me, imparting it into me.... We're not saved by a certain amount or quantity of sanctification."[3]

Similar sentiments were shared by Des the following month in the Ryde Civic Centre, Sydney.[4] More meetings followed in quick succession.

Among them, the week-of-prayer meetings at Fulton College, Fiji, in July. One college staff member reflected soon after, "We have never had such a good turnout of staff members at staff worship and the main meetings than what we had last week.... The students have expressed how much spiritual blessing they have gained throughout the week."[5]

Later, Des spoke at the Melbourne Youth Congress and then flew to the Christchurch Youth Congress in New Zealand to present the same gospel messages.[6] The pace grew hectic. All these extra appointments were in addition to his regular teaching assignments at college.

Robert Parr, having been at Palmdale too, was able to speak from firsthand experience at prayer meetings in Melbourne. Attendance swelled whenever he advertised that he was going to talk about the meetings. Allegedly, he was asked on one occasion, "Did Doctor Ford lose his temper at Palmdale?" "Only when I out-jogged him in our early morning runs," quipped Parr, who once referred to himself as "His Sublime Corpulance."[7]

Back in America Kenneth Wood abused his position as the denomination's chief editor, claiming that perfectionism held the higher moral ground in the debate. He had also attended Palmdale, but deliberately tried to nullify any advances toward the apostolic gospel, something that Duncan Eva of the General Conference promised Des would never happen. Peddling his own views in one editorial, Wood suggested:

> Those [meaning to include himself] who hold sanctification to be a part of righteousness by faith seem to place greater emphasis on holy living than do those who exclude it; also, they seem to give greater emphasis to humanity's part in cooperating with divinity in the plan of salvation. This is perhaps because they consider the gospel not merely as good news that through Christ repentant souls may have a new standing before God, but that through Him sinners may be transformed.[8]

In another editorial Wood argued for the sinful nature of Christ, selectively quoting from Ellen White *(Desire of Ages,* p. 117; *Selected Messages,* book 1, pp. 408 and 409) to substantiate his view that Christ overcame His sinful nature. He concluded by urging:

> With the tremendous challenge of Christ's perfect sinless life

before us, surely we should study earnestly how to imitate it. We should seek the power of the Holy Spirit, surrender wholly to God, and assimilate the divine nature through Bible study, prayer, and meditation.[9]

Wood's position begs the questions, "How much of God's nature had he himself assimilated at the time of writing?" Given that the divine nature is infinite Spirit, how much of Wood's corporeality was transformed into God's nature? Was he, in any way, part-Spirit? Or was Wood thinking of God's infinite moral qualities, His righteousness? If that was so, then how much of Wood's nature was changed into the perfect moral righteousness of God? Was he less than a mere shadow of God's righteousness or getting close to moral perfection? If he was close, then how soon could we expect him to be as righteous as God?

Wood may have pled that he could only expect to reach perfection in the human sphere, not absolute perfection. But questions persist. What criteria would he use to measure success in his enterprise? Would he use the Ten Commandments of Exodus 20, or those in Exodus 34, or the values from the Sermon on the Mount? What could be the height of righteousness in the human sphere? Could it be the righteousness exhibited in the humanity of Jesus? If that is so, then what set of criteria could we expect Wood to use as he compared his righteousness to Christ's? Had he fully appreciated the gravity and breadth and depth of each element of Gods law that Christ kept? As he got closer to the rainbow, did he increasingly realize how distant was the reality? Did he have any appreciation of human depravity and the lofty standard of God's law and Christ's example? Did he realize his constant need of Christ's imputed righteousness? These are serious questions. The answers provided by perfectionists are always shallow and hackneyed.

This fact was illustrated when Parr objected to Wood's editorials and Wood defended himself, seeking refuge in semantics. Wood replied, "While you [Parr] continually state we [Wood and like-minded ones] believe that Christ 'had' a sinful nature the truth is that we do not believe this. We say that Christ 'took' our sinful nature."[10]

Parr threw up his hands in despair. He passed Wood's reply to Des, attaching his own summation, "The most recent poke in the unsanctified eye from K. H. W[ood],—Please explain to me the difference between 'having' and 'taking' a sinful nature. If I take a cold, I have a cold. If I take a drink, I have a drink.... He's playing with words, and I have told him so."[11]

With good intentions church administrators continued the dialogue behind closed doors. One colloquium was held at Nosaca Pines youth camp, South Carolina, in February 1978, but Des did not attend.[12] Instead, he made some suggestions for improvements to the agreed draft hammered out at the meeting. Another gathering took place at the Potomac Conference branch office, August 1978, when about twenty administrators and Bible lecturers, including Des, met together for a week. The report cited some of the questions aired:

Is the need for imputed righteousness gradually reduced or eliminated by receiving imparted righteousness? Is salvation identically and equally dependent on justification and sanctification? Is salvation dependant on justification, with sanctification appearing as the fruitage of the faith relationship to Jesus? Does the true believer ever cease to need justification? What will carry one through the judgment-justification alone, justification and sanctification, or sanctification alone?[13]

These questions are elementary to the gospel of Jesus Christ. It is surprising that a church group would be found still debating the basics more than 130 years after its inception!

When Neal Wilson replaced Robert Pierson as General Conference president, the indecision continued. In June 1979 Wilson wrote a letter to all church leaders, proposing that because the theology was "complex," it "need not be settled in detail." He pled for time, promising that a wide spectrum of laity, administrators, pastors, editors, historians, and biblical scholars would meet to arrive at a consensus, and then the church at large would be obliged to accept their verdict. In the meantime, he said, every member should "earnestly study the Bible and the inspired writings of Ellen G White."[14]

A perceptive theology student at Andrews University had earlier written to Des, "Much of this perfectionistic exegesis seems to start with Spirit of Prophecy [White's writings] and work towards Scripture, instead of vice versa. One of the crucial areas we seem not to have settled (and seem reluctant to settle) is that of revelation and inspiration, especially the treatment of the Spirit of Prophecy."[15]

Wilson's promised colloquium was convened on October 3 and 4, 1979, and Des was among the 150 individuals to gather there in the General Conference chapel.

The published report said, "No vote was taken on any document," "brevity of time prevented in-depth work," and there was a "need for more such sharing." It concluded with the statement, "We dare not stop our evangelistic thrust."[16]

At first it seemed that officials wanted everyone to keep running with their trousers still snagged on a barbed wire fence. It appeared later, however, that the denomination was breaking free with an encouraging statement titled, "The Dynamics of Salvation." When this was issued it patched up some of the split.[17]

Conflicting Concepts

The divide had been exacerbated after Palmdale with John Clifford and Russell Standish publishing a 160-page document they called "Conflicting Concepts of Righteousness by Faith." George Burnside reportedly printed a thousand copies of the book for distribution.[18] A brief summary had been hastily dispatched to the Palmdale meeting. [Sent to Pierson, Wood and Duncan Eva. The first two responded positively.]

The tome began by repeatedly referring to "Dr. Desmond B. Ford." Des was never blessed with a second Christian name, so we are left to conjecture what the authors meant by the initial B. Did they intend "Biblical," "Beloved," or "Brave"? Knowing the mind of its authors, we have to assume it was a Freudian slip for "Babylonish" or some unmentionable B-word. Whatever they meant, it was not a good omen for accuracy in the remaining pages. Its Catholic, or Tridentine, platform was categorically stated in the preface—after citing two excerpts from Ellen White they wrote, "Imparted Righteousness is the crucial factor in salvation."[19]

Des wrote a reply that was endorsed by the Biblical Research Institute at Australasian headquarters. In it he deplored the writers' dissident attitude to Palmdale, Avondale College, and administration in general. After dissecting their arguments, he joined with the BRI to declare:

> We believe in the great earnestness of Brethren Standish and Clifford, but we do not believe in their thoroughness. We would urge these brethren to forsake their practice of superficial research and hasty conclusions and only write when thorough examination of a topic has taken place. We venture to add by that time their intended

writing will be both irrelevant and unnecessary.[20]

Gill, too, issued a hefty volume, "Law, Guilt and Grace," that was really a set of ten talks she had given soon after Palmdale. The series was meant to inform her local church friends of some of the foundational issues avoided at Palmdale, such as the depths of humanity's inherited sinful nature.[21] In the talks she covered some ground she had already covered in previous publications. The collection was not intended for wide distribution, and only a small number of copies were issued privately.

An astute theology student at Avondale College, Ken Nicholls, addressed Clifford and Standish directly in his publication, *The Biblical Concept of Righteousness by Faith.* Nicholls was devastating in his attack, demonstrating the affinity displayed by Clifford and Standish with Roman Catholic theology and at the same time their rejection of Scripture and the best of Reformation theology. A fellow student, Calvin Edwards, wrote the introduction. Norman Young, their lecturer, added a statement of his own personal belief, and Des penned the closing pages.[22]

Robert Brinsmead also made a telling rebuttal. A fellow Christian, David McMahon, wrote in the introduction: We believe that the views expressed by the authors of *C[onflicting] C[oncepts],* and professed by them to be in accordance with the traditional, historic Seventh-day Adventist position, are not only essentially the same as those which were exploded ... at the Reformation, but they are supported by the same arguments and interpretations of Scripture which were then current in the church of Rome.[23]

Alfred Jorgensen, chairman of the BRI, was indignant because Clifford and Standish had dishonestly claimed on the front cover that their book was a "Biblical Research Institute Paper." He had the BRI condemn *Conflicting Concepts,* and a heated exchange of letters ensued.[24]

Neither Clifford nor Standish ever apologized or admitted the deception. Instead, they ducked behind "the General Conference leadership," claiming friends there in high places who supported their positions. (Wood had allegedly agreed with Conflicting Concepts).[25] They then went on to accuse Jorgensen of protecting Des, while at the same time believing in perfectionism. Jorgensen then demanded from them some proof of their accusations. They came forward with four examples, giving names of some witnesses and approximate dates when

Jorgensen was alleged to have been duplicitous. Standish also wrote a lengthy letter to all church leaders in the Australasian Division, a mawkish defense of his protracted stand for tradition. He concluded it with the reaffirmation, "Christ does have toe [sic—a typo for 'the'] power to take all sin from the life."[26]

Jorgensen's comments to Standish demonstrated that he had reached the end of his patience:

Now, Russell, you may fondly imagine that God has called you to lead a mighty crusade against the Australasian Division in general, against Avondale College in the middle distance, and against Dr. Ford in the bullseye.... But let me ask you: Have you ever reflected on how such a crusade could possibly react on Dr. Ford himself? Has it ever occurred to you that you could vitiate his influence, wreck his career, and even destroy the man himself? ... Don't forget that Dr. Ford is after all a man—quite likely a very sensitive man—a man who, despite the resilience he exhibits, may be deeply hurt by the way you and your colleague and all who are like-minded with you apparently leave no stone unturned to create a dismal image of him....

Please don't write to me and tell me that you are only concerned with his theology and not with the man himself. I am a close observer of the current scene. Most of the brickbats that are being thrown fly across my desk and occasionally graze my neck. The plain fact is, my dear Russell, your campaign has alienated people from Dr. Ford and his ministry, and, unless you can justify your action in the sight of God, you will be called to give account of the damage you have done him in the day of judgment....

At this point may I recommend that we bring this present round of correspondence to a close, for I can see nothing to be gained in any further interchanges.[27]

Parr, who had taught the Standish twins in their high school (academy) days, said he knew Colin to be a "character who would crawl backwards over broken bottles to get into a fight." Russell was no different. Like Jorgensen, Parr came to deplore their long, sanctimonious letters of complaint as a "hum-bug, a nuisance."[28]

Russell's frequent expressions such as, "I would be utterly grieved to forfeit your friendship," were taken by Parr to be hollow and mendacious. At the time he replied to Russell:

> Am I numbered among those favored mortals who have your smile of 'Christian affection?' In view of what you have done to Pastor Jorgensen, your dear friend, and your other great buddy, Doctor Ford, I wonder whether such may not be the kiss of death.
>
> I am not the dedicated Christian that my friend Desmond Ford is. You quote him as saying that if you hit him over the head with a crowbar, he would believe that it accidentally fell from your hand.... Not me. If you hit me over the head with a crowbar, I would instinctively duck to avoid the second blow.[29]

Brinsmead gave not only a written response to Conflicting Concepts but also answered its perfectionism in public meetings. Parr attended one such gathering in Melbourne at which Standish and Clifford were also present. Brinsmead spoke for nearly two hours. Parr reported to a correspondent soon after:

> In the very kindest way, Russell [Standish] and John Clifford were absolutely massacred. He left them without a leg to stand on. I expected them to crawl under their seat and not come out until everybody had gone. On the contrary, the whole proceedings went right over their heads, and they came out fighting, even showing no suggestion that their cause had been vanquished and left in shambles.
>
> I really marvel at the obtuseness of these two gentlemen.... It is incredible—there is no other word—that they could even hold up their heads in view of the documented evidence which Brinsmead produced, and which laid them low, after smiting them hip and thigh.[30]

Meetings generated by *Conflicting Concepts* were also held in Sydney. Standish spoke at length to a crowded gathering in a private home on Sabbath, August 28, 1976. During discussion time John Eager, a teacher at the local SDA high school, made the most sagacious contribution of the afternoon by suggesting, "What we really should be debating (if we want to use that word) is whether or not the doctrine is the doctrine according to the word of God or not, not whether this has been the historical doctrine of the Adventist Church."[31]

Des obtained permission from church officials to make a reply in the same house on October 2. He did exactly what Eager suggested should be done, i.e., with Scripture he first built the foundations of the doctrine of righteousness by faith—the nature of sin, the nature of man, and the nature of Christ. He then proceeded to defend Palmdale's decision on the term "righteousness by faith."[32]

An unlikely response to *Conflicting Concepts* came from an Anglican minister, Geoffrey Paxton, who was quietly researching in the background and developing a thesis during his academic studies about the SDA Church and its stance on salvation. In the course of his research, he interviewed church officials and members, in addition to reading extensively in SDA literature. He would issue his findings in 1977.

Prior to the publication of his book, Paxton conducted two meetings in the Church of Christ, Croydon (suburban Melbourne), in January 1977. Many SDAs attended, including Russell Standish. Paxton quoted at length from numerous SDA sources to illustrate his thesis that the SDA Church was traditionally closer to Roman Catholic theology than Protestant theology regarding the basic Christian doctrine of righteousness by faith.

When it came to question time Standish made a rambling statement, finally asking Paxton to comment on two Ellen White quotations that he read out. Paxton politely replied that he was sorry the question was not from the Bible. He had apparently read Conflicting Concepts and offered an objective appraisal of it. "Your publication in its entirety is... fine," he said, "if that's what you want to teach... but please don't call it Protestant."[33]

Clifford and Standish were being assailed from all sides. Their theology (or lack of it) was shown to be paper-thin and fraying at the edges. About this time, they brought forward the argument that the Pharisees considered Jesus to be an unscholarly Nazarene, so it was not surprising that they themselves, the self-proclaimed stalwarts of truth, would be considered unscholarly by Des and Jorgensen and others. "Never have theologians brought real truth and they won't ever do so," Standish fumed.[34]

"How much theology did the dying thief have?" James Kent, another critic, echoed. And what about "the scholarly Pharisee," he continued, "who paraded his theology at Temple prayers when the common sinner went home justified?"[35] Clearly, when presented with sound biblical exegesis, the critics resorted to smearing their opposition. They had no other answer than the argument of anti-intellectualism. They were whipped, and they knew it. So, like little boys, all they could do was throw mud.

Wood and the Australian mossbacks matched each other in their attempted erosion of Palmdale. Wood's editorials did not go unchallenged. One clear-headed American reader wrote to him:

> You were at Palmdale and must have agreed to that accord. But in FYI-2 [Review editorial, Oct 28,1976] you take issue with it.... Our dilemma is that while we say that we are true Protestants and that our claim is to [be] upholding and maintaining the fundamental truths of that faith, yet in our doing we turn around and distort the very truths we are professing to uphold. If we cannot hold to the Protestant concepts of righteousness by faith... what on earth did we ever see in Protestantism to make us wish to identify with it at all?[36]

The same writer objected to Wood's trust in church tradition— Waggoner and Jones and Ellen White: "That position is so biblically vulnerable," he wrote, because "we significantly erode the other Protestant pillar of *sola scriptura.*" "We had better be prepared," he chided, "to stand up and honestly say that in two fundamental, crucial, bedrock areas we are no longer Protestants."[37]

Some American perfectionists at the highest level resorted to duplicity to promote their cause. Pierson, for example, urged unity but practiced division. On the one hand he sent a clear message to some fellow leaders in Australia:

The question of doctrinal unity is a very important one in the church today, when there are so many divergent elements seeking to pull this old world apart. I do not want the [SDA] Church to suffer some of the vicissitudes that other Christian denominations have and are passing through. I am anxious that we stay together on the major doctrines of this church. I am sure that all of you men agree.[38]

At the same time, however, Pierson was overseeing the planning of one of the most divisive Sabbath School lesson quarterlies in the history of the church. Herbert Douglass wrote the manuscript that came to be titled *Jesus, the Model Man,* issued for study in the second quarter of 1977. It reasoned from the platform of the sinful nature of Christ to His victory over sin as a model for us to copy and also promised power for believers to keep God's law perfectly in the process of sanctification. Pierson should have known this enterprise would exacerbate disunity.

Jorgensen and Alwyn Salom read the manuscript prior to publication and expressed strong opposition.[39] As soon as the printed version arrived in Australia, Parr voiced his concerns with Australian church administrators Alfred Jorgensen and Keith Parmenter, predicting, "Our people are going to get a distorted view and a very one-sided picture of Christ."

"I am disturbed to think that many of them will complete the series of lessons, believing that they can be as good as Jesus was," he explained. "Many people of impeccable church loyalty and considerable theological intelligence have already looked at this lesson quarterly and have come away shaken with what they have read and with what they have not read."[40]

Archibald Hefren was appalled by the quarterly and vowed to counter its contents in every Sabbath School class he conducted. Parr suggested someone quickly write lesson helps that could be inserted in the Record each week to answer the perfectionism; as editor, he was prepared to print them. Nothing came of this idea because it was scotched by Pierson.[41] The quarterly was allowed to proceed, strengthening the hand of the likes of Standish and Clifford. Furthermore, it did nothing to forge unity, the goal Pierson claimed he so desperately wanted. He was spiking the drinks of his opposition with sleeping powders and injecting vitamins into the arms of his own players.

Disquiet over the quarterly was not confined to Australia. One outraged Californian church member wrote bitterly to Des, with copies to Pierson, Wood, and five other officials. She confided:

> After reading this present quarterly (Jesus the Model Man), I became so depressed that physical symptoms really manifested themselves. How dare people who call themselves servant[s] of the Most High serve HIM in this manner. How dare they—no greater crime can be perpetrated against the Master of the universe than to misrepresent His love for us and His unblemished character.... If there were a fire going in my fireplace I would have joyfully thrown the quarterly in after I read it from cover to cover.[42]

This was the era when, in many respects, the SDA Church came of age. Richard Nixon's Watergate Affair had sharpened the American psyche to include a healthy distrust of leadership. Political figures were no longer necessarily looked up to as icons of virtue. Cynicism of administrative processes and of administrators themselves increased.

SDA Church dignitaries were not exempt. Members began to question long-established customs. Specifically, there was the Merikay Silver/ Lorna Tobler wages discrimination lawsuit that the church finally had to settle out of court in favor of the two women.[43]

Church leaders felt further under siege with the publication of Ronald Numbers' *Prophetess of Health: A Study of Ellen G White.* Numbers was the son of a minister and a professor in the history of medicine and science at the University of Wisconsin. His excellent book rattled the gates of the White Estate, clearly demonstrating that White had borrowed much from her contemporaries. This dispelled White's own assertion and traditional hagiology that she obtained her wisdom directly from visions. The White Estate offered a rebuttal, but Numbers made a fine reply.[44]

General Conference officials scrambled to reduce the growing chorus of academics that was finding diminishing veracity in church tradition. The officials organized a conference of West Coast Bible teachers and lecturers from Loma Linda University, Pacific Union College, and Walla Walla College. Two prepared documents were discussed, one on the doctrine of inspiration and another on creationism. The ensuing discussion opened a Pandora's box, and both documents were rejected. Instead of discussing the full agenda, much time was spent debating the wisdom of issuing such statements. And along the way the subjects of academic freedom and the priesthood of all believers rose to the fore, topics that many church administrators believed would undercut their power.[45]

Willis Hackett, who had helped to organize the conference, stubbornly urged the viewpoint that official statements of belief should be adopted on themes such as Ellen White, the sanctuary, creationism, historicism, ethical standards, and remnancy. His reasoning was twofold—the statements would serve as benchmarks when employing people, and such unity of faith and practice, he said, would "be rewarded by the latter rain experience."[46]

Charles Scriven, co-editor of *Spectrum,* had published what appeared to be the direct opposite of Hackett's brief. Scriven argued for the ongoing revision of doctrine in the Protestant mode of thinking. If theology is to be bound to unchanging propositions, then theology has doubtful validity, he contended. We cannot afford, he declared, to adopt the idea that "the Spirit of truth lies buried in the cemeteries of New England and Battle Creek [where the SDA pioneers rest] "[47]

Maintaining a sense of an infallible past, which underpinned the thinking of Hackett, Wood, Pierson, and other bellwethers, could only lead the church to Death Valley. It would make the ministry of the Holy Spirit largely irrelevant and better exegesis of Scripture unnecessary. It assumed that all the church had to do was walk backwards and pitch its tent in the nineteenth century. Des was decidedly in the mold of Scriven. He believed there was a need to continually listen to the Spirit and move forward, pulling up stakes and pitching camp closer to the Promised Land, after spying out the prospects with scholarly investigation.

Plans for Transfer

The continuing debate brought no relief for Des personally. It simply isolated him further as American officials and Australian critics united in their push for perfectionism. Some administrators imagined the transfer of Ford from Avondale College would provide the answer to the problem. Time would prove that this was a short-sighted resolution.

Avondale had an affiliation agreement with its sister institution, Pacific Union College in California. Both colleges felt that the agreement was for mutual benefit. Among other features it involved a regular exchange of lecturers.

John ("Jack") Cassell, Jr., president of PUC in 1976, claims he received a suggestion from Avondale College for Des to be a part of that exchange program. General Conference officials warmed to the idea.[48] (The real origin of the plan is difficult to prove. General Conference officers or Australasian Division officers may have first floated the idea informally). John Staples, a PUC lecturer visiting Avondale at the time in company with Duncan Eva, discussed the possibilities with Des.[49] [John Staples told us that the originator of the idea of Des's going to PUC came from Erwin Gane, but he changed his mind when he found out Des and him had theological difference.] The plan was for Des to spend two years at PUC, the normal length of an exchange period, while Des retained the title of head of the theology department at Avondale.[50]

Both Des and Gill were happy about the prospect of transfer.[51] The constant battle with mossbacks had discouraged Des at times because it was so time-consuming and apparently fruitless. A change of paddock presented some hope of relief. Des understood, however, that the move would be made on two conditions—that he would be invited to sit on the American BRI, a committee designated to resolve problems relating to the sanctuary doctrine, and that his return to Avondale College would be guaranteed after the two-year stint. American and Australasian church officials were generally agreed on the deal.[52] No written contract was thought necessary, because all previous transferees had returned according to plan after two years absence.

The arrangements for Des to begin lecturing at PUC in September 1977 were made at the time when Robert Frame was being replaced as Australasian Division president. It should not have made any difference to the terms under which Des went to America, because the replacement, Keith Parmenter, was Frame's assistant and, as such, was conversant with the agreement. Parmenter even reassured Gill that Des would return to Avondale when the two-year term finished. Parr, however, had a premonition of dark days ahead. In a postscript to Des, October 1976, he added, "Tragic news about Bob Frame! This has horrific possibilities for the Australasian Division."[53]

Parr knew Frame to be a highly principled man, but it was known in some circles that Parmenter, although a chairman par excellence, was not of the same mettle. Was there a real chance he would not honor the promises and Des might never be brought back to Avondale?

When word reached California that Des would be teaching at PUC, it created genuine excitement in some quarters. One church member who had read some transcripts of talks given by Des was thrilled that another gospel voice was coming into their midst who might stem the tide of perfectionism. He sang the praises of his own church pastor, who preached the Reformation gospel. However, he warned that there was a small, vocal minority that promoted Robert Wieland's perfectionism. Wieland himself lived further south at Chula Vista, near the Mexican border.[54]

Another cloud on the otherwise sunny horizon was the fact that Erwin Gane, of the same ilk as Wieland, vigorously opposed the coming of Des to PUC. (Wood had done likewise). Prior to Dess arrival Gane canvassed all the board members at PUC and numerous college and church officials in a vain attempt to reverse the transfer agreement.[55] Indeed, he informed Des:

> I have taken the position that it would be unwise for you and me to be together in the same Bible department. Hence I am opposing your coming to PUC. If our board votes to have you come, I will hand over my work to you and will take some other position at least for the period of your stay.[56]

146

Des did not see Gane's petulance as an insurmountable problem. He was quite happy to work alongside someone with a different viewpoint. Des was an optimist, always believing that the Spirit could persuade anyone to accept the gospel. After all, he had witnessed the dramatic turnabout in the Brinsmead family. Perhaps Gane would accept the gospel too.

On May 25,1977, just before his departure for America, Des addressed the Division staff in their morning devotional. His parting gospel message ended with these moving words:

> We cannot climb to heaven by the quaking sides of Sinai. The way is too narrow, one slip will destroy us, but the path of grace is so broad, brethren, that whosoever will, may come. And you come just as you are, but you never remain just as you are after you come. Never. A new creature is born, patterned after the likeness of Christ Jesus. There is only one book in the Bible that has got the name "works" [i.e., acts] attached to it, and it is a very important book, and it follows the four books on the cross and that is always the order. Our acts for Him follow our belief in His acts for us. Our sacrifices are only acceptable when we have received first God's great sacrifice.[57]

End Notes

1   Desmond Ford, Chapel talks, transcripts, Avondale College, May 18, 25, 1976.
2   Desmond Ford, Chapel talk, May 18, 1976, p. 1.
3   *Ibid.,* pp. 12, 13.
4   Desmond Ford et al., *Crisis: The Church,* transcript, June 4, 1976.
5   Rosie Wong to Desmond Ford, July 12, 1976.
6   Robert Parr to Desmond Ford, Oct 18, 1976.
7   Robert Parr to Desmond Ford, July 1, Nov 9, 1976.
8   Kenneth Wood, "F. Y. I." *RH,* Oct 21, 1976, p. 2.
9   Kenneth Wood, "F. Y. I.—4," *RH,* Nov 18, 1976, p. 3.
10 Kenneth Wood to Robert Parr, Dec 11, 1978.
11 Robert Parr to Desmond Ford, Jan 25, 1979.
12 Anon., "The Righteousness by Faith Consultation," *Ministry,* Dec 1979, p. 13; Duncan Eva to Desmond Ford, May 17, 1978.
13 Gordon Hyde, "Righteousness by Faith Consultation in Washington," *RH,* Sept 7, 1978, p. 24.

14 Neal Wilson, "An Open Letter," *Ministry,* June 1979, p. 10.

15 Bernard Brinsmead to Desmond Ford, May 22, [ca. 1976].

16 Anon., "Righteousness by Faith Consultation," *Ministry,* Dec 1979, p. 13.

17 First published in *Adventist Review,* July 31, 1980, pp. 3–8, soon after as a pamphlet.

18 Lowell Tarling to Robert Pierson, Oct 30, 1976.

19 John Clifford, Russell Standish, *Conflicting Concepts of Righteousness by Faith,* [Wahroonga, Australia: Burnside Press, 1976], pp. ix, x.

20 Desmond Ford, "Observations on Conflicting Conceptions [sic] of Righteousness by Faith," n.p., [ca. 1976], p. 45.

21 Gillian Ford, "Law, Guilt and Grace," n.p., [ca. 1976]

22 Ken Nicholls, *The Biblical Concept of Righteousness by Faith,* n.p., [ca. 1977], p. 52–74.

23 Robert Brinsmead, "An Answer to 'Conflicting Concepts of Righteousness by Faith in the Seventh-day Adventist Church'," (Sydney: Wittenburg Steam Press Publishing Association, 1976), p. x.

24 Alfred Jorgensen to Russell Standish, June 28, 1976; Alfred Jorgensen to John Clifford and Russell Standish, July 21, 1976.

25 Robert Parr to Desmond Ford, July 13, 1976

26 John Clifford, Russell Standish to Alfred Jorgensen, July 29, Aug 25,1976; Alfred Jorgensen to John Clifford, Russell Standish, Aug 4, 1976; Russell Standish to Australasian Division Officers *et al.,* Aug 20, 1976.

27 Alfred Jorgensen to Russell Standish, Sept 22, 1976.

28 Robert Parr to Desmond Ford, June 18, Sept 8, 1976.

29 Robert Parr to Russell Standish, [ca. Sept, 1976].

30 Robert Parr to Desmond Ford, Oct 7, 1976.

31 "The Dr. Standish Meeting," transcript, Aug 28, 1976.

32 [Desmond Ford],"An Answer to Dr. Russell Standish," transcript, Oct 2, 1976.

33 Quoted in, "A Babylonian Attacks Seventh-day Adventists," [Wahroonga, Australia: Burnside Press, ca. 1977], p. 35.

34 Russell Standish to Lowell Tarling, Sept 9, 1976.

35 James Kent to Robert Parr, Jan 24, 1977.

36 Douglas Ort to Kenneth Wood, Dec 1, 1976.

37 Ibid.

38 Robert Pierson to Robert Frame *et al.,* June 17, 1976.

39 Quoted in, "The Ford-Brinsmead Link Confirmed," [Wahroonga, Australia: Burnside Press, ca. 1977], p. 13.

40 Robert Parr to Alfred Jorgensen *et al.,* Feb 10, 1977.

41 Ibid; Robert Parr to Desmond Ford, Feb 24, March 31, 1977.

42 Daisy Stanley to Desmond Ford, March 31, 1977.

43 Douglas Welebir et al., "Church Settles Court Cases," *Spectrum* 9:2 [March 1978], pp. 1–5.

44 Ronald Numbers, *Prophetess of Health: A Study of Ellen G White,* (New York: Harper and Row, 1976); Ronald Numbers, "An Author Replies to his Critics," *Spectrum* 8:2 [Jan 1977], pp. 27–36.

45 PUC Religion Department, "A Response from PUC" *Spectrum* 8:4 [Aug 1977], pp. 43, 44; Loma Linda Division of Religion *et al,* "The West Coast Bible Teachers: A Statement of Concern," *Spectrum* 8:4 [Aug 1977], pp. 44–47.

46 Willis Hackett, "Preserve the Landmarks," *Spectrum* 8:4 [Aug 1977], pp. 39, 40.

47 Charles Scriven, "The Case for Renewal in Adventist Theology," *Spectrum* 8:1 [Sept 1976], p. 4.

48 Jack Cassell to Trevor Lloyd, Dec 20,1998. Note: Cassell's memory of the exact sequence of events may be questioned here because it is known that some at Avondale College saw little wisdom in the prospect of Des going to PUC.

49 Arthur Ferch to Desmond Ford, Sept 16, 1976; Gillian Ford, interviewed by Trevor Lloyd at Cooranbong, Jan 1, 1997.

50 Cree Sandefur to Roy Davies, Feb 27, 1977.

51 Gillian Ford, interviewed by Lloyd, Jan 1,1977.

52 Gordon Hyde to Desmond Ford, Nov 10, 1976; Desmond Ford to Keith Parmenter, March 2, 1977; Desmond Ford, interviewed by Trevor Lloyd at Sydney, March 12, 1995.

53 Parr to Ford, Oct 18, 1976.

54 Jack Mallory to Desmond Ford, May 19, 1977.

55 Jack Cassell to Trevor Lloyd, Jan 1, 1999.

56 Erwin Gane to Desmond Ford, Jan 7, 1977.

57 Desmond Ford, Division Devotional, transcript, Wahroonga, May 25, 1977.

Chapter Nine:
Lecturing at Pacific Union College

When Doctor Ford left Avondale College, his colleagues were heartened by the belief that he would soon return. Little did anyone realize, least of all Ford himself, that his gospel ministry would be magnified in ways that confounded his critics.

Mid-1977 found Des, Gill, and Luke settling into their new campus surroundings at Pacific Union College. Des would walk the mile or so to classes or pedal his bicycle. The Americans welcomed them wholeheartedly. "We had a wonderful time at PUC," Gill later recalled.[1]

Robert Brinsmead's lecture tours throughout America had aroused interest in the righteousness by faith emphasis, despite the cold water that Kenneth Wood and others were throwing over it. PUC president John Cassell was aware of this interest and saw great value in having Des come to the campus to provide a parallel thrust, even take the lead, in promoting the apostolic gospel.[2]

In his first academic year, 1977/78, Des was given a teaching load of forty units. The heavy assignment included Pauline Epistles, Life and Teachings of Jesus, Daniel, Revelation, and Hebrew Prophets of the Post-Babylonian Era.[3] The only adverse criticism from the students was his lack of availability, because speaking appointments took him away from the campus so often. His style was the same as at Avondale— energetic, stimulating, and Christ-centered. Whenever possible he was accustomed to taking his classes out into the healthy sunshine and fresh air. His bonhomie won the hearts and minds of his students.[4]

"Des's presence on campus was felt almost immediately," Cassell recalled. "Theology students flocked to his classes," he said, and when Des also "agreed to teach a Sabbath School class on campus soon after his arrival, it did not take long before there was standing room only." Cassell himself attended on several occasions and remembered enjoying the lessons. He commented that "soon members of the community were flocking to the class, and we had to remove to the largest lecture room on campus in the Science complex." "Students, faculty, retired ministers, and visiting parents," he added, "were enthralled by his presentations."[5]

Des was also invited to conduct a series of twelve week-of-prayer meetings on campus, October/November 1977. He titled them "The Gospel—Weight or Wings?" Fred Veltman, theology department head and fellow lecturer at PUC, spoke of Ford as "a preacher par excellence." He regarded him as "a revivalist" both in and out of the classroom, best suited to the proclamation of the gospel and less inclined to spend many hours correcting grammar and lack of logic in student essays.[6]

Speaking invitations began to flood in from all over America and Europe, far too many for Des to accept. Weekend engagements found him away from the college more often than not. These received warm accolades from church officials and members, but some on campus began to complain that he was absent too often. Just as in the days of Lawrence Naden and Avondale College, Cassell had to restrict the times Des could be away on appointments. Cassell himself would field the numerous requests coming in.[7] Des happily complied. During Des's second year at PUC, however, it was agreed that he would travel out of state only once a month and to venues within the Northern California Conference twice a month. He was still away from the campus three out of four weekends. Additionally, he was permitted to take two separate weeks-of-prayer per year at other SDA institutions. In view of the good name Des brought to PUC at these speaking appointments, he had his teaching load reduced to thirty-four units for the 1978/79 college year, so that he would not become emotionally exhausted.[8]

Off-campus appointments during Des's first year at PUC had included the winter quarter week-of-prayer at Walla Walla College;[9] three lectures on righteousness by faith at Andrews University during a weekend in February 1978;[10] a series of eighteen meetings at Monterey Bay Academy and Loma Linda University;[11] and a summertime Nebraska camp meeting. In his second year his appointments included a series in Alaska[12] and week-of-prayer meetings at Atlantic Union College. One writer reported glowingly in the college newspaper:

> Ford presented Christ and His merits with a strength and clarity I've seldom, if ever, heard. The impact of his messages still echoes in my mind, and the freedom with which he exalted the crucified and risen Christ gave an undeniable evidence that God's Spirit was with us throughout the weekend. Many students remarked that they had seen Christ in a totally new way.[13]

"I received many positive responses from educational institutions and North American unions and conferences regarding his positive impact on his audiences and expressing support for his emphasis on justification," Cassell commented later. "I believe American Adventists were hungry for the revival of this historic Christian doctrine and were tired of the attention to such minutia as skirt length, wedding rings, public display of affection, rigid Sabbath observance, etc."[14]

Des also addressed SDA members of the Society of Biblical Literature in New Orleans, November 1978. This, of course, was of a more scholarly nature. He offered a paper, titled "A Hermeneutic for Daniel—the Apotelesmatic Principle." William Shea, of Andrews University, presented a different viewpoint.[15]

Was Des invited to sit on the Biblical Research Institute committee as promised? Yes, but only on one occasion. The committee convened on the PUC campus January 1 and 2, 1978. William Johnsson was there to present a paper on the Book of Hebrews, especially Chapter 9, where references to the sanctuary "veil" are found.[16] Traditional SDA interpretations were at odds with most biblical scholarship. Adventists generally maintained that "the veil" referred to the first, or outer veil, in the heavenly sanctuary, through which Jesus entered at His ascension. They wished to explain that Jesus did not go through the inner veil into the Most Holy Place until 1844. On the contrary, most non-SDA scholars argued that Hebrews 9 has Jesus passing through the inner veil at His ascension, making the date 1844 irrelevant.

Johnsson's presentation was timid and skirted the real issues, prompting Des to categorically outline the problems. Des's response was confrontational and perhaps caused Johnsson to dig deeper later.[17]

The following winter, while Des was preoccupied with research of his own, the BRI committee met at Loma Linda, and Johnsson presented a second paper on the same topic. Only this time he admitted that the non-SDA view had the vast weight of evidence on its side. In most instances, he said, the Hebrew and Greek references to "the veil" do, indeed, refer to the inner veil through which Jesus entered into the Most Holy Place of the heavenly sanctuary at His ascension. In his conclusions he qualified his findings with the explanation that Hebrews is not really concerned with the "when" (Ascension or 1844) of Christ's ministry but rather with the "quality" (the efficacy of Christ's sacrifice was far better than the Old Testament sanctuary services in total, even the high point,

Yom Kippur).[18] Johnsson's qualification, however, neither challenged the non-SDA view nor endorsed the traditional SDA view.

Some Try to Undermine Des's Influence

Inevitably Des would stir some opposition. Erwin Gane had already scattered tares before Des set foot on campus.[19] But these lay dormant in the field of instant popularity for Des. How galling it must have been for Gane.

Gane earned the reputation of being a prima donna. Administration had told him his resignation would be accepted if he did hand it in because of Des coming to PUC. At the same time, they knew he desperately wanted to keep teaching.[20] They called his bluff, and he did not carry through on his threat to resign. He lingered in the theology department with a down-in-the-mouth attitude and continued to sow seeds of discontent. On a number of occasions, Cassell called the department faculty together to discuss the righteousness by faith issues. Gane resented having to attend these meetings. No harmony was achieved, and all remained locked into their own views.[21]

Des made a personal approach to Gane, pleading, "Can't we walk together at PUC, even though we disagree?" "No," was Gane's retort.[22]

Gane treated Edward Heppenstall with a similar attack of the grumps. It troubled Heppenstall and led him to confront Gane with a gracious letter:

> Whenever I have had speaking appointments at PUC or more particularly study sessions with the men in the Bible Department and at the retreats with your theology students, you have invariably absented yourself. Naturally, I asked openly, 'Why this attitude on your part?' Time and again I was told by your fellow teachers that since you disagreed with me theologically on certain points, and thereby disapproved of me, that this was your way of registering your opposition to me. Now, if this is true, it is incredible to me, since such an attitude would be so far removed from what I personally find essential in Christian fellowship and understanding. But this was the consensus, not of just one man in your Bible department, but of almost all of them. I do not like this kind of alienation.[23]

Gane had one or two sympathizers, the most prominent being Morris Venden, pastor of the PUC campus church. Des was often away and missed some of Venden's jibes from the pulpit. Gill, however, sat through most of them. In one sermon she listened to a Venden parable about an Edsel car. She was unfamiliar with an Edsel, so the story went completely over her head. Later, a church member explained to her that the car was a Ford model taken off the market because it was no good.[24] Cheap shots like this were unworthy of any man, especially one who preached perfection of character. Members of the congregation repeatedly visited him, asking him to stop his attack, but their pleas went unheeded.

Venden habitually gathered Ellen White quotes and then used Scripture to support them. In one sermon he used at least twenty White excerpts, while expounding on "Be ye therefore perfect" (Matthew 5:48). He spoke glowingly of Waggoner and Jones, highlighted the idea of Christ dwelling within us, and asserted that it was "possible to obey God's law perfectly."[25] It was vintage perfectionism—with a dash of Indian mysticism, having great emphasis on the surrender of the willpower.

Des wrote to him, pressing for proper methods in biblical preaching. "By all means," he said, "use E. G. W[hite] to illustrate truth clearly stated in Scripture, but she should never be used as a basis for doctrine." In conclusion he thanked Venden for his "patience with an impatient Australian. Your preaching warms my heart, but it also troubles me," he added. "If you think it's worthwhile to discuss these things, I am at your service."[26]

Venden, however, exhibited a certain swagger, and Des could make little impact on his pie-in-the-sky perfectionism.

Cassell observed that Ford never actively solicited support for his views in order to mount a *blitzkrieg* on his opposition.[27] He always presented a phenomenal resilience to his antagonists, confidently going about his teaching and preaching with infectious buoyancy. And, of course, his literary output left him no time for cabal or politics.

Des Continues Writing and Publishing
Drawing on some of the topical and typical questions posed by young minds in the classroom, Des published a paperback in 1977 with the title, *Answers on the Way,* which Pacific Press Publishing Association had asked him to write. It posed questions and offered answers on perfectionism, justification, and the prophecies of Daniel. The most vital question he entertained was, "Does life have meaning?' "It only

makes sense through Christ," Des answered.[28]

This was the era, too, when some of the cream of his research and thinking on the books of Daniel and Revelation surfaced for general readership. Des had written the manuscript for his commentary on the Book of Daniel while at Avondale, after returning from Manchester. Richard Coffen, book editor at Southern Publishing Association had requested the work but ran the gauntlet of censorship during its preparation. As a result, Coffen developed a stomach ulcer.[29] The editing and acceptance of the book took five years (1973–1978).

Duncan Eva, vice president of the General Conference, was initially very cautious about Des's manuscript, expressing the view in 1976 that the church was super-sensitive about the controversial aspects of Daniel. He also judged Coffen and Don Short, another resident editor, to be inexperienced. For these reasons he wanted Gordon Hyde at the Biblical Research Institute to check the manuscript. Hyde did read it through, along with Robert Olson, Robert Spangler, Siegfried Horn, and Graham Maxwell.[30] In Australia Robert Parr ploughed through the hefty work with an editorial eye, and Eric Magnusson, Norman Young, and Arthur Patrick also checked large sections of it.[31] Horn and Maxwell vigorously supported its publication. The task of revision and editing was long and arduous, including a small team being dispatched to libraries to double check quotations Des had used.[32]

The contents of the commentary had been popularized by Des in his articles that had earlier aroused the ire of Jones and company. Professor Bruce wrote the foreword, a fact that was likely to further convince Jones that Ford was now a confirmed Futurist. The chapters were filled with new explanations for the traditional mind, but Des insists that wherever there was some doubt about the exegesis of a text, he would favor the traditional SDA view. It was in the footnotes that he aired the alternative positions. There he made it plain that if the Jews had accepted Christ, time would not have been prolonged to 1844 and beyond. In other words, the fulfillments of Daniel's prophecies were adequate by about the end of the first Christian century.[33]

Des even persisted with the traditional explanation that the seventy weeks of Daniel 9:24 were cut off (as a sub-division) from the 2300 days of Daniel 8:14. Later, Raymond Cottrell convinced him that the better translation is "determined" or "allotted" or "decreed." It is the only point, and a vital one in many respects, that Des would edit if a reprint were ever made.[34]

Coffen and his editors anticipated some controversy on publication. Short took comfort in the knowledge that Ellen White had said, "The fact that there is no controversy or agitation among God's people should not be regarded as conclusive evidence that they are holding fast to sound doctrine" *(Counsels to Writers and Editors,* p. 39).[35]

In a review of the book, Vern Heise, a minister in Australia, observed:

> Dr. Ford's work has brought a breath of fresh air into the somewhat stuffy atmosphere of prophetic interpretation. Believing as he does, that truth is never static and the light "shines more and more unto the perfect day," the author has capitalized on the best research over the centuries and made his own very considerable contribution to this area of study.
>
> He has been careful to use sound principles of interpretation, not the least of which has been to avoid the pitfall of interpreting Daniel according to the morning newspaper! The author believes that the Bible is still its own best interpreter.[36]

Heise concluded with the prophetic words, "Should Dr. Ford find himself in the fiery furnace or the lions' den, he will also find much consolation in the fact that Daniel's companions were delivered from the furnace, and the prophet himself was delivered from the den of lions unscathed."[37]

In conjunction with the Daniel commentary, Des published another series for Ministry magazine, the articles appearing bi-monthly, beginning in May 1978.[38] Unlike Wood at the Review office, Ministry's editor, Spangler, like Coffen and Short, was clearly more openminded to unorthodox interpretations.

During the winter months of 1978/79, Des was granted a sabbatical to do further research for his companion volume on the Book of Revelation. He spent days in the Library of Congress, Washington, D.C., trawling through ancient and modern commentaries on the Book of Revelation. He discovered an unmistakable tendency to interpret Revelation in terms of contemporary events. Every commentator found fulfillments in current plagues, current wars, current persecutions, and the like. Des began to realize more than ever that this method of interpretation, extreme Historicism, was prone to fall into the pit of alarm, reading Revelation (or any apocalyptic literature) between the lines of newspaper print. He concluded that it was more responsible to admit multiple fulfillments of the prophecies—historic peaks in the past, in the present, and in the future. His research culminated in the publication of *Crisis!* his commentary on Revelation.

Reflecting on the finished manuscript he confessed, "When I wrote *Crisis,* I made it plain that all attempts by Historicists to find political events to match exact dates in the Book of Revelation are non-biblical and not exegetically correct. At that point 1844 fell apart."[39]

This brought Des to the brink in 1979. Back among his colleagues at PUC, writing and lecturing again, he confided in some of them and Gill, saying he could lose his job when the commentary was published.[40]

Ford had also written studies for a Sabbath School lesson quarterly scheduled for publication in 1980.[41] The series canvassed the prophetic role, with sections on Elijah, Daniel, New Testament prophets, and latter-day counterfeits. Countless hours went into the draft, including editing by Alwyn Salom and General Conference personnel. Des also wrote a book to supplement the pamphlet series of studies. When the series was in an advanced stage of production, the enterprise was abandoned, but the book itself was issued under the title *Physicians of the Soul.* Des made numerous inquiries to find the cause of aborting the pamphlet series. He concluded that the evidence pointed to Keith Parmenter.[42] If that was true, it was an early sign that some official efforts were being made to strangle Des's influence.

Into the mix of researching, writing, teaching, and preaching, the arrival of humorous letters from Parr fell like the summer rain on parched earth. There was reason for continual contact, because Des was still a regular contributor to the Australian church magazines. Apparently, Parr learned that Des's teenage son, Luke, was a keen marathon athlete. Neither Des nor Gill had urged Luke to adopt the sport, but Parr made light of the news, writing to Des:

I notice that you have Luke on this running business. I beg of you, get the child to desist! And you, too. You are fifty now, remember.... To have a small child run twenty-six miles under the threat of getting no food unless he finished first, that is too much! You are the most intemperate man I ever met. God gave you legs to walk upon, but you must run. He gave you the nights to sleep, but you must get up and study.... He gave you children to bring you joy and gladness, and you send them out on twenty-six mile runs. Shame on your worthless head!... Twenty-six miles indeed! I think twice before I go that far in the car!⁴³

Further Resistance Down Under

Parr also relayed to Des some of the ongoing criticism—criticism that Parmenter had hoped would peter out when Des left Australia. It was relentless. Whenever a General Conference official visited Australia and gave ear to it, the detractors were further encouraged.

Walter Scragg, Sr., lamented that White's *Great Controversy* was being "pushed aside," when in the same stroke of the pen he said, "Sis[ter] White was not infallible." Did he want White to be upgraded or downgraded? His position seemed inconsistent. And his stand on White's fallibility was not shared by his fellow critics. Arthur Jacobson, however, echoed Scragg in some respects, calling for a renewed preaching of the anti-Catholic sentiments in Great Controversy.⁴⁴

The poison pen of Raglan Marks never ran dry. He wailed to Des:

> Get back to the plain straightforward books printed by this people [SDAs]. Forget the so-called scholars and great scholars and commentators and the like who have always rejected God's message and many of whom are out-and-out Liberals and Modernists, Roman Catholics and Plymouth Brethren, and even thinly veiled agnostics. And what do you produce? A lot of confused, wearisome nonsense.⁴⁵

It was difficult to spot one scintilla of Christianity in this sectarian diatribe. The letter served to demonstrate that Marks himself probably had never read anything apart from his own denominational literature. And he addressed but little of substance in Des's writing, indicating that he had only a slender grasp of the theology under discussion. He may even have had difficulties defining some of the terms he used, such as "Liberals" and "Modernists." All he could manage was pejorative language and name calling.

Llewellyn Jones was less vitriolic, but still persisted with his absurd claim that Des was a Futurist and that he had absorbed it from F. F. Bruce.⁴⁶ Alfred Jorgensen published a defense of Des in this regard,⁴⁷ his hand being mightily strengthened by a letter from Bruce himself who categorically denied that Des and he were Futurists.⁴⁸

Frank Breaden continued with Robert 's early masthead, "Complete victory over sin is possible."⁴⁹ Pastor Austin Cooke agreed, preaching in a Sydney service:

While it may be true that we might only partially keep God's commandments now, as we grow in grace we will come to the place where we will literally keep them, by the close of probation....

Righteousness from Christ is imparted to us through the Holy Spirit, imparted to us—it's not our own, it comes from without, it's implanted within.[50]

Cooke then denied he was Roman Catholic! Apparently unaware of the phraseology of the Councils of Trent he did, however, echo those sentiments.

Colin Standish visited Australia from America in the southern summer of 1978/79. It was during that time that George Burnside and James Kent were banned from preaching because they were becoming so strident in their denunciations of officialdom.[51] They still wanted Des axed. The ban was quickly lifted due to pressure from the other critics. This vacillation by Parmenter only encouraged Standish. He came well informed of the American situation, where there was a developing polarization. His tactic was clearly to enlist the help of his friends in General Conference circles and thus bring further pressure to bear on Parmenter to act against Des and Avondale College.[52]

On Sunday, February 11, 1979, a meeting of the mossbacks from all over the eastern states of Australia convened at Turramurra, suburban Sydney. They drafted sixteen resolutions covering every contentious topic—the age of the earth, the attitude to White's writings, the nature of sin, the nature of man, the nature of Christ, the heavenly sanctuary, justification and sanctification. They called on the General Conference to review the doctrinal situation in Australia.[53] Parmenter and Jorgensen, both of whom Standish believed were in league with Des, were being set up for a "Please Explain" from the General Conference. Standish dutifully delivered the document of resolutions to church headquarters in America. Jorgensen was unruffled because he was soon to retire, but Parmenter began to buckle.

The move was a tad hypocritical. At the time Colin Standish was actively promoting a college of his own design. It was to be separate from denominational control, non-accredited, and with the aim of returning, he said, to White's "blueprint" or model training institution.[54] (He had wanted to move Columbia Union College into a rural "blueprint" situation but met with stiff opposition from his board). The inference, of course, was that much of the SDA educational system that employed him had degenerated into apostasy, both by its methodology and its teachings.

Parr, with his usual astuteness, reported at the time what he thought of the Standish twins: "They were, if you understand, with us but not of us. However, they bounded about, glad handing everybody, and giving the impression that they were in no doubt about the fact that they were the benefactors of the human race."[55]

Colin returned to Australia again in November 1979, addressing a layman's convention in co-operation with Burnside.[56] Signs of a Standish splinter group emerging were then more evident. Egotism and dogmatism prevailed at the convention. Colin endeavored to woo the SDA constituency to accept his leadership as opposed to the Australasian Division and drove a wedge between American and Australian church officials. His group continued to disguise the source of much of their divisive literature. They held meetings at the same time as regular SDA services and collected offerings that were not passed into regular church channels.[57] Before long they were conducting their own camp meetings, and the rift grew wider.

Some Agitation in America

In America Ford's critics were found in isolated pockets and were not marshaled under one banner, unlike Australia. Ralph Larsen at Loma Linda Campus Hill church was known to preach the sinful nature of Christ, deliberately contradicting Heppenstall and Ford.[58]

Paradise Church, near PUC, was perhaps the most sharply polarized group at the time. Some members had paid for Russell Standish to travel from Australia to address them, but their conference president put a stop to it. Des was also invited to speak at Paradise, but on learning of the divided nature of the congregation he chose to decline the offer, not willing to inflame the situation.[59]

A lady in Canada became upset about Des and what she termed "the new orthodoxy" at PUC. Challenging Cassell she asked, "Is there any assurance that PUC is going to purge itself from any and all faculty members who oppose what I choose to call historic Adventism, or which I might define by saying that which the *Review* upholds?"[60]

Cassell made a good defense, concluding with these words: "If you have a complaint against Dr. Ford, Mrs. Rabuka, I would suggest you follow the biblical injunction in approaching Dr. Ford directly in an effort to better understand his theology, and to become better acquainted with a man who, in my opinion, is a dedicated Seventh-day Adventist minister of the gospel."[61]

The real source of opposition to the preaching of righteousness by faith still lay at headquarters. Parr received a copy of a letter sent by Larsen to Ormond Anderson in Australia, which allegedly told of how Wood and Hackett, during a visit to Larsen's church, vowed "that the Ministry [editor Spangler, specifically] was going to be straightened out," and that Des was "going to be taken care of also."[62] The knives were out and sharpened, waiting for the opportunity. Perfectionism, some believed, had to be preserved at any cost.

Vital Support Withdrawn

In Australia Parmenter did little to counter the critics. There were tell-tale phrases in his letters, indicating he was in accord with their theology. He spoke of the "purified remnant of God," "the victorious life of obedience," "the imparted righteousness of Christ" and the Christians decided ability to keep God's law.[63] These were the shibboleths of perfectionism. There was no evidence that his understanding approximated the apostolic gospel, unlike that of his two predecessors, Frame and Naden.

In his letters Parmenter also passed on to Des the critics' complaints, as if he were chiding him. For example, in mid-1978 Parmenter complained that tapes of Des's sermons were being freely circulated in Australia. Des responded, "There is no copyright on talks given by Adventist ministers, and anybody can reproduce them. PUC church tape library has sent out thousands of my talks to folks in distant countries as well as America."[64]

Parmenter also whined about an allegation that only one Australian (Parr) was involved in the editing process of the Daniel commentary. In actual fact there were four Australians who assisted with the draft manuscript. He quibbled, too, about Gill's *Soteriological Implications*, finding a place in Avondale's library when it hadn't been vetted by church censors. Des reminded him that there were "thousands of books in that library never scrutinized by religious censors." Furthermore, Des said, the contents of Gill's tome had found favor at Andrews University and had been reprinted in America and England.[65]

The very fact that Parmenter raised these issues with Des indicated that he had no answers of his own to give to the critics when they blew in his ear. Or was he compiling a rationalization to keep Des overseas?

Des was into his second year at PUC when Parmenter fired his torpedo. He wrote:

It is felt that it would be best for you to continue your service overseas for a longer period if this can be arranged. If not, we may need to study the possibility of using you in evangelism or pastoral work for a period of time.[66]

Clearly, the promise of "a two-year period, commencing mid-1977," was an empty one. Parmenter was not going to honor the actions voted by the Avondale College Board and the Division Executive Committee.[67]

Parmenter, at the time, was critical of the "controversial and aggressive" manner, the "methodology" in which Des preached the gospel. He also complained of Des using Professor Bruce to write the preface to Daniel, believing it strengthened the allegations that Des was a Futurist. And he began to warn Des to distance himself from Brinsmead. He became increasingly insistent about the need for "a clear and forthright statement" from Des, denouncing Brinsmead in the Record or Review.[68] Des found it difficult to denounce his enemies and impossible to damn a preacher of the gospel like Brinsmead.

The hearts of both Des and Gill were broken by Parmenter's letter. They wrote impassioned defenses. Gill first told Parmenter, "We already knew that you did not want us to return. I had spoken to Dr. Cassell and knew you had made an official request for us to stay here another year."[69] Gill rehearsed some of the rumors, the absurd accusations, the lies made about Des and then remarked:

My surprise is that intelligent people, once knowing the caliber of the attack and the attackers, even listen.... Why does what they say have such power to damn?... Why does administration take so much notice?... It seems that wrong is going to triumph.[70]

Des was justifiably hurt by Parmenter's criticism of his method of preaching the gospel and replied:

To come to your conclusions before hearing the accused is somewhat surprising. Did you ask men who had heard me take a series of meetings or men who had responded on the basis of gossip? Are you prepared to take a step of some magnitude on the ground of unfair accusation which has never been thoroughly sifted? Did you, for example, inquire of Duncan Eva, J. R. Spangler, or any of the presidents who had actually been in my meetings?[71]

Des listed some of the American conference presidents who had spoken favorably of his gospel sermons. None of them had interpreted them as "controversial" or "aggressive." He continued:

You also blame me because the fruitage of witnessing for Christ is not evident in the North American Division, as though the ripple of the presence of one speaker, [myself], for a year could be intended to reverse the legalistic thrust of a century! I cannot believe you are serious. Please note E. G. W[hite] says the reason for the paucity of converts is that justification is not preached enough. As you think on the evangelistic results in Australia, could this statement have some relevance?[72]

Parr knew that the accusation of a Ford-Brinsmead collusion weighed heavily with Parmenter and so he, too, cautioned Des to be very careful not to do anything that might strengthen the allegations. (Des had merely said he admired Brinsmead because he had the courage to say he was wrong when preaching perfectionism.)[73]

Having all the criticisms in mind, Magnusson also gave this advice to Des at the end of 1978: "Nobody who knows you like we do could stick any of those pins in, but you have some enemies who would do it happily, and you may have to give up jogging as an exercise in favor of bending over backwards."[74]

At the same time, Parmenter was talking of Des staying not just one extra year but "at least another two years."[75] Young, in Avondale's theology department, noted what was happening around him and became apprehensive, witnessing the erosion of all the promises made to Des in 1977. He confided in Des, saying he thought the promise of remaining head of the Avondale theology department while at PUC was effectively dead in the water.[76] By early 1979 plans were already afoot to appoint another head [Arthur Ferch]. Parr, too, was predicting that Des would never return to Avondale.[77] He could read Parmenter's mind.

Some sought clarification when the rumors began to fly among Australian ministers that the original terms of the PUC stint were nullified. Max Hatton, a minister in Sydney, was deeply upset by the "un-Christian attitude" of the critics and wrote to Parmenter asking, "Is it true "that the Division had told Des he cannot return to Avondale College?"[78]

Parmenter used the ploy of rewording the question so he could deny it. The rumor "that Des Ford will not be allowed back to the Australasian Division or Avondale College ... is completely untrue," he replied. Parmenter changed the question a second time, concluding with the words, "The rumor that he [Des] will never be allowed back to Avondale College is false." (Emphases supplied).[79]

Parmenter's request for Des to stay beyond the usual two years had placed Cassell in a dilemma because he had already allocated his staffing for the upcoming year. Having Des as an extra was going to place a strain on their budget. Cassell, therefore, asked Parmenter if the Australasian Division would provide two-thirds of Des's salary. Parmenter agreed to the proposal but wanted the payment disguised as a general payment to the PUC affiliation program. "Do so without making it so specifically for the support of Des," he requested.[80] Apparently, he wanted no critic to learn of the deal. Burnside and company, having detected a soft spine, were already twisting Parmenter's tail.

A Sojourner's Appraisal
As noted earlier, an Australian Anglican clergyman, Geoffrey Paxton, was intrigued by the SDA claim that saw themselves as the modern-day church still keeping alive the flame of the Protestant Reformation. As a research project he quizzed many SDA leaders in order to test the claim, especially in relation to the Reformation's foundations—Scripture alone (sola scriptura) and faith alone (sola fide).

When Paxton published his findings, *The Shaking of Adventism*, in 1977, and then barnstormed through Australia and America advertising the book, it was he who created a shaking of no small proportions. His thesis portrayed the SDA Church as one deep in Roman Catholicism on the fundamental doctrines of salvation and the authority of church tradition.

Paxton may be faulted for the fact that he went along with the traditional SDA view that *sola fide* was preached by Waggoner and Jones in 1888. And he gained a much more complimentary picture of White than other onlookers. But it was the views of Pierson, Wilson, Wood, Douglass, Venden, Clifford, Gane and the Standish twins that led him to declare that Adventism had cozied up to Catholicism. He singled out Gane as the one who gave the "clearest expression" of Roman

Catholicism.[81]

His assessment could not be taken lightly for he had no axe to grind, no personal animus against any of those he dubbed perfectionists. His educated judgment was reasonably objective. With reference to the tenor of the 1970s he summarized:

> This is perfectionism with unprecedented intensity. Never before in the history of Adventism has it received so much stress and such explicit expression. Naturally enough, the corresponding sinful nature of Christ motif and the denial of original sin are also given unrestrained expression.[82]

On the other hand, Paxton pictured Des as a significant gospel voice within the SDA Church. "Ford has set his face against the perfectionism of contemporary Adventism," he declared, "as being a false gospel which is inimical to the movements goal of finishing the work of an arrested Reformation."[83]

On Brinsmead he placed a similar stamp of approval, saying:

> From outside official Adventism Robert Brinsmead exercises a marked influence within Adventism against the perfectionist teaching....
> Brinsmead has made it clear that perfectionism is unbiblical and contrary to the sound testimony of Reformation Protestantism.[84]

Understandably, Paxton's thesis angered church officials. It also evoked diverse book reviews. Hans LaRondelle chose to disagree with Paxton's definition of Reformation gospel, seeming to prefer Calvin's idea of the indwelling Christ that "transformed by the Holy Spirit unto willing obedience to all God's revealed will."[85] This in itself gave the impression that La Rondelle had abdicated from his anti-perfectionism stand, but that was not the case.

Herbert Douglass, in his review, reiterated the traditional SDA perfectionism, thus giving credence to Paxton's claims. Douglass considered that Venden, Wood, Pierson and Wilson were not perfectionists "but they do believe that by God's help men and women can live without sinning"[86]—a paradox invented in order to dodge the truth.

Johnsson's thrusts against Paxton were easily parried. In his review he complained that Paxton misunderstood the SDA claim about being heirs of the Reformation, because it did not hinge on justification by faith but, instead, on sola scriptura.[87] But if it did not hinge on justification by faith, then Adventism had missed much of the import of the Reformation! Furthermore, to imply that Adventism was a paragon of virtue with respect to sola scriptura denied the truth about Adventism's heavy dependence on Ellen White's writings and church tradition.

"Paxton's portrayal of the Reformation," Johnsson continued, "is oversimplified" because he does not consider Roman Catholic sacramentalism and their idea of merit.[88] But Johnsson himself was guilty of oversimplifying Paxton, whose thesis was not that Adventism was identical to Roman Catholicism, but rather that it was akin to it. Therefore, there was no need for Paxton to identify sacramentalism or the idea of merit in Adventism.

Johnsson also noted, "It is significant that the Wesleyan revival is ignored in his [Paxton's] book."[89] The complaint is based on the common SDA fallacy that John Wesley improved on the model of earlier reformers, when in fact Wesley muddied the gospel, especially sanctification, and Adventism inherited that confusion. Paxton, quite rightly so, compared Adventism to better reformers than Wesley.

Justification is a theme used almost exclusively only in Romans and Galatians, Johnsson argued further, therefore the concept does not command the importance Paxton gives it.[90] That charge was incredible. Johnsson, being a New Testament scholar, knew that the topic of justification is seminal to a great deal more than just Romans and Galatians. Titus 3:4–7, for example, is one of the most succinct gospel statements in the New Testament. If Johnsson were to apply his argument to the doctrine of the seventh-day Sabbath in the New Testament, he would have to make the unpalatable conclusion that it is one of the least important doctrines.

Paxton "has brought out the divergence of Adventist thinking concerning the gospel," Johnsson declared. "Perhaps this variety in itself is not a bad thing." Seeking to diminish Paxton's thesis he added, "there are pockets of agitation and disturbance but not the pervasive shaking suggested by this book."[91]

Cloistered in the Seminary, Johnsson may not have been aware of the extent of disquiet Paxton and Brinsmead were effecting. Eighteen years later Johnsson changed his mind. In his own book he deplored not just a shaking but a fragmenting of Adventism. And it was not just in

Australia, as he incorrectly thought it was in the 1970s, but in America too, and gospel issues were not excluded.[92]

Much more could be decried about Johnsson's important critique. What is so unbelievable about it is its overall negativity. If the truth is known, Johnsson's own theology was closer to Paxton's concept of the gospel than he ever was to the perfectionist's model of salvation. So why denigrate and belittle men like Paxton and Brinsmead who had forced the church to take a long and serious look at itself? Why would Johnsson join in the stoning of gospel preachers?

Ford, on the other hand, looked for what was positive in Paxton's book, mentioning a couple of quibbles but finding much that was true. Johnsson believed Heppenstall was the most significant antagonist of perfection in the 1970s, but Des pointed out it was Brinsmead who goaded Heppenstall to attack and therefore his influence was just as important, if not more so.[93]

In defense of Paxton, Des maintained Paxton was correct in apportioning the primacy in salvation to justification by faith rather than sanctification. He also understood Paxton to be comparing Adventism to the refined views of Luther, as found in the Formula of Concord and Luther's chief apologist, Martin Chemnitz. That benchmark is a valid one if Adventism is to be assessed as a movement in the Reformation line, especially an improvement on it, as the church claimed. Of the book in general Des wrote, "I suggest that we should confess its truth, and in so confessing smash the doctrinal and experiential barriers that cripple the progress of the [gospel] work."[94]

Parr later concurred in a private letter to Des:

> I regard Paxton … as a man who is holding up a mirror for us to see ourselves in, and we are too proud and too stupid and possibly too arrogant to appreciate what we are for what we are.... It is when we do not accept the criticisms of the outsider ... that we fall into disarray and are prone to preen ourselves on our virtues and our petty nobilities, while overlooking the warts on our noses.[95]

Overall, Des's critique was the most favorable. It positioned him, along with Paxton and Brinsmead, at the spear tip against SDA perfectionism. The distinct danger, of course, lay in the fact he was the only one of the three employed by the church. It also added to Parmenter's mindset that any friend of Brinsmead's was no friend of the church. For the sake of the gospel Des was courageous in the face of such high stakes. Others would not jeopardize their salaries for the truth they held in their hearts. Instead, they condemned the messengers—Brinsmead, Paxton and Ford. Parmenter was not happy with Ford regarding the publication of Paxton's book. Rumors were circulating that Ford had incited Paxton to write it and had had a hand in editing it. Once again, Parmenter believed a canard and challenged Des about it. Des flatly denied the rumors. Later, Brinsmead revealed it was he who did the editing.[96] Malicious rumor had confused Des with Brinsmead.

In April 1979, soon after Des had returned from the Library of Congress, he received a confidential note from John Brinsmead. His brother Robert, John said, was about to pour scorn on the SDA doctrines of the Investigative Judgment and the idea of an inerrant Ellen White. "Some attempt may be made to implicate yourself," he warned Des.[97]

About the same time John Brinsmead went to Parmenter with a similar report. He mailed the same message to Wilson. Robert's ploy, John alleged, was tied to Des's thinking.[98] Des's involvement with Robert Brinsmead's venture was mere supposition, but it appears that Parmenter was convinced of the worst, i.e., that Robert and Des were working in cahoots to smash some foundation stones of the church. Parmenter's estrangement from Des therefore intensified. The Standish twins sensed that they now had the full attention of Parmenter and his close associates. It was a formidable bloc. Parr read the signs. In desperation he forcefully wrote to Des:

> Russell and Colin Standish are not above underhanded means for achieving their purposes.... They are dedicated to getting rid of you, and they mean to do that, come hell and high water.... Setbacks only make them madder and more determined. Do not turn your back upon them while they are guests in your home. You may just feel cold steel between your shoulder blades.... Regard these fellows as you would a scorpion between your bedsheets.[99]

Brinsmead Shifts into Overdrive

As Robert Brinsmead circulated in America, he became increasingly aware that the professors at Andrews University Seminary were quietly dismissive of the Investigative Judgment doctrine, unique among SDAs. Other leading thinkers in the church, such as Raymond Cottrell and Don Neufeld, had already abandoned the idea.[100] Heppenstall, too, had said to Brinsmead, "Bob, who invented this terrible thing of [the] Investigative Judgment?"[101]

All agreed the biblical "last days" were upon them, that "the hour of judgment" had come, and that Christ had entered the heavenly Most Holy Place. The burning question was, "When?" The SDA pioneers had answered, "In 1844."[102] Brinsmead returned to the doctrine's genesis, an article by James White published in 1857. He found White had placed his own interpretation on four texts, 1 Peter 4:17,18; 1 Timothy 5:24; 1 Peter 4:5–7 and Acts 3:19, all of which refer to the apostolic era, not 1844.[103]

Further study convinced Brinsmead that "the time of the end" began in the days of the apostles (Acts 2:17; Hebrews 1:1,2; 9:26; 1 Peter 1:20). He also found the New Testament remnant motif applied first to the apostolic community (Acts 15:14–18; Romans 9:27–29; 11:1–5) and not necessarily restricted to SDAs after 1844.[104]

His close exegesis of Hebrews 9 and 10 also convinced him the cross was the complete fulfillment of Yom Kippur. The context, he realized, clearly spoke of Christ entering the Most Holy Place at His ascension, not in 1844. Surprisingly, he found support for his assertions in the *SDA Bible Commentary* and a paper written by Young at Avondale College.[105] Essentially, Brinsmead had arrived at the same conclusions as Robert Greive in the 1950s and William Fletcher in the 1930s.

Finally, Brinsmead declared that the judgment, spoken of by Daniel, was interpreted by the New Testament writers to have already begun in their days and for that reason they used the present tense. (1 Peter 4:7; Revelation 14:6, 7).[106]

This accumulation of evidence forced Brinsmead to the conclusion that the Investigative Judgment was not scriptural and both Ellen and James White, along with a long list of SDA leaders, were quite wrong to manufacture and promote the tenet.

Back in the 1950s, while college students, Des had told Brinsmead that the Day of Atonement was fulfilled at the cross.[107] Des held to that belief, but at the same time wanted to find strong arguments to support the Investigative Judgment. For two decades he tried to see his way clear, but in early 1979 he experienced the conviction that it was an impossible task. Brinsmead had taken twenty years to reach the same conclusions, and because he was independent of the church, he could afford to publish his misgivings. Des, on the other hand, was reluctant to broach the subject. His battle was still with perfectionism. He didn't want to open a second front.[108] Nevertheless, over the next few months circumstances converged that pressured him to address the issues Brinsmead was airing.

End Notes

1   Gillian Ford, interviewed by Trevor Lloyd at Cooranbong, Jan 6, 1997; Fred Veltman, interviewed by Trevor Lloyd at Sydney, Nov 5, 1999.
2   John Cassell, Jr., to Trevor Lloyd, Jan 1, 1999.
3   Academic Load Assignment Form, Curriculum and Academic Efficiency Committee, [PUC], May 30, 1978.
4   *Campus Chronicle,* PUC, March 9, 1978, p. 1; James Scott, Associate Academic Dean, PUC, Teacher Evaluation Results, Feb 14, 1979.
5   Cassell to Lloyd, Jan 1, 1999.
6   Week of Prayer leaflet, PUC, Oct 25,1977; Veltman, interviewed by Lloyd, Nov 5, 1999.
7   Cassell to Lloyd, Jan 1, 1999.
8   Academic Load Assignment Form, May 30, 1978.
9   "Week of Prayer to Begin," *The Collegian,* Walla Walla College, Jan 19, 1978, p. 5.
10 Desmond Ford, "Current Issues in Righteousness by Faith," sermons and lectures at Andrews University, transcript, Feb 10, 11, 1978.
11 Desmond Ford to Trevor and Ellen Lloyd, April 26, [1978].
12 Robert Parr to Desmond Ford, June 29, 1978; William Woodruff to Desmond Ford, Aug 22, 1979.
13 Tim Poirier, "Ford Says Christ is All-sufficient," *Lancastrian,* March 6, 1979, pp. 1, 2.
14 Cassell to Lloyd, Jan 1, 1999.
15 Desmond Ford, "A Hermeneutic for Daniel—The Apotelesmatic Principle," paper read at SBL Convention, New Orleans, Nov 1821, 1978; Veltman, interviewed by Lloyd, Nov 5, 1999.
16 William Johnsson, "The Interpretation of the Cultic Language of Hebrews," paper presented to BRI, Jan 1, 2, 1978.
17 Desmond Ford, interviewed by Trevor Lloyd at Sydney, March 12, 1995.
18 William Johnsson, "The Significance of the Day of Atonement Allusions in the Book of Hebrews," paper presented to BRI, Jan

17–21, 1979.

19 Cassell to Lloyd, Jan 1, 1999.

20 Veltman, interviewed by Lloyd, Nov 5, 1999.

21 Cassell to Lloyd, Jan 1, 20, 1999.

22 Desmond Ford, interviewed by Trevor Lloyd at Caloundra, Jan 7, 2001.

23 Edward Heppenstall to Erwin Gane, Aug 28, 1978.

24 Gillian Ford, interviewed by Lloyd, Jan 6, 1997.

25 Morris Venden, "Obedience of Faith," sermon transcript, [ca. 1979].

26 Desmond Ford to Morris Venden, [ca. 1979].

27 Cassell to Lloyd, Jan 1, 1999.

28 Desmond Ford, *Answers on the Way,* (Mountain View, California: Pacific Press Publishing Association, 1977).

29 Ford, interviewed by Lloyd, March 12, 1995.

30 Duncan Eva to Desmond Ford, Oct 15, 1976; Richard Coffen to Duncan Eva, Feb 23, 1978.

31 Robert Parr to Richard Coffen, Feb 9, [1978]; Desmond Ford to Keith Parmenter, June 19, 1978.

32 Richard Coffen et al., "Daniel Discussed," AR, Aug 20, 1979, p. 14

33 F. F. Bruce to Desmond Ford, May 30, 1978; Ford, interviewed by Lloyd, March 12, 1995.

34 *Ibid.*

35 Coffen, *AR,* Aug 20, 1979, p. 13.

36 V[ern] Heise, "Books Across My Desk," AR, Aug 20, 1979, p. 12.

37 Ibid.

38 Desmond Ford, "The Lamb is the Hinge," *Ministry,* May 1978, pp. 5-7

39 Ford, interviewed by Lloyd, March 12, 1995.

40 Gillian Ford, interviewed by Lloyd, Jan 6, 1997. Note: The three-volume publication was not issued until 1982.

41 Richard Coffen to Desmond and Gillian Ford, Oct 25, 1978.

42 Desmond Ford, Lesson Pamphlet manuscript, [ca. 1979]; Ford, interviewed by Lloyd, March 12, 1995.

43 Robert Parr to Desmond Ford, April 17, 1979.

44 Walter Scragg, Sr., to Desmond Ford, [ca. July 1978]; Arthur Jacobson to Duncan Eva, Feb 1, 1979.

45 Raglan Marks to Desmond Ford, Jan 25, 1979.

46 Llewelyn Jones to Keith Parmenter, Dec 12, 1978.

47 Alfred Jorgensen, "Some Comments and Observations on 'Dr. D.

Ford Versus E. G. White on the Vital Subject of the Man of Sin,"' unpublished paper, Nov 15, 1978.

48   F. F. Bruce to Alfred Jorgensen, Nov 25, 1978.

49   Frank Breaden, "The Traditional Seventh-day Adventist Platform on Righteousness by Faith," unpublished paper, April 1979.

50   Austin Cooke, "Is the Adventist Church in Danger?" sermon transcript, Sept 15, 1979.

51   Ken Bullock to Greater Sydney Conference Ministers, Dec 18, 1978.

52   Colin and Russell Standish, "The Crisis in the Adventist Church," Bangkok tapes, March 17, 1979.

53   Walter Hansen et al,, "Report of Meeting held February 11, 1979," transcript

54   Robert Parr to Desmond Ford, Jan 30, 1979.

55   *Ibid.*

56   "Faith Triumphant," program brochure, Nov 16–18, 1979.

57   Notes taken at the meetings by the author.

58   Ralph Larsen, "Who Needs Original Sin?" sermon transcript, [ca. 1978]; Ralph Larsen, "The Fraud of the Unfallen Nature," n p., [ca. 1978].

59   Cree Sandefur to Paradise SDA Church member, March 6, 1979; Philip Follett to Neal Wilson *et al,,* March 6, 1979.

60   Gladys Rabuka to PUC Administration, April 29, 1979.

61   John Cassell, Jr., to Gladys Rabuka, May 16, 1979.

62   Parr to Ford, April 17, 1979.

63   Keith Parmenter to Desmond Ford, June 27, Oct 30, 1978.

64   Keith Parmenter to Desmond Ford, June 12, 1978; Ford to Parmenter, June 19, 1978.

65   Parmenter to Ford, June 12, 1978; Ford to Parmenter, June 19, 1978.

66   Parmenter to Ford, Oct 30, 1978.

67   "Flashpoint," *AR,* May 2, 1977, p. 16.

68   Keith Parmenter to Desmond Ford, Oct 30,1978, Sept 6, 1979.

69   Gillian Ford to Keith Parmenter, [Nov 1978].

70   *Ibid.*

71   Desmond Ford to Keith Parmenter, Nov 3, 1978.

72   *Ibid.*

73   Robert Parr to Desmond Ford, Nov 30, 1978; Robert Parr to Desmond and Gillian Ford, Aug 28, 1978.

74 Eric Magnusson to Desmond Ford, Dec 6, 1978.

75 Keith Parmenter to John Cassell, Jr., Dec 29, 1978.

76 Norman Young to Desmond and Gillian Ford, April 27, [1979].

77 Robert Parr to Desmond Ford, Sept 8, 1978.

78 Max Hatton to Keith Parmenter, Nov 28, 1978.

79 Keith Parmenter to Max Hatton, Dec 5, 1978.

80 John Cassell, Jr. to Keith Parmenter, Nov 30, 1978; Parmenter to Cassell, Dec 29, 1978.

81 Geoffrey Paxton, *The Shaking of Adventism,* (Wilmington, Delaware: Zenith Publishers, 1977), pp. 55, 140.

82 *Ibid.,* p. 144.

83 *Ibid.*

84 *Ibid.,* p. 145.

85 Hans LaRondelle, "Paxton and the Reformers*,"* *Spectrum* 9:3, July 1978, pp. 45-57.

86 Herbert Douglass, "Paxton's Misunderstanding of Adventism," *Spectrum* 9:3, July 1978, p. 34.

87 William Johnsson, "An Evaluation of The Shaking of Adventism, *Focus,* Spring 1979, p. 31.

88 *Ibid.*

89 *Ibid.,* p. 32.

90 *Ibid.,* p. 33.

91 *Ibid.,* pp. 34, 35.

92 William Johnsson, *The Fragmenting of Adventism,* (Boise, Idaho: Pacific Press Publishing Association, 1995), pp. 93, 94.

93 Desmond Ford, "The Truth of Paxton's Thesis," Spectrum 9:3, July 1978, p. 38.

94 Ibid., pp. 41, 43.

95 Parr to Ford, Nov 30, 1978.

96 Parmenter to Ford, June 12, 1978; Ford to Parmenter, June 19, 1978; Robert Brinsmead to Gillian Ford, Nov 17, 2005.

97 John Brinsmead to Desmond Ford, [ca. April 18, 1979].

98 John Brinsmead, interviewed by Trevor Lloyd at Duranbah, April 8, 1996; Claude Judd, interviewed by Trevor Lloyd at Wahroonga, ca. July 15, 1996.

99 Robert Parr to Desmond Ford, Oct 19, 1979.

100 Robert Brinsmead, 1844 Re-examined: Syllabus, (Fallbrook, California: IHI Press, [ca.1979], p. 9.

101 Robert Brinsmead, interviewed by Trevor Lloyd at Duranbah, April 18, 1996.

102   Brinsmead, "1844 Re-examined',' pp. 11, 12.
103   *Ibid.,* p. 87.
104   *Ibid.,* pp. 80, 81.
105   *Ibid.,* pp. 82–84.
106   *Ibid.,* p. 85.
107   Ford, interviewed by Lloyd, March 12, 1995.
108   Brinsmead, interviewed by Lloyd, April 18, 1996

Chapter Ten:
A Pivotal Course

Over the years, as Des had shepherded SDA churches and mingled with members at camp meetings, he became acutely aware that very few could say, "Praise the Lord, I'm saved." There was little sense of assurance for these Christians. It troubled him. He tried to focus his ministry on a remedy that would bring joy and gratitude into their hearts. One, like the grateful leper, readily expressed appreciation:

> I have been richly blessed by hearing your presentation of the gospel .... Our household and certain friends in the community with whom I have shared some of your tapes and who have experienced new joy from this "good news" would like to say, Thank you.[1]

Others did not respond in a similar manner. They seemed to be bound by the delusions of grandeur in perfectionism and remnancy. Their condition was grounded in two major misunderstandings. One was their interpretation of the doctrine of sanctification. They believed it entailed a lifetime process of good works, gradually becoming more righteous and more acceptable to God because of their law keeping. The emphasis was on what they did, not what Christ had done. Therefore, there was little objectivity or finality to what had to be done for personal salvation. Instead, for them the Christian life was a saga of sweaty palms and long nights of insomnia, forever pacing the floor wondering if they were good enough to be saved.

The second cause of uncertainty lay in the fabricated doctrine of the Investigative Judgment. In it lurked the danger that one's name could be raised without notice in the heavenly judgment and take a Christian unawares. The individual was always shadowed by the specter of doubt. "Would I be good enough if my name suddenly came up today?" dogged the trembling soul.

These two misunderstandings, of course, are closely related. Both radically lower the significance of Christ's part in salvation and lift the importance of human effort to impossible heights. The perfectionist's retort is that God's assistance is the key to attainment. That is, they claim, the indwelling Holy Spirit will empower the Christian to keep

God's law and reach perfection.

On the other hand, the apostolic gospel asserts that Christ alone is the Perfect One. It also declares that Christ's righteousness is accepted by the Father as totally sufficient. If then, the believer claims Christ's righteousness by faith for personal justification and sanctification, all uncertainty vanishes. The dread of God's judgment and the timing of God's judgment therefore have no sting or significance. The fact that Christ has been judged worthy means that those who remain as His can always bask in that worthiness. This trust is not grounded in presumption. Its rock is solidly based on faith in Christ alone. Any ethical behavior, any obedience to God's law, that transpires from that abiding trust arises from gratitude for salvation. It carries no merit for salvation, no righteousness that is added to Christ's perfection. This was the message that Des came to realize and preach. It found widespread acceptance in an SDA community nurtured on perfectionism.

To Speak or Not to Speak?
The teaching of perfectionism brought with it a lingering sense of frustration for some church members and an air of self-righteousness for those who believed they had virtually achieved the goal. However, the doctrine of the Investigative Judgment carried gloomy prospects for everyone. Members' minds wrestled with the teaching that the heavenly records of personal sins might militate against their salvation.

The difficulty of finding biblical evidence for the Investigative Judgment seems to recur in every generation of SDAs. Problems arise with mistaken concepts about the Jewish sanctuary services. Doubtful elements can be sourced to literalism and the use of Scripture out of context. Poor translation of Hebrew and Greek words also feature together with the excesses of Historicism. Wrong assumptions are piled one on top of the other to reach the height of dubious conclusions.

When, in 1979, Robert Brinsmead published his treatise *1844 Re-examined,* he unashamedly exposed the soft underbelly of this much-disputed SDA tenet. The book, together with Brinsmead's own promotion of it throughout America, touched a raw nerve within Adventism. The church community became quite divided over the issue. Wherever Des spoke he was bombarded with questions about it. He believed he did have some answers, but he was really placed in the unenviable position of trying to defend the indefensible. The debate was something he would rather have avoided publicly.[2] But because of the intense topical interest, he was asked to speak about it in a meeting sponsored by the Angwin Chapter of the Association of Adventist Forums. The group met regularly on the PUC campus.

Initially, Des refused the offer, knowing the topic was a hot potato. Colleagues who were members of the Forum committee, Adrian Zytkoskee and Wayne Judd, urged him to reconsider, pointing out that at Forum meetings there was academic freedom to express all viewpoints. Fred Veltman, chairman of the theology department, considered the topic to be a ticking timebomb and preferred that Des not address the Forum, sensing that the real danger would present itself during the question time.[3]

Veltman was one of the many academics who did not believe in the Investigative Judgment, and he considered resigning from his job over the doctrine at the time of Glacier View, but Des had persuaded him against the move.[4]

Des weighed his options. Speaking on tour he could face the incessant questioning from the pew and get into trouble with honest answers. He could beat around the bush and obfuscate, leaving listeners further in doubt. Or he could face the issue and offer his solutions for the SDA dilemma.

The context of the era lured him to accept Forum's offer. After decades of frustration waiting for officialdom to admit the problems of SDA exegesis and correct them, he realized they often had no resolve to do it or were ignorant of the situation. Some had apparently opted to shelve the issue, hoping that the doctrine would die a natural death in time. Others were content with the *status quo.* Hope of the doctrine withering away in a fundamentalist environment was fanciful. Despite silence from academics, many officials of the church were forever reinforcing and promoting the fallacy. No change of thought at either the administrative or even grass roots levels was ever going to take place, either suddenly or piecemeal.

Des also realized his vital support base at Australasian headquarters had vaporized. Keith Parmenter, apparently, had quashed the publication of his projected Sabbath School quarterly and did not want him back as a teacher at Avondale. Parmenter had capitulated. With hands in the air, he was being marched forward by the mossbacks. Des knew, too, that Neal Wilson was showing signs of believing black dispatches from the Australian critics.[5]

Furthermore, Des anticipated that the future publication of his commentary on Revelation, *Crisis,* would bring about his dismissal because it did not follow the traditional lines of Historicism. Fundamentalist critics would have a field day.

With all this in mind Des felt the request to address Forum might be his last opportunity to clearly outline the weaknesses of the Investigative Judgment doctrine and at the same time explain a more credible platform for prophetic interpretations.

It was a fact that Raymond Cottrell, another respected SDA scholar of long-standing who did not believe in the Investigative Judgment, had recently spoken on the topic at Andrews University (later repeated at Loma Linda). His audiences were largely composed of academics. He was forthright but what he said attracted no censure.[6]

The Critical Moment

The Forum meeting was scheduled for the Sabbath afternoon of October 27, 1979. Initially, the venue was advertised as PUC's music hall. Judging by previous Forum meetings, Des and others thought only a small crowd would attend. However, word rapidly spread far afield, and some drove from as far away as Paradise, which is four hours north of the campus. Many local SDAs, including conservative retired ministers living in the Angwin area, also flocked to hear the presentation. Brinsmead supporters were there too. At the last moment organizers switched the venue to the larger Irwin Hall chapel. Over one thousand people attended the meeting, some having to stand around the inside edges of the hall.

Des prefaced his address with some Ellen White quotes that advocated a healthy spirit of inquiry. He also noted that the Daniel Committee had been torn over the Investigative Judgment and many academics had abandoned the doctrine. He tried to pepper his remarks with positive statements, confessing his confidence in White and his belief that the SDA Church was raised up by God. The intent of the sanctuary doctrine, he concluded, was to focus attention on the perpetuity of God's law and the efficacy of Calvary's blood drops on the mercy seat. This gospel emphasis, he had preached, guaranteed the assurance of salvation despite the nagging condemnation of the law.[7]

It was his delineation of the insurmountable problems associated with the church's enunciation of the Investigative Judgment that electrified the audience. Many people had never imagined the enormity and complexity of the problems. (See Appendix A for more details on many of these problems).

First, Des bagged the year-day principle, rejecting it as a blunt tool for prophetic interpretation. He noted a recent *Review* article that admitted the principle could not be applied to all prophecies.[8]

He explained the SDA habit of taking Daniel 8:13 and 14 out of context when talking about the sins of saints defiling the heavenly sanctuary. The passage, he stressed, is really about a wicked power, the little horn, defiling the earthly sanctuary. The word "cleansed" (Daniel 8:14), he added, is a poor KJV translation and has no linguistic link to the description of the Day of Atonement service (Leviticus 16). Furthermore, the SDA idea that sacrificial blood was usually taken into the Hebrew holy place each day, defiling the sanctuary, was false, he asserted. Leviticus, he pointed out, repeatedly described how the blood was poured out daily at the altar of burnt offering, effecting atonement and cleansing rather than defiling. Only on the Day of Atonement was blood taken into the sanctuary proper, indeed into the most inner precincts. This, Des cited, was a major theme of the Book of Hebrews, i.e., Christ figuratively took Calvary's blood into the very presence of the Father as soon as He ascended to heaven.

White was quoted by Des to support these clear teachings of Scripture. One early SDA author, E. E. Andross, had also concluded Hebrews taught Jesus went into the inner precincts at His ascension, Des noted. But Andross, he observed, had then invented the theory that Jesus left the presence of God soon after so that He might re-enter in 1844.

This Book of Hebrews' perspective of the ascension, Des explained, underscored the New Testament view that "the last days" started in the first Christian century. He noted the *SDA Bible Commentary* on Revelation 1 took that view also. In other words, Christ could have returned at any time after His ascension, making irrelevant the SDA explanations of "the 1260 days" and "2300 days."

Des was well aware of White's explanation of the Investigative Judgment in *Great Controversy*, in addition to her entreaties to hold onto the views of the SDA pioneers. But he quoted statements from her hand that divested her of infallibility. Knowing the conservative nature of many of his listeners, he hammered away at the point:

Ellen White's role, my friends, is pastoral, not canonical....
Ellen White's not omniscient, not inerrant, neither is she a divine

commentary on the Scripture. And bang goes a very cherished heirloom.... She said, "The Bible is yet but dimly understood," and she didn't say in brackets, "But if you read all my writings that problem will be solved...."

She said, "When the books of Daniel and Revelation are better understood there will be a revival amongst us." We haven't had the revival yet. Apparently, they are not well understood, and she didn't interpret them for us.[9]

Des could have spoken for hours, detailing more weaknesses in SDA prophetic interpretations. His six or seven salient items were, however, enough to floor the Investigative Judgment. It lay comatose on the canvas.

Many conservatives in the audience were overwhelmed and apparently did not grasp the significance of an alternative view that Des offered. He spoke of the inaugural fulfillment of Old Testament passages and the view that prophecies would find a final consummative fulfillment at the end of time, as outlined chiefly in the book of Revelation. He explained the New Testament reinterpretation, in the context of a broken Hebrew covenant, that portrayed last day events as a worldwide repetition of the microcosm found in Christ's Passion Week. There was no place for an Investigative Judgment in his schemata.[10]

Syme Replies

Eric Syme, a fellow PUC lecturer, was given the right of reply, beginning with the comment:

> So much that Dr. Ford has said in this very eloquent and very lucid presentation I have been teaching myself.... The points that I actually disagree on, I think, are extremely minor and I don't feel that with ten minutes or fifteen minutes it's worthwhile even beginning to dwell on those points.[11]

Syme acknowledged the prevailing attitude to White's writings was a "stupid, literalistic miasma, which has made the Spirit of Prophecy something which it was never intended to be." He also agreed that the vital word "cleansed" in Daniel 8:14, was poorly translated. Des is not denying Adventism, he concluded, he is simply breaking away from "foolish literalism."[12]

Question time was most revealing. Typically, half of the responses wanted clarification about White rather than Scripture. One accused Des of using her too much, others appeared to be reluctant to let go of her apron strings.[13]

Initial Reactions

PUC president, John Cassell, was at Avondale College on business during the Forum talk. In Singapore, on his way home, a colleague who had already received a tape recording of the meeting shared it with him. Cassell agreed with much of what Des had said but suspected it could cause trouble in conservative ranks.[14]

In less than a week a copy was also in Edward Heppenstall's home. He had just listened to recent tapes made by the Standish twins. "I have never in my life listened to such distortions," he wrote to Richard Lesher at the BRI. After listening to Ford's Forum tape, he immediately dashed off a letter to Des, saying, "You express my convictions right down the line. I was worried some when you dealt with the inspiration of Ellen G White. You are bound to get negative reactions. I hope and pray that we have come to the time when these matters can be brought out into the open."[15]

Sure enough, when Ellen Whites grandson, Arthur, listened to the tape he was incensed. He wrote a fourteen-page diatribe against the Forum presentation.[16]

Arthur White drew on statements his grandmother made which laid claim to being led point by point into truth during the pioneering days of the SDA Church. He studiously avoided the words "canonicity" and "infallibility," but that was the position he clearly wanted to portray of his grandmother. "She does claim divine guidance, and she does not call for any corrections," he declared. Making an appeal for tradition he asserted, "What was truth then is truth today."[17] (It is equally true that what was error then is error today.)

The question, "Is the Investigative Judgment Scriptural? was never explored by Arthur White. His only question seemed to be, "How can I preserve my grandmother's popular image? He concluded:

It [the Forum meeting] robs Ellen G. White of her authority and integrity, and reduces *The Great Controversy* to a reflection of Adventist thinking a hundred years ago, with nothing to offer in these closing days of earth's history. All in all, it leaves the Spirit of Prophecy with little more value than good devotional reading.[18]

In the PUC neighborhood negative reactions gathered pace, especially among a few retired SDA ministers and, predictably, a covey surrounding Erwin Gane. They were all of a similar mindset—perfectionist and traditional. A tape was sent to General Conference officers. Des himself had to fulfill a speaking appointment at Andrews University but by the time he returned there was mounting pressure for Cassell and General Conference officials to calm the hullabaloo.

Cassell regretted the fact that the Forum meeting was not restricted to academics, especially men who knew the exegetical problems and either had the breadth of learning to grasp Des's remedies or be content with their own explanations. This type of academic freedom to explore new ideas was anathema to the traditional mold of the SDA ministers who listened to the Forum meeting.

The PUC Proposal

At first Cassell tried to restrict the criticisms to his own college campus. Veltman suggested Des briefly outline his views in a paper for the PUC theology faculty to discuss in a departmental caucus. But the scattering of tapes seeded the black clouds and brought a storm of protest.[19] Russell Standish wrote to Wilson, calling for action against Des. At the same time supporters of Des came forward to plead his case.[20]

Cassell resorted to Plan B. Des, he was persuaded, should have the opportunity to explain his views to a wider group of his academic peers, because he was perfectly qualified to do so, and many of them were saying similar things. Jack Cassell makes clear in his interview with Trevor Lloyd that PUC terminated Des's employment before he left for Washington D.C.[21]

After discussion with General Conference officials, the PUC Board decided on a four-point proposal. Des was told of the recommendation and expressed his satisfaction with it. He would be given a six-month leave of absence to go to Washington, D.C., and prepare a written thesis. He would be given access to the General Conference archives, the White Estate holdings, and resources at the BRI. An academic advisory committee of selected theologians from North American SDA colleges and universities would be appointed to counsel him during the preparation of the thesis. Finally, when the thesis was completed, it would be reviewed by a group of SDA theologians and administrators.[22]

Some faculty members at PUC sniffed the loss of academic freedom in the air. They formed a delegation and took their grievance to Cassell, expressing the view that handing the matter over to the General Conference was tantamount to losing control of the situation. Dealing with it in–house, they believed, was essential for damage control.[23] But Cassell felt the issues raised by Des were broader than PUC, affecting the entire church and the understanding of its mission.

On balance the decision seemed to be the honorable and equitable solution. Nevertheless, both Des and Gill felt the guillotine hung by a slender thread. Would Des receive a reprimand from headquarters? Would his thesis reactivate the Daniel Committee for further serious study of the problems? Did it spell the end of his church career? Was the stage set for a George Custer-like final stand at Little Bighorn with the Sioux chiefs, Sitting Bull and Crazy Horse, circling on horseback?

All things considered the PUC proposal was better for Des than for him to disappear quietly. It would give him an unprecedented opportunity to offer Seventh-day Adventism some credibility. Perhaps it would be a watershed experience, when the church would become truly Protestant, adhering strictly to sola scriptura to preach the apostolic gospel.

The church's craving for Pentecostal power had reached feverish levels in the 1970s. Many administrators thought it could be brought on by perfectionism. Instead, God's way now presented itself in a most unexpected fashion, as it often does. God took the shepherds by surprise. They would now be faced by some of the most momentous decisions made on behalf of the church.

End Notes

1   Levi Kuhn to Desmond Ford, Nov 22, 1979.
2   Desmond Ford to Neal Wilson, Dec 12, 1979.
3   Much of this chapter is based on John Cassell, Jr., to Trevor Lloyd, Jan 13, 1999; Desmond Ford, interviewed by Trevor Lloyd at Sydney, March 10, 1996, and at Caloundra, Jan 11, 2001; Gillian Ford, interviewed by Trevor Lloyd at Cooranbong, Jan 6, 1997; Fred Veltman, interviewed by Trevor Lloyd at Sydney, Nov 5, 1999.
4   Ford, interviewed by Lloyd, March 10, 1996.
5   Duncan Eva to Desmond Ford, March 5, 1979.
6   Note: In an undated letter to Trevor Lloyd, Raymond Cottrell later explained that he spoke from slides at Andrews University and did not have a script. He said he gave the same address at Loma Linda

from the same slides. The latter address is found in the unpublished manuscript, Raymond Cottrell, "1844, The Investigative Judgment, The Sanctuary;" transcript, Forum presentation, Loma Linda, Feb 8, 1980.

7   Desmond Ford and Eric Syme, "Investigative Judgment Forum," transcript, Oct 27, 1979.

8   Don Neufeld, "Bible Questions Answered," *Adventist Review,* April 5, 1979, p. 6.

9   Ford and Syme, Forum transcript, pp. 25, 28.

10   *Ibid.,* pp. 28, 29; Ford to Wilson, Dec 12, 1979.

11   Ford and Syme, Forum transcript, p. 30.

12   *Ibid.,* pp. 30, 36.

13   *Ibid.,* pp. 37–53.

14   John Cassell, Jr. to Trevor Lloyd, Jan 13, 1999.

15   Edward Heppenstall to Richard Lesher, Nov 2, 1979; Edward Heppenstall to Desmond Ford, Nov 3, 1979.

16   Arthur White, "Comments on the SDA Forum Presentation at Pacific Union College," unpublished paper, Nov 18, 1979, ACHR, Cooranbong, Australia.

17   *Ibid.,* pp. 7, 11.

18   *Ibid.,* p. 13.

19   Desmond and Gillian Ford, *The Adventist Crisis of Spiritual Identity*, (Newcastle, California, 1982), p. 25.

20   Russell Standish to Neal Wilson, Nov 26, 1979; Geri Lobdell to John Cassell, Jr. and Gordon Madgwick, Dec 3, 1979.

21   John W. Cassell Jr., to Trevor Lloyd in response to Lloyd interview question c.18: FAX, dated Jan 13, 1999: "The six-month writing assignment was our proposal and did not come from the GC. We proposed the following:
     1. Des would be terminated as a visiting PUC faculty member.
     2. He would be given a 6-month leave of absence and must
        move to Washington, D.C...."

22   PUC Board minutes, Dec 6, 1979.

23   "Board Votes on Fords Leave of Absence Today," *Campus Chronicle,* Dec 6, 1979, p. 3.

Chapter Eleven:
Momentous Decisions at Glacier View

It was tornado season at General Conference headquarters. Damage had already been inflicted when the Merikay Silver and Lorna Tobler industrial wages case turned against the church.[1] Threatening black clouds were swirling again in the skies above, whipped up by church financial scandals dubbed "The Davenport Affair." For a number of years, some North American church unions or conferences and leading administrators had been investing large sums of money in Donald Davenport's property developments with the promise of high interest returns. [Those who invested church funds were rewarded with higher interest on their own contributions.] Contrary to church policy, many of these investments or loans were not properly secured. When Davenport later filed for bankruptcy, it was estimated the church unions lost $21 million apart from other monies lost by church officials. The fiasco raised serious accusations of cavalier methods when handling church funds. It also pointed the finger at conflict-of-interest issues, because some church officials who had their own money in the scheme also sat on committees making decisions about church investments with Davenport.[2]

In addition, Spectrum magazine had published long-lost papers from the 1919 Bible Conference that cast doubts about Ellen White's inerrancy.[3] And Walter Rea's research uncovered compelling evidence of her prolific plagiarism, when she herself had apparently denied it, presenting another menacing vortex.[4] Church officials were beginning to board up the fragile glass tower they had erected under White. Their defense included prevarication. For example, the committee that was sent to California to examine Rea's research concluded honestly, "We recognize that Ellen White, in her writing, used various sources more extensively than we have previously believed." But Harold Calkins, a member of that same investigating group and president of the Southern California Conference, reported to his constituency, "The committee did not discover dependence upon other authors in the Spirit of Prophecy writings."[5]

The ongoing debate about White's authority caused one SDA

medical doctor to write to his friend, Richard Lesher, at the BRI, saying, "It is hard for me to believe that there has not been some sort of cover-up all these years." He was dismayed by the church's attacks on Rea. Linking the issue with the crisis surrounding Des, he went on the attack with these words:

> I consider Desmond Ford the consummate theologian in the Adventist Church today. I have seen continued efforts made to stifle, suppress, and thwart his teaching of the gospel of the forgiveness of sins. All the while the editors of the *Adventist Review* have been unrestrained in their presentation of an unbiblical view of righteousness by faith, sinless perfectionism, and our traditional position on the Investigative Judgment. I personally believe we need new editors for our general church paper.[6]

Church administration was clearly under pressure to hide the facts from church members in an age when communication channels were proliferating. The storm generated by the October 27 Forum meeting at PUC only added to headquarters' dilemma. Fully recognizing the situation, Des wrote to Neal Wilson in mid-December:

> This result of my attempt to pick up the pieces after R. D. B[rinsmead]'s Californian meetings was a surprise to me and a matter of deep regret....
> I apologize for unintentionally bringing this upon you....
> I will not be talking on the topic again until G[eneral] C[onference] has studied it in committee. This pledge I will keep.[7]

Wilson himself was well aware that many SDA Bible scholars had grave doubts about the veracity of the Investigative Judgment. For example, it is said that Leroy Froom, on his deathbed, had confided in Wilson, describing especially the problem that Hebrews 9 posed for the traditional SDA view. Wilson was also aware that Eric 149

had basically agreed with Des at the Forum meeting, and Raymond Cottrell had expressed similar views at Andrews University. Cottrell himself told Wilson that most of the biblical scholars were in harmony with Des. Fred Veltman, too, confessed to Wilson at Glacier View that he didn't believe the Investigative Judgment tenet, and Wilson is reported to have replied, "That's OK, but don't go public."[8]

When the controversy from the Forum meeting swept into Wilson's office, he took up the PUC proposal and began to plot his own strategy. A number of avenues were open to him. He could create an atmosphere favoring scholarly opinions, one of tolerance and further extensive study of the issues. He could defend the *status quo*. He could go on the offensive and fight for the fundamentalists. He chose something akin to the latter. As the saga unfolded, the weight of evidence pointed to a rationale that pressed for silencing the clarity of Des's anti-perfectionism, his view of a fallible Ellen White, and his interpretations of prophecy.

Ford Prepares His Thesis

Des left PUC for Washington on January 7, 1980.[9] Gill followed later in the month, leaving Luke with friends so that he could complete his school year with a minimum of interruption. In Washington they were housed in a cockroach-infested apartment on Flower Avenue, Takoma Park. Des was given some office space in a basement room at church headquarters.[10] He was among the first to arrive for work each day and applied himself diligently. A friend in California, Grethe Hartelius, had given him a large poster of a koala clinging to a tree branch. Des pinned it to the wall. Significantly, the words on the poster read, "Sometimes you have to go out on a limb."[11]

Wilson and top officials selected men to act as a consultancy for Des. The group of twelve became known as the Guiding Committee. They included: Fred Veltman, James Cox, William Johnsson, Richard Lesher, Gerhard Hasel, Fritz Guy, Kenneth Strand, Gerard Damsteegt, Duncan Eva, Robert Olson, Donald Yost, and Richard Hammill. Hammill, a General Conference vice president, acted as chairman.[12] From the start it was clear some names were padding. Lesher and Yost, for example, were not trained biblical scholars and could not be expected to have any significant input.

The members of this committee were as diverse in their thinking as the 1960s Daniel Committee who were disbanded because they could not reach agreement. It was impossible for Des to be constructively advised by them. Instead, it was inevitable that he would be pulled in all directions. Indeed, the three occasions when they met, April, May and June, were fiery at times. In one exchange an exasperated Johnsson is reported to have snapped at Damsteegt, "Be quiet. You're talking rubbish!"[13] (Damsteegt was the junior member of the team who seemed to think he knew a lot).

"I am not entirely pleased with what we did at the first session," Veltman admitted to Des.[14] Perhaps uppermost in his mind was the decision to tape the meetings. This move caused some scholars to clam up, too afraid to have incriminating evidence of their divergent views on permanent record. The tapes have never been released from the General Conference archives—if that is where they ended up. Their release for the sake of transparency and honest discussion is imperative, but it is more likely they will be marked "Top Secret" for many years.

Hammill requested arch conservative Hasel to present his views at one meeting on how sacrificial blood defiled the Hebrew sanctuary, recognizing that it was a key issue. After Hasel finished reading his prepared thesis, Hammill admitted, "You see, we haven't got much [evidence], have we?" On another occasion Hammill commented, "The more we chew on these problems, the bigger they become."[15]

Most members of the committee failed to make any critique of chapters as Des submitted them. Others caused despair for him because they could not bring themselves to comment on where they agreed. They simply picked at nits like typographical errors and, in one instance, a dangling participle.[16]

Johnsson was the most faithful. On one area of his expertise, the Book of Hebrews, he reported to Hammill:

> Des and I agree on what is the bottom line of the document. The disagreement is at the level of the parts and their relation to the whole, not over the whole itself. Further, Des has many scholars in support of his views—probably the majority, in fact.[17]

Despite his mixed messages later, Johnsson did not really change at heart. Guy, too, made some salient confessions. He admitted the use of the year-day principle rested on weak foundations. He decried the customary use of White's writings to establish doctrine. In fact, he identified this problem as the major hurdle in all SDA "theological methodology." Hammill, and even Wilson, agreed. Guy concluded by saying, "I want to make clear my conviction that Des's work is not a problem for the church at this time, but an opportunity for it to grow in its theological understanding."[18]

As Des worked on his thesis there were mixed omens in the Washington air. One of the most significant was the publication by the BRI titled, "The Dynamics of Salvation." It was the product of the

Righteousness by Faith Consultation, consisting of 145 members, who were given the mandate to formulate a statement on the doctrine of salvation in the wake of the Palmdale Conference. Des, together with Brinsmead and Paxton, had goaded church officials to declare their hand. It proved to be the most comprehensive and succinct statement on the topic issued by the church. Except for a couple of phrases, it was also the most Evangelical. Its greatest weakness was that it lacked the courage to declare a position on the nature of Christ. Nevertheless, it upheld and surpassed the Palmdale Statement. Perfectionism, under the auspices of Pierson in the 1970s, was dealt a powerful, but not fatal, blow. It appeared that the church was striding back to Protestantism. Having declared the apostolic gospel, perhaps it would exercise sola scriptura too.[19]

These outcomes were no cause for celebration among the traditionalists. They had reason to rally, put on their rusty armor, and ride out to combat foes both real and imaginary. They continued to joust with Rea.[20] They knew Des would soon come riding over the horizon, so they deliberately positioned the troops to their advantage.

Wilson was apparently aware of the academic climate. A majority of the Andrews University Seminary faculty had openly declared themselves to be in agreement with the basic positions Des had taken on the Investigative Judgment.[21] Hammill, presumably, would have informed him of the strong support Des had from some men on the Guiding Committee. Hammill may even have handed over a letter from Harry Lowe, a veteran Bible student and member of the earlier Daniel Committee who, confessed:

> There must be something needing study when these questions come with almost cyclic regularity. Since our small Daniel committee, I have asked myself whether I have been able over the years to teach, write, or preach a series of studies on our full sanctuary teachings without the help of Ellen White. I have to admit that I always have need of Ellen White quotations to prove some of the salient parts of the Investigative Judgment. If all the truths necessary for salvation are found in the Bible and the Bible only, one is left to wonder if a knowledge of the judgment-sanctuary details is essential for salvation.[22]

Wilson must have realized that Des could win the day by a majority of scholars. Or, perhaps, the scheduled colloquium would reach no agreement, as the Daniel Committee had experienced. Both of these options were apparently considered unacceptable. Wilson, therefore, arranged for a gathering where administrators would far outnumber the biblical scholars, guaranteeing a victory for tradition.

Wilson announced in July a colloquium that came to be known as the Sanctuary Review Committee. It was scheduled for August 10–15, 1980, at Glacier View Ranch, a summer youth campsite of the Colorado Conference. Up until that time, when the manuscript was completed, Des was under the impression he had been writing a thesis chiefly for biblical scholars.[23]

Des deserved better warning. Every writer needs to know his readership in order to cut his cloth to fit. An audience with a majority of non-biblical scholars called for brevity and no discussion of Hebrew and Greek nuances. As time would tell, about a third of the readership could be classed as real scholars. And in that group only a fraction were biblical scholars of various specialties. Considerably less than a baker's dozen were experts in apocalyptic prophecy, the area they were expected to assess.

PUC president, John Cassell, later commented, "The case against Des was stacked and already decided .... I am fully convinced that Neal Wilson ... intended to load the dice against Des Ford."[24]

Wilson also made no provision for Des to explain or defend his views at the upcoming meeting. He was well aware of Des's awesome debating skills and apparently wished to deprive him of that edge.

Furthermore, Wilson arranged for the Sanctuary Review Committee to meet immediately prior to a Theological Consultation at the same venue. Was this intended to hose down the inevitable tumult? Twelve scholars were asked to prepare papers for reading at this after-meeting.[25] These minds, together with a number asked to write papers for the Sanctuary Review Committee itself,[26] were thus preoccupied with the production of their own monographs. Delegates were swamped with some of these papers, most of which were merely peripheral to the thrust of Dess manuscript. In this manner Wilson effectively engaged many minds into charging downhill on unnecessary reconnaissance missions.

A rallying flag was essential for the battle, something tangible around which the troops could pledge allegiance with the cry, "Victory or death!" A committee was already operating that would serve Wilson's purpose in this regard—one rephrasing the elements of SDA beliefs.

They had a draft that was sent to the Seminary scholars who undertook a radical makeover. Their finished document was then sent out to executive committees throughout the world for revision. By the time it was voted in at the Dallas General Conference Session in April 1980 it bore little resemblance to the Seminary document. Many scholars did not agree with the product, especially with Article 23 on the sanctuary. The document was Adventist but not scholarly. Introducing the document at Dallas, Wilson boasted, "It should be clear that we are not adding anything nor are we deleting anything in terms of historic Adventist theology."[27] What, then, was the purpose of the extensive exercise? It seems Wilson's speech was a clear declaration of the *status quo.*

One significant change to Article 23 did, however, manage to sneak under the guard of administration—a phrase undoubtedly written by Seminary scholars. Previously the purpose of the Investigative Judgment was always stated as a sorting process to determine who would be saved. The new reworded statement, rightly or wrongly, declared the Investigative Judgment was to vindicate the justice of God. It is surprising that this change was not spotted, but perhaps administrators did not understand the subtle difference.

The 27 Fundamental Articles were adopted at Dallas, and Wilson was given the flag he basically wanted. With one or two exceptions few lessons were learned from past theological discussions. Scholarship, so dearly bought and nurtured by the church, was virtually cast aside. The frayed Nineteenth Century flag of Adventism was shaken out of its mothballs, given a few new threads and hoisted aloft. Prior to leaving for Glacier View Keith Parmenter, intimidated delegates at his Division Session, calling on them to stand in salutation of the 27 Fundamentals.[28] No one dared to remain seated. The creed had become more important than Scripture, and thus a vital element of early Adventism was abused.

How was Wilson to prepare his troops in the flanks? In collusion with Kenneth Wood and other colonels he allowed the publication of articles in the church press espousing views to counter Des. Prior to the Glacier View meetings, the Review carried about twenty articles, mainly editorials, specifically highlighting the usual arguments in support of the Investigative Judgment. There were frequent inferences of Satanic attacks disguised as new theology and appeals to hold fast to tradition.[29]

Wood published a series of leading articles in this vein by Lesher on Albion Ballenger, a convicted SDA heretic of the past.[30] It was like posting "Wanted: Dead or Alive" signs around the nation with Des's mug shot alongside Ballenger's.

An American group of ministers objected to Wood's prejudice. Wood responded sharply:

> This church is not in doubt concerning what it believes. For more than 100 years it has preached the doctrine of the heavenly sanctuary and the investigative judgment. This position is not on trial. Those who take a different position are on trial.... [Ford's] present leave of absence is not to help the church find new light but to give Dr. Ford opportunity to step back and see the danger to himself in the course that he is following.

In the same reply, Wood inferred that Des was a "wolf" and "the enemy."[31]

One astute student of church history at Andrews University complained to Lesher at the BRI that the church's official reply to Ballenger acknowledged that his interpretation of Hebrews was correct—the same interpretation held by Des. On the other hand, White's denunciation of Ballenger, he continued, arose from Ballenger's non-Christian views regarding the mediation of angels, in addition to his unorthodox teachings about the Melchizedek priesthood. It was inaccurate and dishonest, therefore, to insinuate that Ballenger's views were parallel to those of Des.[32] Another student commented about a similarly biased article in the Australasian Record, declaring it is "a typical example of how the actual content of the Bible in Hebrews 9 is obscured by not being able to get past the writings of Ellen G. White." In addition, Arthur Patrick of the Ellen White Research Centre at Avondale College privately challenged an inaccurate editorial by Parmenter that appeared to advocate originality and inerrancy for White.[33] However, these cries for balance and precision were met with stubborn rebuffs.

There is some evidence that General Conference officials shared inside information that Des was about to lose his license as a credentialed SDA minister. Neil Dower, for instance, is reported to have told Edward Heppenstall and a Puerto Rican minister of this prediction. Carl Henry is reported to have said the same to a young minister at the Fortuna camp meeting in California. Robert Olson is said to have shared similar sentiments while speaking to Yugoslav members in Europe. Charles D. Brooks and Ralph Thompson, while on a tour of duty in Australia, spoke in the same manner. And Arthur Delafield, in an unguarded moment with a taxi-driver en route to the Glacier View meeting, apparently forecast the same outcome.[34]

Just before, during, and immediately after Glacier View, an Australian student at Andrews University was doing research at General Conference headquarters. He was told the outcome of Glacier View was predetermined. "One of the presenters at that convocation," he revealed later, "described how the outcome was known before the group from Washington left the office, having been decided by a core of administrators before the meetings had convened."[35]

Luke, on completion of his school year in California, rejoined Des and Gill in Washington. When Gill arrived at the airport to travel to Colorado with 14-year-old Luke, she asked was it all right to bring him along? Neal Wilson said, "I'll leave it up to you, but his father is going to have a hard time!" Gill replied that Luke was old enough to understand what was going on."[36]

Back in Australia, even in remote Papua New Guinea, the rank and file spoke of a prejudged outcome for Des. They sensed something was wrong when Robert Parr, editor, and Eric Magnusson, college president, were relieved of their positions by Parmenter's executive committee just before the Glacier View meeting.[37] Neither of these two men were derelict in their duty. On the contrary, they were outstanding in their fields. Their only crime was support for Ford. Parmenter, therefore, already had a couple of skins nailed to his log cabin before arrival in America. The events surrounding Parmenter's two trophies were well known Down Under, and many feared Des would be his third skin.

Originally, General Conference officials selected about 106 delegates to attend at Glacier View. Hammill commented later that it was surprising how many people came forward pleading their case for inclusion.[38] By June 25 the number had risen to 120. The final figure was 125 but with absentees the actual head count turned out to be just over one hundred. Erwin Gane was one of the last to be given permission to attend.[39] He was in frequent contact with Wood, who was in a position to inform him of the mind of General Conference administration. Further, forty-five of his peers at PUC, who also suspected the prejudged outcome, had sent a telegram to Wilson pleading against the defrocking of Des.[40] Would Gane have bothered to attend if he believed Des was about to be exonerated?

Many were convinced the fate of Des was decided before Glacier View. There is no smoking gun. That probably lies off-limits in the bowels of the General Conference archives. But when all the dots are joined up, some top officials appear to be guilty. Some may dismiss the pointers as mere conspiracy theories, but in the light of the weighty circumstantial evidence it is hard not to take the cynical view. Wilson, it seems, marshaled the entire military in order to ambush one lone sharpshooter.

By the beginning of June, Des had completed the major draft of his manuscript. A period of typing and revision followed. It was, he said, "mainly an enlargement of materials in my Daniel commentary and the October 27 Forum meeting."[41]

Des and Gill took a brief beachside holiday in Florida, friends opening an apartment to them. Des was uncertain of what the result at Glacier View might be, writing to friends in Australia, "There is a good chance we could come home in September or October—but to what I know not." Maintaining his faith in Christ he paraphrased the psalmist with the words, "He still prepareth a table before us in the presence of our enemies."[42]

They returned from Florida to find a letter from Manchester University in their post box. It was a message from Des's professor friend, F. F. Bruce, encouraging them with these words: "As you contemplate the denominational enquiry this month no doubt you feel somewhat as Paul did when he wrote the first chapter of Philippians. We can pray at least that the outcome may be for the furtherance of the gospel, and also that both of you will be able to thank God for it."[43]

At Glacier View

Introducing the proceedings at Glacier View, Wilson deliberately stated that Des was not on trial[44]—Was this political speak for "I now declare the official trial of Des Ford open?"

During the morning sessions the delegates met in seven pre-arranged groups to discuss a portion of Des's thesis, verbalize their responses in a joint session, and a Steering Committee and Drafting Committee wrote a summary in a point-by-point consensus statement.

A brilliant job was done dividing the delegates into balanced groups. Ivan Blazen sat down with Erwin Gane in group one. Group two had Raymond Cottrell and James Cox in dialogue with Kenneth Wood and Jean Zürcher. Fred Veltman was allotted with Gerhard Hasel in group three. The fourth group contained Edward Heppenstall and Herbert Douglass from opposite ends of the perfection debate. Group five contained forward-thinking Fritz Guy and ultra-conservative Frank Holbrook. William Johnsson and William Murdoch found themselves among group six with Keith Parmenter and Arthur White. Group seven included shy theologian Hans LaRondelle and ambitious Athal Tolhurst.[45] This exercise illustrated that church officials were well aware of the theological stance of each delegate. The presence of an overwhelming majority of traditionalists was therefore no accident.

Des walked and talked with many of the men after meals. There was an ambience of friendship and good will.[46]

Wilson emphasized from the start of the gathering that the crucial point of discussion was the role of Ellen White in doctrinal matters.[47] Perhaps his statement could be construed to mean, "Were her writings to be dismissed when found to contradict Scripture? Or were they to be accepted above Scripture or as a reinterpretation of Scripture or as an addition to Scripture?" Wood aptly exhibited the traditional response when he said in his discussion group, "You can bury all the scholars if an inspired writer [like White] has spoken."[48] The question of Scriptural authority and White's authority had, however, already been decided at Dallas with only Scripture declared as "infallible." So, why did Wilson see the need for further discussion on the issue? Was he anxious to see the adopted principle applied at Glacier View? If that was his virtuous aim, he was to be sorely disappointed.

Lesher distributed a Cottrell quiz during the first session and a second poll was taken later in proceedings. The results spoke volumes. The exit poll showed 86 percent believed White's inspiration was equal to the biblical prophets, 89 percent believed none of her teachings contradict the Bible, and 92 percent were convinced her writings have the highest doctrinal authority. The delegates were asked, Is the concept of the Investigative Judgment supported by Scripture? Eighty-four percent answered, Yes. A similar percentage believed the year-day principle is biblical and that the cleansing of the heavenly sanctuary began in 1844.[49]

Apart from the majority views of the delegates there were a number of other factors that militated against an unprejudiced outcome for Des. Cottrell reported that one General Conference administrator had not read Des's manuscript because he already knew Des was a heretic. Cottrell confided to Des that most attendees, in fact, had not read the thesis. Veltman said no one in his group brought the thesis with them and neither was it discussed directly.[50] It was therefore a tall order for them to change their minds in only four days of hearings. The General

Conference promise to dispassionately study the document was not adequately fulfilled.

Furthermore, not all of the reporting from discussion groups truly reflected the majority view. Later, Cottrell, who was in the habit of recording everything in shorthand, related one example from his study group when twelve of the sixteen comments made about an issue favored Des. But when his group's secretary, a vice president of the General Conference, read out the group's report to the plenary session, he presented it as against Des. We are left wondering why Cottrell and other members of his group did not complain at the time and correct the wrong or appoint a different secretary. On the same discussion point Cottrell observed in the plenary session that eleven out of fifteen speeches that were made did agree with Des but the chairman, Wilson, took the consensus to be against Des.[51]

Administrators tended to sit toward the front and repeatedly expressed their agreement with choruses of Amens when points in favor of tradition were lodged. Scholars increasingly sought the rear seats, where they looked on in fearful silence.[52]

On Thursday afternoon Wilson played a late trump card. He arranged the reading of a letter from his predecessor, Robert Pierson, an absentee delegate. It was an eight-page appeal to stand by the traditional viewpoints. "Have the past generations of Seventh-day Adventists, and we today, all been duped?" Pierson pled.[53] That, of course, was a very real possibility, but he could not bring himself to admit error. He was uncompromising. He sought to blacken Des by associating his name with Dudley Canright and Albion Ballenger, demonstrating his ignorance of the real views of these men. He saw only the similarities and not the differences between Des's views and theirs. Des was offering a constructive solution to the problems in an effort to be loyal to the church, whereas Canright's and Ballenger's work were principally destructive.

Pierson also peppered his appeal with false accusations. The thesis put forward by Des, he alleged, attacked the nature of man and the nature of salvation—justification and sanctification. In this he betrayed his real animus. He wrongfully accused Des of teaching "cheap grace," "Calvinist predestination," "a new doctrine of original sin," "a life of spiritual defeat," and "lowered standards." Des had no opportunity to reply to these false accusations. These issues were not discussed in the thesis for Glacier View. These were the topics from the righteousness by faith versus perfectionism debate of the 1970s, in which Pierson and his comrades had fared badly. His wounds were apparently still ulcerous, and he wanted Des's gospel voice eliminated at any cost. His diatribe undoubtedly strengthened the resolve of the traditionalists. At this point Glacier View was no longer all about the Investigative Judgment and White's authority. Instead, it had become payback time for the gospel emphasis that Des had consistently manifested against perfectionism.

Wilson's ploy to read Pierson's letter was not even-handed. No other absentee's thoughts were read to the assembly, nor were they sought. There were a couple of absentees who could have raised the positive stakes for Des. Harry Lowe, a knowledgeable participant in the Daniel Committee of the 1950s, had written a favorable letter, but Wilson chose not to share it.[54] It suited Wilson to have someone of note like Pierson to air negatives, even slander and falsehood.

It was this prejudice that troubled the scholars from the start. Heppenstall, for one, tried to compensate. He went directly to Wilson at the beginning of Glacier View and asked, "Why isn't Des allowed to speak to the assembly? I came to hear this boy." Wilson gave an inch and allowed Des to answer questions in three late afternoon sessions.[55] Both Wilson and Parmenter then used these occasions to publicly attack him. "Why don't you listen to your peers?" Wilson angrily shot at Des on one occasion. The friendly face presented at the outset turned menacing, prompting one to remark after the meeting, "There is no hope." Another had walked out in tears. Others could not sleep well. Even young Luke, sitting alongside Gill, turned to her and said, "Boy, Elder Wilson rough rode dad."[56] Neither Wilson nor Parmenter demonstrated any inclination to learn anything from the discussions.

Every day a group of academics met clandestinely after lunch to work out ways to maximize biblical views of the issues,[57] as opposed to traditional arguments that were being espoused by a few hand-picked Bible teachers. It is clear from the minutes that some concerned scholars spoke up in favor of Des's views, but as time went on and administrators made critical comments, they grew quiet, sensing the promised immunity was phoney.[58]

Of an evening some close colleagues would meet with Des, trying to persuade him to be less polemical. They suggested he openly challenge the administrators to read his manuscript. After all, they said, those untrained in exegesis hardly understood the problems, let alone Des's suggested answers. Church officials were more interested in White's quotations than Scripture and doctrinal matters.[59]

Jack Provonsha, of Loma Linda University, sensed the hardening of opinions. The minutes record his saying that he believed Des was "more right than wrong." The church was like a tree, he said, dependent on its roots, but it could not remain merely roots. He related his own experience of changing his boyhood views passed on by his forefathers. He felt there were better ways of dealing with their differences. Badgering Des to resign and hand in his credentials, as Parmenter was doing, would not make the issues go away. He publicly asked Parmenter if he would work for healing. "The situation needs surgery," Parmenter countered. Provonsha suggested a better method would be to have Des agree not to discuss the Investigative Judgment until further study and reflection could take place. It was very brave, constructive diplomacy by Provonsha that went unheeded by administration.[60]

The final plenary session, Friday morning, was prefaced with remarks from Wilson, who confessed he found it difficult to know when to choose firmness as opposed to largesse, but that there was "a limit to kindness." Bert Haloviak, archivist, then asked that they seek the Lord's guidance and Grady Smoot, Andrews University president, led the assembly in prayer. Did they have the blessing Haloviak craved?

A lengthy oral reading of two Consensus Statements occupied the agenda for the morning session. After the reading of the first statement, one delegate asked for proceedings to be fast-tracked, because some had to leave by noon. Wilson called question on each page of the document and "assumed" there was agreement. After the reading of the second statement, regarding White's writings, "question was called on the whole statement." The minutes do not record that a formal vote was taken on either of the documents. Instead, they indicate Wilson assumed everyone consented. Des turned me and said, "This is great; I can live with this"). Shortly afterwards Des and Gill were asked to leave the room. In haste, Wilson then presented a third document, descriptive of ten points where Des appeared to diverge from the Dallas Statement of Fundamental Beliefs. The document was not circulated among the delegates, and they were not encouraged to comment on it or correct it. "More study needed to be done on the document," the minutes stated.

Delegates were taken by surprise with this alarming development. Veltman, sensing that all the hard work expended on the Consensus Statements was to be nullified, sprang to his feet, objecting to the fact that the Ten Point Statement pushed "beyond the Consensus Statement[s]." Dr. Louis Venden said the Sanctuary Committee had not "approved" the critique. Guy asked the leading question, "What authority does this document have?" He also asked, "Would orthodoxy be determined by the ten-point critique?"[61] Wilson fobbed them all off, saying, "It is the intention that study should continue. When you get the document you should react to it and let it be known where you disagree." That is, he conceded, its nature was tentative and certainly of minimal authority in comparison to the Consensus Statements.[62] Later, many interpreted his words to be a lie, because within hours he was using the Ten Point Statement as a criterion for Des's dismissal. Furthermore, within days it was printed in *Ministry*. Before it entered the public domain no one had a chance to "react to it" or to let it be known how they disagreed.

The Consensus Statements were a pot of goulash, everyone throwing in their own dime's worth of ingredients. When they came hot out of the oven there was something to tempt everyone's taste. The traditionalists savored morsels such as, "The year-day relationship can be Biblically supported" and "We believe that our historic interpretation of Daniel 8:14 is valid."[63]

Other major tidbits reflected views proposed by Des. These included:

a) The year-day principle "is not explicitly identified [in Scripture] as a principle of prophetic interpretation."

b) The New Testament does possess a "strong and widespread sense of the imminent second advent." Therefore, the New Testament does not anticipate fulfillments of Daniel's prophecies in the same way that SDAs interpret them.

c) The blood of sacrificial animals in the Hebrew services was a symbol of cleansing and purification of sin, not of defilement.

d) The biblical phrase "within the veil" is "the symbolic language of the Most Holy Place," not the Holy Place.

e) The word "cleansed" (Daniel 8:14 KJV) basically means made right, justified, vindicated, or restored.

f) There is "not a strong verbal link between this verse [Daniel 8:14] and the Day of Atonement ritual of Leviticus 16."

g) In Daniel 8 it is the little horns desecration of the sanctuary that "occasions the need for its restoration or purification," not the accumulation of sins of the people.

h) We are left with the subjective choice of determining when Ellen White is exegetically correct on Scripture passages, for "at times she employs Scripture homiletically."[64]

Cottrell's summation of the consensus said it was "internally inconsistent with itself, affirming opposite concepts out of both sides of its literary mouth."[65] The Glacier View colloquium, like the former Daniel Committee, tacitly admitted it had not resolved the serious problems that existed with some distinctive SDA doctrines. It would therefore have been wiser and fairer to defer judgment on Ford's weighty thesis. In time, the Consensus Statements were buried, as administrators gradually realized they contained remarkable agreement with Des on vital points.

The Ten Point Statement

Wilson and Parmenter showed no interest in the parallels between Des's thesis and the Consensus Statements. Perhaps they had little capacity to understand them. It seemed clear to many by the end of the meetings that the sole reason for the gathering was to find a pretext for firing Ford.

To achieve this Wilson, apparently acting without committee approval, had arranged at Glacier View for six delegates to write the synopsis of ten points where Des allegedly failed to meet traditional expectations or went beyond the Dallas Statement. Those writers were Robert Spangler, Herbert Douglass, Arthur Ferch, Norman Young, James Londis, and Raoul Dederen. These hapless men understood their task was to prepare something that would provide a basis for ongoing study and discussions. Young, one of Des's closest friends, was horrified when he later realized Wilson had duped them all, using their statements to sharpen his knife.[66] Hammill later commented that the Ten Point Statement "was a serious mistake in tactics" and "an affront to the members of the Sanctuary Review Committee."[67] He could say that because the Ten Point Statement contradicted the Consensus Statements in a number of areas. (See Appendix B for summaries and rebuttals of each point).

The grave overall weakness of the Ten Point Statement was that it had no provision for rebuttal. If the writers had been asked to weigh both sides of the arguments, the document would have been balanced and accurate. As it stood it was prejudiced, even unorthodox and dishonest in some respects. It should never have been used as an execution weapon. Wilson was a wily charmer, the "master of connivance," as Parr dubbed him.[68] Furthermore, he showed little capacity for equity. For example, SDA Bible teachers and administrators who taught and preached perfectionism were never confronted with the view of righteousness by faith found in the BRI document, "The Dynamics of Salvation," published in 1980. Instead, for six months Wilson and his henchmen worked at creating a climate for the conviction of Des, climaxing in a flawed ten-point document that had neither biblical evidence nor church endorsement. His claim that "there are no dictators at 6840 Eastern Avenue, Takoma Park [church headquarters]" looked extremely hollow.[69]

Des felt comfortable with the Consensus Statements. Sitting with Gill on the Friday morning at Glacier View as the documents were read out, Des whispered excitedly to her, "I can live with this." The fact that it incorporated some of his views was cause for celebration. Cottrell noted later, it did not prove Des's views were unscriptural and it did not prove the veracity of the traditional SDA interpretations.[70] When reports in the church press later that month trumpeted "Ford Document Studied: Variant Views Rejected,"[71] it could only have been a reference to the variant views found in the Ten Point Statement. To give the impression rejection referred to the Consensus Statements was disingenuous spin.

A voice from Down Under summed up the week's meetings in these words:

> Never once did I hear, in all the hoo-haa [uproar] about Glacier View, that truth would be the criterion. It was always the church and its unity that was the main consideration. While ever that is the thinking, God help us all. Glacier View will go down [in history] as an exercise in administrative infamy and prearranged skullduggery. NOTHING, but NOTHING, will convince me that the whole thing wasn't orchestrated in advance."[72]

Cottrell was just as blunt. "Glacier View was a farce;" he reflected later, "it never dealt with the real problems to which he [Des] was calling attention."[73] It was nothing more than a Pyrrhic victory for Wilson and his associates. By sinking Ford's end of the boat, they sank theirs too. All administrative credibility evaporated.

What further actions would SDA Church officials take to solve the twin dilemma of White's doctrinal authority and her endorsement of the Investigative Judgment theory? Would the next few years witness any bridging of the deep chasm between scholars and administrators? Ford's views seemed to have gained a mixed reception. As it was prior to the gathering at Glacier View, so it was at the meeting itself, with antagonists and supporters deeply divided. The news of Ford's fate was imminent and heralded a time of schism.

End Notes

1   Tom Dybdahl, "Court Verdict on Pacific Press Case," *Spectrum* 11:1, p. 14.

2   Kenneth Emmerson to Harold Calkins, April 10, 1979; Neal Wilson *et al.,* to Union Conference Presidents *et al.*, Aug 10, 1979; Tom Dybdahl, "Bad Business: The Davenport Affair," *Spectrum* 12:1, pp. 50–61.

3   Molleurus Couperus, "The Bible Conference of 1919," *Spectrum* 10:1, pp. 23–26.

4   Douglas Hackleman, "G. C. Committee Studies Ellen White's Sources," *Spectrum* 10:4, pp. 9–15.

5   [Harold Calkins], "Update from the President," *Pacific Union Recorder,* Feb 11, 1980, p. 2; Jerry Wiley to Harold Calkins, March 18, 1980.

6   Hershel Lamp to Richard Lesher, Feb 20, 1980.

7   Desmond Ford to Neal Wilson, Dec 12, 1979.

8   Desmond Ford, interviewed by Trevor Lloyd at Sydney, March 10, 1996.

9   "Dr. Ford Leaves for Washington, D.C.," *Campus Chronicle,* Jan 10, 1980, p. 4.

10 Gillian Ford, interviewed by Trevor Lloyd at Cooranbong, Jan 6, 1997.

11 Desmond Ford to Milton Hook, March 29, 2007.

12 Richard Hammill, *Pilgrimage,* (Berrien Springs, Michigan: Andrews University Press, 1992), p. 188.

13 Desmond Ford, interviewed by Trevor Lloyd at Caloundra, Jan 7, 2001.

14 Fred Veltman to Des and Gillian Ford, April 15, 1980.

15 Ford, interviewed by Lloyd, Jan 7, 2001.

16 Desmond Ford to Richard Hammill, April 2, 1980, in Desmond and Gillian Ford, *The Adventist Crisis of Spiritual Identity,* (Newcastle, California: Desmond Ford Publications, 1982), p. 30.

17 William Johnsson to Richard Hammill, March 19, 1980.

18 Fritz Guy to Richard Hammill, May 11, 1980; Richard Hammill, "Spirit of Prophecy Authority a Major Issue in Ford's Sanctuary Question," *Sligonian,* March 7, 1980, pp. 7–10.

19 Richard Lesher, ed., "Dynamics of Salvation," *Adventist Review,* July 31, 1980, pp. 3–8.

20 Neal Wilson to Walter Rea, July 2,1980; Harold Calkins to Walter Rea, July 10,1980; Walter Rea to Neal Wilson, July 28, 1980.

21 Graeme Loftus to John Godfrey, Feb 6, 1980.

22 Harry Lowe to Richard Hammill, July 28, 1980.

23 Neal Wilson, "Update on the Church's Doctrinal Discussions," *Adventist Review,* July 3,1980, p. 24.

24 John Cassell, Jr. to Trevor Lloyd, Jan 20, 1999.

25 Lawrence Geraty, "First Adventist Theological Consultation Between Administrators and Scholars," *Review and Herald,* Oct 16, 1980, pp. 15–17.

26 E.g., Raymond Cottrell, "A Hermeneutic for Daniel 8:14," unpublished paper, [1980]. Note: Some of these documents were listed in Ministry, October 1980, p. 23. Cottrell's document and two others (one by Alfred Jorgensen on W. W. Fletcher and another by Bert Haloviak on A. F. Ballenger) were not listed, apparently because they discussed unorthodox material.

27 Ron Taylor, "What, No Creed?" Sydney Adventist Forum transcript, Nov 1, 1980.

28 Ritchie Way to Milton Hook, Aug 11, 1980.

29 E.g., Kenneth Wood, "Satan Versus the Church," *Adventist Review,* Jan 24, 1980, p. 13.

30 Richard Lesher, "Landmark Truth Versus 'Specious Error,'" *Adventist Review,* March 6, 1980, pp. 4–7; Richard Lesher, "Truth Stands Forever," *Adventist Review,* March 13, 1980, pp. 6,7.

31 Kenneth Wood to SDA Ministers of the Philadelphian Area Ministerium, May 27, 1980

32 Gilbert Valentine to Richard Lesher, March 27, 1980.

33 Loftus to Godfrey, Feb 6, 1980; Arthur Patrick to Keith Parmenter, July 30, 1980; Keith Parmenter, "The Ellen G White 'Borrowings':— What are the Facts?" *Australasian Record,* July 28, 1980, p. 4.

34 Ford, Adventist Crisis of Spiritual Identity, 1982, p. 66.

35 John Waters to Barry Oliver, Aug 30, 2001.

36 Gillian Ford, interviewed by Lloyd, Jan 6,1997.

37 Robert Parr to Dean Jennings, July 17, 1980; Robert Parr to Desmond Ford, July 17, 1980; Way to Hook, Aug 11, 1980; Avondale College Board minutes, Aug 7, 1980.

38 Hammill, *Pilgrimage*, 1992, p. 191.

39 Note: Gane's name did not appear on the original list or on the revised list of June 25, 1980.

40 Eric Anderson et al. to Neal Wilson, Aug 7,1980; Cassell to Lloyd, Jan 20, 1999.

41 Desmond Ford to Trevor and Ellen Lloyd, July 4,1980.

42 Ibid.

43 Frederick Bruce to Desmond and Gillian Ford, Aug 8, 1980.

44 William Johnsson, "Overview of a Historic Meeting," *Adventist Review,* Sept 4, 1980, p. 6.

45 "Discussion Groups for the Sanctuary Review Committee," unpublished paper, Aug 10–15,1980.

46 Gillian Ford to Neal Wilson, Oct 27, 1980; Gillian Ford, interviewed by Lloyd, Jan 6, 1997.

47 "Sanctuary Review Committee Meeting, First Session," minutes, Aug 10, 1980.

48 Raymond Cottrell, "Group Dynamics at Glacier View," unpublished paper, [ca. 1986], p. 8.

49 "Sanctuary Review Committee, First Session," minutes, Aug 10, 1980

50 Ford, *Adventist Crisis of Spiritual Identity,* 1982, p. 67.

51 Cottrell, "Group Dynamics," [ca. 1986], p. 19.

52 [Gillian Ford], "Impressions of Glacier View," unpublished paper, [ca. 1982].

53 Robert Pierson, "An Appeal to the Sanctuary Review Committee," Aug 10–15, 1980; "Sanctuary Review Committee, Eighth Session," minutes, Aug 14, 1980.

54 Ford, *Adventist Crisis of Spiritual Identity,* 1982, p. 76.

55 Ford, interviewed by Lloyd, March 10, 1996; Gillian Ford, interviewed by Lloyd, Jan 6, 1997. Gillian Ford, 'Glacier View, My View,' Letters written from Glacier View to Marie Webber, 12 Aug 1980 (7 pp.)

56 Cottrell, "Group Dynamics," [ca. 1986], p. 7; Gillian Ford, "A Statement on Glacier View," unpublished paper, [ca. 1983].

57 Cottrell, "Group Dynamics," [ca. 1986], p. 9.

58 Compare "Sanctuary Review Committee, Second Session" with "Sanctuary Review Committee, Sixth Session," minutes, Aug 11, 13, 1980.

59 Cassell to Lloyd, Jan 20, 1999; Fred Veltman, interviewed by Trevor Lloyd at Sydney, Nov 5, 1999.

60 "Sanctuary Review Committee, Eighth Session," minutes, Aug 14, 1980.

61 Cottrell, "The Sanctuary Review Committee, *Spectrum,* vol. 11, No. 2, Nov 1980, p. 15, col. 2.

62 "Sanctuary Review Committee, Ninth Session," minutes, Aug 15, 1980.

63 "Christ in the Heavenly Sanctuary" and "The Role of Ellen G. White Writings in Doctrinal Matters," *Adventist Review,* Sept 4, 1980, pp. 12–15.

64 *Ibid.*

65 Cottrell, "Group Dynamics," [ca. 1986], p. 16.

66 Norman Young, interviewed by Trevor Lloyd at Cooranbong, April 24, 1997

67 Hammill, *Pilgrimage,* p. 194.

68 Robert Parr to Desmond Ford, Nov 9, 1983.

69 Neal Wilson, "Response to an Open Letter," Ministry, Feb 1980, p. 20.

70 Cottrell, "Group Dynamics," [ca. 1986], p. 12.

71 "Ford Document Studied; Variant Views Rejected," *Adventist Review,* Aug 28, 1980, p. 32.

72 Robert Parr to Desmond Ford, Sept 30, 1981, [ca. Nov 25, 1982].

73 Raymond Cottrell to Vern Heise, June 20, 1993.

Chapter Twelve:
Justice Brazenly Flouted

Many of the delegates at Glacier View were buoyant as they left for home on Friday afternoon. They took comfort in the Consensus Statements, understanding that some advances were made in the enunciation of the sanctuary doctrine. And the promise of further study and progress seemed real. Within hours their euphoria was dashed.[1]

Lunch over, the President's Executive Advisory Committee (PREXAD) and a few additional American administrators, together with Keith Parmenter and Arthur Duffy, ministerial secretary for the Australasian Division, met in consultation with Des. Gill joined Des an hour into the discussions. The American squad consisted of administrators Neal Wilson, Robert Spangler, Duncan Eva, Charles Bradford, Francis Wernick, Charles Hirsch, and Ralph .[2] (was one who allegedly prejudged Des.) There was not a single biblical scholar on this bench of judges. It was as if Des was called before the Supreme Court of Lilliput.

PREXAD was relatively uninterested in the Consensus Statements and their points of agreement with Des. When Des tried to explain some places of agreement, Wernick asked, "Are you saying the Consensus Statements move towards your position?" "Yes," said Des. "Well, if I'd known that I would have voted against them," Wernick retorted.[3] In other words he came to Glacier View with a closed mind, prepared to vote against anything favorable toward Des. It also appears Wernick didn't have a clue what was going on theologically, not understanding the nuances in the Consensus Statements.

Pressure was brought to bear on Des from several quarters. One PREXAD member even alleged that Edward Heppenstall thought Des had psychological problems (as if Heppenstall was qualified to assess that!). They claimed, too, that almost all scholars disagreed with Des.[4] That was manifestly untrue, as time would tell.

The Ten Point Statement was used as the pièce de resistance. The document had no consensus or official status, and Des reminded them that it had no evidence attached to it. Spangler chimed in with the promise that the evidence would appear in the forthcoming issue of

Ministry. Des asked if he could see the article before publication, and Spangler said, "Yes." Spangler failed to produce the evidence and did not show any articles to Des before going to press.[5] Furthermore, Des was taken off the mailing list for *Ministry* before it was published and so never received the published article. He had to borrow a copy.

Neal Wilson was also livid that Des had allowed Robert Brinsmead to distribute 50,000 of the tapes made of the Forum meeting. The committee was sorely embarrassed that the weaknesses of SDA viewpoints were getting a wide airing. Des reminded them that the tapes were not sent out on his initiative or with his permission.[6] General Conference administrators were obviously frustrated, because they had no control over Brinsmead. It seemed as if they wanted to arouse guilt in Des in order to enlist him in their endeavors to hobble Brinsmead. Or did they plan to make Des the fall guy because Brinsmead was untouchable?

Whatever the case might have been, they were in a hurry. There was no debriefing of the Glacier View meeting. They left no time for further study and meditation over the documents. There were no prayer sessions. They invited no biblical scholars into their deliberations. They acted precipitously. It appeared as if the PREXAD meeting was planned well beforehand and was indeed perfunctory.

Duffy insisted on the inerrancy of Ellen White's sanctuary doctrine. Ford apologized for his different view and four times offered to publicly enjoin others not to follow him. But the offer was ignored and Parmenter threw down his gauntlet, a letter prepared in his own hand listing four ultimatums. Under criticism later, he claimed he had discussed the substance with two or three others, including Wilson.[7] In the letter Parmenter demanded Des resign by surrendering his credentials if he did not act on the following:

a) Publish in the Review a statement confessing he was out of harmony with the Dallas creed.
b) Change his mind, say he was wrong, and teach and preach in harmony with the Dallas creed.
c) Publicly acknowledge the PUC Forum talk and his Glacier View thesis contained doctrine out of harmony with the pillars of Adventism.
d) Publish a denunciation of Brinsmead and cease to be associated with him.[8]

On conscience grounds Des could not agree to Parmenter's demands. Knowing that academia in general agreed with him, and realizing that the Consensus Statements made significant concessions toward his views, he was certainly not going to throw it all away. He would have to lie to make the public confessions asked of him, and continue to live the lie when preaching and teaching.

Furthermore, the thought of denouncing a fellow gospel advocate like Brinsmead was outrageous. Des found it impossible to speak evil of his enemies and could never say a word against a friend, even though he didn't agree with everything Brinsmead taught.

Wilson sensed that Parmenter's letter was a hasty move. He suggested that Des think about his reply for a couple of weeks.[9] Parmenter backed off and waited for a further opportunity to handcuff Ford, put him in a tumbrel and haul him to the guillotine.

Des declared that he did not need weeks to make a decision. He understood that Wilson's offer was death by a thousand drawing pins. He would, instead, accept the guillotine. He and Gill had prayed about matters beforehand. If the theological advances made at Glacier View were going to be swept under the carpet; if the Dallas Statement was going to be used as a creed; if tradition was going to prevail in preference to honest ongoing study of the problem issues; if Ellen White was going to be forever eulogized and canonized ad nauseam, then there was no point in a theologian lingering in the vestry. Des declared he could not accept the ultimatums, but he did not resign. Together with Gill he left the meeting, believing an executive vote of dismissal was inevitable.[10]

Some scholars who had remained behind for the Theological Consultation meetings heard of PREXAD's actions and Parmenter's demands. They were furious and notified friends. The single telephone at Glacier View became clogged with incoming protest calls for hours, people citing Wilson's now-empty promise that Des would not be tried. About fifty faculty and staff back at PUC sounded the red alert and signed a telegram to John Cassell, urging him to oppose PREXAD's move. It arrived in Cassel's hand at Glacier View before the weekend was over.[11]

Within hours news spread around the world. A Melbourne member rang Parmenter the following day, Saturday, and roasted him for his treatment of Des. Parmenter broke down and wept, realizing his isolation, having alienated a respected section of his constituency and at the same time being denied the immediate resignation of Des.[12]

Telegrams demanding Parmenter's resignation began to pile up, adding to his dilemma.[13]

Parmenter wrote a second letter, softening his ultimatums. He desperately wanted a signed promise from Des to take back to Australia, but he was frustrated further. Des, accepting Wilson's former advice, changed his mind about the guillotine and said he would consider this second letter from Parmenter.[14]

Des and Gill returned to Washington, Parmenter to Australia. In Washington Des wrote to Parmenter:

> Gladly I can both teach and preach in harmony with its [Consensus Statements] new direction and to the same extent as the majority of my fellow teachers present at Glacier View. To that end I pledge myself to seek that unity of spirit in the church for which Christ prayed in John 17. I am prepared to refrain from preaching on the sanctuary in any area that might bring perplexity while we all continue the study so well begun at Glacier View.[15]

Wilson persuaded Des not to mail this response, still advising that it was better to wait and properly assess the situation after a fortnight.[16] Wilson was shrewd. He could hear the shrill voices of protest rising from significant quarters. He knew PREXAD had hustled their decision, but he did not want to be seen in that poor light. He would rather, of course, be judged as patient and magnanimous.

On Sabbath, August 23, panels at Loma Linda University, Walla Walla College, Andrews University, and PUC gave reports to church members about Glacier View.[17] Different perceptions were expressed. Scholars were careful not to incriminate themselves.

The Australasian delegation made similar presentations back home the following week. Parmenter, in Sydney, skirted theology and spent most of his time explaining the protocol followed at Glacier View. Alwyn Salom, however, finding the courage that deserted him and others at Glacier View, explained to Adelaide ministers where the Consensus Statements agreed with Des.[18]

When Parmenter visited Papua New Guinea early in September he made the mistake of inviting ministers to quiz him about the Investigative Judgment. He quickly found himself out of his depth and promised to send a scholar. Dr. Arthur Ferch and Arthur Duffy were sent with a brief that, according to the local mission secretary, "closed the door to a free and frank discussion of the major issues." Parmenter had phoned the secretary in a torrid frame of mind, making it clear that his head office would frame the questions and supply the answers. But the ministers persisted with their questions. It came to the point where, in private, Ferch begged them not to embarrass him in Duffy's presence. Ferch wanted to give his own answers, but felt that he would lose his job if he was candid.[19] Parmenter's two emissaries were only stooges.

At an Avondale College meeting, both Parmenter and Athal Tolhurst met with the stiffest opposition, as expected. It appeared to at least one lecturer that Tolhurst's comments smacked of political grandstanding. Nevertheless, Tolhurst was met by some unflinching interrogation by faculty members and principal Eric Magnusson's wife, Nainie (Tolhurst's sister), a special invitee. Parmenter tried to shake off the lecturers by falsely claiming that sixty percent of the delegates at Glacier View were biblical scholars, and all were united against Des.[20] This attempt to portray those at Avondale as out of step with Adventist scholarship was a nefarious strategy.

Believing that the Glacier View manuscript yielded too much to the traditional view, Brinsmead wrote to Des:

> The whole 1844 doctrine is an exegetical monstrosity, an embarrassment to the church and unprovable from the Bible.... None has tried harder than you to reconcile the 1844 doctrine to the facts derived from sound biblical scholarship. But even your Herculean efforts cannot reconcile the 1844 theology to the New Testament gospel. This is no time to go on with a synthesis theology [a mix of the traditional SDA view and Des's suggested alternative put forward at Glacier View]. Only those with minds like Philadelphian lawyers will be able to follow the fancy double talk of a synthesis theology. Give me rather the apostolic gospel, which is clear and certain as well as final and all-sufficient.[21]

This letter may not have impacted on Des's mind at all. He was still optimistically looking forward to the church applying itself to more study of the doctrinal problems.

On Tuesday, August 26, Duncan Eva sat down with Ford to rewrite a response to Parmenter. Des's unsent letter was used as a basis, but important additions were made. These included an apology similar to the one Des had sent Wilson soon after the Forum meeting. Des also conceded that his solutions to the sanctuary doctrine "could be wrong." This took the sting out of accusations that Ford was inflexible. But he concluded by maintaining:

I cannot compromise in my understanding of the doctrinal issues. Inasmuch as the Adventist Review has now published to the church and the world acknowledgments of the accuracy of certain points of my sanctuary manuscript [in a postscript he listed the twelve points of agreement], to withdraw such would be to repudiate the Consensus Statements and bring confusion confounded.[22]

Wilson read this letter and telegrammed Parmenter:

I am not satisfied with his answers. He uses some very gracious words and makes some good statements primarily written for him by Eva. But he then makes so many disclaimers and leaves so many escape hatches, it really boils down to very inconclusive answers to your specific questions and the letter concludes by listing what he describes as twelve key points where he tries to show the church has come his direction. He avoids saying anything about two crucial matters in my judgment, namely the role of Ellen G White and his own relationship with Bob Brinsmead. I intend to take this matter to a full meeting of PREXAD next Tuesday.[23]

Parmenter wired back to Wilson before Des's letter reached him, reaffirming that unequivocal answers from Des were expected. I "would appreciate [a] written statement of advice from your [PREXAD] meeting," he concluded. Ron Taylor, Parmenter's executive secretary, also sent a message to Wilson with the information that he had received two unsigned letters from groups in Australia, pledging their support for Parmenter.[24] Such anonymous letters, in Taylor's estimation, were apparently regarded as strong evidence of widespread support for Australian leadership.

In Ford's absence PREXAD duly met and echoed Wilson's original response to his letter, claiming it contained "qualified answers, ambiguities, and reservations." They swept aside the advances made in the Consensus Statements, still insisting the Sanctuary Review Committee rejected Des's arguments and conclusions. They were unforgiving, too, because Des had advertised the weaknesses of the traditional views of the church and would not publicly denounce Brinsmead. This they interpreted as a serious failure to take counsel from administration. Taking the hard line, they virtually insisted Des surrender his conscience and be servile. They recommended Des resign. If he did not, then they would advise the Australasian Division to withdraw his ministerial credentials and dismiss him.[25]

Des did not resign. Wilson immediately wired Parmenter who, in turn, notified his executive committee of a meeting to deal with PREXAD's recommendation for dismissal. About the same time PREXAD scuttled an offer from the Northern European Division to employ Des as an evangelist in the New Gallery, London.[26]

Des, Gill, and Luke returned to California as messages of support for Des continued to flood in.[27] They heard that 140 church members met in Melbourne to register their dismay over the outcome of Glacier View. One Australian wrote six pages addressed to "Dr. Des Martin Luther." A married couple in Oregon telegraphed, "We praise God for your firm stand, your messages have brought hope and encouragement to us." Another American couple, an elder and deaconess who realized that church credibility had crumbled, resigned from church office.[28]

Wilson, justifiably, became a target. One likened him to Caiaphas.[29] Another found a parallel in Napoleon of Orwell's Animal Farm. In anguished tones he lamented:

> I thought that Seventh-day Adventism had grown up. I thought that we were tolerant and pluralistic enough to handle Ford. I could tolerate Herbert Douglass' perfectionism.... I could tolerate almost anything, just so long as we had sermons on the cross. And now you've axed the man who spearheaded the movement which brought Calvary into Seventh-day Adventism, the man who impressed me to stay with this church when I was young and ready to leave.[30]

Another alluded to the high-level lies, deceptions, and intrigue of Richard Nixon's Watergate, predicting, "Glacier Gate will be recorded in annals of church history as a day of infamy and shame May God have mercy upon your souls for the fatal error of denying the sole and final authority of the Scriptures."[31]

All these responses came from the pew, where many understood the theological debate better than some administrators. The sky was raining radioactive dust on Washington church headquarters. Wilson, in his communications to the constituency, cried crocodile tears. Many of the scholars who had attended Glacier View were confirmed in their belief that he had deceived them and used them to provide a facade of credibility, sending about 250 letters of protest to him.[32] Religion teachers at Southern Missionary College asked the loaded questions:

> Are Dr. Ford's views now officially considered heresy? When and by whom was such judgment made? The consensus document seemed to be mutually agreed upon. What happened to it? How should the scholars now view the time and effort put into developing the consensus document?[33]

One professor of religion commented:

> I never sensed that his [Ford's] views had been judged by the Sanctuary Review Committee to be so divergent that the mere holding of them unfitted him for the ministry. This seems to be what PREXAD has concluded. I hope we are not setting a dreadful precedent by so narrowly defining Adventist orthodoxy as to stifle the theological task among some of our brightest minds.[34]

Twenty-six PUC scholars put their signatures to a letter, saying their representatives at Glacier View now believed their attendance was used to legitimize "something they were specifically told would not be carried out, namely a heresy trial." They objected to the use of the Ten Point Statement, "a document publicly acknowledged not to represent a voted consensus," as a weapon against Des. As chairman of the religion department at PUC, Fred Veltman wrote six pages to Wilson, complaining of the bias exhibited by Kenneth Wood in the Review and the misuse of the Ten Point Statement. He also deplored PREXAD's rejection of scholarly opinion regarding the points made by Ford in his Glacier View manuscript.[35]

The weightiest and most forthright objection came from Andrews University. Thirty-nine scholars at that institution signed a document saying, in part, "we deplore the rending asunder of Christ's body by what we consider to be the unjust recommendation that Dr. Desmond Ford not be employed in denominational service." The Consensus Statements, they reminded Wilson, proved Des was "in harmony with his brethren." The same statements, they added, agreed with the "major biblical concerns" outlined by Des. Then they went on the offensive, asking for the *Review* to explain the advances Des had contributed to the sanctuary theology, and recommended that a new committee be established to review the action of PREXAD as a start to a healing process between scholars and administrators. Both requests were ignored.[36]

Some scholars further afield wrote personal letters to Wilson. One was Wesley Amundson, chairman of the religion department at Southeast Asia Union College in Singapore.[37] Adrian Zytkoskee wrote a blistering analysis of events, asking the following leading questions:

[Regarding the article in] the Pacific Union Recorder headlined, "Historical Sanctuary Theology is Reaffirmed," where do we find the reaffirmation? If Ford was expected to move his position, where was he expected to move it to? Did not his willingness to accept the voted consensus statement[s] indicate flexibility on his part? Is it pastoral for scholars and administrators to leave questions unanswered for decades? Was not Ford's [Forum] discussion pastoral in nature because it did offer solutions rather than simply raising questions?[38]

Knowing the groundswell of support for Des, Gill told Wilson, "We see the tables turned on the accusers."[39] There had been a mustering of worldwide church officials in a show of authority, only to bring that authority into disrepute. Considering the damage that followed PREXAD's decision Raymond Cottrell claimed later, "The General Conference repeated on a world scale the very indiscretion that Ford committed on the campus of PUC."[40] PREXAD's action forever blighted the legacy of Wilson's term of office. The protests did not soften his determination to endorse tradition. He had cut his cloth to fit a suit of the 1800s. In future, any scholar who publicly shared the faults of the Investigative Judgment doctrine, or reduced Ellen White, or preached the apostolic gospel with too much enthusiasm against perfectionism, would think twice about it lest he be axed. That was Wilson's salient message to the scholars. His legacy was a weakened academia and an army of obsequious ministers.

Closure Draws Near
While protests multiplied the wheels of the tumbrel rolled on relentlessly toward the guillotine.

After the PREXAD judgment Parmenter promptly called a joint

meeting of the Australasian Division Executive Committee and the Avondale College Board for September 18. As the time approached, Kenneth Eastman, the Division attorney, became increasingly apprehensive. He was aware of legal precedents when clergymen, after dismissal, had successfully sued their employers[41] but he thought it unlikely Des would consider the same action. Eastman was not a Fordian disciple. He was primarily dedicated to seeing natural justice (due process) given to Des.

Early in 1979, as Eastman reflected on the legal problems of the church in America, he had written to a fellow SDA attorney, Lloyd McMahon, and posed the question, "The SDA Church sues people so why can't SDAs sue the church?" He had in mind defensive actions similar to Paul's appeal to Rome for legal protection. Top officials in the Australasian Division office, he observed, subscribed to what he called "The Divine Right of Adventists," a belief that they were above the law. He believed they counted on others not to sue them while at the same time reserving the right to sue others and even tread on natural justice.[42]

Eastman concluded that PREXAD's meeting with Des on the Friday afternoon at Glacier View was certainly a trial hearing with the verdict pronounced on September 2. He analyzed the proceedings and found many legal irregularities. The Consensus Statements, he noted, never directly referred to Des; therefore, they could not be used as a basis for his dismissal. The Ten Point Statement could not be used, because neither the church nor the colloquium had voted agreement on it. PREXAD had therefore acted unilaterally and admitted at least two hostile witnesses into their meeting, Parmenter and Duffy. At the meeting Des was not given legal representation and Parmenter had submitted an unauthorized prejudicial letter. In his letter Parmenter's use of the plural "us" and "our" deliberately misled, giving the impression he had been asked by an authorized committee to write it. Eastman was convinced, too, that PREXAD was acting as both accuser and judge; therefore, they could not be regarded as unbiased.[43] He thought it was a kangaroo court, a show trial where the procedures are manipulated for expediency.

The upcoming combined meeting of September 18 posed further illegalities in Eastman's mind. He believed church constitutional law did not allow for a combined meeting of the two committees. His interpretation only permitted it if both committees agreed beforehand that it should take place.[44] Parmenter had not gained that permission. Parmenter knew that the Avondale College Board on its own, perhaps unanimously, would block a conviction of Des, so the only way to get an adverse judgment was to have a joint committee where the College Board would be outnumbered.

In addition, Parmenter invited twenty handpicked extras to participate in the committee discussion, presumably without voting rights. Why the extras? The expression of their conservative views would evidently sound better than coming from his lips, and it would discourage pro-Fordians from holding the floor. Eastman believed that these invitees should be approved by both committees.[45] The official minutes of the meeting began with a listing of all those present. The list was apparently constructed to make it look as if it was simply a Division Executive Committee with a long list of special invitees scattered throughout. Avondale College Board members were not identified as such, hiding the reality of a combined committee. The ploy appeared to be a deliberate camouflage.

Eastman also noted that Parmenter had published an article called "Wedges" in the church paper, which could be classified as having prejudicial bias. In it Parmenter had given the distinct impression that those questioning church tradition were dim wits and satanic. Church magazine headlines such as "Variant Views Rejected" and the post-Glacier View public meetings that discussed the results, he thought, were also in the same category of prejudice.[46]

The number of illegalities continued to mount in Eastman's mind. Des was not advised of the time and place of the meeting. He was not asked to be present and certainly would not be speaking on his own behalf. There was a tape from Wilson to be played as a hostile witness. And there were no provisions in place for the right of appeal. It could not be proved that members of both committees had not been prejudiced by defamatory literature against Des. There were possible grounds for conspiracy and blackmail because of reports some church members were withholding tithe until Des was sacked. And the only reasons for dismissal allowed by British law in New South Wales were immorality, willful disobedience, and habitual neglect, none of which were in the brief against Des.[47]

Hal McMahon, a Melbourne physician, wrote to Eastman and Parmenter, expressing his concerns from a church members viewpoint. The SDA interpretation of prophecy is not the real issue, he claimed. The central point is "the supremacy of Scripture." "Dr. Ford," he continued, "should be reassigned to head a team to organize and mobilize the laity to take the gospel to the world." He saw the struggle in cosmic terms, with Satan rejoicing because the failure of the church to accept biblical truth would delay his own eternal destruction.[48]

More letters of support for Des came in from all quarters, especially Avondale College, urging Parmenter, Eastman, and other committee members not to follow through with PREXAD's recommendation.[49]

"Ford is the greatest exponent of the gospel that our church has known in modern times," one Avondale lecturer maintained. Withdrawing his credentials will "not help to solve the theological problems," he cautioned.[50] Another observed that "a careful reading of Des's letter to PREXAD affirms that he has offered to do all that a reasonable group of administrators would expect of him."[51]

History professor, Noel Clapham, reminded Parmenter that, "spirited horses serve best, even if they buck a bit; they are not, unless very bad rogues indeed, sent to the knackers .... Do you think it too late to exercise the statesmanlike qualities of mercy and good sense to avoid a dismissal, to me unnecessary and impolitic?"[52]

A week before the crucial meeting, after seeking other legal counsel in Sydney, Eastman put his concerns to Parmenter in writing. He was aware of a groundswell of support for Des among the laity. He believed Brinsmead would make great capital out of perceived illegalities. And he feared subsequent court actions. Nevertheless, neither Parmenter nor Taylor thought there was anything to worry about and brushed the concerns aside.[53]

Gathering at the Guillotine

The combined committees convened, as scheduled, on the afternoon of September 18, 1980, and proceedings extended into the evening, lasting approximately six hours. About one-third of the time was taken up by hearing the case against Ford. Accusations were put forward by Parmenter and strengthened by the tape from Wilson, describing PREXAD's recommendation of dismissal. No time was given for a structured defense.[54]

Eastman was so worried he had not slept well the previous night. In the meeting he felt "second-class treatment" was given to Des and proceedings were "rigidly controlled." "Every time," he later recalled, "some thought was expressed as to some alternative to taking the credentials, either Ron [Taylor] or K. S. P[armenter] immediately countered with a comment or speech to defuse any trend away from the instructions from PREXAD."[55] "The Avondale Board was swamped by the size of the A[ustralasian] Division] executive," a board member declared, "and did not have the freedom to discuss the matter of Des's employment without pressure from the majority. Furthermore, Wilson's taped message made it very clear that he wanted only one outcome and expected us to be compliant."[56]

Trans-Commonwealth Union Conference president, Claude Judd, courageously made a brief summary in support of Des.[57] When a motion was made that Des's credentials be revoked, Eastman proposed an amendment not unlike a preface. He wanted the vote to be subject to an assurance from the Division's Sydney firm of lawyers, Allen, Allen and Hemsley, that no breach of natural justice had taken place.[58] Eastman knew the lawyers would easily spot the illegalities and the meetings vote would then be voided. This amendment to the motion was carried.

Apparently sensing that a message from the lawyers might undo all his scheming, Parmenter called a recess. When everyone reassembled, a fatal loophole was suggested. Hospital superintendent Herbert Clifford proposed that when the assurance was received from the lawyers that the process of dismissal was legal or otherwise, then the matter might be handled "administratively," i.e., as administration saw fit. Ultimate control was therefore handed to Parmenter. Eastman conceded, loyally believing that Parmenter would follow legal advice.[59]

Parmenter wanted an open ballot on the principal motion, but when someone moved that a secret ballot be taken, it was seconded and carried. The main vote was then taken. No result was recorded, but it was later alleged to be sixty percent in favor of revoking Des's credentials.[60] The special invitees were not asked to leave the room prior to the vote. Some or all may have voted, even though they were not entitled to do so.

Parmenter was not satisfied. He desperately wanted an open ballot to get a higher percentage to relay to American headquarters. It would also serve to clearly identify his opposition. After the vote he moved quickly to ask, "Can we make this unanimous?" He then called for all to raise their hands in agreement with the motion. But five brave hands went up when "Against" was called.[61] These men became pariahs in the eyes of administration. About fifteen others abstained. This duplication of voting, one by secret ballot followed by an open ballot on the same motion, was irregular, of course.

Eastman was later called into Parmenter's office and told that his amendment to the motion was a "severe embarrassment" to administration.[62] Neither the amendment nor Clifford's proposal were recorded in the official minutes. However, Taylor and another church official dutifully visited the lawyers with Eastman to make a show of compliance. Taylor was designated to do the talking, but he carried no documents with him. Evidently Taylor hoped to make light of the case with a verbal description only. Eastman, on the other hand, went well prepared. When the lawyer noticed Eastman's papers he asked if they could be left for him to study. Eastman glanced at Taylor and received a nod of approval. He handed over the dossier, including a page listing his own perceived irregularities of the case. He felt sure the lawyers would agree with him.[63]

News of the axing immediately went to press. Eastman protested, "We haven't heard back from the lawyers yet. If they say our decision violated the law then we will have the embarrassment of revoking the committee's decision and telling the church about the illegalities."[64] His plea fell on deaf ears.

For months Eastman kept asking administration for that vital letter from the lawyers. Parmenter began to hedge, even claiming that the amendment was never put forward. Eastman believed the exact wording of the entire meeting would be on tape and asked for it. Taylor had indeed made one but would not release it to him or anyone else.[65] Clearly, the lawyers had communicated their agreement with Eastman, but Parmenter and Taylor remained quiet, for fear it would undo their conspiracy. Eastman kept asking the question. Eventually he was again called into Parmenter's office for a scolding, Parmenter becoming so abusive his face turned purple. Taylor was there, too, with a hidden tape recorder strapped to his leg. Eastman spotted him fiddling with it and said to Parmenter, "Excuse me, but I don't remember giving permission to record my comments." There was a deathly silence. Parmenter realized their subterfuge was exposed. With a smirk on his face he tried to make peace, saying, "Well, I suppose we are all brothers in the cause and should work together." However, Eastman was never told the outcome of their visit to the lawyer's office.[66]

The guillotine had fallen. Eastman had done his best to snag the rope, but Parmenter and Taylor brought down the blade "administratively."

End Notes

1   Dave Collings, "Ford Defrocked," *Campus Chronicle*, Sept 25, 1980, pp. 1, 8.

2   Neal Wilson, tape-recorded at Glacier View, Colorado, Aug 17, 1980; Desmond and Gillian Ford, *The Adventist Crisis of Spiritual Identity*, (Newcastle, California: Desmond Ford Publications, 1982), p. 76.

3   Gillian Ford to Neal Wilson, Oct 27, 1980.

4   Desmond and Gillian Ford, *Adventist Crisis of Spiritual Identity*, p. 60.

5   *Ibid.*, p. 61.

6   *Ibid.*, p. 63.

7   David Spencer Clark Diary, Aug 25, 1980.

8   Desmond and Gillian Ford, *Adventist Crisis of Spiritual Identity*, p. 60; Keith Parmenter to Desmond Ford, Aug 15, 1980.

9   Desmond and Gillian Ford, *Adventist Crisis of Spiritual Identity*, p. 62.

10 *Ibid.*, pp. 62, 64.

11 Collings, *Campus Chronicle*, Sept 25,1980, p. 9.

12 Robert Parr to Desmond Ford, Aug 18,1980.

13 Athal Tolhurst, interviewed by Calvin Edwards by phone, Aug 23, 1980

14 Gillian Ford to Neal Wilson, [late Sept 1980]; Collings, *Campus Chronicle,* Sept 25, 1980, p. 9.

15 Desmond Ford to Keith Parmenter, Aug 18, 1980.

16 Collings, *Campus Chronicle,* Sept 25, 1980, p. 9.

17 Ibid.; Adrian Zytkoskee, interviewed by Jim Caldwell, "The American Series," 1981.

18 E.g., David McMahon, "Glacier View Report," transcript of meeting at Wahroonga Church, Aug 27,1980; Alwyn Salom *et al.,* South Australian Conference Workers Meeting, tape-recording, 1980.

19 Ritchie Way, "Glacier View and Its Outcome," *Good News for Adventists,* Nov 2005, p. 6.

20 David Spencer Clark Diary, Aug 25, 1980.

21 Robert Brinsmead to Desmond Ford, Aug 19, 1980.

22 Desmond Ford to Keith Parmenter, Aug 26, 1980; Collings, *Campus Chronicle*, Sept 25, 1980, p. 9.

23 Neal Wilson to Keith Parmenter, Aug 27, 1980.

24 Keith Parmenter to Neal Wilson, Aug 28, 1980; Ron Taylor to Neal

Wilson, Aug 29, 1980.

25 PREXAD Report to Keith Parmenter, [ca. Sept 2, 1980].

26 Ron Taylor to Members of Division Executive Committee and Avondale College Board, Sept 5, 1980; Desmond Ford, interviewed by Trevor Lloyd at Caloundra, Jan 7, 2001.

27 Collings, *Campus Chronicle,* Sept 25, 1980, p. 9.

28 Helen Meissner to Desmond and Gillian Ford, Aug 24,1980; Garry Webster to Desmond Ford, Aug 27, 1980; Irwin and Hazel Wagner to Desmond Ford, Aug 29, 1980; Jack and Thelma Mallory to Paradise SDA Church Board, Sept 11, 1980.

29 Hally Baker to Neal Wilson, Sept 28, 1980.

30 Lowell Tarling to Neal Wilson, Sept 6, 1980.

31 Albert and Mrs. Watson to Neal Wilson, Sept 8, 1980.

32 Raymond Cottrell, "Group Dynamics at Glacier View," unpublished paper, [ca. 1986]; Neal Wilson, tape recorded at Glacier View, Aug 17, 1980.

33 Division of Religion, Southern Missionary College, to Neal Wilson, Sept 8, 1980.

34 Lorenzo Grant to Neal Wilson, Sept 8, 1980.

35 Larry Mitchel et al. to Neal Wilson, Sept 10, 1980; Fred Veltman to Neal Wilson et al., Sept 15, 1980.

36 An Open Letter to President Wilson from Concerned Pastors and Scholars at Andrews University Seminary and Graduate School, Sept 10, 1980.

37 Wesley Amundson to Neal Wilson, Sept 18, 1980.

38 [Adrian Zytkoskee], "Glacier View and Desmond Ford," [ca. Sept 1980].

39 Gillian Ford to Wilson, [late Sept 1980].

40 Cottrell, "Group Dynamics," [ca. 1986].

41 Kenneth Eastman, "Natural Justice and Church Disciplinary Process," draft, [ca. 1980].

42 Kenneth Eastman to Lloyd McMahon, March 30, 1979.

43 [Kenneth Eastman], "Notes for Paper on Natural Justice," unpublished paper, [ca. 1980].

44 Kenneth Eastman to Australasian Division Officers, Sept 12, 1980; [Kenneth Eastman], "Questions, Points of Order," unpublished paper, Sept 14, 1980.

45 Ibid.

46 Keith Parmenter, "Wedges," AR, Sept 8, 1980, p. 4; [Eastman],

"Notes on Natural Justice," [ca. 1980].

47   [Eastman], "Notes on Natural Justice," [ca. 1980].

48   Hal McMahon to Keith Parmenter, Sept 10, 1980; Hal McMahon to Kenneth Eastman, Sept 11, 1980 .

49   E.g., Robert Hosken to Kenneth Eastman, Sept 9, 1980; Joy Hallam to Kenneth Eastman, Sept 11, 1980; Gary Mankelow to Ormond Speck, Sept 11, 1980; Trevor Lloyd to Keith Parmenter, Sept 15, 1980.

50   Don Hanson to Ormond Speck, Sept 10, 1980.

51   Robert Cooper to Ormond Speck, Sept 11,1980.

52   Noel Clapham to Keith Parmenter, Sept 12, 1980.

53   Eastman to Division Officers, Sept 12, 1980; Kenneth Eastman to Ron Taylor, Sept 19, 1980; Kenneth Eastman to Lance Butler, Feb 9, 1981.

54   Australasian Division Executive Committee [and Avondale College Board] minutes, Sept 18, 1980.

55   Kenneth Eastman to Lance Butler, Feb 9, 1981.

56   Arnold Reye to Milton Hook, Dec 28, 2005.

57   Robert Parr to Desmond Ford, Sept 30, 1981.

58   Kenneth Eastman to Keith Parmenter, Sept 26, 1980.

59   *Ibid.*

60   Kenneth Eastman to Milton Hook, Dec 5, 2006.

61   Trevor Lloyd, interviewed by Milton Hook at Sydney, Jan 7, 2006; Arnold Reye to Milton Hook, Feb 6, 2006.

62   Kenneth Eastman to Lance Butler, Feb 9, 1981.

63   [Kenneth Eastman], "Notes: Points and Queries to be Raised with Messrs. Allen, Allen and Hemsley," unpublished paper, Sept 25, 1980; Eastman to Parmenter, Sept 26, 1980; Kenneth Eastman to Trevor Lloyd, Aug 19,1997; Kenneth Eastman to Milton Hook, Dec 8, 2006.

64   Kenneth to Ron Taylor, Sept 19, 1980.

65   Kenneth Eastman to Ron Taylor, Oct 30, 1980; Kenneth Eastman to Thomas Andrews, Dec 22, 1980; Eastman to Butler, Feb 9, 1981; Kenneth Eastman to Australasian Division Officers, Feb 18, 1981.

66   Kenneth Eastman to Keith Parmenter *et al,* Nov 19, 1980.

Chapter Thirteen:
Ebb and Flow After High Tide

I hope we can all learn to disagree without being disagreeable," Ford declared, as he pondered on the Glacier View meetings.[1] Robert Parr was not so charitable. "I have great difficulty," he fumed, "in restraining myself from praying the prayer, Lord, do not forgive them, for they know exactly what they do."[2] Later, in a pensive mood, Raymond Cottrell remarked:

> How fervently we await the dawn of a new day—a day when the church will be willing to accept the Bible and the Bible only as our authority in matters of faith and doctrine, in fact, as well as in profession... but events since Glacier View appear to indicate a reversion to the dark decade of the 1970s and with the prophet Habakkuk we cry out in distress of soul, "How long, O Lord."[3]

Glacier View evoked numerous reactions—disbelief, defensiveness, prophecies of doom, triumphalism, a sense of vindication, a sense of betrayal, disgust, despair, anger, fear, a reversion to traditionalism, and, in some cases, an enlightenment with increased understanding of the gospel. What was Ford himself to do in its wake? Naturally, Des was emotionally exhausted. The homeland beaches of Queensland beckoned seductively. Oh, for a swim in the gentle breakers and the soft sand underfoot. But the urge to keep on preaching in the Lord's army was irresistible.

Robert Brinsmead invited Des to join him in his ventures. Des refused, knowing that to do so would widen the gulf between himself and Adventism. He wanted to stay as close to his church as possible.[4] Californian friends, especially Zane Kime and Don Muth, floated ideas for supporting Des as a hospital chaplain, or a speaker for health seminars, or in a gospel ministry on radio. They recognized the extensive harvest of souls that could be made by his gospel witness.[5]

Des accepted this development as the leading of the Spirit because at last he would be able to preach the gospel without snipers firing at him.[6] There is nothing more soul-destroying for an enthusiastic preacher than having to break your shotgun over your arm simply to avoid attracting flak. He would not have to breathe the fumes of perfectionism. He would not have to suffer the darts thrown into his back by the traditionalists. He could brush aside the casuistry, chicanery, and cultism of his church and preach a message based squarely on Scripture alone. Vern Heise's prediction that Des would be delivered from the lion's den, made twelve months earlier, was fulfilled.[7]

In response to Kime's offer, Des and Gill returned to California. Except for Erwin Gane and one or two others, the PUC community remained supportive of Des and Gill. In a hall off-campus a large crowd gathered to welcome them back from Washington. During the function, Henry Brown, formerly of the General Conference, expressed enduring respect for Des and made a presentation gift of a Bible.[8] It was a warm-hearted response toward the Fords and at the same time served as an act of defiance against PREXAD. Des and Gill found rented quarters at Penryn, near Auburn.[9] First priority was to obtain testimonials from a score of close associates in order to submit them for a permanent visa application. These routines went smoothly.[10]

In the meantime, the church was processing its paperwork regarding financial settlement with Des. For almost thirty years of service church policy allowed him fourteen months' salary, plus return airfares to Australia, in addition to a baggage allowance. The total amount enabled Des and Gill to make a deposit on a home of their own in California.[11] It was a comfortable house, but not luxurious. At least they had a roof over their heads. Before the end of the year Des was speaking on radio and in halls in the local area. He had also started writing a book in defense of the Saturday Sabbath.[12] Brinsmead was beginning to argue against the doctrine.

Some Official Responses

At Washington headquarters church officials wore happy masks. Neal Wilson dismissed all the theological controversy as "Satan's subtle sophistry and cunningness."[13] Surely, he didn't mean that it was he and his associates who were using Satanic sophistry. He must have meant that Des and his associates were under the influence of the devil. How could Wilson be so sure when so many disagreed with him?

Sensing the end of the world, church officials published a series in the *Review,* urging the constituency to pray for the latter rain because of the imminent shaking time.[14] It was reported that the church "could sustain the loss of 70,000" members in the shaking,[15] cleansing it of so-called apostates and purifying the remnant for translation to heaven. For the perfectionists it meant they were left with little time to achieve worthiness for their Shangri-La. These sanctimonious fantasies all fell apart. There was no high tide of revival. Instead, trusted leaders were disciplined or dismissed over the mismanagement of funds and conflict of interest concerns during the Donald Davenport bankruptcy hearings.[16] An Adventist lecturer in legal matters wrote at the time that the findings made the upper echelons of the church look like "a collection of feudal barons who combine to keep a weak king in office."[17]

Kenneth Wood continued to misuse the columns of the *Review* to proclaim tradition. Some laity sent protest letters, one accusing him of the "intentional suppression of truth."[18] A significant number of the Seminary faculty at Berrien Springs lodged a complaint with Wilson, calling for Wood's head, and they obtained approval to publish their own paper in order to bypass the Review.[19] Ten editors of SDA student newspapers across North America, at an annual conference on the campus of PUC, called for more objective news releases from Wood's office. They cited, among other things, his bias against Des.[20] This, and more widespread concern, was also voiced in the "Atlanta Affirmation," a consensus of seventeen leading lecturers at SDA colleges and universities in America.[21]

The "Atlanta Affirmation" came in the wake of a silly editorial by Wood that proposed that the church should ignore all criticism of the Investigative Judgment view and just get on with preaching it to the whole world. His crass conjecture about the seemingly long interval between 1844 and the culmination of the heavenly judgment was that "perhaps they [the angels] need considerable time to do their assigned tasks." "And after they have done their work," he speculated, "is it possible that there are review boards or superior courts in heaven to make sure that each case has been dealt with fairly?"[22]

Well, well! So that's why the Investigative Judgment was taking such a long time. With millions of briefs to process and seven heavens through which to trundle with those heavy books, or computers, it could well be more than one eternity before the Second Coming. And what if the angels get a virus in their computers? Or, worse still, what if the power fails and the angels lose all their files and they then have to depend on God's memory alone? The angelic barristers would then have to declare, "In God We Trust."

William Johnsson, too, joined in the bunkum. In a *Review* editorial he welcomed the publicity given to the Investigative Judgment theory occasioned by Glacier View. "The world needs to hear it," he wrote. It is an "unparalleled opportunity" to witness, he continued.

Those outside the church, he surmised, have "unconscious stirrings of future participation [in or with our church]."[23]

There was, however, no spring tide of acceptance in the wider Christian community, neither of the Investigative Judgment teaching nor the charismatic authority of Ellen White (another focal point of Johnsson's dreams). Two decades later, he claimed that "great good emerged" from "the triple challenge posed by Ford, Davenport, and Rea." Yes, a more mature view of White's role took root in some limited quarters, and there was a tightening of church fiscal procedures in the wake of the Davenport fiasco. But Johnsson also wrote, "the questions posed by Ford brought a renewed emphasis on Bible investigation," and "Christ and the gospel were given new emphasis."[24] In this respect he was whistling in the dark, and some readers told him so.[25]

Other church magazines similarly squandered their credibility with colorful spin. The *Ministry* editors reported on Glacier View in biased terms, which displeased Richard Hammill. For example, it deliberately cast the Ten Point Statement as a consensus statement, though it was never put to the vote.[26]

Later, *Ministry* editors ran articles with muddied messages about sanctification. Morris Venden, for example, wrote a piece in 1982, stressing again the imperative of mystical self-surrender in order to achieve "perfect obedience," indeed, "spontaneous obedience" to God. He used a parable, Matthew 13:45 and 46, to suggest that selling everything we possess means total surrender of the self, but quickly qualified it to exclude the surrender of our power of choice.[27] Did he mean the power of choice is untouched by inherent sin? Surely the power of choice is the basic human element eroded by the inherited sinful nature. If, as he alleged, we are expected to surrender self, then the enterprise must include the power of choice.

When David Newman came to the editorial chair of *Ministry*, he brought a sharper focus to the apostolic gospel with his editorials that gave no room for perfectionism.[28] The Evangelical view was well represented.[29] Unfortunately, his shining emphasis faded with his successors.

For editor of the Australian church paper, the *Australasian Record,*

Keith 's personal preference to replace Parr was Geoffrey Garne, apparently brought from the South African editorial office to revive traditional Adventism. Garne claimed in his first editorial that he had received his mandate by reading from an Ellen White book en route to Australia high above the Indian Ocean in a jumbo jet.[30] Not every reader was persuaded by his claim. One deplored the fact there was no thanks for his predecessor and wished his mandate were expressed as a Christ-centered one instead of focused on tradition.[31] The West Australian Forum group complained there was no mention of a commitment to Scripture in his mandate, only of Ellen White.[32]

Readers did not have to wait long for Garne to show his hand. He published an article by Gane that reiterated the flimsy assumptions traditionally made when trying to connect Daniel 8:14 to Daniel 9:24–27, culminating in an Investigative Judgment in 1844.[33] He resurrected a 1969 series called "The Sanctuary Truth," prepared by the White Estate, in which the heavenly sanctuary was depicted in very literal terms.[34] These articles were followed by ones on the year-day principle by arch-conservative Jean Zurcher.[35]

From his own pen Garne rehearsed Ellet Waggoner's view that God can infuse us with power to keep His commandments. "What a thrilling possibility! What a heart-warming, awe-inspiring assurance!" he enthused as he quoted Ezekiel 36:26, 27, calling it the "new covenant promise."[36] Of course, it was not the new covenant. He was quoting a renewal of the old covenant in Old Testament times, offered primarily to the Hebrew nation—a covenant that lapsed because of their natural human frailty. The perfectionist stance always fails to underestimate the height of God's righteousness found in His law, together with the impotence of human depravity and the imperative to trust in Christ's imputed righteousness alone. Garne, perhaps ignorantly, was coaxing the constituency back to the Roman Catholic Councils of Trent and the second blessing of Wesleyanism, the two sources that advocated self-generated righteousness with God's assistance as the essence of sanctification.

Garne was also an accessory to a series portraying Australasian church leaders as affirming their belief in the Fundamental Statements of the SDA Church. Parmenter, well known as a proponent of creedalism, was probably the instigator of the idea and was featured in the leading article.[37] The aim of the series was unclear. If it meant to calm the conservative group, it failed miserably, because their carping only became more strident and widespread, as they called for a vigorous purge of so-called heretics. If the series was designed to bring left wing critics into line, then it was a flop, for they were not so gullible. Was it designed to reinforce the status quo? It certainly demonstrated a dogged intention to maintain Nineteenth Century lines of argument. There was little expressed desire to continue to search for truth as promised at Glacier View. Why would anyone be motivated to dig deeply into the Scriptures when there prevailed an overwhelming conviction that, as one writer put it, "our early history reveals that the foundations of our teachings were laid carefully."[38] This mentality only required a thorough study and endorsement of Nineteenth Century SDA sectarianism. Any fresh thoughts or corrections that the Spirit may have introduced since the early decades of the church could not be entertained.

The BRI Responds to Ford's Manuscript

This back-to-the-good-ol'-days frame of mind was bolstered by a series of weighty volumes published under the auspices of the Biblical Research Institute. Various SDA scholars were called on to write chapters defending the traditional SDA interpretations of prophecy, their sanctuary doctrine with all its date setting, and conclusions about the Investigative Judgment. These books were designed as a direct answer to Ford's Glacier View manuscript.[39] In a brief critique Des was kind to Ivan Blazen for his timid contribution that "half-heartedly" suggested some "thin threads of argument" for the Investigative Judgment. And he noted that Gerhard Hasel admitted that the actual wording of the command of Artaxerxes I of 457 BC makes no mention of any order to rebuild the city of Jerusalem.[40] That pivotal admission was enough to bring down the whole Investigative Judgment construct.

Des saved his most scathing criticisms for Arthur Ferch's contribution that tried to establish the veracity of 457 BC as the starting point for the seventy-week prophecy of Daniel 9. Des noted that the chief characteristic of the article was "its exceeding tentativeness." It frequently used words such as "assuming," "appears to be," "presumably," "suggests," "implied," "seems," and the like.[41] Establishing doctrine on such a precarious pile of pick-up sticks simply illustrated that it was impossible for SDA scholars to bring credibility to the Investigative Judgment.

With rare satire Des rephrased John 3:16 for Ferch in these words: "It is possible, even likely, that God so loved the world, that it appears he gave His only begotten Son. This presumably implies that whosoever believeth in Him (it seems) might not perish, but, in all likelihood, have the most acceptable reward—eternal life (though no explicit proclamation to this effect is available)."[42]

Cottrell challenged Johnsson's contribution, which tried to argue that the prophecies of Daniel had nothing to do with God's covenantal promises and judgments and therefore were unconditional prophecies. Cottrell pointed out that Johnsson contradicted himself when he asserted that significant parts of Daniel did, indeed, contain covenantal elements. Johnsson's contribution was disappointing, and he was being subjective by taking the party line, Cottrell alleged.[43] It certainly did appear that a fine scholar had exchanged his birthright, like Esau, for a bowl of pottage.

Des had always agreed with Cottrell's article in the *SDA Bible Commentary* that argued for conditionality in Daniel on the basis that human choice, whether it was Hebrew or Gentile, operated while probationary time lasted. Alden Thompson, professor of biblical studies at Walla Walla College, agreed with Cottrell and Des.[44]

These efforts by the BRI to revive respectability for Adventism's prophetic interpretations did not touch the laity. For them the pseudo-scholarship was chloroform in print, putting readers to sleep. Furthermore, despite Johnsson's hopes that the new costuming and set for the preaching of the sanctuary doctrine would attract many into SDA pews it was, instead, panned in the press, both popular and scholarly.

One prominent Evangelical magazine proclaimed: "Traditionally, Adventists are taught they can't be sure of heaven until they have lived lives good enough to have their sins blotted out during the Investigative Judgment. That, in many cases, has spawned an attitude of perfectionism, always striving to be good enough, but never sure just how good that is."[45]

Newsweek reported:

> Church members are suing Adventist officials in an Oregon court for fraud and breach of fiduciary trust, stemming from the 1981 bankruptcy of fellow Adventist Donald Davenport, a Los Angeles developer.... On top of this, the church has been hit by a second scandal: the charge that the theological writings of its most important figure [Ellen White], which rank second only to the Bible, may have been plagiarized from other authors....
>
> Georgetown University ethicist Roy Branson, editor of

Spectrum, an independent journal for church liberals, says flatly that Adventists will no longer be able to appeal to White as "the final authority on a whole range of issues, including biblical and theological interpretation and lifestyle." If so, the Seventh-day Adventists would seem to have lost a resource more precious than the millions that went down the [Davenport] drain.[46]

"The dilemma facing the Adventist Church in 1981 is how to reconcile its commitment to the Bible with its doctrinal dependence upon the charismatic Mrs. White," Newsweek declared. Influential Christian editor, Kenneth Kantzer, even portrayed Des as a modern Martin Luther and the church views of the Investigative Judgment as outside the stream of Protestantism.[47]

A professor in the biblical languages department of the University of Chicago who had apparently been contributing occasional articles to the Andrews University Seminary journal withdrew his support in protest. "I believe," he stated, "that the [SDA] church will either have to come to terms with the Twentieth Century or else wither." He believed the treatment given to Des was "odious." He had concluded that much of the apologetics with respect to SDA tradition, written against Des by men like Hasel under the auspices of the BRI, was "trash."[48]

Omega

Further shame was served on the heads of the church for their publication of Omega,[49] written by Lewis Walton, a Californian SDA lawyer. He employed White's alpha-omega motif *(Selected Messages,* vol 1, pp. 193–208) to pin the charge of heresy on modern anti-perfectionists, critics of the Investigative Judgment, and those against White's inerrancy.

In 1904 White had tagged John Harvey Kellogg's extreme views on sanctification, akin to perfectionism, as the alpha, or beginning, of a path that would soon end in apostasy. It did in a few short years, that is, by about 1910. But Walton deliberately misquoted White in grand prosecution style by omitting the element of "soon,"[50] stretching the prediction to the 1980s so that the *omega,* or end, of the apostasy would fall on Des and his like-minded associates. Robert Pierson had made the same misleading application soon after Palmdale, when he realized that his perfectionism had suffered a major blow.[51]

Walton's extension of the omega to the modern era was accompanied by a proposal that the *omega,* being at the opposite end to *alpha* in the

Greek alphabet, would be an extreme view of justification by faith in view of the fact the *alpha* was an extreme view of sanctification by faith. He did not reflect White's intent that the seed of error found in the *alpha* would naturally flower in the *omega*, i.e., Kellogg's view of sanctification would eventually manifest itself in worse theories about sanctification. Instead, Walton's thesis was a thinly disguised thrust against Des's gospel preaching of justification by faith alone, as opposed to Kellogg's view of sanctification.

As it was at Glacier View, with Pierson and Wilson working in tandem to silence any apostolic gospel voice, so it was with the issue of *Omega*. It was a grubby little paperback that served the General Conference purpose of demonizing Des and the preaching of righteousness by faith alone.

Under the auspices of Parmenter and Garne the Australasian church paper advertised *Omega* as "recommended reading," but no one was brave enough to sign a name to the recommendation.[52] Bert Haloviak, archivist at American church headquarters, had apparently been a lone critic prior to its publication. When it reached the bookstands, a chorus of scholars joined Haloviak, including Cottrell, Robert Johnston at Andrews University and Walter Utt of the history department at PUC.[53]

Veltman's Research

Not all developments, however, were negative. Under the umbrella of the Glacier View promise to engage in further study of the problematic issues, the General Conference appointed Fred Veltman to research the extent of White's source dependency when she wrote *Desire of Ages*. Earlier, at least three scholars had done similar studies.[54] Parmenter informed his staff of this move in October 1980, saying the project would run "for one or two years."[55]

Veltman was perfectly suited for the task, being a specialist in the techniques used for New Testament source analysis. Fortuitously, it also removed him from the backlash directed at PUC in the wake of Glacier View.

Desire of Ages, like a number of White's books, was compiled largely from previous columns she had written in the church papers. When writing those early articles, she had copied portions from other religious writers but did not acknowledge the quotations. Those who have read widely in her diaries and original manuscripts will agree that her writing style had no literary flair. It was repetitious, prosaic, and often ungrammatical. Her secretaries would correct the more obvious errors when typing it out.[56] It would then go through a second editorial process at the publishing house. Those published articles were later gathered together by Marion Davis, one of White's secretaries, then significantly reworked and submitted to White for checking and rewording in places. In this manner *Desire of Ages* was compiled to make a free-flowing narrative. Later, others read the manuscript, or portions of it, and were free to suggest further changes as part of the editorial process. Then it was submitted for a final editing by the book publishers.

It is readily understood that this long editorial process from the original drafts of the early articles to the final book stage would make it extremely difficult to pinpoint in the book the exact passages copied. Words had been substituted, phrases and sentences had been turned on their heads or shifted around. Many deletions and additions had been made in the rewriting, to the point where recognition of the original sources was often impossible. Imagine a thousand manuscripts put through a shredder and then blown out the window in a storm. Veltman's task was to pick up each strand and identify the original source from which it was copied. It took him five years full-time and another three years part-time to achieve a result that was commendable, but that by his own admission, and through no fault of his own, contained inadequacies.[57]

Before Veltman published his results in 1990, the conservative wing of the church, in denial over the very thought of White's copying, claimed that only .002 percent of her works came from other sources.[58] Veltman, in his search of fifteen chapters of Desire of Ages, found 31 percent that was clearly dependent on other sources to some degree. Understandably, in the earlier published articles from which these chapters were compiled, he found a higher level of copying.[59] In other words, if it were possible to go back to the very first stage when White copied the material into her initial article drafts (none exist), before all the editing process began, one would expect to find much more than a 31 percent level of copying.

Veltman's report, published in two issues of Ministry, forced the White Estate to accept reality. His research virtually endorsed all and more that Walter Rea had published. Rea had had his ministerial credentials and ordination cancelled. He deserved an apology and reinstatement but never received either. Robert Olson, a refreshingly honest voice in the White Estate, did not have it within his powers to make amends, but he did project a more objective view of White's copying and the overall nature of her ministry. On the latter he admitted, "I think that there were times when she was an exegete, but those instances are extremely rare. I think usually she was a homiletician. She used Scripture as an evangelist would."[60]

Olson, therefore, echoed a position Raoul Dederen had taken in 1977 when he commented, "As an interpreter of the Bible, Ellen White's most characteristic role was that of an evangelist—not an exegete, nor a theologian, as such, but a preacher."[61] These were courageous words in the climate of the 1970s, reflecting a European SDA view of White rather than a traditional American position. Ford had taken the European view in his 1979 Forum address and at Glacier View. Now, a decade later, Olson, as the voice of the White Estate and as a result of Veltman's research, had to concur with Dederen and Ford.

One important issue was left dangling: "How do we explain the fact that White denied she copied?" Veltman was asked. "As of now I do not have—nor, to my knowledge, does anyone else have—a satisfactory answer," he readily confessed.[62] White's denial will forever haunt her reputation.

A Return to SDA Fundamentalism

Glacier View was a watershed in the SDA Church. Efforts to join the Protestant mainstream, begun in the 1950s, were abandoned in favor of a return to sectarian fundamentalism.[63] Not even the results of Veltman's research took hold among the laity. Some little Jack tars came out of their bunks and pressured "willing captains" to drop anchor in the safe waters of tradition. Sailing off into the horizon only invited disaster, they believed, because one might drop off the edge of the world. The attitude of church officials, especially evangelists, seemed to be, "We will keep preaching our traditional views because it makes good Adventists."[64] It was tantamount to saying, "We are in the business of perpetuating institutionalized error."

Anti-intellectualism was part of the resurgence of fundamentalism. Gordon Thomas, history professor at PUC, reflected on the strong Methodist strand in the SDA Church and noted:

> The Methodist hostility to learning became proverbial. Education was considered a time-wasting luxury at best, and at worst, a stumbling block or tool of the Devil. The Methodist Church in America took pride in 1800 that not a single one of its preachers

was a college graduate....

Most Adventists have not wanted to study or to probe very deeply into complex issues.... This anti-intellectual attitude among our members helps to explain why any speaker who so desires can take the pulpit of an Adventist Church, even a college Adventist Church, and quite successfully ridicule or berate the so-called scholars in our church, play the age-old anti-intellectual song to the galleries, and receive an enthusiastic response from the audience.[65]

One practical example of anti-intellectualism emerged in Australia with a ban on the *Collegiate Sabbath School Quarterly,* because its pages were not peppered with Ellen White quotes and gave space for quotes from various Christian commentaries. This taboo was brought in by Gordon Lee, president of the Western Australian Conference. In a similar vein Ron Taylor of Australian headquarters recommended that the Sydney Adventist Forum be disbanded because their podium was sometimes given to speakers espousing non-traditional views. Similar sentiments emerged at the General Conference level against American Forums and their publication, *Spectrum.*[66]

Fundamentalisms squeeze on academic freedom also became more evident. The issue had been raised periodically in the 1960s and 1970s.[67] Administrative control tightened dramatically in the 1980s. The BRI and Geoscience Research Institute continued to be stacked with undistinguished men prepared to say what General Conference officials wanted to hear.[68] For this reason their pronouncements became inconsequential. Scholars outside the parameters of the fundamentalist mind-set resigned under pressure or were eased into positions where they had no impact on the training of the next generation. Smuts van Rooyen resigned from the Seminary. Frank Knittel, Lorenzo Grant, and Jerry Gladson resigned from Southern College. Ed Zackrison was fired. James Cox, Fritz Guy, and Lawrence Geraty were transferred out of the classroom and into executive chairs.[69] John Cassell resigned from PUC, fed up with fundamentalists attacking the theological integrity of the college.[70] (Van Rooyen, Grant, and Zackrison were eventually re-employed by the church.)[71]

There is nothing more destructive of a preacher's talent than subordinating it to goals that have nothing to do with the apostolic gospel. At the local church level many gospel-preaching American ministers, 150 or more, resigned or were forced out.[72] In Australasia about 180 ministers, forty percent of the work force, were fired or resigned under pressure.[73] Others found refuge in the denomination's hospital chaplaincy work, hospital systems, marriage counseling, health education, or trust services. Usually, this provided less direct involvement with theology.

In the long term the attrition caused such a talent drain that the church was left with substandard leadership at all levels. Ministerial trainees in Australia declined in quantity and quality. The healthy flow of Australasian postgraduate students virtually dried up. The pulpits rapidly ran out of gospel fire. Despite the proliferation of committee meetings, planning sessions, and training seminars, the end results indicated that the church structure had become almost dysfunctional, withering in the extremities away from its major centers and suffering inertia elsewhere.

Much of the purge was instigated by little old Miss Muffets and her brothers, stirring their curds and whey in the presence of fundamentalist administrators. The laity stoned the preachers while officials looked on. As Parr prophesied in 1980, "having once tasted [Des's] blood, they are not likely to be satisfied with a vegetarian bone."[74]

Ministers on the front line rapidly learned that there were quislings in their own ranks who would relay rumor and confidences to church officials. Ministerial camaraderie dissipated. Some administrators, more prone to suspicion than others, made insinuations that unsettled their pastors. For example, a gospel preacher in Western Australia was asked by his president, "Why do people flock to your pews when other SDA churches are emptying?" A senior gospel preacher in New South Wales was interrogated when an administrator noticed that the young pastors were seeking his counsel.[75] Both confrontations carried the implication that these preachers were magnets for dissidents.

The most unmerciful administrator in the Australasian Division was Athal Tolhurst, nicknamed without affection "The Ayatollah." He was the quintessential fundamentalist, advocating a literal heavenly sanctuary[76] and posturing as a biblical scholar.

Tolhurst openly attacked Des in a *Record* article on Daniel 8 and 9.[77] It contained many of the dubious assumptions traditionally used to arrive at the date 1844 as the beginning of an Investigative Judgment—the type of twaddle the innocent laity love to hear rehearsed. It appeals to their ego. It says, "You're smart. What you were clever enough to accept twenty years ago still stands as the impregnable fortress of truth.

You do not have to reinforce the mortar or replace any stone. Truth it was and truth it will forever be." With this mindset there is no compulsion to humbly ask the Spirit to lead into further truth. Instead, arrogance is displayed with the assertion, "We already have the truth."

Des wrote a reply to Tolhurst's effort, highlighting the assumptions and noting that the piece ran counter to previously published *SDA* literature. Like any fundamentalist Tolhurst had insisted on the literal meaning of Daniel 9:24, arguing for the translation to read as "cut off." Des agreed that "cut" is the root meaning, but he pointed out that the idea of "off" was added. Furthermore, Des observed that the context suggested the legitimacy of the cognate meanings "determined" and "decreed." For that reason, modern translations provide that sense. It was Tolhurst's only foray into the academic chambers, for, according to one report, he was advised by Australian administration to leave these weightier topics to the scholars.[78]

Fundamentalism's hand was mightily strengthened by the promotion of lecturer Gerhard Hasel to the dean's chair at Andrews University Seminary on September 1, 1981. A very small minority of lecturers had advocated the move. On the other hand, prior to the vote, delegations of professors and students had urged university administrators not to elect Hasel. They disliked his "authoritarian personality," his "rigid theological views," and "his penchant for undermining the reputations of his colleagues." But on decision day only Hasel's name was put forward to the board. Two members dissented, but their challenge was not enough to reverse the Board's preference for Hasel.[79] On hearing the news, Parr from afar teased Des with tongue-in-cheek: "I noted Hasel's elevation to the peerage, and shook in my shoes. I wondered for one puckish minute whether you had nominated him. Then I doubted it; you wouldn't be among those present, would you?"[80]

Walter Specht, of Loma Linda University, dispatched a scathing letter to Wilson:

> I view with great alarm the appointment of a new dean of the SDA seminary, with instructions, the rumor is, to clean up the seminary faculty. I hope that you will not allow yourself to be deceived into thinking that unity can be achieved and preserved by enforcing a uniformity of belief on everyone.... Unity cannot be legislated or forced.

Dr. Hasel is known to be an extreme right-winger in Adventism....
One of his weakest points is his personal relationship with colleagues
and students.... He is essentially a loner.... He has had little, if
any, pastoral experience.... He comes across to many people as a
conceited and arrogant Prussian.... It seems to me incredible that
the judgment of the vast majority of the seminary faculty should be
completely ignored.... No wonder the morale in the seminary is at its
lowest level during its history.[81]

Such courageous candor did not sway Wilson. Hasel remained dean
until 1988, when his "pretentious theological omniscience" could not be
tolerated any further. He did not go graciously. Instead, he polarized the
SDA academic community by establishing the Adventist Theological
Society, in opposition to the Andrews Society for Biblical Studies.
Membership of ATS is only by invitation. There is a strict screening
process, and a signed loyalty statement is required, renewable every year.
Would that be in case further enlightenment by the Holy Spirit might
change a member's beliefs? It is, one scholar observed, "the Mafia"
within Adventism that seeks total control of theological thought.[82]

It seems that by 1988 church officials were beginning to realize that
when they embraced fundamentalism at Glacier View, they had a tiger
by the tail. They took note of the drop in college enrolments, tithing, and
attendance at church services.[83] They were dismayed by the proliferation
of splinter groups and their literature, much of it extremely scurrilous
scribbling in the same vein as that directed at Ford in Australia during
the 1970s and Cassell at PUC after Glacier View.

In an effort to control the runaway situation, administration tried
knocking some of the teeth out of the tiger. Gane, despite his protests
over his dismissal by the Board for his relentless campaign of criticism
against colleagues, was summarily extracted from PUC and placed in a
lower profile office in the White Estate.[84] One of the first molars to lose
his ministerial credentials in Australia was Austin Cooke,[85] followed by
an American incisor in the person of Charles Wheeling.[86] The tiger's two
front teeth suffered the same fate when Colin and Russell Standish were
disciplined.[87] Perhaps it was these drastic measures that led Tolhurst to
conclude later that the church had "bowed to the wishes of the liberal
elements...and frowned on the more conservative class as legalists."[88] In
some respects it was an inaccurate assessment, but he was obviously in
pain, adjusting to the loss of some fellow fundamentalists.

The reality is that nowadays Adventism can be characterized as The Owl and The Aging Tiger. The Owl is on the endangered list, but occasional sightings still happen. One was an Alden Thompson variety called *Inspiration,* spotted in America.[89] And a Kai Arasola species, *The End of Historicism,* was seen in Europe.[90] A few small colonies are said to exist. Being shy, nocturnal creatures, they are difficult to trace.

On the other hand, the Aging Tiger still roams at large. He has appeared in the form of author Clifford Goldstein's unbelievable publications;[91] Gerhard Pfandl's implausible Sabbath School Lesson quarterly, "Daniel," [92] and Erwin Gane's quarterlies, especially "Enlightened by the Spirit," in which he wrote:

> As long as we permit the Holy Spirit to reign in our hearts and control our minds, we are kept from sinning. The tendencies of fallen nature and acts of sin can be overcome through total dependence on Christ.... The Holy Spirit cleanses us spiritually when we respond to the Word; in the same divine act He makes us right with God.... [It's a "making" righteous, not an imputation of righteousness]. The Holy Spirit's gift of righteousness makes them [i.e., believers] holy. They [believers] have habitual victory over evil.... We may reflect His love and live without committing sin.... By Christ's grace, the living believers will be obeying all His commandments.....[93]

Are these the claims of a screwball? It is unproductive to ask perfectionists, "Are you perfect yet?" They could very well be delusional. The burning question, "Does Erwin ever sin?" should be put to his closest associates. Gane's view implies that if you are not perfect then it is clear you don't have the Holy Spirit in your life; you haven't made a full spiritual surrender; and you are not totally depending on Christ. It is guilt induction at its best. Further, it is no wonder that conspiracy lovers allege there is a Jesuit infiltration into the SDA Church. Gane's phraseology was vintage Roman Catholicism from the Councils of Trent. It was also the raw Wesleyan perfectionism that caused Cottrell, after Glacier View, to wring his hands in dismay, predicting a reversion to its emphasis of the 1970s.[94]

With Pierson's urging, under the auspices of Wilson, the church at Glacier View made its choice to grimly grip the tail of the Aging Tiger and restrict the Owl to isolated habitats so it could not breed easily. What are the prospects of attracting lots of visitors into the viewing galleries at the Nature Reserve where the chief attractions have been replaced by cardboard replicas with nothing to say?

End Notes

1   Dave Collings, "Ford Defrocked," *Campus Chronicle,* Sept 25, 1980, p. 9.
2   Robert Parr to Desmond Ford, Oct 6, 1981.
3   Raymond Cottrell, "Our Present Crisis: Reaction to a Decade of Obscurantism," [Aug 1981].
4   Desmond Ford, interviewed by Trevor Lloyd at Sydney, March 12, 1995; Gillian Ford, interviewed by Trevor Lloyd at Cooranbong, Jan 6, 1997.
5   Zane Kime to U S Immigration Department, Sept 19, 1980; Ford, interviewed by Lloyd, March 12, 1995.
6   Desmond Ford, interviewed by Trevor Lloyd at Sydney, March 10, 1996.
7   Vern Heise, "Books Across My Desk," *AR,* Aug 20, 1979, p. 12.
8   Desmond Ford to Milton Hook, April 3, 2007.
9   Robert Parr to Desmond Ford, Oct 14,1980; Gillian Ford to Milton Hook, Jan 6, 2006.
10 Desmond Ford, "Andrews University Forum meeting," Nov 22, 1980; Letters to US Immigration Department from Zane Kime, Kenneth Hance, Gerald Fuller, Eric Magnusson, John Cassell, Edward Heppenstall, James Staples, Richard Coffen, Frederick Bruce, Norskov Olsen, Roy Branson, Duncan Eva, Robert Frame and James Londis, Sept 1980.
11 Thomas Andrews to Desmond Ford, Sept 23,1980; Delmer Wood to Desmond Ford, Nov 17, 1980; Robert Parr to Desmond Ford, Dec 29, 1980.
12 Ford, "Andrews University Forum meeting," Nov 22, 1980.
13 "Beset by Critics, Adventist Official Cites 'Satanic Influence,'" *Christianity Today,* Nov 20, 1981, pp. 64, 69.
14 E. g., Neal Wilson, "Results of the Reception of the Latter Rain," *Adventist Review,* Oct 9, 1980, pp. 22–24.
15 Bernard Merrill, "Open Letter to Neal Wilson," *Student Movement,* March 4, 1981, p. 5.
16 Bonnie Dwyer, "The General Conference Overrules Commission on Davenport Disclosure," *Spectrum*, March 1983, pp. 2–13; Bonnie Dwyer, "Disciplining the Davenport Offenders," *Spectrum,*

June 1983, pp. 32–42.

17 Jerry Wiley to Neal Wilson, April 7, 1983.

18 Skip Baker to Eugene Durand, Aug 27, 1981.

19 Gilbert Valentine to Milton Hook, Jan 19, 1981; Desmond Ford to Trevor Lloyd, March 24, 1981. Note: Wood left the editorial chair in November 1982.

20 Donna Rubano *et al,* "An Open Letter to the G C," ˆ May 21, 1981, p. 4.

21 John Craven, ed., "Atlanta Affirmation," *Limboline,* Aug 22, 1981, pp. 3–5.

22 Kenneth] W[ood], "The Message for Today," *Adventist Review,* March 19,1981, p. 3.

23 W[illiam] J[ohnsson], "Looking Beyond Glacier View," *Adventist Review,* Oct 16, 1980, p. 14.

24 *Idem,* "Twenty-Year Perspective," *Adventist Review,* Nov 1999, p. 5.

25 Vern Heise to William Johnsson, Dec 6, 1999; Lynden Rogers to William Johnsson, Aug 16, 2003.

26 Richard Hammill, *Pilgrimage,* (Berrien Springs, Michigan: Andrews University Press, 1992), p. 193; "Participants and Committees," Ministry, Oct 1980, p. 25.

27 Morris Venden, "What Jesus Said About Sanctification," *Ministry,* Jan 1982, p. 7.

28 E.g., David Newman, "Confused Over the Basis of Salvation," *Ministry,* July 1991, p. 4,5. Note: Newman lasted in the editorial office until Sept 1995.

29 E.g., Michelle Rader, "Adventists and Evangelicals: Another Viewpoint" *Ministry*, June 1993, pp. 18, 19.

30 Ron Taylor to Russell Standish et al., Aug 5,1981; Geoffrey Garne, "My Mandate," *AR,* Feb 2, 1981, p. 4.

31 Peter Lawson to Geoffrey Garne, Feb 5, 1981.

32 "My Mandate," *Valnews,* March 1981, pp. 2,3, quoted from Logos 1:5, 6.

33 Erwin Gane, "The Bible Doctrine of the Sanctuary," *AR,* Feb 23, 1981, pp. 6,13.

34 Ellen G White Estate, "The Sanctuary Truth," *AR*, March 30, pp. 6,7; April 6, 1981, pp. 6,7; April 13, 1981, pp. 6,7.

35 Jean Zurcher, "The Year-Day Principle—1," *AR*, April 27, 1981, p. 6; Jean Zurcher, "The Time Prophecies of Daniel 9," *AR,* May 4,

1981, pp. 10,11; Jean Zurcher, "Astronomical Evidence Sustains the Year-Day Principle," *AR*, May 11, 1981, pp. 10,11.

36 Geoffrey Garne, "Sanctification by Faith," *AR,* May 4, 1981, p. 4.

37 Keith Parmenter, "Our Leaders Affirm Their Faith—1: My Commitment," *AR,* Sept 21, 1981, p. 1f.

38 Claude Judd, "Our Leaders Affirm Their Faith: Gratitude and Praise," *AR*, Sept 28, 1981, p. 6.

39 Frank Holbrook, ed,, *Symposium on Daniel,* (Washington, D.C.: BRI, 1986); Frank Holbrook, ed., "70 Weeks, Leviticus, Nature of Prophecy," (Washington, D.C.: BRI, 1986); Arnold Wallenkampf, Richard Lesher, eds., The Sanctuary and the Atonement, (Silver Spring, Maryland: BRI, 1989).

40 Desmond Ford, "A Response to the Daniel and Revelation Committee," *GNU,* Nov 1990, special edition, p. 5.

41 *Ibid.,* pp. 5, 6.

42 *Ibid.,* p. 6.

43 Raymond Cottrell, "Conditional Prophecy in Relation to Apocalyptic," unpublished paper, [ca. 1987], p. 1.

44 Alden Thompson to Desmond Ford, Dec 26, 1991, Jan 20, 1992.

45 E.g., "The Adventist Showdown: Will it Trigger a Rash of Defections?" *Christianity Today,* Oct 10, 1980, p. 76.

46 Richard Ostling, "The Church of Liberal Borrowings," *Time*, Aug 2, 1982, pp. 38,39.

47 Kenneth Woodward, "A False Prophetess?" *Newsweek*, Jan 19, 1981, p. 72; Kenneth Kantzer, "Editorial," *Christianity Today*, Oct 24, 1980, pp. 1210, 1219.

48 Dennis Pardee to Lawrence Geraty, Sept 20, 1982.

49 Lewis Walton, *Omega,* (Washington, D.C.: Review and Herald Publishing Association, 1981).

50 *Ibid.*, pp. 49–51.

51 Robert Pierson, "The Omega of Apostasy," *Ministry,* Oct 1977, p. 8.

52 "Recommended Reading," *AR*, July 27, 1981, p. 10.

53 Arnold Reye to Milton Hook, Sept 23, 1981; Raymond Cottrell, "Thoughts on Omega," *West Coast Forum Newsletter,* Oct 1981, pp. 6, 7; Robert Johnston, "A Theological View," *Spectrum,* Dec 1981, pp. 53–57; Walter Utt, "An Historical View" *Spectrum,* Dec 1981, pp. 5762.

54 They were Don McAdams, Walter Specht and Raymond Cottrell.

See Eric Anderson, "Ellen White and Reformation Historians," *Spectrum*, July 1978, pp. 23-26; Don McAdams, "Shifting Views of Inspiration: Ellen G. White Studies in the 1970s," *Spectrum*, March 1980, p. 37.

55 Keith Parmenter to fellow workers, Oct 13, 1980.

56 A published example appears in Robert Olson, *101 Questions on the Sanctuary and on Ellen White,* (Washington, D.C.: Ellen White Estate, March 1981), pp. 90, 91.

57 Fred Veltman, "The Desire of Ages Project: the Data," *Ministry,* Oct 1990, pp. 108, 109.

58 Robert Wieland, "Ellen Whites Inspiration; Authentic and Profound," *AR,* May 31, 1982, p. 9.

59 Fred Veltman, "The Desire of Ages Project: the Data," *Ministry,* Oct 1990, p. 110.

60 Fred Veltman, "The Desire of Ages Project: the Conclusions," *Ministry,* Dec 1990, p. 11–15; Robert Olson, "Olson Discusses the Veltman Study," *Ministry,* Dec 1990, p. 17.

61 Raoul Dederen, "Ellen White's Doctrine of Scripture," *Ministry,* July 1977, supplement, p. 24H.

62 [Fred Veltman], "Personal Postscript," *Ministry,* Dec 1990, p. 14.

63 Jack Cassell to Trevor Lloyd, Jan 20, 1999.

64 Raymond Cottrell, "The Future of Adventism," [ca. 1987], p. 34.

65 Gordon Thomas, "Anti-intellectualism: How to Succeed Without Really Thinking," *Campus Chronicle,* May 27, 1982, p. 30.

66 "Gordon Lee to my dear Adventist friends," Dec 1982; Ron Taylor to John Pye, June 3, 1983; Cottrell, "The Future of Adventism," [ca. 1987], p. 14.

67 Earle Hilgert, "To What Degree Can Critical Thinking be Promoted, or Even Permitted, on an Adventist Campus?" Quadrennial Council for Higher Education, Official Report, (Washington, D.C.: GC Department of Education], 1968), pp. 380–382.

68 Cottrell, "The Future of Adventism," unpublished paper, [ca. 1987], pp. 10,11.

69 "Resigns*,"* *The Journal Era,* May 20,1981, p. 1; Jerry Gladson, "The Crime of Dissent," [ca. 1987], p. 5; Cottrell, "The Future of Adventism," [ca. 1987], p. 48.

70 Kent Seltman, "Adventist Colleges Under Siege: Report on Pacific Union College," *Spectrum,* Dec 1982, pp. 4–6.

71 Raymond Cottrell, "The Adventist Theological Society: Its Ethos

and Hidden Agenda," unpublished paper, Feb 20, 1992, p. 5.

72 E.g., H. J. Harris to Bernard Merrill, Nov 14, 1980; John Zapara to Woodside SDA Church members, Jan 6, 1981; "Fear of Dismissal," *Limboline,* June 11, 1983, p. 17.

73 [Peter] Harry Ballis, "Wounded Healers," *Adventist Professional,* Sept 1992, p. 31. Note: The most comprehensive analysis of the Australasian attrition is by Peter Ballis, in *Leaving the Adventist Ministry: A Study of the Process of Exiting,* (Westport, Connecticut: Praeger, 1999).

74 Parr to Ford, Dec 29, 1980.

75 Rita Clark to Milton Hook, Dec 1984; Vern Heise to Trevor Lloyd, Jan 14, 1998.

76 Athal Tolhurst to J. W. Harvey, Dec 21, 1987.

77 Athal Tolhurst, "'Cut Off' or 'Determined'?" *AR,* Oct 22, 1983, pp. 6, 7, 14.

78 Desmond Ford, "Comments on the Record Article Re 'Cut Off,'" [1983]; Arthur Ferch, interviewed by Milton Hook at Sydney, May 21, 1984.

79 "Opposition to New Seminary Dean," West Coast Forum Newsletter, Oct 1981, pp. 7, 8.

80 Robert Parr to Desmond Ford, Sept 30, 1981.

81 Walter Specht to Neal Wilson, Sept 12, 1981.

82 Cottrell, "The Adventist Theological Society: Its Ethos and Agenda," pp. 3–8

83 E.g., Donald Lee, "Enrolment at NAD Colleges," *Adventist Review,* Dec 29, 1983, p. 23; Cyril Miller, "Sending Tithe to Independent Ministries," *Ministry,* April 1992, pp. 22–24; "Gordon Lee to brethren and sisters," April 12, 1983.

84 Seltman, "Adventist Colleges Under Siege," *Spectrum,* Dec 1982, pp. 5–8.

85 "Current Comment," *The Anchor,* Sept 1989, p. 15

86 R. R. Hallock to General Conference president *et al.,* Feb 8, 1991.

87 John Gate to Ministerial Association Secretaries *et al.,* June 17, 1991; Laurie Evans to administrators et al., June 23, 1994.

88 Quoted in Roy Davies to Jan Paulsen, Oct 24, 2001.

89 Alden Thompson, *Inspiration,* (Hagerstown, Maryland: Review and Herald Publishing Association, 1991).

90 Kai Arasola, *The End of Historicism,* (Sigtuna, Sweden: Datem Publishing, 1990).

91 E.g., Clifford Goldstein, *Graffiti in the Holy of Holies,* (Nampa, Idaho: Pacific Press, 2003).

92 Gerhard Pfandl, *Daniel,* (Warburton, Victoria: Signs Publishing Company, 2004).

93 Erwin Gane, *Enlightened by the Spirit,* (Warburton, Victoria: Signs Publishing Company, 1995), pp. 17, 20, 39, 47, 56, 60, 100.

94 Cottrell, "Our Present Crisis: Reaction to a Decade of Obscurantism," [ca. Aug 1981].

Chapter Fourteen:
Good News Goes Global

The time came when men did not put up with sound doctrine. Instead, to suit their own desires, they gathered around themselves teachers to say what their itching ears wanted to hear. They turned their ears away from the truth and turned aside to myths. But you, Des, kept your head in all situations, endured hardships, did the work of an evangelist, and discharged all the duties of your ministry (2 Timothy 4:3-5, adapted).

Sustained denunciation from extremists and trials like Glacier View would have crushed a person with an eggshell ego, but Des was resilient. However, there comes a time when answering criticism that is ill-advised no longer remains a moral duty. Ford recognized there were more pressing urgencies, primarily the preaching of the apostolic gospel. After dismissal he devoted all his energy to preaching and writing about the deep-seated gospel themes he carried in his heart.

Friends made while at PUC gathered around Des to form a think-tank and strategy for gospel evangelism. Californians Zane and Sharon Kime, together with Don and Vesta Muth and a few others, joined Des and Gill in the engine room of an organization that came to be known worldwide as Good News Unlimited. The name was Des's brainchild. Vesta interacted with many SDA ministers in America who came under fire for preaching views parallel to Des's.[1] It was reported that twenty to thirty congregations hived off from the Adventist Church to form their own fellowships under the leadership of these ministers.[2] They looked to GNU as their spiritual hub, but each group controlled its own activities. The GNU Board was not intent on starting its own denomination. Des and Gill continued to attend SDA churches whenever they could.

Des received invitations to speak both locally and across the country. He was banned from most SDA churches and institutions but wherever a door closed ten others beckoned. One of the earliest openings was the GNU-sponsored meetings in the Berrien Springs public academy near Andrews University in November 1980. Des climaxed the occasion with an address to the Andrews University chapter of Forum. All meetings were crowded out. There was so much interest generated that the Question and Answer period at the Forum meeting lasted over three hours.[3]

Speaking appointments took Des to many quarters. More than 1,800 crammed a hall to listen to him address the Loma Linda/La Sierra chapter of Forum in February 1981. Then he flew to Florida to give six lectures to the Seventh-Day Baptist's Convention where his theme was "Understanding Adventism." These were followed by services with the Church of God Seventh Day in Colorado.[4] Des would frequently speak to scattered congregations of this latter group in the coming years.

Later in 1981 Des was invited to speak at meetings in Puerto Rico. Groups in England, Scandinavia, South Africa and Australia had to be scheduled into the 1982 itinerary because there was just not enough time to respond to every request.[5]

Des conducted meetings at Mindanao University in the Philippines. When he went to Germany, he learned that Neal Wilson had sent messages ahead of him, telling church officials he was not to speak in SDA churches. Nevertheless, members came to hear him at the German SDA Forum group. In Denmark he addressed the nursing class at the SDA Skødsburg Sanitarium. Australian Ray Stanley, conference evangelist, happened to be staying there at the time and frantically tried to put a stop to the meeting, but he found no sympathy with the local president. When Des went to Sweden, one of the cleanest countries in the world, he succumbed to food poisoning after being taken out to eat at a restaurant by a friend. He vividly remembers later having to climb up into a high pulpit in Finland in his weakened condition and grimly hang on to the lectern lest he fall.[6]

From the outset tape recordings were made of some of these meetings. These were made available for a modest fee to those who were unable to attend or who wished to review the meetings and share them with others. This form of ministry rapidly gained popularity, becoming a major avenue for the gospel. By about March 1981 similar messages were being aired on six different radio stations.[7]

Don Muth was instrumental in publishing the earlier GNU magazines. The first issue appeared in April 1981.[8] Throughout the 1980s the editions were printed in black and white at Auburn Oaks Printing, operated by Lowell and Pat Erickson, and later at J and M Printing.[9] The masthead proudly carried the four tenets of the Christian faith that GNU emphasized—"Sola Christos, Sola Fide, Sola Gratia, Sola Scriptura."

Inside the covers was an elaboration of GNUs objectives, a three-part statement of faith highlighting the gospel of Jesus Christ, the authority of Scripture, and the priesthood of all believers.[10] Sectarianism was studiously avoided. The thrust of their Christian witness would span chasms in order to be pan-denominational.

Vesta Muth enlisted her sister-in-law, Marian Fritz, to serve as bookkeeper and office manager.[11] Fritz was experienced and efficient, an indispensable foundation stone who rarely appeared in the limelight but was vital to the solid performance of GNU.

During 1981 three key men provided added impetus to the GNU organization. Noel Mason, an Australian minister who had resigned from the Oregon Conference, came to shepherd the local Auburn Gospel Fellowship and became increasingly involved with GNU. His wife, Jillian, struggled with health problems, and eventually, he found other employment to fund ongoing specialized treatment.[12] The six years that Mason gave to GNU, with his preaching and editorial work, enriched the gospel emphasis.

Another Australian, Calvin Edwards, joined in 1981 and brought additional editorial skills. He also showed management capabilities that were displayed in the organization of significant gospel congresses, conducted first in Monterey, California, then in Atlanta, Georgia. A further series was conducted in Australia during early 1982 and a number of others were later held in America. Meetings in Australia became an annual feature.[13]

In May 1981 Smuts van Rooyen resigned from the faculty of Andrews University Seminary and united with GNU almost immediately. Van Rooyen was an incisive gospel preacher who, like Des, had received many invitations to speak at large SDA gatherings throughout North America. He was a sharp thorn in the side of the perfectionists and traditionalists. At the BRI, the church's watchdog, Richard Lesher's estimation of van Rooyen was that "he is as Ford as Ford."[14] That reputation brought great pressure to bear on him, and he finally saw no point in trying to lecture under a cloud of suspicion. Even though other SDA institutions wanted to employ him, van Rooyen decided he could best serve by preaching the gospel under the auspices of GNU.[15] For two years he traveled extensively to spread the good news, sharing with Des the heavy schedule of speaking engagements.[16] After that, the family returned to South Africa in order for Smuts complete his PhD and, later, they returned to pastoral work in large Adventist churches in

Southern California.

The duplication of cassette recordings and the technicalities required to produce a high-quality product for radio transmission brought to Auburn another talented man, Stan Bisel, from the Andrews University campus. Bisel, like Fritz in the office, became a long-term stalwart behind the scenes, whose expertise proved to be invaluable. His wife, Carolyn, well known at Andrews University for her dazzling soprano solos, continued her performances at GNU gatherings.[17]

By 1982 the GNU Board found itself in dire need of office space to accommodate its vibrant expansion. Blueprints for a building were drawn up by September 1982, and on June 9, 1983, a fine representative building of 3,000 square feet was officially opened.[18] Later, in 1991, a retired preacher, Paul Alderson, headed a building committee that raised funds and supervised additions to the original structure.[19]

Ordination Annulled

The success of GNU apparently attracted hostility both from Robert Brinsmead's organization and some quarters of SDA administration. There was resentment that Des and his associates were attracting Adventists in Europe, South Africa, Australia, New Zealand, Canada, and the United States. Strong alternative worship services emphasizing the gospel were proliferating. Naturally, freewill offerings were being redirected from SDA coffers into support of the radio, cassette, magazine, and seminar ministries of GNU, even though the organization did not actively solicit funds. Des had a policy that his was a faith ministry, and funds would come in as the Spirit moved listeners to make donations.[20]

Keith Parmenter, especially, had initially thought the Glacier View storm would prove to be a passing summer shower, but now realized he was up to his knees in rising floodwaters.[21] He thought he might engineer a solution, transforming the rain into a rainbow by annulling Des's ordination. He failed to recognize that the ordination that matters is not the stamp of a committee but rather the Spirit's endowment. That anointing of an individual is patently obvious to all observers.

While visiting General Conference headquarters for consultation meetings in 1982, Parmenter apparently asked officials for advice regarding Des's ordination, keen to expunge it from Australasian records and diminish Ford's status. Parmenter returned to Australia and presented a rationale to his executive committee for the annulment he desperately sought. It was specifically cast in the context of GNU's forays into Australasian territory.[22]

Parmenter's rationale was flimsy. He accused Des of accepting tithe. That was unproven and positively untrue. He said that Des had misrepresented the facts (told lies) about church ministers, administrators and a majority of denominational scholars. No examples were cited, and Des himself categorically denied the charges. And he alleged Des had drifted further away from the doctrines of the church, compared with his Glacier View manuscript. That, too, was false. Nevertheless, Parmenter relayed his committees ill-founded disquiet to American headquarters.[23]

Consequently, Duncan Eva, Robert Spangler, and Lesher met with Des and Gill on July 28 and 29, 1982. The General Conference men concluded that Des had not radicalized his views since Glacier View and so assured Parmenter. The meeting concluded that further steps should be taken to discuss some narrow fields of disagreement. Four provisos were established, i.e., Des and his associates preach within established SDA beliefs; they do not criticize church administration, either publicly or privately (the latter would be difficult to police without elaborate bugging!); "they keep a low profile in the Australasian Division"; and they continue to seek healing and unity.[24]

In view of these developments the GNU Board postponed seminars in Australia that were planned for the first half of 1983. They wanted to keep a low profile in Australia, in accordance with the agreement.[25]

Athal Tolhurst interpreted the "low profile" as a total ban on entering Australia. When Edwards visited Australia to privately brief two core groups of supporters regarding the postponement of meetings and the discussions with church officials, Tolhurst hit the red alert button. "It appears like a flagrant violation of the conditions," he claimed.[26]

Robert Parr advised Des of the development. He himself did not see it as a breach of the proviso but suggested Des personally assure Wilson that Edward's visit was definitely within the meaning of "low profile." A full explanation appeared in the GNU magazine.[27] The outcome was not damaging to the agreement because Wilson did not echo Tolhurst's alarm.

The incident simply exposed the raw nerve among some Australian administrators. Parmenter continued to turn the screws, his committee voting to recall all of Ford's publications from Adventist sales outlets. These included books such as the black *Daniel* and *Physicians of the Soul*—the latter written to accompany his Sabbath School lesson quarterly that was scotched by the church. In 1980, before the

Glacier View meetings, it had been published by the denominational press in Tennessee. The Signs Publishing Company in Australia was compensated from church funds for all stock withdrawn from its book centers.[28] The recalled stock was apparently destroyed. It was quite clear that Parmenter was hell-bent on destroying any memorials to Des, regardless of the rapprochement efforts.

Wilson initially seemed to be at cross-purposes with the GNU group. He wrote to Des saying that he only wanted to negotiate with him, not his associates. Edwards made it clear that any General Conference delegation would be dealing with all the principals in GNU.[29] Wilson also tried to steer the discussions away from doctrine, saying he believed the main problem was one of relationships.[30] This was a gross oversimplification of the situation. He had conveniently forgotten about the doctrinal content of the Ten Point Statement. Once again, Edwards reflected the wish of his board, stating they were only interested in doctrinal discussions.[31] For that reason Des prepared a list of almost eighty objections to the allegation that the Investigative Judgment was biblical.[32] And Edwards communicated to Eva his board's list of nine suggested doctrinal topics for discussion, adding the names of ten SDA scholars who were specialists in the issues tabled.[33] Only one, Niels-Erik Andreasen, was eventually accepted by church officials.

The GNU Board added that they could see no logical reason why Australian seminars could not proceed while discussions were ongoing.[34] They sensed a plot that discussions could be purposely prolonged by church officials so that Australian seminars would be delayed indefinitely, and gospel interest would peter out.

Finally, it was agreed the discussions would be doctrinal and would involve the GNU principals, Des, van Rooyen, Edwards, and Mason. The General Conference contingent would include Duncan Eva as chairman, Niels-Erik Andreasen, Dick Lesher, Bob Spangler, William Johnsson, Gerhard Hasel and Enoch Oliveira.[35] Edwards, with his usual efficiency, came prepared with duplicated copies of written material for all. On the other hand, only Hasel in the General Conference group brought a script for his own reference. Church officials interpreted this situation as a concerted attempt by GNU men to ambush them.

The meeting began at the El Rancho Motel near San Francisco International Airport on Friday, January 14, 1983, and continued over the weekend.[36] The general topic was "What are the Methods and Principles of Biblical Interpretation, Especially as they Relate to Prophecy?"[37] This was a wise choice because it was foundational. If the question had been resolved prior to 1979 then little controversy might have arisen.

Des and Gill have vivid memories of Eva and Spangler apologizing to them in front of all present for the way matters were handled at Glacier View. This took place after the decision was made to discontinue the meetings. It was explained to them that at the Glacier View meetings pressure had come from Parmenter, and for this reason a hasty reaction had been made against Des. This, therefore, portrayed Wilson and PREXAD as weak-willed in the face of Parmenter. In retrospect, there seemed to be a tendency for the Americans to blame the Australians and for the Australians to blame the Americans. However, the evidence indicates that they were working in unison, with Parmenter and Wilson leading from the front.

Now, in 1982 in California, Eva was under instructions from Wilson not to review the Investigative Judgment doctrine or the authority of Ellen White. Eva made this clear in his opening remarks at the rapprochement meeting.[38] It was, however, unavoidable that their discussions would skirt similar issues. Johnsson, for example, stated during the proceedings that the New Testament teaches that Christ could have come in the first Christian century. Des immediately shot back, "That's what I said at Glacier View!"[39]

Hasel, Wilson's heavyweight theological champion, did much of the talking. He tried to define and redefine the term "apocalyptic prophecy" to suit his own conclusions. He wanted to argue that prophecies about foreign nations are unconditional (Jonah's message to Ninevah is one notable example that nullifies that idea!) and, further, that since Daniel and Revelation are all about foreign nations, all the apocalyptic prophecies in those books are unconditional.[40]

Hasel's argument was in direct opposition to the *SDA Bible Commentary*. It was also radically diluted when he had to admit, under cross-examination from Des and his associates, that Daniel 9 and Revelation 2 and 3, for example, were definitely not about foreign nations and contained provisos for repentance: therefore, they were conditional. Hasel was simply reiterating some of the cheap rationalizations that he and the BRI had invented for their publications after Glacier View.

The GNU group pressed the point that Hasel's definition of apocalyptic prophecy, limiting it to foreign nations, was too narrow and did not stand the test of Scripture. The prophecies of Daniel and Revelation were not just about foreign nations, they stressed, but instead were focused on "the saints" and how they fared at the hands of foreign nations—with eventual victory for the saints and vindication at the end.[41]

Wilson's champion bobbed and weaved without landing a blow. Three Aussies and a Boer were as blunt as three Aussies and a Boer can be without being rude. Eva was surprised that Hasel didn't storm out and go home mortified.[42] The GNU group quickly sensed that the General Conference concept of a bridge between them was one-way traffic from church to reformatory. The church was not in the business of restudy, as it professed. Instead, it was all about re-education of naughty boys who asked embarrassing questions.

Eva informed headquarters that their prized fighter was bloodied and bruised in the first round. Wilson threw in the towel, saying that any further meetings "probably would prove to be unproductive."[43]

In his reply to Wilson, Des admitted there was a vast gulf between his rules for interpreting Scripture and Hasel's rules. Des agreed with the *SDA Bible Commentary*; Hasel had a private view. Des reminded Parmenter in another letter that Ellen White made the comment that SDA leaders have frequently taken the wrong side of an issue. "I believe the last instance was Glacier View," he declared.[44] To the three men involved in the early stages of the attempted rapprochement—Eva, Spangler and Lesher—Ford remarked:

> So long as we ignore the overwhelming evidence of doctrinal fallibility in E. G. W[hite] we shall never be truly Protestant and never make progress. When Israel made a wrong use of the brazen serpent, given them of God, He had it ground to powder—which things are an allegory for us. And I, who give this warning, may be one who in practical terms takes E. G. W[hite] much more seriously than most of my critics.[45]

Wilson informed Parmenter that the talks had broken down. Parmenter quickly called an executive committee together and Ford's ordination was annulled, and he was called apostate.[46] The same punishment was meted out for Noel and Smuts who were ordained SDA ministers—just for attending the meeting.

The guillotine man behind the black balaclava had disposed of the body, only to be haunted for the rest of his life. The same punishment for Noel and Smuts who were ordained—just for attending the meeting. It was reported in the *Review and Herald*.

Good News Unlimited Consolidates

In 1983 the Board of GNU searched for a minister who would provide strong leadership for their gospel outreach in Australasia. They found their man in the person of Ron Allen. Within nine months he had arranged for the broadcasting of GNU messages over seven radio stations in Australia.[47] He stayed with the organization and matured into a fine leader and exponent of the good news.

Allen received strong backing from a core Australian committee, chaired for many years by Bruce Johanson. Bill Sinclair was another key individual, taking on the printing of the Australian magazine at his Western Australian business, Spartan Press.[48]

At times Allen did some of the editorial work for the Australian magazine. Often, it was others who shouldered this responsibility—capable individuals such as Jean Bedford, Brad McIntyre, Paul Porter, Robert Cooper, Roger Jones, and Ritchie Way.[49] Flora Collett, alias Flora Mia, wrote many of the children's stories.[50] In the office at Tweed Heads, Patricia and Dennis Tedman, together with Carolyn Wagemaker, gave years to the gospel cause in the day-to-day operations of GNU.[51]

In the Californian office, when Mason departed, Roy Gee took over as editor of the main magazine in 1987. Gee had sat in Edward Heppenstall's classes and gave his best years to the preaching of the gospel, sharing the load of speaking appointments all over America and Canada.[52] Des said of Gee, "What he does he does with all his heart and with a good mind."[53] Gee and Allen, more than any others besides Des himself, brought stability to the GNU organization because of their robust pastoral talents over a long period.

About the same time, 1987, Gill began to take a more prominent role in the production of the magazine. She had learned typesetting at a local printing shop and then took up this kind of work for GNU.[54] Since 1983 she had written most of the children's stories. Some later ones were simple homilies written by observing her pet dog and cats.[55]

The regular publication of the GNU magazines, together with the seminars and cassettes, served as spiritual meat for hungry gospel lovers. They also provided a sense of family for fellow believers who had found Christ and joined the invisible church. The magazines "Letters [to the Editor]," especially, spoke of the appreciation that the network of readers experienced. One very familiar name appeared in the July 1983 issue—Ruth Bird, who had given Des his first Bible many years earlier and was now in her sunset years. She expressed a real sense of Christian community among GNU readers when she wrote, "I trust this scribbled note finds you all full of courage. God bless, guide and strengthen each one."[56]

Frank Steunenberg, son of the man murdered by well-known Harry Orchard, shared his conviction with Des: "My courage is good in the Lord and His blessed Word. I sense that yours is too, perhaps brighter than mine. So be of good courage, Brother Desmond, and carry on. Some day, I will walk the streets of gold with you."[57]

By 1988 GNU was airing television programs on four American channels. Quarter-hour radio features could be heard on seven American stations and fourteen Canadian outlets. Three years later these avenues increased to five television programs and thirty-six radio stations—seventeen in America (including Hawaii), eighteen in Canada, and over shortwave Christian radio in Tennessee that reached to Africa, Europe and the Middle East.[58] Many radio stations gave a series of approximately 250 short talks by Des that were spread over a twelve-month period. These media outlets and the frequent gospel seminars were complementary, adding impetus to each other in gospel evangelism.

Speaking appointments for Des thrust him into a hectic schedule year after year. For example, his 1991 travels included eight seminars in Australia, one in New Zealand, two in Canada, and seventeen in America. In addition, he addressed five separate Adventist Forum meetings across America.[59]

The periodic visits to Australia gave Des a window of opportunity to spend a few weeks with close family members. In 1987, for example, he visited his mother, jogged and swam with his brother, Val, and met son Paul's Japanese girlfriend, Mina, discovering her to be "a talented, pleasant girl." Paul and Mina later married. He cooked meals for Paul and helped in his plant nursery for a few days. With fatherly concern he came to believe Paul was working too hard. He "may spend his health to get his wealth and then the reverse," he shared with Gill, but Paul's health was preserved. And daughter Elènne, now a barrister-at-law (a lawyer), who was so excited as a teenager when Des bought her a new pair of shoes, spared no expense to purchase a top-quality pair for her dear father.[60]

During these visits to Australia those who had known Luke as a child often asked about his welfare. Des would reply, "He is arguing with his father on philosophical issues plus doing a little schooling, radio, and landscaping." Des's frequent letters to Gill and Luke usually finished with words such as "I think of you both often" or "I think of and pray for you both regularly." He sorely missed them. They had affectionately nick-named him "Cookie" because of his culinary exploits. When away from home he would playfully remind them of his soon return to their kitchen. "Beware," he warned, "the potato man is coming back—so you had better live it up while you can. Avoid potatoes, lentils, beans, avocadoes—then [on my homecoming] they will return in all their glory. But don't spend too much time cooking. I want to be wanted!" He was known to bake twenty-four pounds of full grain bread and biscuits in one day.[61]

If Gill happened to be overseas, on the occasional visit to her mother in New Zealand, they would correspond two or three times a week. "We love you—that's no platitude—it's for real," Des enthused on behalf of Luke and himself.[62] A wry smile no doubt crept over Gill's face as she read further:

> Missing you. Who was that angel living in our house these past days? You had not been gone long and I thought of those invaluable counsels I should have passed on before you left. I cannot conceive that you have safely made it without these—don't talk to strange men. Remember to say your prayers and.... Ah well, it is a mystery how you reached four decades full without such an original counselor.[63]

When home in California Des would exercise by sometimes walking fourteen miles a day and cycle to church on Sabbath. In his words, "a more leisurely day" included reading the essence of two books, preparing a sermon, writing letters, jogging and hosing the garden thoroughly.[64] He continued to have a heavy load of correspondence. Some of it was in the course of maintaining contact with friends within the SDA Church, including Spangler[65] and Heppenstall. Soon after Glacier View the Fords had visited the Heppenstalls and enjoyed warm fellowship. In their last letter to Des and Gill before Ted's debilitating illness prevented him writing any more, they pled, "We love you; better believe it. ... Do come and see us. We never forget you."[66]

Newsy Christmas letters were exchanged regularly with Professor Bruce, Des's colleague at Manchester University. Des also sent him tapes of a few of his sermons. Bruce's name was on the GNU magazine mailing list. "It is always refreshing," he responded, "to see the central message of the gospel emphasized so plainly ... in every issue of GNU."[67]

Des also found new friends in the Evangelical Christian community, some of them prominent leaders in their denominations. One was Gordon Moyes of the Uniting Church in Sydney, who contributed articles to the GNU magazine[68] and later interviewed Des on Australian radio. Another was Walter Martin, renowned for his writings on Christian cults. Des shared speaking appointments with him at various venues and on radio. They prayed together and laughed together. When Martin passed away in 1989, the memorial service included a written testimonial from Des. Martin's widow, Dareene, wrote to Des and Gill, "I thank the Lord for our friendship. May He continue to bless and use you both to His glory!"[69]

Trip to Russia

The 1992 preaching itinerary in Russia took in the region near Chernobyl, where Des saw and learned much about the lethal results of the nuclear disaster that brought tragedy to many families. Traveling in Russia proved to be the most grueling trip of all for him. Eating and sleeping conditions were primitive and irregular. Hygiene was poor. He was advised to boil all his drinking water and eat only cooked food. Fruits and salads prepared by hand were liable to carry gastric disease. Despite all the precautions he contracted what he thought was food poisoning. Sheer fatigue and low blood pressure could have been contributing factors that led to a fall.

While speaking at an appointment, he was overcome with weariness and hot flashes. He knew he was going to faint, so he quickly drew his sermon to a close with John 3:16 and tried to sit down. But it was too late. He collapsed and tumbled forward into the orchestra pit, gashing his chin and bruising his elbows, hips, legs, ribs, and back. He regained consciousness quickly and refused an ambulance. That night he vomited repeatedly and only catnapped. A local evangelist stepped in for the next meeting in the series, but the following night Des managed to preach while sitting in a chair.

"It is a small price to pay for the privilege of preaching the gospel in Russia," Des reflected when he returned home. "What happened is a trifle to what might have been. I am whole, and I consider that miraculous—and I thank God."[70]

For over four years Des took the precaution of either sitting down or walking to and fro while preaching in order not to experience dizziness. The Russian experience shook up his system so badly that he never knew, having started a sermon, whether he was going to finish it. There were, however, no relapses and gradually he fought his way back to a measure of health. His walking regimen aided his recovery, but the accident left him with a traumatized pancreas.[71]

In 1997 Lynden Rogers, then president of Sydney Adventist Forum, coordinated a special visit to Australia by Des and Gill. Alumni of Avondale College were celebrating the institution's centenary year. Rogers knew Des and Gill would be warmly welcomed by many during the nostalgic weekend. Des had been invited to address the alumni, but church officials had intervened. Nevertheless, during Sabbath School, Trevor Lloyd called on Des, seated in the audience toward the front, to stand while he welcomed him. With Des on his feet in full view, the majority gave him a prolonged standing ovation.[72] It was clear that administration could not stymie the gratitude for spiritual enlightenment that many experienced from Ford's ministry.

During the same visit Des conducted a service in the Castle Hill church in Sydney, despite the administration's ban on his preaching. The local church board deliberately ignored the official taboo, insisting Des address them in the Sabbath-morning service. He had recovered from his fall and was back to standing and delivering sermons in scintillating style. Rogers had arranged for both Des and Gill, under the auspices of Forum, to speak in the same church during the afternoon. Gill recalled the human side of Glacier View. Des cast his mind forward in a talk titled, "My Vision for the SDA Church."[73]

The passing years clearly demonstrated the richness of GNU's ministry in comparison to the very ordinary fare found in most SDA congregations and publications. Thousands of testimonials verified the fact that SDA and non-SDA listeners and readers depended on GNU resources for gospel nourishment. Most of them attended various churches, even SDA churches, but their intellectual and devotional roots found the water of life in GNU.

Spectrum's 1994 testimonial began with the words:

Over the past 25 years, Desmond Ford, more than any other one person, made Adventists care passionately about theology. Even before this period, Ford, following in the footsteps of his teacher, Edward Heppenstall, assured Adventists that their salvation was certain not because of their own works, but because of Christ's work on the cross.[74]

257

Ford, himself, was gratified when he looked back over his shoulder. By 1992 GNU's annual budget was US$500,000. "If at any time the money dries up," Des said, "we would take that as a signal from the Lord to move on into other ministries and resign from this one."[75] With Glacier View in mind he observed later, "Because of good helpers all around the world, other doors have opened. While Glacier View may have seemed a tragic affair, in some ways it opened up the way for the gospel, the everlasting gospel, the Pauline gospel, Christ's gospel—the gospel we seek to preach at GNU."[76]

Des was pleased that the GNU magazine, now in full color, was distributed to eighty different countries.[77] His parish was the world— and, more so, with the 1998 establishment of a web site.[78] This facility provided magazines, sermons, individual articles and pastoral letters online. Transcripts of interviews, a question and answer page, radio and speaking schedules, book and DVD listings and other features brought GNU resources within reach of a vast audience.

Books

The website, [now desmondford.org] in general, provides snippets of the gospel message. Weightier or more comprehensive coverage is to be found in Ford's advertised books. Those from the post-1980 era begin with his Glacier View manuscript. *The Adventist Crisis of Spiritual Identity*[79] an assessment of Glacier View, followed in 1982, together with his three-volume commentary on the Book of Revelation, titled *Crisis,* which proved to be his bestseller.[80]

Ford continues to adhere to the Saturday Sabbath, as did Raymond Cottrell. Both men could be critical of some views held by their church, but they tenaciously defended the Sabbath. Des's 1981 book, *The Forgotten Day,* is a classic apologetic for this doctrine.[81] From time to time he buckled on his armor, as in the day of the Burgin debate, and rode out against Sabbath antagonists, both from the pulpit and through the media.[82]

Other books Des published in the 1980s were a two-volume set titled *A Kaleidoscope of Diamonds* (now republished as *The Murder of the Prince of Life),* which was of a Christian apologetic nature;[83] and a hefty volume applying Ellen White's practical principles of living called *Worth More Than a Million,* which was offered to viewers of a television series featuring Ford that began in 1986.[84]

Four smaller works appeared in the early 1980s. These booklets included *Coping Successfully with Stress, How to Survive Personal Tragedy, Good News for Adventists,* and *Will There be a Nuclear Holocaust?*[85]

In the 1990s Des issued *Daniel and the Coming King*[86] and *Right with God Right Now—A Commentary on Romans.*[87] Departing from theology later, he also condensed a lot of research from scholarly journals on the topic of diabetes, for he himself was battling with a form of it. He first sought to understand the disease and then find credible natural remedies. His findings are published in *Eating Right for Type 2 Diabetes.*[88] Ford's latest work, *In the Heart of Daniel,* offers a very credible interpretation of Daniel 9:24–27, a passage Des describes as one "with as many problems as there are cells in a honeycomb." The book serves as a corrective for Ford's *Daniel* because it clarifies and expands on the single point in that book which he has since revised in his thinking. He cites many reputable Bible commentators to support his amended view that these verses from Daniel must first be interpreted in the context of other Hebrew prophets such as Jeremiah, Isaiah, and Haggai, and then understood in the light of the first advent of Christ in addition to the promise of the Second Advent.[89]

Having traveled the equivalent of forty times around the globe preaching the gospel, Des, in his seventies, felt it was wise not to push the boundaries of his health too far. By 2000, after two decades closely associated with GNU headquarters in California, Des and Gill decided to return to Queensland in Australia. This brought about the relocation of Ron Allen from Australia to California. He joined Ford's colleague, Roy Gee, to maintain the gospel outreach in North America. At the same time, it was planned that Allen would visit Australia on a regular basis to share GNU seminars with Des.[90]

Robert Pierson and Neal Wilson thought the gospel could be buried at Glacier View, but it rose phoenix-like from the ashes created. During the 1980s and 1990s, Des never harped on the unscriptural nature of the Investigative Judgment. He only addressed the issue when questioned and occasionally wrote something about it. He continued, instead, to stand by his published commentaries on Daniel and Revelation in which he presented an alternative explanation of latter-day events. His parallel theme was, of course, the apostolic gospel, presented in a stirring and memorable manner.

We can only guess what might have happened if SDA administration had taken the prudent path and allowed Des to preach at the New Gallery in London under the auspices of the church. How many thousands would have joined the gospel throng? How many bright and energetic SDA ministers might have been saved? How many congregations would have remained united in the fold of the denomination? Would the camaraderie of SDA academics have been preserved? Would the SDA Church now be known as a leading evangelical gospel exponent? Or would it remain deeply divided and bogged down in the sands of Nineteenth Century sectarianism?

Furthermore, we are left wondering whether it might have been wiser for Parmenter to tame the tiger in 1979, or earlier, while Des was on the campus of PUC. Instead, church officials decided to keep feeding the fundamentalist animal whose clumsy efforts to explain the Scriptures trod on the best of biblical exegesis. All along, Des continued to preach the gospel from an enlightened viewpoint.

End Notes

1   Gillian Ford to Milton Hook, March 1, 2006.
2   Joel Thurtell, "Heretic Questions 'Pillar' of Adventist Church Doctrine," *The Journal Era,* Nov 26, 1980, pp. 1, 28, 32.
3   *Ibid.;* Lori Pappajohn, "Forum Questions Views, Background," *The Journal Era,* Nov 26, 1980.
4   "Progress of the Gospel," *GNUB,* April 1981, p. 3.
5   "Dr. Ford's Itinerary," *GNUB,* April 1981, p. 4; "A Special Request," *GNUB,* April 1981, p. 3.
6   Milton Hook, interview with Desmond Ford, June 28, 2006.
7   "Announcements," *GNUB,* April 1981, p. 4; "Radio Broadcasts," *GNUB,* April 1981, p. 3.
8   *GNUB,* April 1981, p. 2.
9   Life Sketch, "Patricia Erickson," *GNU,* Feb 1993, insert, p. ii; Gillian Ford to Hook, March 1, 2006.
10   *GNUB,* April 1981, pp. 1, 2.
11   Gillian Ford to Hook, March 1, 2006.
12   "Noel Mason Joins GNU," *GNUB,* Aug 1981, p. 7; Roy Gee, "Word to the Wise," *GNU,* Feb 1987, p. 2.
13   "GNU Acquires Director," *GNUB,* Aug 1981, p. 9; "Announcements," *GNUB,* May 1982, p. 9.
14   "Van Rooyen Resigns: 'Under Pressure but No Ultimatum,'" *Evangelica News,* [May 1981], p. 1; June Franklin (for Charles Watson) to Ron Taylor, telex, Nov 11, 1980.

15 Desmond Ford, "Smuts van Rooyen Joins Staff of Good News Unlimited," *GNUB,* July 1981, p. 1

16 E.g., "With Christ Into the Holiest of All," *GNUB,* Oct 1981, p. 1.

17 "New Staff Member," GNU, Aug 1983, p. 10; "Remembering," *GNU,* Jan 2003, p. 13; Desmond Ford to Gillian Ford, July 8, 1987.

18 "Odds and Ends," *GNU*, Sept 1982, p. 10; "Odds and Ends," *GNU,* July 1983, p. 11.

19 Roy Gee, "GNU Building Addition Progress," *GNU Newsletter,* Sept/Oct 1999, p. 1:

20 Athal Tolhurst to R. J. King et al., March 25, 1982; Gillian Ford to Neal Wilson, July 30, 1982.

21 Keith Parmenter to fellow workers, Oct 13, 1980.

22 "Odds and Ends," *GNU,* Dec 1982, p. 14; Australasian Division Executive Committee minutes, May 19, 1982.

23 *Ibid.*

24 Neal Wilson to Keith Parmenter, telex, Aug 6, 1982; Duncan Eva, "Report of Discussions with Desmond Ford and Associates," *Adventist Review,* Jan 13, 1983, p. 23.

25 "Odds and Ends," *GNU,* Dec 1982, p. 14.

26 Athal Tolhurst to R. J. King, *et al.,* Dec 17, 1982.

27 Robert Parr to Desmond Ford, Dec 31, 1982; "Odds and Ends," *GNU,* Dec 1982, p. 14.

28 Robert Parr to Desmond Ford, [ca. Nov 25, 1982].

29 Neal Wilson to Desmond Ford, Nov 11, 1982; Calvin Edwards to Neal Wilson, Nov 18, 1982.

30 "Interview with Dr. and Mrs. Desmond Ford and Calvin Edwards, Nov 1, 1982," Correspondence, Memos and Publications Relating to the GC–GNU Meetings, Jan 14–17, 1983, (Auburn, California: GNU, [1983]), [pp. 10–12]

31 Edwards to Wilson, Nov 18, 1982.

32 Desmond Ford to Neal Wilson, Feb 9, 1983; James Hefley, "Adventist Teachers are Forced Out in a Doctrinal Dispute," *Christianity Today,* March 18, 1983, p. 23. Note: The points are found in Desmond Ford *et al., Good News for Adventists,* (Auburn, California: GNU, 1985), pp. 52–54.

33 Edwards to Wilson, Nov 18, 1982

34 *Ibid.*

35 Eva, "Report of Discussions," *Adventist Review,* Jan 13, 1983, p. 23.

36 Adrian Zytkoskee, "Ford and Van Rooyen Lose Ordinations," *Spectrum,* March 1983, p. 14.

37 Eva, "Report of Discussions," *Adventist Review,* Jan 13, 1983, p. 23

38 Desmond Ford to Duncan Eva et al., April 25, 1983.

39 Desmond Ford, interviewed by Trevor Lloyd at Caloundra, Jan 7, 2001.

40 [GNU representatives], "Summary of Problems and Progress of Discussion on Friday, January 14, 1982 (sic)," (California: GNU Publications), [ca. January 16, 1983].

41 *Ibid.*

42 Duncan Eva to Desmond Ford, June 6, 1983.

43 Duncan Eva, "G. C. Representatives Meet with Ford Group," *Adventist Review,* Feb 17, 1983, p. 23.

44 Ford to Wilson, Feb 9, 1983; Desmond Ford to Keith Parmenter, Feb 24, 1983.

45 Ford to Eva *et al.,* April 25, 1983.

46 Australasian Division Executive Committee minutes, Feb 1, 1983. See W. D. Eva, "Report of discussions with Desmond Ford and associates," *Adventist Review,* Jan 13, 1983; Duncan Eva, "G. C. Representatives Meet with Ford Group," "Statement on Ford Group," *Australasian Record,* Feb 26, 1983, p. 5. See also Adrian Zytkoskee, "Ford and Van Rooyen Lose Ordinations," *Spectrum Magazine,* Vol. 13, March 1983, pp. 14–16. In Zytkowskee's article he mentions the timely adoption of a new policy, no doubt produced with the 1983 meetings in mind. He stated: "Termination of the two men's ordinations was based on a new policy adopted in October of 1982 at the Annual Council of the General Conference held in Manila, Philippines. According to that revision of the General Conference Working Policy, a minister who 'openly expresses significant dissidence regarding the fundamental beliefs of the Seventh-day Adventist Church' may lose his credentials. The status of his ordination will be reviewed at an appropriate time. If he persists in dissidence, he may 'make void' his ordination, moving him into the category of an apostate. It then becomes the 'duty' of the local church where he is a member to administer discipline, possibly including disfellowshipping."

47 "Minister Appointed," *GNU,* Nov 1983, p. 11; "Odds and Ends," *GNU,* Aug 1984, p. 11.

48 E.g., Ron Allen to friend, Feb 1988; *GNU,* Jan 1988, p. 2.

49 ["Editorial"], *GNU,* March 1984, p. 2; ["Editorial"], *GNU,* Feb 1983, p. 2; ["Editorial"], *GNU,* March 1985, p. 2; ["Editorial"], *GNU,* April 1988, p. 2; Roger Jones, "Editorial," *The Good Newsletter,* July 1999, p. 1; Ritchie Way, "Editorial," *The Good Newsletter,* Jan 2004, p. 1.

50 E.g., Flora Mia, "Snakes," *Good News Australia,* July 1988, p. 14.

51 E.g., "Transition," Good News Australia, No. 3, 2000, p. 9; Ron Allen, "Dear Friend of the Gospel," Good News Australia, No. 5, 2003, p.7.

52 Gee, "Word to the Wise," *GNU,* Feb 1987, p. 2; [Roy Gee], "Dr. Edward Heppenstall," *GNU,* Oct 1994, p. 13; Roy Gee, "Word to the Wise," *GNU,* June 1987, p. 2.

53 Desmond Ford to Gillian Ford, July 19, 1987.

54 Gillian Ford to Hook, March 1, 2006.

55 E.g., Gillian Ford, "The Tale of the Tonsils," Good News for Kids, *GNU,* Aug 1983, insert, pp. 3, 4; Gillian Ford, "Banished," *GNU,* Oct 1988, pp. 12–14

56 Ruth Bird, "Letters," *GNU,* July 1983, p. 12. Note: Ruth Bird passed away in 1990 aged eighty-nine.

57 Frank Steunenberg to Desmond Ford, Nov 13, 1983.

58 "Tune in With Good News Unlimited," *GNU,* Jan 1988, p. 6; "Radio and TV Log," *GNU,* Dec 1991, insert, p. iv.

59 *Ibid.,* p. ii.

60 Desmond Ford to Gillian and Luke Ford, [March 22, 23–25, 27, April 3, 7, ca. April 1987].

61 Desmond Ford to Gillian and Luke Ford, [March 22, 27, ca. March, ca. April, July 4, 1987].

62 Desmond Ford to Gillian Ford, [July 20, 1987].

63 Desmond Ford to Gillian Ford, [July 3, 1987].

64 Desmond Ford to Gillian Ford, [July 3, 7, 20, 1987].

65 E.g., Desmond Ford to Robert Spangler, Oct 18, 1982, Jan 27, 1991,

66 Edward and Margit Heppenstall to Desmond and Gillian Ford, Christmas 1991.

67 Frederick Bruce to Desmond and Gillian Ford, Dec 18, 1984.

68 E.g., Gordon Moyes, "Authentic Faith—Counterfeit World," *Good News Australia,* June 1988, pp. 4,5.

69 Dareene Martin, Thank you card, [ca. July 1989].

70 Desmond Ford, "Good News Unlimited in Russia," *GNU,* Nov

1992, pp. 6, 7.

71 Desmond Ford, "Marvel and Mystery of Prayer," *GNU,* June 1999, p. 11.

72 Avondale College Homecoming Weekend, Aug 30, 1997, tape-recording

73 "Historic Tapes Available," *GNU,* Oct/Nov 1997, p. 12.

74 Editors, "Desmond Ford: Herald of Gospel Theology," *Spectrum,* Dec 1994, p. 4.

75 Michael Saucedo, "Good News Keeps on Going and Going," *Spectrum,* March 1992, p. 9.

76 Ford, "Marvel and Mystery of Prayer," *GNU,* June 1999, p. 12.

77 *Ibid.*

78 Advertised as www.goodnewsunlimited.org, *GNU,* July 1998, p. 6.

79 Desmond and Gillian Ford, *The Adventist Crisis of Spiritual Identity,* (Newcastle, California: Desmond Ford Publications, 1982).

80 Desmond Ford, *Crisis,* 3 vols., (Newcastle, California: Desmond Ford Publications, 1982); Saucedo, Spectrum, March 1992, p. 10.

81 Desmond Ford, *The Forgotten Day,* (Newcastle, California: Desmond Ford Publications, 1981).

82 E.g., Desmond Ford, "Is the Seventh-day Sabbath Christian?" *Adventist Today*, July/Aug 1996, pp. 1–14.

83 Desmond Ford, *A Kaleidoscope of Diamonds*, 2 vols., (Newcastle, California: Desmond Ford Publications, 1986).

84 Desmond Ford, *Worth More Than a Million,* (Auburn, California: Good News Unlimited, 1987); *GNU Catalog*, 1988, p. 4.

85 Desmond Ford *et al., Good News for Adventists,* (Auburn, California: Good News Unlimited, 1985); *GNU Catalog,* 1988, pp. 8, 10.

86 Desmond Ford, *Daniel and the Coming King,* (Newcastle, California: Desmond Ford Publications, 1996).

87 Desmond Ford, *Right with God Right Now,* (Newcastle, California: Desmond Ford Publications, 1999).

88 Desmond Ford, *Eating Right for Type 2 Diabetes,* (Lincoln, Nebraska: iUniverse Inc., 2004).

89 Desmond Ford, *In the Heart of Daniel,* (Lincoln, Nebraska: iUniverse Inc., 2007).

90 "Transition," *Good News Australia,* No. 3, 2000, p. 9.

Chapter Fifteen:
Back Home in Australia

Numerous friendships were forged by Des and Gill during the almost quarter of a century they spent in America. Those ties would never be broken. Instead, they would simply be stretched by the distance across the Pacific Ocean.

During the closing months of 2000, Des and Gill settled into a home at Shelly Beach near Caloundra, Queensland. Son Paul helped with the unpacking. Luke had chosen to remain in California. The new quarters were situated alongside daughter Elènne's home and within a stone's throw of the beach. Des added swimming to his walking regimen, even in the cooler winter months.[1]

Reluctantly, Des and Gill severed membership with the PUC campus church. It was the noble thing to do because they would no longer be able to attend. At the same time, they felt it would not be wise to regularly attend an SDA Church near Caloundra, because it would place the local preacher, no matter who he was, under suspicion of being a sympathizer.[2] Des accepted invitations to speak at Baptist churches, including the large Metropolitan Tabernacle in Brisbane. He also spoke on occasion at a charismatic church whose minister attended Des's meetings at St Francis Theological College, Brisbane. Eventually, the way opened for Des to conduct Sabbath services every fortnight in a farm chapel at nearby Peachester. These meetings were deliberately scheduled for Sabbath afternoons in order not to compete with regular Adventist morning services.[3]

Despite deliberately keeping at arm's length from SDA churches, an official warning was issued in May 2001 from Wahroonga headquarters that under no circumstances should SDA ministers invite Des to preach. The ban cited Des's alleged sin of accepting tithe. As a gospel preacher he was, of course, entitled to do that, but the accusation was false. Furthermore, officials believed he would unsettle the laity.[4] That much was true.

If ever a church group needed unsettling it is the SDA Church. They are still unconvinced about the nature of the seal of God—Is it the Sabbath or is it the Holy Spirit?[5] The director of the BRI still publishes silly articles about a literal sanctuary in heaven—"a majestic structure," he describes as if he has visited, with "no less than two rooms."[6] Headquarters continues to confound its ministry by republishing the widely divergent views of Erwin Gane and Edward Heppenstall on perfection.[7] And they are still limping with two opinions about basics such as the nature of Christ, the nature of sin, and the nature of man.[8] Sanctification is still defined in the denominations Fundamental Statements as "imparted" righteousness. Indeed, the Roman Catholic idea of internalized righteousness is clearly expressed in a recent *Ministry* article:

> It is His work to write the law inwardly through His Holy Spirit. Thus, the law becomes internalized within the believer, an integral part of the believer's will, permeating it so as to make the human will and the divine law conform perfectly with each other.[9]

These continued attempts to express the gospel in perfectionist terms demonstrates that the denomination's perception of righteousness by faith alone remains dull. While some may claim the church has matured in the last half century, the evidence indicates it is still deeply fractured and not seriously intent on a gospel path. The church cannot claim to have a list of illustrious gospel preachers. Even the scholars within the church remain divided between two theological societies that are hardly on speaking terms.

A notable exception to the Laodicean spirit and malaise within the church was the gospel statement adopted by Campus Hill Church at Loma Linda University in 2001.[10] Unfortunately, there were no widespread repetitions.

The preaching ban imposed against Des by the Australasian church outraged many members, provoking a storm of protest letters from as far afield as England.[11] Many came from the Avondale College campus church in addition to others from elsewhere on the eastern seaboard of Australia. They were all looking forward to his unfettered ministry. With deep disappointment some reasoned:

> I admire the fact that Des has not undermined confidence in the church or leadership. I admire his patience, his persistence and integrity. Des has much to teach the church about suffering as a Christian. He has much to contribute to making the church foremost

in uplifting Christ before the world.[12]

Instead of that cold shoulder, should we not see a sincere attempt to come to a mutual understanding and extend the hand of fellowship again? Surely that ought not to be too difficult for a mature church![13]

We need from our leaders and from our church, here in Australia, an expression and experience of grace. It is only the power of the gospel that can unite us in this familial fellowship.[14]

He [Ford] is one of the most powerful and compelling speakers of our time—worldwide. He is the most insightful preacher on the subject of righteousness by faith, a truth most needed in the church at this time.... You gentlemen [Division officers] need to take hold of the fortitude necessary to do the Christian thing. Des Ford should not only be fully restored to his church, but unashamedly championed. Only then will our church move forward in this country, away from the disgraceful day we rejected the truth of righteousness by faith and along with it, many feel, the Holy Spirit.[15]

Des experienced a similar church ban when he was scheduled, by invitation from the PUC associate minister, to return to the Monterey area in California at the end of 2005. A local group, the board of Adventist Today, arranged for him to speak at the Hyatt Hotel. Erwin Gane heard of it and stirred up opposition, twisting the tail of Don Schneider, president of the North American Division, to proclaim a taboo. However, the gospel cannot be silenced by wormwood. The meetings proceeded with a little help from the free advertising given by the SDA Church's taboo.[16]

By words and actions over more than two decades the church's leaders showed their true colors. They marched around Jericho a couple of times and then scurried back to Egypt for the fishing haunts of their ancestors. Perhaps they have much to fear about the future, for it seems they have forgotten the way the Lord has led them in the past.

Des soldiered on. Having settled into his new home, he accepted appointments, under the auspices of the Christian Lawyer's Association in Brisbane, speaking twice a month at breakfasts attended by physicians, lawyers, and businessmen.[17] He also taught classes at the Baptist Bible College, the Brisbane School of Theology, Mueller College, and St Francis Theological College.[18] These activities were in addition to annual seminars he conducted for GNU throughout Australia. Furthermore, his policy has always been to respond when Christians call upon him to conduct baptisms, weddings, and funerals.[19] It remains part of his pastoral calling and ministry. At the same time Gill established a consultancy to assist women with hormonal difficulties as she had experienced earlier.

Sydney Adventist Forum engaged Des to speak on occasions. One historic meeting in 2005 was devoted to remembering the famous gathering at Glacier View in 1980—a twenty-fifth anniversary with mixed emotions. Norman Young, a delegate at the 1980 assembly, contributed a paper in absentia, and Arthur Patrick offered an analysis of the event. Alwyn Salom and Ford himself recounted some of their vivid recollections. Des also conducted the Sabbath morning worship service, a moving discourse from biblical prophecy. "Jesus has been judged worthy," he reminded his listeners. "Rest assured," he concluded, "those who are in Christ are also judged worthy and do not have to wait for some investigative process to determine their eternal fate." At that point his audience broke into sustained applause.[20]

Des also shared two memorable presentations that took place in Gordon Moyes's Wesley Theatre, an inner-city auditorium in Sydney. The first, a debate, was with Brian Wilshire, a well-known atheist on Sydney radio.[21] Another was a symposium held with Michael Denton, pitched around the theme of creationism and evolution.[22] Hundreds of listeners were attracted to these various meetings.

Retirement has naturally allowed for more family time and reflective hours that are devoted to writing, some for *GNU*. In 2003 Gill's aging mother was brought into their home for care.[23] She passed away peacefully in 2006.[24] Des maintains contact with his ailing brother, Val. Elènne and Paul, together with their families, are close by. A network of many friends, some known for decades, surround them.

Recently, Des established his own Web site, www.desmondford.org, principally for the purpose of sowing his gospel sermons in near and far-flung fields. The themes correspond, of course, to those on the GNU site.[25]

Conclusions

Prophecy is more difficult than history. To speculate on the future is generally futile. It is more edifying to ponder the past and present rather than the distant unknown. Des looks back and gratefully remembers the godly men and women who shaped his destiny. They were numerous. Some were church luminaries. Others were unsung saints. Many more, long gone, witnessed to him from the pages they had written and the lives they had lived. More than a few were Christian martyrs. It is, however, the pre-eminent martyr, Jesus Christ Himself, who remains his paramount contemporary. Jesus has led him through trying and miraculous circumstances. Des speaks of Him continually. He has not betrayed Him.

The teenage memories of crowds spilling from the Sydney underground railway station never left Des. They evoked a divine ordination in his marrow. Despite numerous distractions of the devil and the scheming of devious men, he has explained the Scriptures to a vast throng around the world. His detractors were like little boys throwing pebbles at a speeding train. The Spirit brought conviction to his preaching. Thousands now testify of the unlimited grace of God in their lives. For them the assurance of their salvation is sweet and real. His legacy will continue to enrich many.

End Notes

1   Gillian Ford, "Waiting for Heaven," *GNU,* Nov 2001, pp. 13, 14; Desmond and Gillian Ford, "Keeping in Touch," *GNU,* Sept 2002, p. 11.
2   Desmond Ford to Milton Hook, Aug 10, 2005.
3   "Mango Hill Farm," *The Good Newsletter,* Sept 2003, p. 11.
4   Ron Allen, "SDA Church Acts Against Dr. Desmond Ford," *Good News Australia,* No. 4, 2001, p. 13; Denis Tedman, "Ford Judged, Found Guilty and Sentenced," *Good News Australia,* No. 4, 2001, insert.
5   E.g., "Letters," *AR,* Dec 2, 2000, p. 13.
6   Angel Rodriguez, "Is the Heavenly Sanctuary Really Real?" *Adventist Review,* Dec 2002, p. 15.
7   Erwin Gane et al., inserted reprint of Oct 1970, *Ministry,* Aug 2003
8   E.g., "Letters," *Ministry,* Feb 2005, p. 3.
9   Michael Hasel, "Old and New: Continuity and Discontinuity in God's Everlasting Covenant," *Ministry,* March 2007, p. 20.
10   Desmond Ford, "Campus Hill Congregation, Loma Linda, Votes Gospel Statement," *GNU,* Sept 2001, p. 17 .
11   Mary Trim to Barry Oliver, Dec 16, 2001.
12   Douglas Martin to Barry Oliver, Oct 23, 2001.
13   Flora Aris to Barry Oliver, [Nov 26, 2001].
14   Calvin and Yvonne Stewart to Barry Oliver, Nov 17, 2001.
15   Kevin Ferris to Barry Oliver, Aug 7, 2001.

16 Dick and Kay Paulson to Desmond and Gillian Ford, July 11, 2005; Desmond Ford to Milton Hook, Sept 3, 2005.

17 E.g., "Regular Meeting with Dr. Desmond Ford," *The Good Newsletter,* Jan 2001, p. 9.

18 Desmond and Gillian Ford, "Keeping in Touch," *Good News Australia,* No. 3, 2002, p. 11; Desmond Ford, "Letter from Desmond Ford," *GNU,* June 2003, p. 8; "Dr. Fords Speaking Engagements," *The Good Newsletter,* Jan 2003, p. 9.

19 Desmond Ford to Gillian and Luke Ford, [ca. 1992]; "Weddings," *AR,* Oct 1, 2005, p. 13; "Obituaries," *AR,* June 28,2003, p. 13, *Desmond Ford: Reformist Theologian, Gospel Revivalist.*

20 Two reports appear on atoday.com under Archives, Dec 2005, Jan 2006.

21 Desmond and Gillian Ford, "Keeping in Touch," *Good News Australia,* No.3, 2002, p. 11.

22 "Genesis and the Age of the Earth Revisited," *The Good Newsletter,* July 2002, p. 5.

23 Gillian Ford to Milton Hook, Dec 22, 2003.

24 Gillian Ford to Milton Hook, Nov 16, 2006.

25 Desmond Ford, The Great Invitation, Feb 2005, [p. 4]; Desmond Ford to Milton Hook, July 16, 2005.

Chapter Sixteen:
Appendix A: Twenty-Eight Fundamental Statements

[These points do not necessarily represent Des's viewpoints. These are the explanations of the author.]

The Daniel Committee, meeting intermittently from the 1930s to the 1960s, was established by the General Conference to test and, if needs be, recommend corrections to SDA interpretations of Scripture. Their discussions canvassed Scripture passages such as Leviticus 16, Daniel 7 to 11, and Hebrews 9, especially as these chapters related to the Day of Atonement ceremony and the denominations teaching about an Investigative Judgment that began in 1844.

The visions of Daniel were central to their discussions. These visions culminate with the kingdom of God triumphant. With regard to the specific visions of Daniel 8 and 9, so vital to the SDA identity, there are some unquestionable similarities between them. Both relate to God's chosen people. Both speak of the destruction of the destroyer of God's people and a restoration of God's people. Both have their foundation in God's covenant of grace with the saints. However, many of the problems with the SDA interpretations lie in the obvious separateness of the two visions, removed from each other by approximately twelve years. The Daniel Committee published no papers and made no recommendations. Where they hoped to establish solid foundations for their views, they discovered only sandcastles.

Des was aware of the unstable nature of the SDA views, but spent the 1960s and 1970s defending them while at the same time trying to find better arguments for them. He finally had to admit some radical changes had to be made.

The following is a survey of some of the more important sandcastles, together with some alternative views that may withstand the test of closer examination.

The End Notes chiefly cite Nineteenth Century references. The Adventist Church has adopted a few modifications since that era, but the essential lines of argument remain. It is helpful to compare and contrast the early references with relatively recent publications such as the volumes published by the Biblical Research Committee soon after Glacier View together with *Seventh-day Adventists Believe,* (Hagerstown, Maryland: Review and Herald Publishing Association, 1988), pp. 41, 314–331, 347. A remarkable similarity exists, despite the passage of time. It serves to illustrate the irony that the SDA Church prefers to cling to some threadbare traditions while praying for added enlightenment.

General

1. **Seventh-day Adventists traditionally literalize the heavenly sanctuary, spoken of in Hebrews 8:1, 2, thinking of it as a building with similar rooms to the Hebrew earthly model, but on a grand scale.[1]**

This view trivializes the nature of God and the heavens, reducing both to the human level. It confines God to a building in the sky, indeed, to a room within that alleged building, whereas Hebrews speaks of Christ entering not a building but "heaven itself" (Hebrews 9:24).

Solomon, at the dedication of his glorious temple, was under no illusions about the truth of the matter. He prayed, "The heavens, even the highest heaven, cannot contain You. How much less this temple I have built!" (1 Kings 8:27).

Biblical descriptions of God, who is Spirit (John 4:24), and His heaven are of necessity couched in human terms and bear no resemblance to heaven's reality. Persisting with anthropomorphic images of God and His dwelling place, accomplishes little except on a kindergarten level.

2. **Seventh-day Adventists misunderstand some basic functions of the Hebrew sanctuary, both daily and annual services. One of the common misconceptions is the function of sacrificial blood. They teach that the daily sacrificial blood, bearing the sin, was usually taken into the Holy Place. They teach that this brought moral defilement to the inner sanctum during the daily services, and this defilement was cleansed by sacrificial blood during the annual Day of Atonement service.[2]**

Is it not a stark contradiction to teach that sacrificial blood tainted with sin cleanses the sanctuary only during the Day of Atonement service, but defiles the sanctuary during the daily services throughout the rest of the year?

When one thinks of the earthly or heavenly sanctuary, is it not grossly inappropriate to depict God dwelling in a defiled building? The Hebrews even thought it inappropriate for the earthly sanctuary. That is why there were so many rules ensuring ceremonial cleanliness. Strict taboos existed to maintain this cleanliness of the sanctuary and priesthood. Foreigners, commoners, women, ceremonially unclean priests, semen, menstrual blood, unfit and non-sacrificial animals, and fire from the common hearth were all strictly forbidden in the holier places. Does it not seem pointless to maintain such extraordinary care with the constant ceremonial cleanliness of the sanctuary, if the Holy Place was inevitably and simultaneously defiled by sins carried on sacrificial blood? If defilement of the sanctuary was taking place on a daily basis, it would force the necessity of a continual cleansing ceremony, not just once a year on the Day of Atonement.

Scripture itself repeatedly testifies that sacrificial blood, even that in the daily service, made an atonement or cleansing from sin (Leviticus 1–7). It was also used to consecrate priests (Exodus 29:19–21). If sacrificial blood effectively defiled, then we would have to assume the contradiction that the priests were defiled in their ceremonial purification ceremony!

It is worth noticing, too, that the blood of most sin offerings was not carried into the Holy Place or first apartment of the sanctuary, contrary to traditional SDA teaching. The blood of burnt offerings was either sprinkled or drained out at the altar in the courtyard (Leviticus 1). Sin offerings of members of the community and their leaders were administered in the same manner (Leviticus 4: 22–35).

Furthermore, it is important to consider the Day of Atonement service as not utterly different from all the other Hebrew services. It was a zenith of the festal year, but in essentials it differed little from the other atonement services. It was when atonement was thoughtfully and joyfully celebrated in all its aspects—confession, substitution, efficacy of sacrificial blood, cleansing from sin, freedom from guilt and reconciliation with God in the covenant relationship. The vital point is that it was done on a national level during the Day of Atonement (Leviticus 16:34). In fact, all annual services were national reconsecrations of the sanctuary and the people within the covenant relationship. They were interpretations of God's simple plan of forgiveness, reiterated each time with sacrificial blood.

One of the last festivals of the Hebrew calendar, the Feast of Tabernacles, brought to another pinnacle: the application of cleansing sacrificial blood with the offering of 200 or more bulls, rams, lambs, and goats, more than at any other ceremony (Numbers 29:12–40). This event was so important it was one of three mandatory services for males (Deuteronomy 16:16). Surprisingly, the Day of Atonement, considered by Adventists to be the most important ceremony, is not mentioned among the mandatory festivals.

Adventists have the notion, too, that sin has some vital physical properties that are extracted from the sinner at atonement, carried in the sacrificial blood, and locked down securely like nuclear waste, awaiting transport to some final remote dumping site. Forgiveness of sins is highly literalized. Furthermore, they find it hard to believe that atonement means a complete atonement there and then. They assume it is a prolonged process. This is in sharp contrast to the sense given in Leviticus 1–7.

3. **Seventh-day Adventists have an atypical view of God's judgment. They divide the judgment into two phases, a lengthy investigative period beginning in 1844 and an executive event at the end of time with the destruction of the wicked. The heavenly ministry of Jesus is also divided into two phases. They teach that prior to 1844 Christ's heavenly ministry was solely one of intercession. An individual could receive forgiveness of sins in this process, but it was conditional, dependent on a final and absolute examination of personal morality. That mother-of-all Supreme Court sessions began, they say, in 1844 when Jesus took on the additional role of judge to assess individually first the dead and then the living.[3]**

This teaching leaves the Christian believer standing in a perpetual state of apprehension, pacing up and down with sweaty palms, fidgeting and sighing. None can be sure of their standing before God until their name comes up for final judgment. And none knows when their name will come up for judgment. The mental picture of the Investigative Judgment is quite foreign to New Testament descriptions of the judgment—"Rejoice that your names are written in heaven," Jesus said (John 10:20), and those who love God "will have confidence on the day of judgment,"

John assured his readers (1 John 4:17).

When Jesus was predicting His death, He said to His audience, "Now is the time for judgment on this world; now the prince of this world [Satan] will be driven out" (John 12:31). Calvary, He said, would precipitate a cosmic judgment, condemning Satan and vindicating Himself. Jesus and the apostles, therefore, spoke of the judgment in the present tense, as something that already belonged to their day (John 16:8–11; 1 Peter 4:17; Revelation 14:7). It follows that because Jesus has already been judged as the Worthy One (e.g., Revelation 5:12), any disciples who are in a covenant relationship with Jesus will then be judged as having that same worthiness imputed by faith. That is what brings Christian assurance. It is the joy of heaven already begun. There need be no sweaty palms, no fidgeting, no uncertainty. It is paramount that Christians remain in the covenant relationship. Then any judgment by God loses its sting, whether it is at death or instantaneously at the end of time.

4. **Seventh-day Adventists consider their own days, from the inception of their church in the Nineteenth Century and onwards, as the biblical period of "the time of the end." This KJV phrase is preferred by the denomination.**[4]

Different translations of Daniel 1:18; 8:17, 19; 10:14; 11:35, 40; 12:4, 9 express the time variously as "the last days," "the latter days," "the time of the end," "days to come," "in the future," or "at the appointed time." Generally speaking, these phrases mean "in God's own good time," for God is in control of history. There is the element of open-endedness in the phrases.

It is clear from Scripture that God's kingdom, which Jesus so frequently spoke about, was inaugurated with His first advent (e.g., Matthew 3:2; 4:17; 10:7; 12:28; Mark 9:1; Luke 10:9, 11). Likewise, New Testament writers clearly refer to their own era as "the last days" (Acts 2:1–17; Hebrews 1:2; 1 Peter 1:18–20; 1 John 2:18). With God's kingdom established in the first Christian century, the time of the end immediately prior to the Second Advent was always imminent, always a possibility. Therefore, any prophecies relating to the time of the end were always in a position to be fulfilled. They did not have to extend to 538 or 1798 or 1844, or any other specific date that an interpreter might apply.

It is a legitimate exercise to look for and expect fulfillments of Daniel's prophecies at any time after he received them, even in his own day and certainly by the first century AD, when Christ's kingdom was inaugurated. SDAs have not used the New Testament to full advantage, especially when interpreting the prophecies of Daniel. Christ's references to the kingdom of God are His applications of Daniel 2:44, 45; 7:13, 14; 8:14 and 9:24.

5. **Seventh-day Adventists apply what is traditionally called "the year-day principle" to certain time elements in apocalyptic prophecy. Numbers 14:34 and Ezekiel 4:6 are used to verify its use. It is not a consistent application, for they do not apply the principle to the Millennium.**[5]

The book of Numbers is a book of history, not apocalyptic prophecy. The verse under question addresses a punitive judgment for past sins, one year of suffering allotted to the Israelites for each day of unbelief while exploring Palestine. It was a one-off judgment not intended as a general rule applicable to all judgments. And it had one eye on the past. It was not solely a simple projection into the future. What lay ahead for Israel was given as forty literal years, not in terms of days.

The prophet Ezekiel was instructed by God to act out a mini-drama, reclining on his left side for 390 days and on his right side for 40 days. These days represented the 430 years of Israel's past sins and foreshadowed a coming siege of Jerusalem. It was, of course, impossible for Ezekiel to spend 430 years reclining on his side. The day-for-a-year allocation was designed solely for the practical purpose of an extended play. The time element referred to the past. It was not a principle for interpreting future events.

More importantly, if the year-day theory is a legitimate tool of prophetic interpretation, we would expect it to be applied by the inspired New Testament evangelists. But they never used it, despite the fact they repeatedly appealed to Old Testament passages to prove Jesus was the Messiah. How convenient and conclusive it would have been to quote Daniel 9:24–27, using the year-day principle, to establish the dates 27, 31 and 34 AD as SDAs do! Almost the entire Hebrew nation, especially the learned rabbis, would have accepted Jesus without question if the passages were to be understood in the way SDAs interpret them.

The year-day theory was introduced by Christian commentators, centuries after the close of the New Testament canon. It was used to rationalize the unexpected and lengthy delay of Christ's Second Coming, with interpretations unheard of in apostolic times.

The use of the year-day theory has prompted SDAs to put forward dubious dates as fulfillments of Bible prophecy. E.g., 538 AD to 1798 AD are proposed as the *termini* for papal supremacy in fulfillment of the 1260 days prophecy (Revelation 11:3; 12:6).

The starting date of this prophecy is chosen because it is the era when Emperor Justinian declared the Pope to be head of all the Christian churches and his general, Belisarius, defeated the Ostrogoths, thus removing a threat to the papacy. SDAs ignore the reverses experienced at this same time, i.e., Belisarius thought Pope Silverius was in league with the Ostrogoths and had him exiled in 537 AD.; the Ostrogoths recaptured Rome in 541 AD and did not lose control until 562 AD; and in the meantime, Emperor Justinian harassed Pope Vigillius and summoned him to court. These facts do not indicate that there was any significant rise to power in practical terms by the papacy at that time.

Thereafter, the papacy experienced an up and down existence. In 653 AD Pope Martin was exiled in chains. In 799 AD Pope Leo III fled to France because he was attacked by Roman aristocrats. Pope Stephen VI was imprisoned and strangled to death in 897 AD. Six years later the same fate occurred to Pope Leo V. In 928 AD, Pope John X was imprisoned and smothered to death by Roman aristocrats. Pope John XIII was imprisoned by Roman aristocrats in 965 AD Pope Benedict VI was imprisoned and strangled to death in 974 AD In later years similar reverses involving murder, imprisonment or exile were suffered by Pope John XV (996 AD), Pope Benedict IX (1044 AD), Pope Gregory VI (1047 AD), Pope Gelasius II (1119 AD), Pope Innocent II (1133 AD), Pope Alexander III (1167 AD), Pope Boniface XIII (1303 AD), Pope John XXII (1328 AD), Pope Pius III (1503 AD), and Pope Clement VII (1527 AD). The division of the Christian church into East and West in 1054 AD; the setting up of antipopes in France and Spain during the 1300s; and the Protestant Reformation of the 1500s all weakened the power of the papacy. The arrest of Pope Pius VI in 1798 AD, fades as a significant date to end papal supremacy, especially when one considers the annexation of the lucrative Papal States by Napoleon in 1809 AD and their confiscation by the Italian government in 1870 AD, actions far more devastating than the arrest of Pope Pius VI in 1798.

The dates 538 AD and 1798 AD are arbitrarily chosen by SDAs to fit a bankrupt theory.

Similarly, the dates proposed for the prophecy of Daniel 9 are dubious. The date 457 BC is chosen to begin the fulfillment on the strength of the decree of Artaxerxes in Ezra 7. However, this decree only allowed for some Temple utensils to be returned, the donation of some precious metals, the tax exemption of the priesthood, and the formation of the judiciary in Jerusalem. There is no mention of a physical restoration and rebuilding of Jerusalem involving bricks and mortar, as the prophecy seems to specify.

A better date is the decree of Cyrus issued at the end of the seventy years of captivity, about 538 BC, permitting the rebuilding of the Temple, taking for granted that, as the builders worked on the Temple, they also built their own houses to live in. In fact, according to Haggai 1:4, some eighteen years later, they were living in luxurious homes. It is evident, therefore, that the physical reconstruction of Jerusalem began as soon as the returning exiles arrived back from Babylon. It makes better sense that God would allocate the probationary 490 years from the start of the captives return to Jerusalem rather than waiting about eighty years before beginning the countdown. This would mean that the 490 years of probationary time was due to expire about 48 BC. The moral condition of the nation at that time was far removed from the covenant expectations in the prophecy—"finish transgression," and "to put an end to sin." It appears that God, because of His patience and abiding love for His people, extended His period of 490 years of grace. No being in the universe could therefore ever accuse God of acting precipitously against His beloved people.

The exactness of the end dates given by SDAs for the termination of the 490 years also presents difficulties. They insist on 27 AD for the baptism of Christ, 31 AD for the cross, and 34 AD for the end of Israel's probationary time. The last date is marked variously as the stoning of Stephen, the conversion of Saul, and the proclamation of the gospel to the Gentiles.

Scripture identifies the start of John the Baptist's ministry (Luke 3: 1, 2), thought to be 26/27 AD. For how long did he preach before baptizing Jesus? No one can be sure. Not having an exact date for the beginning of Christ's ministry means that the exact year of the cross is unknown. How long after the cross was it before Stephen was stoned or Saul was converted? No one can be sure. There is, therefore, a degree of uncertainty with the use of these dates. Furthermore, it is worth asking,

Did God bring an end to Israel's probationary time when the Temple was utterly destroyed in 70 AD? Only those prophetic interpreters who insist on knowing the day and the hour of God's activities would insist on punctilious mathematics. They do it with the use of the year-day theory.

Any theory of prophetic interpretation must pass the pragmatic test. Ideas must be tested. Ever since the year-day theory was proposed it has been tried by many interpreters in attempts to set a date for the Second Advent. In every instance, of course, it has failed. Yet SDAs still persist in using it, not to set a date for the coming of Christ, but to establish 1844 as the beginning of an Investigative Judgment in heaven. It is a case of rotten apples—the choice of arbitrary dates, the distortion of historical facts, and hopes dashed time and time again. The so-called year-day principle profoundly fails the pragmatic test.

Furthermore, SDAs use of the theory defies the purpose of prophecy. When biblical prophecy finds its fulfillment, it endorses the validity of the prophet's message. That can only be done when the fulfillment takes place on earth in some historical event. Only then is it objectively verifiable. However, SDAs use the theory to try and prove that something happened in heaven in 1844, an event impossible to verify objectively. No one can use the idea of an Investigative Judgment beginning in 1844 as verification that Daniel was a true prophet. Instead, demonstrable historical facts should be used to verify his divine inspiration.

The Book of Daniel

6. **Seventh-day Adventists traditionally ignore the primary meaning of Daniel's prophecies, pouring latex into them, and stretching them to culminate in the era when the Seventh-day Adventist Church was established. They regard themselves as the saintly focus of the prophecies in the Nineteenth Century and onwards.[6]**

In the visions of chapters 7 to 12, Daniel repeatedly refers to "the saints," "the holy people," "my people" and "your [God's] people" (Daniel 7:18, 21, 25, 27; 8:24; 9:5–24; 12:1, 7). It is clear from the context these phrases refer to Daniel's own kin, the Hebrews, highlighting the post-exilic period, the status of the Jerusalem temple and services, and how foreign nations will affect the temple. In view of this the prophecies

279

should be interpreted primarily in the context of the Hebrew nation rather than Western history in the Christian era.

Applying the passages to Gentiles in a secondary sense is legitimate in view of two principles of prophetic interpretation—conditionality and recurring fulfillments—providing the primary meaning is put in place first. If the primary meaning is ignored, the excesses of Historicism and Futurism then take over and phrases such as "the saints" are interpreted primarily as Christians or even Seventh-day Adventists.

In view of the fact Daniel's prophecies range over four successive kingdoms, the last fragmenting at the end, it should be expected also that a momentous event like the first advent of the Messiah would be depicted in some of his visions. Indeed, that is the case. But SDAs, correctly or incorrectly, interpret only Daniel 9 in this manner. Their interpretation of Daniel 2 is the best example of stretching the vision to the Second Coming while ignoring the first advent as a prior fulfillment.

Daniel 2

7. **Seventh-day Adventists traditionally use Daniel 2 as the launch pad for their exegesis of apocalyptic prophecy. The interpretation is then used as a model to interpret the remaining visions of Daniel. Daniel 2 is projected solely to the Second Coming of Christ and other visions of Daniel are forced into a mould with the same end.[7]**

The denomination has never taught that a primary fulfillment of Daniel 2 can be found with the takeover of the Babylonian kingdom by the Medo-Persian kingdom. Daniel told Nebuchadnezzar, "You are that head of gold" (Daniel 2:38). Possibly, no SDA would interpret the succession of metals in the entire image to begin with Nebuchadnezzar then proceed to Amel-Marduk (chest of silver), Nergal-Shar-Urur (thighs of brass), Labashi-Marduk (legs of iron) and the dual monarchy of Nabonidus and Belshazzar (the feet of iron and clay). The Babylonian kingdom, according to Daniel's description, was then to be replaced by a Jewish kingdom that would not fail.[8] An alternative ending, therefore, positions the Medes and Persians, under Darius and Cyrus, as the meteor that destroyed the image. But this interpretation, cited by Baldwin and a few other commentators, is not a popular one.

The more commonly accepted view is to extend the fulfillment from Babylon to the Seleucids. Jews of the second century AD had interpreted the kingdoms as Babylon, Medo-Persia, Greece, and Syria, later adding Rome. Devastations by Antiochus Epiphanes and later the Romans prompted these views.[9]

There is cause to make this latter fulfillment by interpreting the metals to signify a succession of nations in general, i.e., Babylon, Medo-Persia, Greece, and Rome, culminating in the first advent of Christ. This explanation is in harmony with the New Testament view that Christ inaugurated His kingdom in the first century AD, incorporating all earthly domains. This view is not welcomed by SDAs, because it permits no space for their date setting in subsequent centuries. They allow only one fulfillment, a view that the meteor represents the Second Coming. Having established that narrow view, it forces a dogmatic exegesis of the remaining visions of Daniel that generally traverse a similar succession of kingdoms.

Daniel 7

8. **Seventh-day Adventists traditionally teach that the papacy is prefigured in the prophecies of Daniel, only implicitly in Daniel 2, but explicitly in Daniel 7, 8, and 11. The papacy is seen as a fulfillment of "the little horn" (7:8) of the fourth beast; "the little horn" and "a king of fierce countenance" (8:9, 23) that emerges from the four divisions of the Grecian kingdom; and the power that "shall take away the daily sacrifice" (11:31). They attempt to strengthen the assertions by citing the phrase "it was diverse" (7:7) or different and then by arguing that the difference came about when the political power, pagan Rome, became a religious power or papal Rome about the sixth century AD.[10]**

First, the obvious should be noted. That is, pagan Rome was pagan and hence religious. Yes, they followed a pagan religion, but a religion nevertheless and therefore not a political system exclusively. Therefore, to assert that pagan Rome was political and papal Rome was religious is an artificial dichotomy.

It should also be noted that it is the entire fourth beast of Daniel 7 that is referred to as "different," not just the little horn. The context suggests this difference is extreme because of the intense ferocity toward God's people and God's temple in comparison to the three previous powers. The difference therefore is not between a political power and a religious power. The contrast lies in the degree of opposition to the Hebrew people, the fourth beast being the most aggressive against the Hebrews.

Furthermore, the context of Daniel 7 indicates that the little horn arises from the fourth power, pagan Rome, but the little horn of Daniel 8 emerges during a late development in the history of a provincial Grecian power. Neither of them refers primarily to papal Rome. The little horn of Daniel 7 could find an application to pagan Rome, specifically regarding the campaign against the Jews by Titus that culminated in the destruction of the temple. The little horn of Daniel 8 could find an application to Antiochus Epiphanes.

Identifying the emergence of papal Rome at Daniel 11:31, as Uriah Smith did, is problematic. The Jews saw Antiochus Epiphanes as the little horn of both Daniel 7 and 8 and the heart of Daniel 11. No historian of note interprets the latter as primarily meaning papal Rome. The elements of the prophecy match Antiochus Epiphanes so conclusively that some commentators, especially those reluctant to admit predictive elements, are led to assert that the passage was written after the events, i.e., as history in the guise of prophecy, penned after 165 BC.

Daniel 8

9. **Seventh-day Adventists traditionally maintain that "the sanctuary" of Daniel 8:14 is a sanctuary in heaven. They assume that the prophecy of Daniel 9:24–27 is joined to Daniel 8:14. They further assume that the fulfillment of the two passages begin at the same time. The denomination then calculates "the 2300 days" (KJV) to be 2300 years, conjecturing a starting point at 457 BC so that the prophecy finds fulfillment in 1844 AD. The observation is then made that the date is too late to be applied to the earthly Jewish temple, destroyed by the Romans in 70 AD, and so it therefore must apply to a heavenly temple.[11]**

This is a specious and serpentine argument, remarkable for its many assumptions along the way. Ford listed over twenty of the assumptions in his Glacier View manuscript.

It is important to ask, "What would Daniel think 'the sanctuary' meant?" The answer is quite obviously his nation's place of worship in Jerusalem. As an exile, the restoration of those temple services must have preoccupied his prayers.

Basic exegesis of Scripture, like any other literary analysis, involves study of the context and linguistics, with the help of some historical background. There is no reason whatsoever, contextually, linguistically, or historically, to conclude that "the sanctuary" of Daniel 8:14 refers to a "heavenly sanctuary," whatever that term may mean. On the other hand, there is every reason to believe "the sanctuary" refers to the Jerusalem temple, contextually, linguistically, and historically. In the broader application it could even be a symbol of the kingdom of God.

10. **Seventh-day Adventists traditionally point out that no starting date for the "2300 days" is given in Daniel 8. They insist it must be found in order to complete the vision. They maintain it is found in Daniel 9:25.[12]**

The quest is an unnecessary one. The vision of Chapter 8 remains completed without either a starting or finishing date. Gabriel did not see fit to be so exact.

SDAs regard Daniel 7 as complete in itself, despite the fact no starting or finishing date is given for the "time, times and half a time" (7:25). And Daniel's final vision is regarded by SDAs as complete without starting and finishing dates for the 1290 years and 1335 years being mentioned in the texts. Consistency is a virtue.

11. **Seventh-day Adventists traditionally argue that Daniel didn't understand the meaning of the "2300 days." For that reason, it is alleged, Gabriel returned in Chapter 9 to specifically clarify the meaning of that time period.[13]**

There is nothing in Chapter 9 to indicate that Daniel is concerned about the "2300 days." Instead, the context strongly suggests his mind is preoccupied with the prophecy of Jeremiah 29 and its implications for future Hebrew prospects.

From Daniel's perspective the substance of his vision in Chapter 8 runs counter to his common understanding. In the back of his mind there are no doubt the promises of other Hebrew prophets that speak of a renewed Israel after the Babylonian captivity. These promises depict a period of consummate glory and a close covenant relationship with God.

Gabriel's message regarding a period of persecution and destruction among the Hebrews is alarming and goes against the grain for Daniel, because it sounds like a repetition of the Babylonian captivity or worse.

Daniel has good reason to be "appalled," not just about the "2300 days" but also about the whole of the vision. Why does the devastation occur? Have my people not learned anything from the Babylonian captivity? Is the projected persecution caused by a repetition of our sins? Is Israel's covenant with God irrevocably broken? The entire situation was beyond Daniel's understanding, not just the time element.

Context clearly indicates the inadequacy of the assumption that it was only the "2300 days" causing uncertainty in Daniel's mind. Gabriel chose not to give further details on many points.

12. Seventh-day Adventists traditionally argue that the translation "2300 days" (KJV) is the best interpretation of the original language.[14]

The Hebrew term is not used to describe a day of twenty-four hours, therefore the KJV translation is a poor one. The expression is best translated "evenings-mornings" or "evenings and mornings" (NIV). In Daniel 8:26 the article is repeated and could be translated "the evenings and the mornings." This highlights the sense of evening sacrifices and morning sacrifices, two separate groups of functions within the regular daily sacrifices.

The Jewish sanctuary service, specifically the daily sacrifices and their unholy desecration by a foreign power, is the focus of this vision. In that context "2300 evenings-mornings" is better understood as 2300 daily sacrifices. With two occurring each day, the time period would be 1150 days, an era when the temple sacrifices were evidently to be suspended due to foreign aggression.

Modern scholarship, as reflected in the more recent Bible translations, has little place in the traditional SDA scheme of prophetic interpretation. For this reason, ultra-conservative SDAs of today are known to condemn modern translations, insisting that the KJV is the only reliable one. They slay the more athletic messengers because they don't like the messages.

13. Seventh-day Adventists traditionally argue that the word "cleansed" (8:14 KJV) is the best translation. Then they insist this is a clear reference to the Day of Atonement service

outlined in Leviticus 16. They then interpret the antitypical Day of Atonement service as beginning in a heavenly sanctuary in 1844, a service they call the Investigative Judgment.[15]

The Hebrew word TAHAR (cleanse) is used in Leviticus 16, but in Daniel 8:14 the Hebrew word is TSADAQ and is best translated "justified" (Revised Version, margin). The NIV renders it "reconsecrated," interpreting the period as a specific reference to the desecration of the temple by Antiochus Epiphanes and a subsequent reconsecration of the premises. No matter what word is used in the modern translations, the fact remains there is no direct linguistic link between Daniel 8 and Leviticus 16.

Furthermore, the context of Daniel 8 does not contain any direct references to the Day of Atonement service. The context specifically refers to the daily services, but because of the length of time involved (1150 days, or more than twelve months) it would, by implication, also include all annual ceremonies like the Day of Atonement. The real point of concern for Daniel lies primarily in the very thought of more desecration for the Jerusalem temple rather than any particular Hebrew ritual or festivity.

14. **Seventh-day Adventists have traditionally placed great emphasis on the words "seal up the vision for it concerns the distant future" (8:26). They have linked it with the similar instruction, "close up and seal the words of the scroll until the time of the end" (12:4). From this platform they then claim the infant SDA Church cracked the code on the seal, enabling it to explain the proper meaning of the "2300 days." But at the same time, they say Daniel was shut out from understanding the meaning of the "2300 days" because it was sealed until he was given the explanation in the vision of 9:24–27.[16]**

If the mystery of the "2300 days" was to be broken in "the time of the end," and Daniel was given the meaning in 9:24–27, then "the time of the end" would have commenced with that revelation to Daniel, i.e., ten to twelve years after the vision of Chapter 8.

On the other hand, if the vision of Chapter 8 was indeed sealed until the SDA Church began, then 9:24–27 cannot be a divine explanation of the "2300 days." Instead, the explanation would have come in the

Nineteenth Century.

The better way to explain the phrases is to highlight the true meaning of the verb "to close up" or "to seal."

The sealing of a vision does not necessarily mean its substance is not understood. It could indeed be very well understood to the point of causing grave concern. The instruction "to seal" has more to do with making a written record, rolling it up and applying an official seal to it, then preserving it as a valuable document for the archives so that, if needs be, it can be consulted in the future. It is in the future, perhaps the distant future, when the contents will come to pass and be verified and grant veracity to the prophet's message. It is tantamount to saying, "Daniel, you don't necessarily have to understand all of it now. Just preserve it and you will be vindicated in the future." This harmonizes with sentiments in the closing verses of the Book of Daniel.

The act of sealing does not force the necessity for Daniel to have an unsealing and further explanation in his day. The emphasis is on the vision's intrinsic value.

15. Seventh-day Adventists traditionally argue that all of the vision of Chapter 8 was explained to Daniel except the time element, the "2300 days."[17]

In reality, Daniel is not told the name of "the first king" of Greece (v. 21), or the identity of the "four kingdoms" (v. 22) that emerge from Greece, or the person depicted as "another horn which started small" (v. 9). All is sketched in broad outline only, sufficient to alert Daniel of trouble and deliverance in the future.

From our perspective today we may understand much more than Daniel, but to say that Daniel had it all explained to him except the "2300 days" is a gross over-simplification.

16. Seventh-day Adventists traditionally argue that Daniel became ill during the vision of Chapter 8, a malady caused by mental and then physical turmoil over the announcement of the very long time of "2300 days," allegedly 2300 years. Illness necessitated, they claim, a postponement of the vision's completion, and that completion came in Chapter 9.[18]

The Scriptural record states that part way through the vision Daniel collapsed into sleep (vs. 17, 18), but Gabriel strengthened him to hear the meaning of the vision (v.18). Gabriel then instructed Daniel to roll up the scroll and seal it because he had obviously finished the explanation (v. 26). Having finished his task, Gabriel had no need to strengthen Daniel any longer. Gabriel then departed. Daniel was therefore left with his elderly physical condition, feeling exhausted and ill after the vision was completed.

Gabriel's strength could have supported Daniel through sickness if there were more information to give. He could have given more information while Daniel slept.

There is no evidence that the time period was a trigger for illness. Daniel's exhaustion is simply caused by the withdrawal of Gabriel's strength. Similar conditions occurred at the end of the earlier vision in Chapter 7 (v. 28) and during the later vision of chapters 10–12 (esp. 10:17).

The allegation that Gabriel broke off his explanation at 8:26 because Daniel suddenly took ill is an unreasonable assumption, a fabrication.

17. **Seventh-day Adventists traditionally argued for a very short period between the end of Chapter 8 and the return of Gabriel in Chapter 9. This was to indicate that the only obstacle to Daniel's understanding of the "2300 days" was his illness which lasted "several days" (8:27). Gabriel was then supposed to have hurried back with the meaning of the "2300 days."**

   Stephen Haskell spoke of the gap as "some days" and "soon." Uriah Smith extended it to "less than a year." Ellen White and others were non-committal, saying "some time afterward" and "later." By the 1930s the gap had extended to "two years." Nowadays, it is admitted the interval is between ten and thirteen years.[19]

The early traditional argument had a hidden agenda—to suggest that Daniel 9:24–27 was Gabriel's elaboration on the "2300 days."

Scholarship has forced the SDA Church to drop the assumption of a short period and accept the fact of a longer gap. With that in mind it seems unreasonable for Gabriel to wait ten years or more to enlighten Daniel. If he did wait that long we would expect Daniel to make some reference to the "2300 days" in his prayer of Chapter 9, indicating he was still waiting for an explanation, but Daniel does not refer back to the vision of Chapter 8. Daniel is apparently content with the information given in Chapter 8. Ten years later he has the prophecy of Jeremiah weighing on his mind, not his previous vision.

The separate visions of chapters 8 and 9 cannot be linked on the basis that there is only a short gap between them. They cannot even be linked on the basis there is at least ten years between them. Any gap does not establish a link per se. Neither Daniel nor Gabriel speaks of any obvious link.

Daniel 9

18. In the 1950s Seventh-day Adventists tentatively put forward a linguistic argument not seen before in their literature. It was designed to weld the visions of Chapters 8 and 9 together, making Daniel 9:24–27 a postscript, or appendix, to Daniel 8:14. The proposal hinged on the meanings of two Hebrew words, CHAZON and MAREH. CHAZON, they said, consistently meant the whole of the vision. MAREH, they claimed, meant only a particular part or parts of the vision. They quoted authorities and an obscure 1764 version of the Bible by Anthony Purver to support the proposal. They followed with the observation that Daniel 9:23 used MAREH and claimed that this referred back to Daniel 8:14 where the "2300 days" was found to be only a particular part of the vision. In other words, Daniel 9:23 was not referring to the whole of Daniel 8 but only the time element that they claimed Gabriel had left unexplained.[20] When Gerhard Pfandl, of the SDA Biblical Research Institute, republished this idea in his ultra-conservative Sabbath School Lesson Quarterly of 2004, all hedging had disappeared. What was tentative in the 1950s became a clear assertion by Pfandl.[21]

People can quote all the lexicons in the world to establish word meanings but what really matters is, "How did Daniel use the two words?" Can it be established by context just what Daniel means by the words?

Accepting the above SDA distinctive definitions of the two words, a listing of their use in Daniel is enlightening. Notice especially the occurrences marked by three asterisks:

Daniel 1:17 CHAZON Generic. All visions as a whole.

Daniel 8:1 CHAZON The whole vision of Chapter 8.

Daniel 8:2 CHAZON (2) The whole vision of Chapter 8:3–12.

Daniel 8:13 CHAZON (2) The part dealing with the little horn.

Daniel 8:15 CHAZON The whole vision of Daniel 8:2–12 or 14.

Daniel 8:16 MAREH The whole vision of Chapter 8:2–12 or 14. ***

Daniel 8:17 CHAZON The whole vision of Chapter 8:2–12 or 14.

Daniel 8:26 MAREH The part that deals with evenings-mornings (v.14).

Daniel 8:26 CHAZON The whole vision of Chapter 8.

Daniel 8:27 MAREH The whole vision of Chapter 8:2–12 or 14. ***

Daniel 9:21 CHAZON The whole vision of Chapter 8.

Daniel 9:23 MAREH The whole vision of 9:22–27, relating to Jer. 29. ***

Daniel 9:24 CHAZON Generic (No definite article). All visions/ prophecy.

Daniel 10:1 MAREH The whole vision of chapters 11, 12. ***

Daniel 10:7 MAREH The whole vision of the heavenly ones, Chapter 10. ***

Daniel 10:8 MAREH The whole vision of the heavenly ones, Chapter 10. ***

Daniel 10:14 CHAZON The whole vision of chapters 11, 12.

Daniel 10:16 MAREH The whole vision of chapters 11, 12.***

Daniel 11:14 CHAZON A small part of chapters 11, 12. ***

Of the twenty-one occasions when Daniel uses these two Hebrew words, about 50 percent of them go against the specialized meanings SDAs want to attribute to them. That is, Daniel 8:13 and 11:14 use CHAZON when it is obvious only a part of the vision is in mind. And in Daniel 8:16, 27; 10:1,7, 8, 16, MAREH is used when it is obvious the whole of the vision is in mind. Daniel does not follow the formula, nor the definitions set by the lexicons. Instead, he uses the two words interchangeably as synonyms.

Consequently, when Daniel writes in 9:23, "Consider the message and understand the vision" (MAREH) he is not necessarily referring to a small part of a vision, specifically the "2300 days" of Chapter 8. On the contrary, the context strongly favors the view that he has in mind the whole vision that is about to follow, i.e., Daniel 9:22–27 in relation to Jeremiah's vision (Jeremiah 29:10–14) mentioned in 9:2.

19. **Seventh-day Adventists traditionally argue that the year-day principle needs to be applied to the "seventy weeks" of 9:24 (KJV); i.e., they regard them as prophetic weeks which, by extrapolation, are 490 prophetic days or 490 literal years.[22]**

Daniel 9:24–27 is perhaps the most debated passage in the entire book of Daniel, mainly because of the curious Hebrew language involved.

The word translated "weeks" in the KJV does not necessarily have that English meaning. The Hebrew word is *SHABUIM* the plural of *SHABUA*. *SHABUA* simply means "a unit of seven." The literal translation, therefore, is "seventy units of seven." Seven what? In the ancient world years were often counted in units of seven or *heptomads*. For example, Aulus Gellius quotes the Roman author Marcus Varro as saying his age was twelve *heptomads* (eighty-four years).[23]

The use of "weeks" in the KJV is purely an arbitrary choice. But it cannot mean seven-day weeks because the masculine plural is used here. (The feminine is required for seven-day weeks). For the Roman mind it would best be translated *"heptomads."* In other words, the full phrase could be read as "seventy *heptomads"* or "seventy units, each of seven years" making a total of 490 literal years.

By focusing on the exactness of the time the modern mind seems to miss the thrust of the expression for the Hebrew mind. The Hebrews thought in terms of seven-year intervals too, just as the Romans did. They had a sabbatical year every seventh year. Thus, the language here in Daniel 9 presents a play on the number seven.

That is, the vision is cast in the context of the Babylonian captivity of seventy years, ten lots of sabbatical years. Gabriel then promises Daniel that God's grace will be extended sevenfold in the up-coming era, not just ten more lots of sabbatical years but rather seventy more lots of sabbatical years. How good is God's grace!

This sevenfold meaning is expressed by Ruth at the birth of Obed, a situation showing God's grace which is interpreted as better for Naomi than having a daughter with seven sons (Ruth 4:15). Hannah expresses similar sentiments when she bore one child, Samuel, but felt God had blessed her sevenfold (1 Samuel 2:5). One dip in the river would have been enough for Naaman to be healed of his leprosy but sevenfold demonstrated a better faith. Peter thought a sevenfold forgiveness might express perfect forgiveness.

The idea of "seventy sevens" (9:24) of God's grace is therefore primarily speaking of a period seven times as long as the Babylonian captivity, indicative of God's long-suffering and fair-mindedness. It is linked to the literal seventy years of captivity and should be likewise regarded as a literal period. The year-day principle does not need to be applied.

This expression "seventy sevens" has no direct linguistic or contextual link to the "2300 evenings-mornings." The former has sabbatical years in mind and the latter has daily sacrificial services in mind.

The arbitrary use of "weeks" (KJV) suits some Christian interpreters of the text because it is used to pinpoint the coming of Jesus of Nazareth. However, a proper appreciation of the Hebrew explains why the Jews see no light in the Christian exegesis. The Jews regard the Christian's translation, "weeks," as biased and incorrect. The NIV reflects a better understanding of the Hebrew language.

20. **Seventh-day Adventists traditionally argue that the Hebrew word CHATAK is to be interpreted in its concrete sense, i.e., "to cut" or "to cut off." (9:24 KJV). They prefer this rather than the abstract meaning, "determined" or "decreed" (NIV), because it fits the idea of the "seventy weeks" being a period cut off from the "2300 days."[24]**

Both the concrete and the abstract meanings are acceptable translations. Philology generally proposes the earlier meaning to be the concrete one but when this word took on an abstract sense is said to be unknown.[25]

The exact meaning of the word in Daniel's time is unimportant. The vital point is that "cut off" does not decisively link the "seventy weeks" to the "2300 days." The question remains, "Cut off from what?" "Cut off" could well mean cut off from some other time period, either a specific length of time or an indeterminate era.

The assertion that the "seventy weeks" is cut off from the "2300 days" is speculative.

21. Seventh-day Adventists traditionally argue that the "seventy weeks" (9:24–27) must be cut off from the "2300 days" (8:14) because there is no other time period mentioned in Daniel from which it can be cut off.[26]

The "seventy weeks" should be understood in the context of the entire chapter. After reading Jeremiah 29 Daniel's mind goes back to the period just after the Egyptian captivity (v. 11). At that time God's covenant was made manifest. The terms of the covenant were spelled out with consequent blessings and curses. No time limit was set for the covenant relationship. Daniel is keenly aware, however, that Israel's sins brought about his own dislocation and the curse of the Babylonian captivity (v. 12).

The purpose of Gabriel's message (vs. 24–27) is to reveal to Daniel there will be an extension of God's grace in post-exilic times, but its extent will be limited. The first evidence of God's renewed grace will be seen with a command to rebuild Jerusalem.

Mention of a time limit indicated that the terms of the post-exilic covenant remained conditional. Failure to respond to God's grace would mean forfeiture of the covenant. Faithfulness would mean a consummation of the covenant as prophesied in messages such as Ezekiel 16:60–63, Jeremiah 32:37–42, and Zechariah 8:13–15. That consummation would be the beginning of a glorious eternity (Daniel 7:27).

In other words, the "seventy weeks" is conceivably decreed or determined by God as a period of grace cut off from eternity, not cut off from the "2300 days." God is virtually saying, "Israel, this is your last chance. Choose between eternal liberty or eternal oblivion."

22. Seventh-day Adventists traditionally argue that the phrase "understand the vision" (9:23) refers back to the "2300 days" of the previous vision. Both Gabriel and Daniel were obviously thinking of the previous vision, they say.[27]

It is, however, not at all obvious. The context is a strong argument that 9:23 is a reference to the immediate vision.

The catalyst is that Daniel has just read Jeremiah and is led to pray for the renewal of the covenant with God in view of the fact that the seventy years captivity is nearing an end. His prayer is immediately answered with the arrival of Gabriel (v. 21) with another revelation. Gabriel prefaces his remarks with the advice to listen carefully to what he has to say.

"Understand the vision" is a reference to the new vision. If Gabriel was talking about the previous vision common sense would demand that he specifically link the new with the old by a clear reference to the old, but there is not the slightest hint that Gabriel has the "2300 days" of Chapter 8 in mind.

23. Seventh-day Adventists traditionally argue that Daniel 9:24–27 is an explanation of Daniel 8:14, because both are dealing with a time element.[28]

True, both mention a time element, but it is purely circumstantial. Use of the same traditional argument could link it also to "a time, times and half a time" (7:25) but SDAs have never been known to do this. They only apply the argument in this instance because of a predisposition to closely link chapters 8 and 9, arguing that the prophecy of Daniel 9 is an added explanation of the "2300 days" of Daniel 8.

24. Seventh-day Adventists traditionally argue that the "seventy weeks" (9:24) form the first portion of the "2300 days," i.e., the two periods start at the same time.[29]

Early Adventist writers appealed to logic in order to have this point accepted by the readers. There is no biblical evidence for it, and it really has no logic to it.

If one time period is a part of another time period, why is it logical for them to begin at the same time? If twenty years is a part of a century, why could not those twenty years be at the end of the century or at any other time within the hundred years?

Furthermore, using Adventist logic it could be proposed that the seventy weeks start at the same time as the "time, times and half a time" (7:25) because there is no starting point for that period either.

25. Seventh-day Adventists traditionally argue that Daniel 9:24-27 is an explanation of Daniel 8:14 because the angel Gabriel

served as the messenger on both occasions.[30]

If a postman delivers a letter to an individual and then ten years later the same postman delivers another letter to the same person, there is no reason to believe the second letter is an explanation of the first, simply on the grounds it was delivered by the same postman. The contents of the messages and what prompted the messages determine whether or not the latter is a further explanation of the former. The same postman is purely circumstantial.

26. **Seventh-day Adventists traditionally apply 457 BC to the phrase "the decree to restore and rebuild Jerusalem" (9:25). This date is used to establish the beginning of the fulfillment of the "2300 days" (years) of Daniel 8:14 and the 490 days (years) of Daniel 9:24–27.**[31]

This interpretation is simplistic. Cyrus is the king spoken of in Scripture as the one who would rebuild Jerusalem (Isaiah 44:28; 45:13). It was about 538 BC when he decreed the captive Hebrews could return to Jerusalem under Zerubbabel's leadership, but restoration was limited to the rebuilding of the Temple (Ezra 1). This task was accomplished (Ezra 6). Later, about 457 BC, Artaxerxes decreed Ezra could lead another group to Jerusalem with finance and temple artifacts, and he was specifically authorized to reestablish the judicial system (Ezra 7). No mention is made at that time of a general rebuilding program for the whole of Jerusalem. About 444 BC, Artaxerxes issued another decree, this time authorizing Nehemiah to rebuild the walls of Jerusalem (Nehemiah 1–6).

It is evident that pinpointing 457 BC to begin an exact chronology defies the facts. The first decree of Artaxerxes, 457 BC, does not specify any rebuilding, and the other two decrees, 538 BC and 444 BC, do not fit the SDA interpretation. If an interpreter is satisfied with approximations, then about 538 BC provides a defensible date as the fulfillment of Daniel 9:24. (Approximations of prophetic time, or chronography, are similar to approximations or abbreviations in Hebrew genealogies, e.g., Matthew 1.)

The best method of interpretation is to use the context. The thrust of the message is that the Hebrews were to be given 490 years to make good the covenant relationship, beginning with their release after the 70 years of Babylonian captivity. If they were faithful the promises of national glory would be realized. But they were not faithful. The desecration of the temple by Antiochus Epiphanes, an experience revealed to Daniel, provided a wake-up call. Tragically, fanatical legalism and corruption in high places, even among the priesthood during the intertestamental period, continued to squander their time of grace. Therefore, the prophecy of Daniel 9:24–27 could not be fulfilled. God's relation with mankind was therefore eventually reoriented. The coming of the Messiah soon after heralded a covenant with a broader spectrum and a re-interpretation of future events.

Daniel 11

27. **Seventh-day Adventists traditionally begin their interpretation of Chapter 11 with the Persian and Greek kingdoms, as vs. 1, 2 specify. In order to stretch the vision to the Second Coming a succession of powers are introduced, first with pagan Rome at v.14, then papal Rome at v. 31. Prior to the Second World War explanations introduced Turkey at v. 40 and even suggested the introduction of Russia at v.44.[32] More recent SDA explanations continue papal Rome to the end of the chapter.**

For its primary fulfillment pagan Rome could perhaps be introduced at v. 40 or even as early as v. 30, but to insert other powers and to propose transitions at the verses suggested by SDAs is an exercise unsupported by context, linguistics, or history. It is arbitrary and highly speculative. The flow of the drama in the chapter does not suggest new kingdoms where SDAs want to insert them.

If there is any relevance to the Christian era in Daniel 11, it should be applied in the light of New Testament revelation.

Hebrews

28. **Seventh-day Adventists traditionally use the Book of Hebrews to teach that Jesus, at His ascension, entered the Holy Place of the heavenly sanctuary but later, in 1844, moved into the Most Holy Place to begin an Investigative Judgment. The KJV of Hebrews 9:12 would seem to support this view. The teaching also rests on the assumption that "the veil" (6:19; 10:20) refers**

to the curtain at the entrance to the sanctuary, not the inner veil that divided the Holy Place from the Most Holy Place.[33]

Some things are certain—The Book of Hebrews portrays Jesus as the archetypal High Priest. The special work of the typical High Priest was to enter into the Most Holy Place on the Day of Atonement. Therefore, Jesus is depicted in Hebrews as fulfilling the Day of Atonement service. Hebrews uses Day of Atonement imagery.

Furthermore, Hebrews places Jesus at the right hand of God (1:3) and that fact, notably, in the first Christian century, not after 1844 AD. Therefore, the NIV uses the term "Most Holy Place" (9:8, 12; 10:19) rather than "holy places," because of the strong case that the context presents.

Hebrews does not differentiate between a Holy Place and a Most Holy Place in the heavenly sanctuary. Rather, the author generalizes with the term "holy places" or Ta Hagia (9:12, 25) and "heaven itself" (9:24). And "the veil," or *Katapetasmatos* (6:19; 10:20), is not specifically identified, except to say it represents Christs body (10:20). Hebrews, instead, is preoccupied with the thought of Christ's ready access to the Father, access which is continual, on an equal footing, and having no walls or curtains as barriers between them. The thought of Christ waiting in a first apartment until 1844 before gaining access to God in a second apartment is totally foreign to the thrust of Hebrews. Furthermore, the depiction does not allow for the idea that Christ entered into the presence of the Father when He first ascended and then went out from His presence, only to re-enter in 1844, as some SDA writers once proposed.

The portrayal of the ascended Christ waiting in the wings, as it were, until 1844, before going into the presence of the Father, is a denial of the fundamental doctrines of God's omnipresence and Christ's divinity. It is inconceivable that Christ, as God, at one and the same time could be in heaven and separated from the Father.

The picture of Jesus presented by Hebrews in the first Christian century is parallel to the one in Revelation. Both depict Jesus as humanity's mediator in the very presence of the Father, a situation that has been so since His ascension. Any digression from that fundamental truth is neither a Christian nor gospel view.

Hebrews 9 is the clearest expression in Scripture that the two apartments in the earthly sanctuary are types of the two eras—precross and post-cross. The Holy Place represented the era of the sacrificial system rendered redundant by Christ's sacrifice at Calvary. The Most Holy Place represented the era ushered in by Calvary and the symbolic presentation of Christ's blood in heavenly places. This demonstration of divine love was the catalyst for the expulsion of the devil and his angels from heaven (Hebrews 9:22, 23; Revelation 12:1–12). With the entire universe as witnesses God had been fully vindicated.

End Notes

1   Uriah Smith, *Daniel and Revelation*, (Battle Creek, Michigan: Review and Herald Publishing Association, 1892), pp. 170–175; F. C. Gilbert, *Messiah in His Sanctuary*, (Takoma Park, Washington: Review and Herald Publishing Association, 1937), pp. 167, 171–173; William Branson, *Drama of the Ages*, (Nashville, Tennessee: Southern Publishing Association, 1950), pp. 227 and 29.

2   Uriah Smith, *Daniel and Revelation*, p. 178; Gilbert, *Messiah in His Sanctuary*, p. 55; Ellen White, *Patriarchs and Prophets*, (Oakland, California: Pacific Press Publishing Association, 1890), p. 354.

3   General Conference [of SDAs], *Church Manual*, 1932, pp. 183–185.

4   James White, *Bible Adventism*, vol. 1 (Battle Creek, Michigan: SDA Publishing Association, [ca.1870]), p. 76; Ellen White, *The Great Controversy*, (Oakland, California: Pacific Press Publishing Association, 1888), p. 356.

5   J. N. Andrews, "The Sanctuary," *RH*, 23 Dec 1852, p. 264; J N Andrews, "The Sanctuary and the Bible," *RH*, 10 March 1874, p. 360; Ellen White, *Desire of Ages*, (Oakland, California: Pacific Press Publishing Association, 1898), p. 234.

6   James White, *Bible Adventism*, vol. l, p. 74; Smith, *Daniel and Rev elation*, pp. 123, 312.

7   Uriah Smith, *Daniel and Revelation*, pp. 60–75.

8   P. R. Davies, cited in Joyce Baldwin, *Daniel*, (Leicester, England: Inter-Varsity Press, 1978), p. 92.

9   Josephus, *Jewish Antiquities*, x., 276, 280.

10   *Bible Readings for the Home Circle*, (Mountain View, California: Pacific Press Publishing Association, 1916), pp. 217, 218.

11   Uriah Smith, *Daniel and Revelation*, pp. 195–214.

12   James White, *Bible Adventism*, vol. l, p. 137.

13   *Ibid.*

14 Uriah Smith, *Daniel and Revelation,* pp. 163, 175.

15 *Ibid.,* pp. 174,175.

16 James White, *Bible Adventism,* vol. l, p. 76. Note: In 1981 an SDA layman, Brian Lynch, surveyed the following institutions— Department of Biblical Studies at the Catholic University of America, Yale University Near Eastern Languages Department, Harvard University Near Eastern Languages Department, Princeton Theological Seminary, Chicago Theological Seminary, University of Michigan Program on Studies in Religion, Andover Newton Theological Seminary, and John Hopkins University Department of Near Eastern Studies. All agreed that the rendering "2300 days" is best translated "2300 evenings and mornings" or "1150 days [of sacrifices]."

17 Uriah Smith, "The Sanctuary," *RH,* 21 March 1854, p. 69; Uriah Smith, *Looking unto Jesus,* (Battle Creek, Michigan: Review and Herald Publishing Association, 1898), pp. 168, 171.

18 Ellen White, *Great Controversy,* p. 325; J. L. Schuler, *The Great Judgment Day,* (Washington, D.C.: Review and Herald Publishing Association, 1923), p. 14

19 Stephen Haskell, *The Cross and its Shadow,* (South Lancaster, Massachusetts: The Bible Training School, [1914]), p. 190; Smith, *Looking Unto Jesus,* pp. 168, 169; Ellen White, *Great Controversy,* p. 325; William Branson, *In Defence of the Faith: A Reply to Canright,* (Washington, D.C.: Review and Herald Publishing Association, 1933), p. 288; *Questions on Doctrine,* (Washington, D.C.: Review and Herald Publishing Association, 1957), p. 270; W. R. Lesher, A. V. Wallenkampf, editors, *The Sanctuary and Atonement:* Biblical, Historical, and Theological Studies, (Washington, D.C.: Review and Herald Publishing Association, 1981), art. "The Relationship Between the Prophecies of Daniel 8 and Daniel 9" by William Shea, p. 239; Mervyn Maxwell, *God Cares,* vol. l, (Boise, Idaho: Pacific Press Publishing Association, 1981), p. 195.

20 *Questions on Doctrine,* pp. 270, 271.

21 Gerhard Pfandl, *Daniel,* (Warburton, Victoria: Signs Publishing Company, 2004), pp. 98, 102.

22 Smith, "The Seventy Weeks and 2300 Days," *RH,* 31 Dec 1857, p. 477; Ellen White, *Desire of Ages,* p. 234.

23 Varro, cited in C. W. Hengstenberg, *Christology of the Old Testament,* (McLean, Virginia: McDonald Publishing Company,

facsimile of 1854), pp. 809, 810 .

24 Smith, "The Sanctuary," *RH,* 17 Feb 1876, p. 52.

25 Lesher and Wallenkampf, *The Sanctuary and Atonement,* art. by Shea, p. 243.

26 Smith, *RH,* 21 March 1854, p. 69, Ellen White, *Great Controversy,* p. 326 .

27 Andrews, *RH,* 23 Dec 1852, p. 263.

28 Smith, *Daniel and Revelation,* pp. 195, 196.

29 *Ibid.;* Ellen White, *Great Controversy*, p. 326.

30 Andrews, *RH,* 23 Dec 1852, p. 263; James White, "The Sanctuary and the 2300 Days," *RH,* 17 March 1853, p. 170; James White, "The Sanctuary," *RH,* 21 July 1863, p. 205.

31 Smith, *Daniel and Revelation,* pp. 197–203.

32 *Ibid.,* pp. 279–298.

33 Ellen White, *Great Controversy,* pp. 420, 421; William Branson, *Drama of the Ages*, p. 253.

Chapter Seventeen:
Appendix B: The Ten-Point Statement and Rebuttals

The full Ten Point Statement appeared in the *Adventist Review,* September 4, 1980, pp. 8–11. The gist of the ill-begotten document was as follows:

1. Dr. Ford's thesis contained "various instances" of references "taken out of context or used indiscriminately."

Rebuttal: No examples were ever given despite the fact they were promised. Ford denied the allegation, but if there was some truth to it then it would be as much a reflection on his Guiding Committee as on himself, because they were there to check his work.

The unfulfilled promise to produce examples raises the question, "Did the examples significantly undermine the thrust of the manuscript, or did they only find nits to pick at that did nothing to alter the main points Ford raised?"

The BRI, intent on countering Ford after the Glacier View meeting, never attempted to marshal the so-called "out-of-context" references in order to embarrass him. If the alleged examples were significant, they would surely have used them as ammunition against him.

2. Dr. Ford taught that the Day of Atonement language in the Book of Hebrews depicts Christ entering the presence of God at His ascension. Adventism, he said, rediscovered this gospel during the 1844 Movement, while at the same time teaching that the end times would climax with a final judgment just prior to the Second Coming. This outline, the Ten Point Document said, was an "unwarranted reduction of Adventist belief."

Rebuttal: This dodged the issue. The important question remains, "Is it Adventist traditional beliefs or Ford's outline that stands the test of Scripture?" For decades church officials had discussed the doctrinal problems behind closed doors, without providing answers. Diverse opinions prevailed on many points, but on the meaning of Hebrews

6:19 and 20; 9:11, 12 and 24–27; and 10:19 and 20, the SDA scholars were generally agreed. The church had no compelling answers for the disarray in their belief structure on other major points. It was foolish to condemn a man offering plausible solutions to their dilemma.

3. **Dr. Ford believed that the phrase "within the veil" (Hebrews 6:19) was symbolic language for the inner veil of the sanctuary. We, the SDA Church, do not believe this "precludes our understanding of Christ's two-phase mediatorial ministry in the heavenly sanctuary." (The two phases being an intercessory phase prior to 1844 followed by an intercessory plus judicial phase from 1844 to the close of probation.)**

Rebuttal: Dr. Ford's critics admitted, "Hebrews neither teaches nor denies" a two-phase ministry, but were unable to offer any scriptural basis for the unique SDA position of two phases during the Christian era, either with categorical Bible texts or types from the Old Testament. In essence, the critics said, "Yes, we admit Ford is right, but we still want to hang onto our traditional belief." The idea of a two-phase ministry in heaven during the Christian era remains SDA fiction. The Book of Hebrews, where we would expect to find it if it did exist, does not speak of it.

4. **The statement complained that Dr. Ford "operates with the presupposition that all Old Testament prophecies were to be fulfilled by the first century AD, which prevents him from using the year-day principle."**

Rebuttal: Ford's modus operandi flows from and is consistent with his belief that the year-day principle "is not explicitly identified as a principle of prophetic interpretation," as the Consensus Statement clearly stated. (However, the Consensus Statement contradicted itself on this point. It was a rash move to convict him on an unresolved issue. The church itself was obviously confused about it.)

The New Testament writers were not in two minds. It is clear that they believed they were living in the last days, and that all Old Testament prophecies had been fulfilled.

5. **Dr. Ford uses the apotelesmatic principle, an acceptance of dual or multiple fulfillments of Bible prophecies, but the SDA**

Church must reject it "because it lacks external control."

Rebuttal: Where, then, do we find the external control for the year-day principle? There is none. Furthermore, isn't it paramount to look for internal scriptural evidence for the apotelesmatic principle (of which there is plenty) before looking further afield? Furthermore, Ellen White used the principle in her Desire of Ages chapter, "On the Mount of Olives." SDA author George McCready Price and the *SDA Bible Commentary* recognized the internal evidence. Why was the Glacier View colloquium abandoning such orthodox sources?

6. **Dr. Ford preferred the translation "justify" or "restore" in Daniel 8:14 rather than the translation "cleanse," admitting no strong contextual or linguistic link with the Day of Atonement ritual in Leviticus 16.**

Rebuttal: The Consensus Statement admitted the same preference in harmony with the best of modern scholarship and modern translations. Whenever there is a range of possible translations of a word, as in Daniel 8:14, then the context must decide the best choice.

7. **Dr. Ford believes that the seventy-week prophecy of Daniel 9: 24–27 is a parallel of Daniel 8:14 rather than being a segment of the 2300-day prophecy.**

Rebuttal: This is an extremely complex exegetical issue and presents a core problem for the traditional SDA interpretation. (See Appendix A.) It was apparently avoided during discussions at Glacier View, for there is no reference to it in the Consensus Statements. It was, therefore, unfair to use this point in judgment of Ford.

8. **Dr. Ford believes that Antiochus Epiphanes was the first and major fulfillment of the "little horn" of Daniel 8 and the "vile person" of Daniel 11. Pagan and papal Rome, he says, are "fulfillments in principle rather than in detail," but we, the SDA Church, teach that only "pagan and papal Rome fulfill the specifications" of the little horn.**

Rebuttal: The SDA position ignores all of the historical evidence presented by the activities of Antiochus Epiphanes, evidence accepted by the best of biblical scholars, including the respected SDA scholar, Siegfried Horn. Ford's view was not destructive of the SDA teaching. Instead, it was an attempt to harmonize the SDA position with history and scholarship. It was also consistent with the principle of recurring fulfillments outlined in the *SDA Bible Commentary.*

9.   Dr. Ford believes that the wicked, especially those symbolized by the fourth beast of Daniel 7, are the subjects of judgment. SDAs believe it is the saints who are judged, i.e., in an Investigative Judgment beginning in 1844.

Rebuttal: The primary focus of Daniel 7 is on the fourth beast. Its frightening nature, together with its war against the saints and near defeat of them, troubled Daniel deeply. The context clearly demonstrates that when God judges these persecutors, they are found to be unworthy and are forever destroyed (v. 26). God's judgment, therefore, leaves the saints untouched and as inheritors of the kingdom. Why? Because they are in the covenant relationship. In the Christian context the saints are similarly in a covenant relationship with Christ and therefore shielded from God's judgment and condemnation because their Lord has been judged worthy. This view taken by Ford is in accord with the context of Daniel 7 and Revelation 14:6–20; 18:10. It is also gospel-centered.

10. Dr. Ford does not believe that Ellen White's writings can be used as an authority for doctrine.

Rebuttal: This was simply untrue. The lie lies in the vital use of the definite and indefinite articles. Ford believes White is an authority but not the authority. The authority, he holds, is Scripture. Notice the clear distinction made with the definite and indefinite articles in the Dallas Statement of Fundamental Beliefs, Articles 1 and 17. In that very orthodox document Scripture is clearly accorded the authority. White is relegated to an authority, i.e., one authority among other authorities, without any levels of value being suggested. Ford was fully in accord with this position. To portray him as unorthodox in this respect was an outrage. His regard for White as an authority was probably much higher than the level applied by many of his fellow academics, but his emphasis was that White's authority was primarily pastoral.

Desmond Ford's Literary Works

Masters Thesis
"Daniel 8:14 and the Latter Days," SDA Theological Seminary, Potomac University, Washington, DC, United States, September, 1959.

PhD Dissertations
"A Study of Selected Pauline Epistles as Written Addresses," Michigan State University, United States, 1960. "The Abomination of Desolation in Biblical Eschatology," Manchester University, Great Britain, 1972 (Print version from University Press of America, Washington, D.C., 1979).

Books
Unlocking Gods Treasury, (Warburton, Victoria: Signs Publishing Company, [1964]). Republished as *Discovering God's Treasures,* (Washington , D.C., Review and Herald Publishing Assoc.). SDA doctrines in a question and answer format.
Answers on the Way, (Mountain View, California: Pacific Press Publishing Assoc., 1977). Adapted from Ford's responses in Australasian Signs of the Times "Question Corner."
Daniel, (Nashville, Tennessee: Southern Publishing Co., 1978). Commentary.
Physicians of the Soul, (Nashville, Tennessee: Southern Publishing Assoc., 1980). The gift of prophecy and its main manifestations throughout the ages.
Daniel 8:14, the Day of Atonement, and the Investigative Judgment, (Casselberry, Florida: Euangelion Press, 1980). Thesis prepared for the Glacier View meeting.
The Forgotten Day, (Newcastle, California: Desmond Ford Publications, 1981). A polemical presentation on the Saturday Sabbath.
Crisis, A Commentary on the Book of Revelation, 3 vols., (Newcastle, California: Desmond Ford Publications, 1982). Volume 3 is an index of volumes 1 and 2, prepared by Dr. Colin Greenlaw.
The Adventist Crisis of Spiritual Identity, (Newcastle, California: Desmond Ford Publications, 1982). Co-authored with Gillian Ford. Personal reflections on the Glacier View meeting and suggestions of

possible causes that led to the event.

Coping Successfully with Stress, (Auburn, California: Good News Unlimited, 1984).

Will there be a Nuclear Holocaust? (Auburn, California: Good News Unlimited, 1984).

How to Survive Personal Tragedy, (Auburn, California: Good News Unlimited, 1984).

Jesus and the Last Days, (Auburn, California: Good News Unlimited, 1984). A brief exposition of Daniel 9.

Good News for Adventists, (Auburn, California: Good News Unlimited, 1985). Discusses in simple language the theological issues highlighted at Glacier View.

A Kaleidoscope of Diamonds, 2 vols., (Newcastle, California: Desmond Ford Publications, 1986). Christian apologetics, especially a focus on Calvary.

Worth More than a Million, (Auburn, California: Good News Unlimited, 1987). Common sense preventive medicine from science and Scripture.

Daniel and the Coming King, (Newcastle, California: Desmond Ford Publications, 1996). Popularized version of Ford's commentary *Daniel*.

Right With God Right Now, (Newcastle, California: Desmond Ford Publications, 1999). Gospel sermons on the Book of Romans.

The End of Terrorism, (Auburn, California: Good News Unlimited, 2004) Current world issues in the context of prophecy and Christian apologetics.

Eating Right for Type 2 Diabetes, (Lincoln, Nebraska: Universe Inc., 2004). A condensation of research from medical journals offering dietary strategies to counter this condition.

God's Odds: How to Win the Wager, (Lincoln, Nebraska: iUniverse, 2006). A Christian apologetic drawing from discussions on the origin and nature of mankind.

In The Heart of Daniel, (Lincoln, Nebraska: iUniverse, 2007). A robust exegesis of Daniel 9:24-27 for mature sheep in the Christian flock.

Jesus Only, (Lincoln, Nebraska: iUniverse, 2008.). A focus on the life of Christ in the four Gospels. Published in a number of revised forms.

For the Sake of the Gospel, (Lincoln, Nebraska: iUniverse, 2009). The sanctuary message reinterpreted by the gospel.

The Coming Worldwide Calvary, (Lincoln, Nebraska: iUniverse,

2009). This is a popularised version of Ford's Manchester thesis on the abomination of desolation.

The Final Rollercoaster: When Elijah and Jezebel Ride Again, (Lincoln, Nebraska: iUniverse, 2010). This is a popularised version of Ford's Manchester thesis on the abomination of desolation.)

How Long O Lord? An Introduction to the Book of Daniel (Lincoln, Nebraska, iUniverse, 25 May 2010).

The Time Is at Hand!: An Introduction to the Book of Revelation, (Lincoln, Nebraska, iUniverse, 12 January 2010).

Your Biography: As Revealed by the Seven Saints of Genesis (Createspace Independent Publishing Platform (30 March 2014). Reading your biography in the experience of the saints of the first book of Scripture.

Why God? (Createspace Independent Publishing Platform (11 April 2014). Does God exist, and what does this mean for our existence.

How to Live in a Topsy Turvy World, (Createspace Independent Publishing Platform (9 September 2014). Keys to living in a threatening world.

Here Is the Answer (published by Good News Unlimited, Australia, 9 June 2015).

Genesis Versus Darwinism: Abridged Version Especially for Adventist, (Amazon Createspace, 9 February 2015).

Genesis versus Darwinism, (2016), Desmond Ford's protest against Darwinian evolution.

The Investigative Judgement and the Everlasting Gospel (Amazon Createspace, 2016). Republished by Good News Unlimited, this is the print version of the talk given at Angwin Forum at Pacific Union College on 27 October 1979, which led to Ford's dismissal.

The Forgotten Day: A Study of the New Testament Sabbath, (Amazon Createspace, 10 March 2018), a reprint of the out-of-print version written c. 1981.

Crisis, Vols. 1 and 2, (reprint of the 1982 version, republished by Good News Unlimited, available on Amazon.com)

Daniel 8:14, the Day of Atonement, and the Investigative Judgment, (Amazon Createspace, 2018 in three volumes). Republication of the thesis prepared for the Glacier View meeting.

The Murder of the Prince of Life Through the Prism of the Cross (Amazon Createspace, 2018 in three volumes). Republication of *Kaleidoscope of Diamonds* in one volume.

Right with God Right Now! A Commentary on the Book of Romans,
(Amazon Createspace, 2018 in three volumes).

Monographs
"The Sealing of the Saints—Before or After the Loud Cry?" n.p., [ca. 1964],
"A Review of R. D. Brinsmead's 'The Timing of Revelation 18 and the Perfecting of the Saints: An Answer to Dr. Desmond Ford and Pastor L C Naden,'" n.p. [ca. 1964].
"Observations on 'Conflicting Conceptions of Righteousness by Faith,'" n.p., [ca. 1964]
"The Cross and Other Sermons," (Steam Press [private], 1977)
"Daniel 8:14: The Judgment and the Kingdom of God," n.p., [ca. 1978]

Magazine Articles
Australasian Record. Occasional articles, 1946–1975.
Signs of the Times [Australasian], Scores of articles, beginning in February 1948. Also, a regular Bible question column, 1952–1980.
Ministry. An average of one article each year, 1964–1978, on the Book of Daniel.
Good News Unlimited. Regular contributions, 1980 until shortly before his death.

Unpublished Papers
"The Reality of the Heavenly Sanctuary," [ca. 1963]
"Nature of Christ: Address at Western Australian Camp-meeting," 1964.
"Report on Manuscript on the Subject of the Nature of Christ," [1960s].
When "Probation Closes: Absolute Loyalty or Absolute Sinlessness?" [ca. 1973].
"Condition of Saints at and After the Close of Probation," [ca. 1973].
"Imputed Sanctification—1 Corinthians 1:30; Romans 8:1; Ephesians 1:6; Colossians 2:10," [ca. 1974].
"An Interview with Ellen G. White on Righteousness by Faith," [ca. 1974].
"A Second Interview with Ellen G. White on the Christian Life," [ca. 1974].

"Ellen G. White and Righteousness by Faith," [ca. 1974].
"Sin in Believers," [ca. 1976].
"Chapel Talk, Avondale College," 1976.
"Post Palmdale Meeting No. 1," 1976.
"Post Palmdale Meeting No. 2," 1976.
An Answer to Dr. Russell Standish, 1976.
Devotional, Australasian Division Office, 1977.
"Current Issues in Righteousness by Faith," Andrews University, February 1978.
"A Hermeneutic for Daniel—The Apotelesmatic Principle," New Orleans, 1978.
"The Investigative Judgement and the Everlasting Gospel," Angwin Chapter of Adventist Forums," 1979.
"Andrews University Forum Meeting, 1980.

Contact Details:

Some books published after 1980, in addition to recorded sermons and magazine subscriptions, can be ordered from:

Good News Unlimited, Australia
Postal Address:
PO Box 973
Penrith, NSW 2751
Australia
www.goodnewsunlimited.com

Others can be found online in bookstores such as Amazon.com.

Gospel Resources can also be obtained in USA from:

Good News Unlimited, USA
Good News Unlimited
P.O. Box 6687
Auburn, CA 95602
(530) 823-9690

gnu@goodnewsunlimited.org

Family Photos

William and Lillian (Simpson) Ford on their wedding day

Desmond and Val, 1930

Desmond, Lillian and Val in Townsville

Desmond, seated third from left, barefoot and having the most fun

Val, Lillian and Desmond in
Townsville about 1937

Cousins Desmond (on left), Keith, Val and
John, 1934

Desmond in Sydney, 1941

Crown Street High School, Sydney, 1941 (Desmond in back row, third right from
center)

Desmond, Lillian and Val in Sydney, 1946.

Lillian visiting Desmond on the
Avondale campus, 1948

Gwen Booth, Desmond's sweetheart

Desmond's Chevrolet Tourer before and after the crash

Desmond and Gwen (Booth) Ford wedding, 1952

Des and Gwen on a camping trip   Des as a young evangelist about 1953

Gwen and Des (holding Elenne) greeting church members

Gwen with Elenne

Des receives his first tertiary
degree, 1958

Des and Gwen with Elenne, Luke and Paul, 1967

Gwen with Des during early stages of her illness

Gwen, at an advanced stage of her illness, surrounded by her devoted family

Des and Gillian (Wastell) Ford wedding, November 1970

Des at his office desk, Avondale College.

Gill with Luke in England, 1971

Elenne Ford

Des training Rollers in devotional studies,
Avondale College, about 1975

Paul Ford

Des and Gill at PUC, 1977

Des and Gill in Washington, D.C., 1980, just prior to the Glacier View meeting

That unforgettable preaching style

Des waits to speak at a GNU gathering   Des on a hike in Canada

Des with Ron Allen of GNU

Proud father Des with Elenne on the day of her admittance to the bar

Des at Lenin's Tomb, Moscow, 1992

Des visiting King's College, Cambridge, England

Dr.Gordon Moyes interviewing guest, Dr. Ford, on his Sydney radio program

Des with Paul, Elenne and Luke

Des addressing a group at an
outdoor baptism

Des with Paul and his family, wife Mina
and daughters Lilly and Hasu (Lotus)

Gill at work on her consultancy

Long-time friends Norman Young and Des in Australia, about 2001

Des at the beach with his brother, Val

Des on his 70th birthday

Index of Contemporaries

Bold numbers reflect more than 2 mentions on a page;
'n' after page number = citation is in endnotes

Topical Index

329

Made in the USA
Monee, IL
26 May 2024

58969795R00190